CONTENTS

FOREWORD

This book, Volume II, of *A Short History of the U.S.S.R.* is the chronicle of the relatively brief period from 1917 to 1964, a span, which, though short, has witnessed many epoch-making events.

The Great October Socialist Revolution inaugurated a new era in the history of the Soviet peoples and of all mankind, and marked the beginning of the transition from the old, exploiter society, to the new, socialist system. After the Revolution had been completed, it took the Soviet Union only two decades, or less than a third of the life span of one generation, to lay the foundations of socialism. Never before had there been such a rapid transition from one social system to another.

The new social system was built under difficult conditions frequently accompanied by momentous and dramatic events. The years after 1917 saw the Soviet people fight international imperialism and internal counter-revolution, uphold the gains of the Revolution, and then, on the labour front, surmount dislocation and famine, restore the economy and carry out radical socio-economic reforms. The Revolution expropriated bourgeois-landowner property and instituted a socialist system of management as the economic foundation of society. Socialist industrialisation and the collectivisation of agriculture required immense creative work and dauntless heroism. Revolutions were accomplished in culture and ideology. Illiteracy was wiped out. The level of education and professional skills rose sharply in both town and country. Millions of people came to adopt the philosophy of Marx and Lenin as their own. With the expulsion of the exploiting classes and the wiping out of old class antagonisms a new community of interests took shape. The Soviet people became united in their aspirations and vital interests and began to build a completely new life. Far-reaching changes took place in the relations between the peoples of the U.S.S.R. Their friendship and co-operation, founded on moral and political unity, common objectives and creative work, were consolidated.

Ever since it emerged the Soviet state has tirelessly championed friendship between nations and co-operation between countries, including states with different social and political systems. The objective of the Leninist policy of peaceful coexistence is to preserve peace as the key condition for building the new society. Supported by the peace-loving forces of other countries, this policy gave the Soviet Union peace for 20 years after the Civil War. In the Second World War, the Soviet people, led by the Communist Party, together with other peoples and all progressive forces allied against Hitler decisively defeated the nazi aggressors.

When the Second World War ended the world balance of forces changed in favour of socialism and democracy. A number of European and Asian countries broke away from imperialism and, together with the Soviet Union, formed a world socialist community in opposition to the capitalist system. In Asia, Africa and Latin America many nations have liberated themselves from colonial oppression and taken the road of independent development.

In the post-war years the U.S.S.R. resumed its interrupted peaceful construction and completed building a socialist society. A new period, that of the full-scale building of communism, was ushered in. The restoration of Leninist standards of Party and social life, proclaimed at the Twentieth Congress of the C.P.S.U., became a powerful stimulus calling forth a further upsurge of the people's creative energy. The Programme of the C.P.S.U., adopted at the Twenty-Second Congress, outlined the methods and timetable for building communism. Firmly confident that their cause will triumph, millions of Soviet people are enthusiastically carrying out the tasks set out in the Programme.

All this is briefly dealt with in this book, which consists of eight chapters giving events in their chronological order. Culture, art and science are dealt with in the last chapter.

* * *

Compilers:
Chapter I–D. K. Shelestov;
Chapter II–D. A. Kovalenko and A. P. Shurygin;
Chapters III, IV, VI and VII (excluding the sections on foreign policy)–D. A. Kovalenko;
Chapter V–A. V. Karasev;
Chapter VIII–V. A. Kumanev;
Foreign policy (1917-18 and 1921-33)–A. O. Chubaryan;
(1934-41 and 1945-63)–I. S. Kremer;
Seven-Year Plan (in Chapter VII)–G. A. Kumanev.

Chapter One

GREAT OCTOBER SOCIALIST REVOLUTION. BEGINNING OF A NEW ERA IN HISTORY (1917-18)

On the Road to the Socialist Revolution

On the evening of April 3, 1917, crowds began to pour into the square in front of the Finland Railway Station in Petrograd. Thousands of workers, soldiers and sailors filled the square to overflowing, but more and more kept arriving and spilled over into the adjoining streets and lanes. Bands played and the beams of searchlights swept over the sea of heads, picking out in the darkness hundreds of banners and placards bearing the words, "Greetings to Lenin!".

Revolutionary Petrograd was turning out to meet Vladimir Ilyich Lenin, leader and founder of the Communist Party, who was returning from emigration.

Only a month before, the February bourgeois-democratic revolution had triumphed in Russia. The insurrection staged by workers and peasants clothed in army greatcoats had overthrown the hated tsarist system. That was a turning point in Russia, a turning point that took place when the development of world imperialism had brought mankind to the epoch of socialist revolutions. When the February revolution broke out, the prerequisites for fundamental socialist reforms had already matured in Russia.

However, the problem of power, the key problem of any revolution, was not solved by the February revolution.

In addition to the Provisional Government, representing the bourgeoisie and the landowners, there was another government, the Soviets. It was in its infancy only and therefore weaker, but there was no doubt about its existence. This was a rare instance of *dual power*. The masses supported the Soviets, set up by the revolutionary workers and peasants, but real power was in the hands of the Provisional Government.

This situation was not accidental. When the revolution broke out the bourgeoisie was, as a class, better organised than the proletariat and the peasants. Besides, the composition of the proletariat, the leading revolutionary class, had changed during the First World War. A considerable proportion of the foremost workers was scattered about at the numerous fronts or was in exile. Hundreds of thousands of politically immature peasants with a petty-bourgeois way of thinking came to work at the factories. Another important factor is that the revolution had brought into politics tens of millions of people who had previously had nothing to do with politics. This gigantic petty-bourgeois wave swept over the proletariat and somewhat weakened its position for a certain time.

The petty-bourgeois Menshevik (Social-Democratic) and Socialist-Revolutionary parties rode on the crest of this wave during the first weeks of the revolution. They won over politically inexperienced sections of working people and secured the vast majority of seats in the Petrograd Soviet and in practically all the other Soviets in the country.

Though the Mensheviks and Socialist-Revolutionaries called themselves socialists, they were very far removed from socialism. They preached a counter-revolutionary bourgeois ideology, which they masked with "socialist" slogans. This ideology was alien to the people. The Mensheviks and Socialist-Revolutionaries considered that the February upheaval had completed the revolution and that certain reforms were all that were now required. Covertly at first and then openly they backed the Provisional Government, taking the road of conciliation with the bourgeoisie and rightly became known as conciliators.

This policy played into the hands of the bourgeoisie and landowners, whose interests were promoted by the Provisional Government, which was itself kept in power by the conciliatory policy of the Socialist-Revolutionary and Menshevik majority in the Soviets. The bourgeoisie and their political parties, primarily the Constitutional Democrats (Cadets) and the Octobrists (Union of October 17), did all they could to hold up the revolution, secure political power and, giving the façade of the old Russian Empire a whitewashing, preserve the former way of life.

However, those who thought that the revolution was petering out were deeply mistaken. Not a single revolutionary demand for which the people had fought tsardom had been fulfilled.

The soldiers were exhausted by the years of slaughter in the name of alien interests and wanted peace. But the Provisional Government had no intention of concluding peace and continued the imperialist war.

The peasants, driven to despair by the shortage of land, poverty and famine, demanded land. But the Provisional Government did all it could to put off settling the agrarian problem and preserve the landed estates.

10

Millions of starving people demanded food. But the ministers of the Provisional Government could do nothing to improve the economic situation. Dislocation and famine, brought on by the war and the piratical economic management by the capitalists and landowners, steadily increased.

The Socialist-Revolutionary and Menshevik conciliators aided and abetted the bourgeois-landowner ministers. They deceived the masses, telling them that the war had now become "different", that the government was defending the "revolutionary mother-land". They called upon the peasants to wait until the Constituent Assembly could be convened to settle the agrarian problem and in their press they trumpeted about "temporary" difficulties, the need for "sacrifices for the revolution", and so forth.

The whole of Russia seethed. The people, having shaken off tsardom, were confronted with the question of what road of development to choose and how to secure the fulfilment of their revolutionary demands. The Mensheviks and Socialist-Revolutionaries took advantage of the people's political immaturity and prepared a new yoke for them under the guise of a bourgeois-democratic republic.

The Communist Party,* the vanguard of the Russian working class, was the only political organisation that championed the interests of the people. It had been prepared for the fierce class battles that started in Russia in 1917. After the February revolution it got its first opportunity (not counting a short period during the first Russian revolution of 1905) to come out into the open and carry on its work legally. It had about 40,000 members, all of whom were steeled by struggle and had close ties with the masses. Early in March, before the smoke of the insurrection against the autocracy had dispersed, it embarked upon extensive work among the people, giving its attention mostly to organising and rallying the proletariat. It called upon the masses to set up Soviets, organised the first detachments of the Red Guards, became active in establishing trade unions and factory committees, constantly called for peace and exposed the imperialist nature of the world war.

When the February revolution broke out Lenin was in Switzerland. Soon the telegraph brought the news that he had set out for Russia. His train was scheduled to arrive in Petrograd on April 3.

It pulled up at the platform of the Finland Railway Station in Petrograd at midnight. The platform was crowded with columns of working people who had come to meet their leader. "Lenin's thickset figure appeared on the steps of one of the carriages," recalled Nikolai Podvoisky, a veteran Bolshevik, who attended the

---

* In those years it was called the Russian Social-Democratic Labour Party (Bolsheviks)—R.S.D.L.P.(B.)—*Ed.*

meeting. "There was a simplicity and composure about him. He had small dark-hazel eyes and his glance was at once alert, penetrating and friendly.

"Coming down to the first step of the carriage, he looked about him, and, taking off his hat, waved it happily. Words fail to describe the enthusiasm of the people on the platform. They gave Lenin a tremendous ovation, shouting out words of welcome.

"The organisers of the meeting indicated that Lenin would speak. There was immediate silence. They were all ears as he uttered his first word, 'Comrades'.

"The intonation was such that everybody felt the depth and force of his love for the working masses. He went on to say that the workers and soldiers had heroically overthrown the autocracy and had, within a few days, turned Russia from a politically backward country into one of the freest democratic states.

"'And now they want to palm off on us another tsar—capital,' he continued. 'But the factories and mills must belong not to the capitalists but to you, and the land must belong not to the landowners but to the peasants.'

"Lenin finished his short speech with the words:

"'Long live the socialist revolution!'

"It seemed as though the workers and soldiers were spellbound. They were not used to hearing such words. Then they broke their silence and applauded and cheered."*

That memorable night the ardent call "Long live the socialist revolution!" was made by Lenin again in a speech delivered from an armoured car in the square in front of the railway station. Soon afterwards it was heard throughout the length and breadth of the country.

On the next day, April 4, Lenin spoke on "The Tasks of the Proletariat in the Present Revolution" at the offices of the Bolshevik faction of the Petrograd Soviet in the Taurida Palace. The lecture was attended by members of the Central and Petrograd Party committees and by the Bolshevik delegates to the All-Russia Conference of Soviets of Workers' and Soldiers' Deputies, which was then in session. Three days later, on April 7, *Pravda* published the theses of this lecture.

These were the famous *April Theses*, in which Lenin brilliantly defined the tasks of the working class and of its vanguard, the Communist Party, in the revolution.

In the *Theses* Lenin outlined the course to be steered to escalate the bourgeois-democratic revolution into a socialist revolution. "The specific feature of the present situation in Russia," he pointed out, "is that the country is *passing* from the first stage of the revolution—which, owing to insufficient class-consciousness

* N. I. Podvoisky, *God 1917* (*The Year 1917*), Moscow, 1958, pp. 8-9.

and organisation on the part of the proletariat, placed power in the hands of the bourgeoisie–to its *second* stage, which must place power in the hands of the proletariat and the poorest sections of the peasants."* Before the February revolution he creatively developed Marxist theory in the new conditions, in the conditions of imperialism, and drew the conclusion that the socialist revolution could triumph in one country, taken singly. Now, analysing the situation in Russia in the spring of 1917, he showed that the proletariat and its ally–the poorest sections of the peasants–had every opportunity to seize power and start socialist reforms in the country.

By moving the Soviets to the forefront, the February revolution had gone further than the usual bourgeois-democratic revolution. This fact and the experience of the 1905-07 revolution brought Lenin round to the conclusion that the best political form of the dictatorship of the proletariat was not a parliamentary democratic republic but a Soviet republic. This conclusion, which marked a step forward in Marxist theory, was precisely worded in the *April Theses*: "Not a parliamentary republic–to return to a parliamentary republic from the Soviets of Workers' Deputies would be a retrograde step–but a republic of Soviets of Workers', Agricultural Labourers' and Peasants' Deputies throughout the country, from top to bottom."**

Lenin said that the Party had to expose the conciliatory policy of the Mensheviks and Socialist-Revolutionaries and patiently explain to the masses that the Soviets were the only possible form of revolutionary government. It had to isolate the conciliators, secure a majority in the Soviets and lead the proletariat and the poorest sections of the peasants to a socialist revolution under the slogan of "All Power to the Soviets!"

Lenin urged the masses not to support the Provisional Government and insisted that they be told of the imperialist nature of its policy and of the hollowness of the promises it was making.

He laid special emphasis on the fact that under the Provisional Government the war continued to pursue predatory, imperialist aims and had nothing in common with "revolutionary defence of the motherland". It had to be shown that the Mensheviks and Socialist-Revolutionaries were preaching "revolutionary defence of the motherland" in the interests of the capitalists, that there was a direct link between capitalism and the imperialist war and that without overthrowing the capitalists no genuinely democratic unforced peace could be secured after the war.

The Communists are portrayed by their enemies as advocates solely of the forceful seizure of power by the proletariat.

---

* Lenin, *Collected Works*, Vol. 24, p. 22.
** *Ibid.*, p. 23.

In the Programme of the Communist Party, adopted in 1961 by the Twenty-Second Congress of the C.P.S.U., it is emphasised: "The working class and its vanguard–the Marxist-Leninist parties–seek to accomplish the socialist revolution *by peaceful means*. This would meet the interests of the working class and the people as a whole, it would accord with the national interests of the country."[*]

In the situation obtaining in Russia in April 1917, Lenin allowed for the possibility of a peaceful transition of power to the working class and its ally, the poorest section of the peasants. The *April Theses* set the course for the peaceful development of the revolution. The Bolsheviks, the *Theses* said, had to win a majority in the Soviets by peaceful struggle and through them change the composition and policy of the government and institute radical social reforms.

While outlining the political tasks of the proletariat in the struggle for the development of the bourgeois-democratic revolution into a socialist revolution, the *Theses* specified the economic demands whose satisfaction would ensure thorough-going social reforms. In the sphere of industry these demands were: the establishment of control by the Soviets over social production and distribution, the immediate merging of all banks into one single national bank and the institution of Soviet control over its activities. On the agrarian problem, Lenin advocated the confiscation of all the landed estates and, on that basis, the nationalisation of all land in the country and its transfer to the Soviets of Agricultural Labourers' and Peasants' Deputies.

The *Theses* ended with a brief formulation of the tasks in Party activity. Lenin suggested that a congress be convened immediately and that the Party Programme be changed in conformity with the new experience that had been accumulated since 1903, when the first Programme was adopted. The Party's name should be changed from Social-Democratic to Communist, thereby emphasising the end goal of its struggle. In conclusion, Lenin urged the convocation of a new, Third Communist International because the Social-Democratic leaders of the Second International had utterly betrayed the working class and had slid into the mire of opportunism and social-chauvinism.

Thus, Lenin's *April Theses* mapped out an all-embracing programme of struggle enabling the proletariat to achieve victory for the socialist revolution under Bolshevik leadership. Under the slogan of "All Power to the Soviets!" they stirred the Russian working class and the poorest sections of the peasants to action aimed at radically reorganising society on socialist lines.

The publication of the *April Theses* sparked off heated discussions in all Party organisations. Within only two or three weeks

---

[*] *The Road to Communism*, Moscow, p. 485.

the whole Party pledged its support for Lenin's programme of socialist revolution. The *Theses* were opposed by only a small group of dissenters (Kamenev, Rykov, Pyatakov and their supporters), who subsequently betrayed the revolution.

The Seventh All-Russia Bolshevik Conference opened in Petrograd on April 24, three weeks after Lenin's return to Russia. It was the first legal Bolshevik conference to be held in Russia, and was attended by more than 130 delegates, representing nearly 80,000 Party members. Shortly after the Party emerged from underground its membership doubled. This convincingly demonstrated the prestige enjoyed by the Bolsheviks among the foremost section of the Russian proletariat.

It would be difficult to overestimate the role played by this conference, which was equivalent to a Party congress. It sat for six days, examined the key problems of the development of the revolution in Russia and, using Lenin's *April Theses* as the basis for its resolutions, called upon the entire Party to agree to Lenin's programme of struggle so that the bourgeois-democratic revolution could be developed into a socialist revolution.

All covert and overt enemies of the revolution gave the *April Theses* a hostile reception. In this respect, particular zeal was displayed by the Menshevik leaders. They made the charge that Lenin had "planted the banner of civil war in the midst of revolutionary democracy".* Georgi Plekhanov said that Lenin's programme of revolution was "absurd". But events showed these unhappy critics to have been cruelly mistaken.

The Crisis Matures

The first major political crisis in Russia broke out in April. It sprang from the foreign policy of the Provisional Government, which led the country to disaster, to the complete loss of national independence and its final enslavement by Anglo-French and U.S. imperialists. On April 18, the Constitutional-Democratic Foreign Minister Pavel Milyukov sent the Entente powers a note, assuring them that the Provisional Government would fight the war "to a victorious conclusion". Naturally, it was sent in secret, but news of it leaked out into the press. Spontaneous demonstrations broke out in Petrograd on April 20. Tens of thousands of workers and soldiers, carrying banners with the words "End the War!", "We Want Peace!" and "Down with Milyukov!", marched to the heart of the city, filling the square in front of the Mariinsky Palace, the residence of the Provisional Government.

That day there was greater activity than usual at the Kshesinskaya mansion, where the Central and Petrograd Party commit-

---

* Lenin, *Collected Works*, Vol. 24, p. 24.

tees had their offices. From there Bolshevik agitators went to the factories and army barracks to tell the workers and soldiers what the true state of affairs was. Addressing rallies of workers and soldiers, they explained that Milyukov's note exposed the policy pursued by the Provisional Government as being against the interests of the people and that every effort should be made to secure the transfer of power to the Soviets.

On the following day, demonstrators carried the Bolshevik slogan "All Power to the Soviets!" The demonstrations continued all day on April 21.

In revolutionary Moscow, too, rallies and demonstrations were held in reply to the Milyukov note. Action against the Provisional Government's imperialist policy was taken in many towns and in the army as well.

This revolutionary upsurge gave the Petrograd Soviet, then the leading Soviet in the country, a real possibility of seizing power. But its Socialist-Revolutionary and Menshevik leaders were even afraid to think of it. They limited themselves to "explaining" the Milyukov note and, on April 21, declared that the incident was over. At the same time, behind the backs of the masses, they had talks with the bourgeois-landowner leaders on reorganising the government with the purpose of strengthening it.

The formation of the first coalition government was announced on May 5. Two of the most hated ministers, the Cadet Milyukov and the Octobrist Alexander Guchkov lost their portfolios. In addition to ten capitalists, the cabinet included representatives of the conciliator parties—the Mensheviks Irakly Tsereteli and Matvei Skobelev, and the Socialist-Revolutionary Victor Chernov and others. The sugar millionaire Mikhail Tereshchenko became Foreign Minister, while the "socialist" Alexander Kerensky took over the War Ministry and Admiralty from Guchkov. Count Lvov remained as Prime Minister. Thus, the Provisional Government that was formed in early March solely of capitalists was able to hold out for only two months. The extremely acute political crisis brought the leaders of the bourgeoisie and the conciliators round to the decision to form a coalition. Mensheviks and Socialist-Revolutionaries were given posts in the government in order to deceive the masses who still believed in these parties. The April crisis was weathered, but the deep-rooted causes that had precipitated it were not removed.

"Socialist" ministers appeared in the Mariinsky Palace but that did not change the government's policy. The capitalist organisations and the Cadet Party supporting them, gradually rallying round itself all the counter-revolutionary forces in the country, were the real leaders of the Provisional Government, while the "socialist" ministers humbly obeyed orders, screening the

V. I. Lenin

May Day demonstration in Petrograd, 1917

Demonstration in Petrograd, June 1917

anti-popular nature of the Provisional Government's policies with "revolutionary" slogans.

Nothing had changed. Millions of soldiers, cursing the war, were rotting in the trenches. The country found itself increasingly dependent on Western imperialists. A special U.S. mission headed by Elihu Root came to Russia in May and reached agreement with the Provisional Government on a further large U.S. loan for the purchase of arms and other war equipment. U.S. capital penetrated ever deeper into Russia's economy. While the government spent thousands of millions of rubles to continue the war, the queues at the food shops grew ever longer. The scale of the economic dislocation became greater than under tsardom. Nothing was done about the agrarian problem.

All this created the objective conditions for an exacerbation of the revolutionary crisis.

The summer of 1917 was marked by a further sharp aggravation of the class struggle. The Russian working class had come forward as the leading revolutionary force in the struggle for social emancipation long before the First World War. It led the masses in the insurrections of 1917. The coalition government set up a special Ministry of Labour headed by Tsereteli. It was to be expected that this ministry would protect the class interests of the workers. But this was far from being the case. The government showed indulgence towards the capitalists, who launched an offensive against the workers' standard of living. The cost of living rose, but wages remained frozen. The government made no effort to control industry and the profits of the capitalists. There was no check on the insolence of the financial and industrial magnates, who, in order to crush the struggle of the proletariat, deliberately dislocated production, shut down factories and mines and dismissed workers by the tens of thousands, dooming them to starvation.

The working class retaliated with strikes in Moscow and Moscow Gubernia, the Donbas, Baku, Ivanovo-Voznesensk and the Urals. An eight-hour working day was started spontaneously in many factories. The working class became more organised. The trade unions, first set up in Russia in 1905-07, became mass organisations. Towards the autumn of 1917 they had more than 2,000,000 members. An important role was also played by the factory committees.* They demanded the institution of control by workers, an eight-hour working day, higher wages, labour protection and social insurance.

---

* These were elected organs of workers and employees at factories and mills. As soon as the bourgeois-democratic revolution of February 1917 took place, they began to organise factory workers. They supported and carried out the Bolshevik demand that workers should have control over production and the distribution of foodstuffs, and worked to secure the transfer of power to the Soviets. In 1918 they became the primary bodies of the trade unions.—*Ed.*

The heroic struggle of the working class had a tremendous influence on the country as a whole, echoing in the countryside and revolutionising the peasant masses. However, because of their political backwardness and petty-bourgeois prejudices the peasants were still strongly swayed by the Socialist-Revolutionaries. Small wonder that the Socialist-Revolutionary leader Chernov became Minister of Agriculture. The bourgeois and conciliatory press played him up as the "peasant minister". In actual fact, the Socialist-Revolutionaries made every effort to extinguish the growing flame of the peasant movement.

The First All-Russia Congress of Peasants' Deputies* was held in Petrograd in May. It was dominated by the Socialist-Revolutionaries, whose speakers exhorted the peasants to disregard the Bolshevik call for the immediate seizure of the landed estates. They recommended postponing the land question until the Constituent Assembly was convened. The Socialist-Revolutionaries imposed their resolution on the congress, seizing the majority in the newly elected All-Russia Central Executive Committee of Peasants' Soviets.

At that congress the small but extremely active Bolshevik group was headed by Mikhail Frunze, a Leninist and professional revolutionary. On May 22 the peasants' deputies were addressed by Lenin, who told them of the Bolsheviks' agrarian programme and urged the immediate confiscation of the landed estates. The speech made a tremendous impression and Lenin was given an ovation by most of the delegates.

The peasant movement mounted in spite of the efforts of the Socialist-Revolutionaries to keep it down. In the summer it spread to 43 of the 69 gubernias. The peasants were most active in the central gubernias, along the Volga, in the Ukraine and Byelorussia, i.e., in areas where the shortage of land was particularly acute. Between June and August there were 2,390 cases of peasants taking over the landed estates, sowing the land, and seizing the meadows and implements, a figure five times the number in the course of the first two months after the February revolution.

The Provisional Government sent punitive detachments to villages gripped by unrest. But the struggle of the peasants went on growing and became one of the key factors in the revolutionary upsurge.

All through the spring and summer of 1917 revolutionary feeling in the army kept increasing. Soldiers' committees were set up in military units at the front as well as in the rear. The soldiers, being drawn from the working class and peasantry, had the same interests as the working people. What they wanted most

---

* In 1917 there were separate Soviets of Workers' and Soldiers' Deputies and Soviets of Peasants' Deputies.—*Ed.*

was peace, and an end to the hated war. In May 1917 General Dragomirov testified: "The dominant sentiment in the army is the desire for peace. Anybody who preaches peace without annexations and the granting of self-determination to nations can easily become popular in the army.... The desire for peace is so overwhelming that recruits refuse to take up arms, saying that they do not intend to fight anyway."[*]

This was not accidental. Deep in the rear the soldiers garrisoning the towns (recruited mostly from the countryside) were powerfully influenced by the proletariat. This influence was a real school of revolution for them. Vladimir Antonov-Ovseyenko, a member of the Bolshevik Party, recalls the Petrograd garrison of those days: "Petrograd was filthy with sunflower-seed husks. It was as though the village had been dragged into the city. But it was an armed village.... It was a huge laboratory where the peasants' political consciousness was refashioned."[**]

This refashioning went on in the army in the field as well. In the summer of 1917 Kerensky toured the firing lines several times, persuading the soldiers to continue the war. For this he was nicknamed the "Persuader-in-Chief". But more and more frequently, his exhortations were met with grim silence. Gradually the soldiers began to realise that the Provisional Government as well as the Mensheviks and Socialist-Revolutionaries, who had seized the key positions in the Soldiers' Soviets and committees, were bent on continuing the war. The soldiers became more and more revolutionary.

The national liberation movement of the peoples of Russia provided one of the major reserves of the proletarian revolution now coming to fruition. For ages the tsarist system had been oppressing the numerous peoples inhabiting the Russian Empire. In the interests of the bourgeoisie and landowners, the tsarist government had pursued a tough colonial policy with regard to the non-Russian peoples and this line did not essentially change when the Provisional Government came to power. Unable to suppress the struggle of the national minorities by force, it hoped to stifle it by minor concessions and leave everything else unchanged. What these concessions were can be seen from the example of Finland, then part of Russia. The Provisional Government refused to extend the rights of the local Sejm or to grant autonomy to the Finns. Instead, it restored the Constitution of the Grand Duchy of Finland, that had been "granted" by Alexander I.

The national liberation movement gained momentum in the Ukraine, Central Asia, Transcaucasia and other areas. The local

---

[*] Iz istorii grazhdanskoi voiny v SSSR (History of the Civil War in the U.S.S.R.), Vol. I, Moscow, 1936, p. 236.

[**] V. Antonov-Ovseyenko, V revolyutsii (In the Revolution), Moscow, 1957, p. 7.

national bourgeoisie took steps to win the leadership of this movement and use it to their own ends. A bourgeois-nationalist Central Rada was set up in the Ukraine during the first months after the February revolution. While making a pretence of demanding autonomy for the Ukraine, it was prepared to accept any minor concessions the Provisional Government cared to make. A so-called National Council, the Shuro-i-Islamiya, and the Moslem bourgeois Ulema Party were formed in Central Asia. A bourgeois-nationalist organisation called Alash-orda appeared in Kazakhstan. In Transcaucasia nationalist feelings were fomented by the Georgian Mensheviks, the Dashnaks (in Armenia) and the Musavatists (in Azerbaijan). The bourgeois nationalists proclaimed that they were out to abolish national oppression. But, like the Russian capitalists, their prime concern was to strangle the revolution. However, following the example set by the Russian proletariat, the working masses of the oppressed nations became increasingly active in the struggle not only for national but also for social emancipation. The revolutionary-democratic forces of the national liberation movement grew stronger and merged into a single torrent.

Thus, the spring and summer of 1917 saw a further aggravation of the revolutionary crisis. The mounting mass movements became better and better organised and infused with political consciousness.

One of the most striking manifestations of this was the growth of the influence and prestige of the Communist Party. The ardent appeals of the Bolsheviks, who urged the masses to establish the power of the Soviets and work for the victory of the proletarian revolution, reached the hearts of the masses and won increasing support.

In the period from April to June the Party membership trebled. Its influence increased particularly among the workers. The Soviets of Ivanovo-Voznesensk, Orekhovo-Zuyevo, Krasnoyarsk, Kronstadt and many others went over completely to the Bolsheviks. True, the number of these Soviets was still small, but the prestige of the Bolsheviks steadily rose in the Soviets, particularly in working-class districts. Their position in the trade unions likewise grew stronger. Their influence was decisive in the trade union councils of Petrograd and Moscow. This was particularly marked in the factory committees. The first Petrograd Conference of Factory Committees sat on May 30-June 3. Its work was directed by the Bolsheviks. The conference demanded that the trade unions and factory committees should be granted the right to control the work of industrial enterprises. Similar Bolshevik demands were made by the workers of many factories and mills in Moscow, Ivanovo-Voznesensk, Kharkov, the Donbas, the Urals and other towns and areas.

Hard as it was to carry on their work in the countryside, the Bolsheviks launched a widespread agitation campaign, urging the peasants to seize the landed estates, i.e., settle the agrarian question in a revolutionary way. Soldiers who supported the Bolsheviks were instrumental in increasing the Party's influence in the country. In their home villages they told the people the truth about the Bolsheviks and Lenin, rallied the poorest section of the peasants around themselves, and pressed for the setting up of Soviets and for the landed estates to be seized without waiting for the Constituent Assembly.

Back in March, the Petrograd Party Committee had formed a Military Organisation, whose task was to unite all Social-Democrat soldiers and officers for a struggle under the banner of the R.S.D.L.P.(B.). In May, when work among the troops was intensified, this body was taken over by the Party Central Committee. Bolshevik military organisations were established in Moscow, Kharkov, Kiev, and Saratov. *Pravda*, the Party's central newspaper, and *Soldatskaya Pravda*, which was published by the Military Organisation of the Central Committee, enjoyed a large circulation all along the front. The Bolshevik newspaper *Okopnaya Pravda* was published on the Northern Front.

In the large towns, particularly in Petrograd, more and more soldiers began to go over to the Bolshevik Party. A considerable section of the Baltic Fleet also sided with the Bolsheviks. The Baltic Fleet Central Committee, headed by a Bolshevik sailor named Pavel Dybenko, was formed at the end of April.

Support for the Party increased among the masses, above all among the foremost workers. The Mensheviks and Socialist-Revolutionaries, naturally, still had considerable influence, but as time went by their position grew weaker. This was convincingly demonstrated by the events of the second political crisis that broke out in mid-June.

The First All-Russia Congress of Soviets of Workers' and Soldiers' Deputies opened in Petrograd on June 3. It was attended by more than 1,000 delegates from over 350 Soviets. The Congress had the support of the masses and could easily have seized power peacefully. But the Mensheviks and Socialist-Revolutionaries held a majority in it. The Bolshevik faction had only 105 delegates. The conciliators spoke of the need to support the Provisional Government. In the Cadet Corps Hall on Vasilyevsky Island, where the Congress sat, they monotonously repeated that "all the forces of the revolution must be united". It seemed as though they had the situation well in hand. But when the question of power was brought up and Tsereteli declared there was no party in Russia that could seize power, Lenin said distinctly from his seat: "Yes, there is!"

Then, taking the floor, he said:

"He said there was no political party in Russia that was prepared to assume full power. I reply: Yes, there is. No party can refuse this, and our party certainly doesn't. It is ready to take over full power at any moment."*

He told the delegates of the Bolshevik programme of struggle for the triumph of the proletarian revolution and showed that only the Soviets could give food to the people and land to the peasants, win peace and lead the country out of ruin.

The majority, however, committed to appeasing the capitalists, saw to it that the Congress endorsed the decisions drafted by the Socialist-Revolutionaries and Mensheviks. But while the Congress was in session an event occurred, which showed that the revolutionary masses were rejecting the Socialist-Revolutionary-Menshevik leadership.

On June 18 the leadership of the Congress planned an organised demonstration under slogans showing confidence in the Provisional Government and the determination to fight the war "to a victorious conclusion". The Bolsheviks decided that workers and soldiers would take part in the demonstration under their own slogans.

The sun shone brightly on Sunday, June 18. Early in the morning the first of the endless columns moved to Mars Field, where heroes of the revolution had been buried. A forest of banners filled the streets. The demonstration became purely proletarian. About half a million people turned out with the slogans "All Power to the Soviets!", "Down with the Ten Capitalist Ministers!", "No Secret Treaties with the Anglo-French Capitalists!" The few slogans calling for confidence in the Provisional Government could hardly be seen.

That day and on the next Sunday, June 25, demonstrations broke out in Moscow and many other towns under Bolshevik slogans.

These demonstrations proved that the influence of the Bolshevik Party was growing. The overwhelming number of people taking part in them had no confidence in the Provisional Government. They created a tremendous impression. Lenin wrote: "As the Socialist-Revolutionaries and Mensheviks themselves admitted on the evening of July 18, a political crisis would certainly have broken out had it not been for the offensive at the front."**

While the workers and revolutionary soldiers were demonstrating their distrust for the anti-popular, imperialist policy, the Provisional Government yielded to the insistence of the Entente imperialists and started an offensive at the front. The High Command headed by General Alexei Brusilov ordered the

---

* Lenin, *Collected Works*, Vol. 25, p. 20.
** *Ibid.*, p. 170.

South-Western Front to attack. It was an abortive offensive. It lasted for ten days and nearly 150,000 men were killed or wounded.

The news of this disaster still further aroused revolutionary feeling among the people. The counter-revolution, too, did its best to utilise the defeat. The baiting of Bolsheviks, started in the spring of 1917, now became more organised and more widespread. The bourgeois press raised a howl that the country had been "betrayed", and began to circulate rumours slandering the proletarian Party.

The atmosphere, particularly in Petrograd, grew tense.

The third, July crisis of the Provisional Government began in that situation. On July 2 the Cadet ministers resigned on the grounds that they disapproved the government's policy on the Ukrainian problem. This measure was taken by the bourgeois leaders in the hope that their resignation would cow the Socialist-Revolutionaries and Mensheviks and make them agree to a programme of bourgeois counter-revolution. But unexpectedly for the Cadets, this manoeuvre was the last straw and it broke the people's patience. On the morning of July 3, the 1st Machine-Gun Regiment, part of the Petrograd garrison, decided to turn its guns against the Provisional Government. Delegates were sent to other army units and to the factories. Workers and soldiers spontaneously staged demonstrations under the slogan of "All Power to the Soviets!" The revolutionary masses of Petrograd were determined to overthrow the Provisional Government.

This spontaneous action, however, proved to be premature. As a whole, the country was not ready for it. Many of the workers were still labouring under the illusion that it was possible to come to terms with the capitalists. Moreover, this was just the pretext the counter-revolutionary forces were waiting for to take action against the revolutionary masses.

Meanwhile, the spontaneous movement of the Petrograd workers and soldiers gained momentum. In the night of July 4, when it became obvious that the movement could no longer be stopped, the Central Committee of the Communist Party passed a decision to head the masses and give their action the nature of a peaceful, organised demonstration under the slogan of "All Power to the Soviets!" Leading Bolshevik agitators were dispatched to the factories and army barracks. They had the difficult task of explaining to the revolutionary workers and soldiers that any armed action of the sort they now wanted was premature and that the movement had to be limited to a peaceful demonstration. This task was carried out.

On July 4, Petrograd witnessed yet another mighty demonstration in which half a million people took part. The columns of workers were joined by soldiers and Baltic Fleet sailors, who marched in military formation. They carried slogans demanding the transfer of power to the Soviets. This time the demonstration headed towards the palace occupied by the All-Russia Central Executive Committee of the Soviets of Workers' and Soldiers' Deputies (A.R.C.E.C.), elected two weeks previously at the First All-Russia Congress of Soviets. Delegates were sent to demand that A.R.C.E.C. take over the reins of government.

The July 4 demonstration was a peaceful one, but the government decided to use it as a pretext for launching an offensive against the revolutionary forces. The Socialist-Revolutionary-Menshevik majority in A.R.C.E.C. acted in concert with the counter-revolution. Firing broke out in the streets of Petrograd and nearly 400 of the demonstrators were killed or wounded.

During the next few days, with the support of the conciliators, the counter-revolution openly started a large-scale offensive. Troops loyal to the government, including Cossack units, had earlier been called into Petrograd from the front. Reprisals began against the revolutionary workers, soldiers and sailors.

Lashed into fury, the counter-revolution directed its main blow at the Communist Party. Lies and slander were hurled at it. The counter-revolutionary press started an unprecedentedly foul campaign of slander against Lenin.

The *Pravda* editorial offices and printing works were smashed up on July 5. On the next day, a gang of military cadets broke into the premises of the Party Central Committee. *Pravda, Soldatskaya Pravda* and a number of other newspapers were closed. Vladimir Antonov-Ovseyenko, Pavel Dybenko, Vladimir Nevsky, Alexandra Kollontai and other active Party members were arrested and imprisoned.

On July 7, the Provisional Government issued a warrant for Lenin's arrest on a trumped-up charge of "high treason". Lenin was thus forced to go into hiding, but this was for the last time. At first he lived at a secret address in Petrograd and then moved out to a place called Razliv on the Gulf of Finland, where he wrote articles defining the Party's tactics and his famous book *The State and Revolution*. While in hiding he continued to direct the Party's activities, maintaining close touch with the Central Committee. In August he moved to Finland.

The July days reverberated throughout the country. Demonstrations and rallies protesting against the Provisional Government's counter-revolutionary policy were held in Moscow, Ivanovo-Voznesensk, Yaroslavl, Nizhny Novgorod, Krasnoyarsk and other cities.

The counter-revolution hurried to crush the revolutionary movement. Kerensky became Prime Minister on July 8. Within a short space of time this little-known, mediocre barrister rocketed up from being a simple member of the State Duma to the post of Prime Minister. The secret of this dazzling career was simple: he showed that he was a devoted servant of the capitalists and landowners. On July 9, the Socialist-Revolutionary-Menshevik majority in A.R.C.E.C proclaimed that the Provisional Government had "saved the revolution" and voluntarily transferred all power to it. The creation of the second coalition government was announced on July 24. Half the portfolios in it went to Mensheviks and Socialist-Revolutionaries.

Dual power came to an end. That was the basic result of the July crisis. The bourgeois-landowner Provisional Government became the sole executive organ of power. The Soviets were subordinated to it, while the Mensheviks and Socialist-Revolutionaries heading them went over to the side of the capitalists, openly aiding and abetting the counter-revolution. "After July 4," Lenin wrote, "the counter-revolutionary bourgeoisie, working hand in glove with the monarchists and the Black Hundreds, secured the support of the petty-bourgeois Socialist-Revolutionaries and Mensheviks, partly by intimidating them, and handed over real state power to the Cavaignacs, the military gang, who are shooting insubordinate soldiers at the front and smashing the Bolsheviks in Petrograd."* This changed the situation and the balance of class forces in the country. The period of the peaceful development of the revolution came to an end. After the July crisis, when the bourgeoisie resorted to force against the masses and dual power was replaced by the single power of the bourgeois-landowner Provisional Government, the proletariat could no longer seize power by peaceful means. It now had to win it by armed struggle against the Provisional Government.

On the evening of July 6, members of the Party Central Committee met at the home of Margarita Fofanova in the Vyborg Side and, with Lenin presiding, analysed the events of July 3-5. At this conference and also in articles written in July ("On Slogans", "On the Political Situation", "Lessons of the Revolution") Lenin mapped out a new tactical line to meet the tasks that confronted the Party and the proletariat after the July crisis.

The decisions of the Sixth Congress of the R.S.D.L.P.(B.) were based on this line. That Congress sat in Petrograd on July 26-August 3, but in face of the real threat of arrest the sessions were held semi-legally. Despite repression, the influence of the Bolsheviks grew steadily. By that time the Party had 240,000 members. The delegates to the Sixth Congress represented 162 Party organisations.

Lenin was in hiding and could not attend the Congress but nonetheless he gave it ideological leadership. The Congress made a searching analysis of the balance of class forces in the country

---

* Lenin, *Collected Works*, Vol. 25, p. 185.

and in the world, and outlined the prospects for the further development of the revolution.

On Lenin's recommendation, the slogan "All Power to the Soviets!" was temporarily withdrawn. The counter-revolution had gained the upper hand and the Socialist-Revolutionary-Menshevik Soviets had become appendages of the bourgeois-landowner government. This slogan had therefore lost the revolutionary significance that the Bolsheviks had attached to it in the period of dual power. "The Soviets *at present*," Lenin said in mid-July, "are powerless and helpless against the triumphant and triumphing counter-revolution. The slogan calling for the transfer of power to the Soviets might be construed as a 'simple' appeal for the transfer of power to the present Soviets, and to say that, to appeal for it, would now mean deceiving the people."* The Bolsheviks withdrew the slogan only as applied to the Socialist-Revolutionary-Menshevik Soviets, which had completely repudiated the revolution.

The Sixth Congress directed the Party and proletariat towards an armed uprising, the overthrow of the bourgeois-landowner government and the victory of the socialist revolution. In the resolution, "On the Political Situation", the Congress declared: "Peaceful development and the painless transfer of power to the Soviets have now become impossible because in fact the power has passed into the hands of the counter-revolutionary bourgeoisie. Today, the only correct slogan can be that of completely abolishing the dictatorship of the counter-revolutionary bourgeoisie."**

The Party Central Committee, elected by the Congress, consisted of Lenin, Andrei Bubnov, Felix Dzerzhinsky, Alexandra Kollontai, Victor Nogin, Yakov Sverdlov, Fyodor Sergeyev (Artyom), Joseph Stalin, Moses Uritsky, Stepan Shahumyan and others, and the candidate-members included Prokofy Japaridze, Yelena Stasova, and others.

In the next few weeks the rapidly developing situation confirmed the Congress's analysis of the course of the revolution. The counter-revolutionaries defeated the July action of the masses and began to prepare the ground for a military dictatorship. The capitalists hoped that a dictator would extinguish the revolution.

The Entente powers had much to do with the preparations for installing a dictator. They interfered in Russia's internal affairs more and more actively, determined to keep her in the war. The ripening military plot was thus the work not only of a handful of monarchist generals. Behind it were both Russian and foreign

---

* Lenin, *Collected Works*, Vol. 25, pp. 189-90.
** *Shestoi syezd, RSDRP(b), Protokoly (Sixth Congress of the R.S.D.L.P.[B.], Minutes)*, Moscow, 1958, p. 256.

imperialists, supported by all the counter-revolutionary forces headed by the Cadet Party.

General Lavrenty Kornilov, a confirmed monarchist and Supreme Commander-in-Chief, was picked out as candidate for the dictatorship. A so-called State Conference was convened by the Provisional Government to legalise the military dictatorship.

This conference opened in Moscow's Bolshoi Theatre on August 12. It was attended by representatives of trade and industrial circles, the landowners, the General Staff, the clergy, former members of the State Duma, and leaders of the Cadets, Socialist-Revolutionaries and Mensheviks. On August 13, General Kornilov arrived in Moscow from Mogilev, where he had his headquarters. The counter-revolution gave him a hero's welcome: army officers carried him from the carriage and Morozova, a millionairess, went on her knees before him, imploring him "to save Russia". It seemed that the organisers of the conference had prepared everything to carry out their plot successfully.

The conference was not convened in Petrograd because the counter-revolution believed that it would be easier to act in Moscow which was "peaceful". But this was an empty delusion. The Central Committee of the R.S.D.L.P.(B.) exposed the counter-revolutionary designs of the State Conference and called upon the people to disrupt them. With the support of the Central Council of Trade Unions, the Moscow Party Committee mobilised the masses for action against the counter-revolution. Organised by the Moscow Bolsheviks, more than 400,000 workers went on strike on the day the conference was opened. This was the reply of the working people of Moscow to the counter-revolutionary conspiracy. In Petrograd, Kiev, Kharkov, Samara and many other towns and cities working people protested against the conference.

The Moscow conference mobilised the counter-revolutionary forces, but in face of the revolutionary actions of the masses these forces could not immediately carry out their designs. The preparations for a counter-revolutionary coup continued with renewed energy after the conference.

On August 25, after having mustered considerable forces, Kornilov began to carry the conspiracy into effect. Instructions to "restore order" in Petrograd were sent from Mogilev. A cavalry corps commanded by General Yuri Krymov moved on the city, where, simultaneously, a counter-revolutionary uprising was being prepared. Kornilov's action served as a signal for activating all the anti-revolutionary forces in the country. With the Kornilov mutiny the bourgeoisie and the landowners, in effect, started civil war, which it was hoped would drown the revolution in blood, and enable them to install Kornilov as dictator.

Kerensky was privy to the Kornilov plot. Troops were moved from the front line to Petrograd with his consent. But when the

27

mutiny broke out and he felt that the masses would sweep him away together with Kornilov, he performed a volte-face, declaring himself opposed to the mutineers.

Angry clouds gathered over the country. News of the counter-revolutionary mutiny stirred the masses to action under the leadership of the Bolsheviks. The Bolshevik Party Central Committee became the headquarters of the anti-Kornilov forces. Nearly 25,000 workers joined the Red Guards in Petrograd. Tens of thousands of soldiers and sailors waited for the signal to defend the city. In Moscow, Minsk, Ivanovo-Voznesensk, Kazan, Nizhny Novgorod and many other towns the working class took effective steps to curb Kornilov's supporters. The revolutionary soldiers of the Western Front also joined in the struggle against the mutiny.

This Bolshevik-led revolutionary upsurge played the decisive role in crushing the Kornilov mutiny. Bolshevik agitators went to meet Krymov's cavalry corps that was advancing on Petrograd. They turned the troops against the corps commanders.

On August 30, when it became obvious that the mutiny had collapsed, General Krymov shot himself. That same day Kornilov was relieved of his post of Supreme Commander-in-Chief and put on trial for the mutiny. That ended the counter-revolutionary conspiracy.

The struggle against the Kornilov mutiny was of tremendous significance to the further development of the revolution. It showed the people where the Provisional Government was leading the country and what the policy of the Mensheviks and Socialist-Revolutionaries really stood for. Increasing numbers of people went over to the side of the proletariat and its Party. This was most vividly manifested in the Bolshevisation of the Soviets, which began as soon as the Kornilov mutiny was put down.

On August 31, the day after the mutiny was quelled, the Petrograd Soviet endorsed its first Bolshevik resolution. This was so unexpected for its Socialist-Revolutionary leaders that they had the voting repeated three times. After the third vote had been counted "we re-entered the hall," recalls S. S. Goncharskaya, a Bolshevik deputy in the Soviet. "The members of the Presidium resumed their places, with pale faces and downcast heads. Chkheidze* held the paper with the voting results in trembling hands. Without raising his eyes he announced in a muted voice:

"'More than 107 deputies have voted for no confidence in the Presidium of the Executive Committee. The Presidium [Socialist-Revolutionary-Menshevik.—Ed.] thus relinquishes its authority.'

"That sparked off virtual panedemonium. It was what people had been waiting for. Nobody heard Chkheidze's last words.

---

* Nikolai Chkheidze, Menshevik, Chairman of the Petrograd Soviet in March-August 1917.—Ed.

Everybody rose and the hall shook with applause and cries of 'This is victory, congratulations!' The soldiers threw their caps in the air embracing, clapping each other on the back and shaking hands. Few saw the members of the Presidium disappear behind the side columns."* The Bolsheviks took over the leadership of the Petrograd Soviet.

On September 5, a Bolshevik resolution was adopted by the Moscow Soviets as well. In the course of September the Bolsheviks won a majority in a large number of Soviets, principally in the main cities and industrial centres. In this situation the slogan "All Power to the Soviets!" was put forward once more. It now became a slogan of insurrection, of calling for the forcible overthrow of the counter-revolutionary dictatorship.

In the autumn of 1917 the nation-wide revolutionary feeling, growing steadily in the seven months since the February revolution, now reached a peak. The country was on the brink of economic disaster. Capitalist rule had brought about further dislocation in industry and transport. Industrial output dropped sharply compared with 1916. The railways were becoming paralysed. The capitalists had deliberately reduced output in an effort to starve the working class into obedience. In August the millionaire Ryabushinsky callously urged that the revolution should be strangled by the "bony hand of hunger". These were not merely words. According to conservative estimates, more than a thousand enterprises were closed and over 360,000 workers found themselves without the means of subsistence in the period from March to October. But even those who held jobs could not provide their families with a living. Famine broke out. Profiteers inflated food prices. To a large extent this was linked up with the crisis in agriculture. In 1917 the grain crop hardly reached half the pre-war level.

In *The Impending Catasrophe and How to Combat It*, written in September 1917, Lenin made a thorough analysis of the economic crisis brought about by capitalist rule and showed that only a socialist revolution could save the country from economic catastrophe. "It is *impossible*," he wrote, "in twentieth-century Russia, which has won a republic and democracy in a revolutionary way, to go forward without *advancing* towards socialism, without taking *steps* towards it. . . ."**

In the national crisis and the mounting economic disaster, the mass revolutionary movement steadily expanded. Revolutionary enthusiasm spread throughout the country. The working-class movement took the form of a mighty wave of strikes. A feature

---

* *Rasskazyvayut uchastniki Velikogo Oktyabrya (Reminiscences of Participants in the Great October Revolution)*, Moscow, 1957, p. 59.
** Lenin, *Collected Works*, Vol. 25, p. 358.

of this period was that most of these strikes were political. In Petrograd, Moscow, the Ukraine, the Urals and other areas workers took over the management of many factories and mills. The working class was gradually working towards a solution of the problem of who should take power.

In September and October, reports on the growth of the peasant movement were constantly on the agenda of Provisional Government meetings. Cases of landowner mansions being set on fire, pulled down or seized became more and more frequent. The country was on the verge of a peasant war against the landowners. The policy of the Bolshevik Party, which demanded an immediate revolutionary solution to the agrarian problem, drew the working peasants over to the side of the proletariat and ensured an alliance between the working class and the poorest sections of the peasants. This alliance was the decisive force of the socialist revolution.

Dissatisfaction was rife among the men in the trenches as well. The war was dragging into its fourth autumn and the end was not in sight. The troops were now convinced that neither the government nor the Mensheviks and the Socialist-Revolutionaries would give them peace. The elected company and regimental committees came under the control of the Bolsheviks. Thousands of soldiers wrote home urging their relatives to support the Bolsheviks. Many of these letters contained leaflets giving a popular exposition of the Bolshevik views. A letter written by a soldier on October 24 and sent to a faraway village in Siberia stated: "I am enclosing a leaflet. From it you will learn about the Party I am joining and advise you to join. It is the Social-Democratic Party, which demands the transfer of all land, forests and factories to the people. It demands the conclusion of peace as soon as possible. It is the Party of Bolsheviks."

The whole vast country was beginning to move.

Under these conditions the ruling parties—Cadets, Socialist-Revolutionaries and Mensheviks—could no longer rule the country by old methods. A crisis of authority set in. This was one of the basic elements of the revolutionary situation in the autumn of 1917.

In the Malachite Hall of the Winter Palace, which became the residence of the government under Kerensky, the ministers debated the situation endlessly. With a view to consolidating capitalist rule, the government tried to introduce bourgeois parliamentarism. On September 1, Russia was proclaimed a republic. A "Democratic Conference" attended by representatives of the conciliator parties, bourgeois-nationalist organisations, city dumas, district councils, Soviets, and so on, was convened two weeks later. It formed a Pre-Parliament (Provisional Council of the Republic), which became the government's consultative organ. At the close of September there was another reshuffle of ministers and the third (and last) coalition government was formed.

The purpose of this ballyhoo was to deceive the masses, to distract them from the revolutionary struggle. In the meantime, plans were secretly drawn for strangling the revolution. "The bourgeoisie drew up two plans of struggle against the masses," wrote A. I. Verkhovsky, who was Minister of War in the last government. "One of these plans was noisily debated at sittings of the Provisional Government and had no significance; the second plan, drawn up jointly by Kerensky, Tereshchenko and Konovalov, was a real strategic programme of struggle. It was implemented without loud words by men with their backs to the wall."[*] This second plan called for another mutiny after the Kornilov pattern. The enemies of the revolution embarked upon the monstrous crime of delivering Petrograd to German troops—a project that was nothing less than high treason.

But the last hour of the counter-revolutionary bourgeois-landowner government had struck. In the autumn of 1917 the national crisis brought the country to the proletarian revolution. On September 29, in an article entitled "The Crisis Has Matured" Lenin wrote: "The end of September undoubtedly marked a great turning point in the history of the Russian revolution and, to all appearance, of the world revolution as well."[**]

Socialist Revolution

On October 10, the Central Committee of the R.S.D.L.P.(B.) held a meeting in Petrograd, in a house on the esplanade along the Karpovka River. Presided over by Yakov Sverdlov, this meeting was attended by Lenin, Bubnov, Dzerzhinsky, Stalin, Kollontai, Lomov, Oppokov, Sokolnikov, Zinoviev, Kamenev and Trotsky. The latter had been admitted into the Party together with the Mezhrayontsi by the Sixth Congress and elected a member of the Central Committee.[***]

This was the first time Lenin had attended a Central Committee meeting since the July events. He had returned illegally to Petrograd shortly before the meeting was convened. In mid-September he had written a letter to the Central, Petrograd and Moscow

---

[*] A. I. Verkhovsky, *Na trudnom perevale* (*At a Difficult Crossing*), Moscow, 1959, p. 364.

[**] Lenin, *Collected Works*, Vol. 26, p. 74.

[***] The Mezhrayontsi were a small group of Trotskyite Mensheviks and former Bolsheviks and were active in 1913-17. In the summer of 1917 they proclaimed their agreement with the Bolshevik policy and were accepted into the Party. V. Volodarsky, Moses Uritsky and some other members of this group became loyal Bolsheviks. But Leon Trotsky, as subsequent events showed, remained an out-and-out opportunist and joined the Party with the purpose of undermining it from within.—*Ed.*

committees, entitling it "The Bolsheviks Must Seize Power". At the same time, he sent another letter, "Marxism and Insurrection", to the C.C. In these two documents he made a profound analysis of the situation in the country and drew the conclusion that the Bolsheviks could and should seize power. "We have the following of the *majority* of the people," he wrote. "*Our victory is assured,* for the people are close to desperation, and we are showing the entire people a sure way out. ..."*

At the C.C. meeting on October 10, Lenin showed that the time had come for an armed insurrection, that such an insurrection was inevitable. "We now have the majority behind us," he said. "Politically, the situation is fully ripe for taking power.... We must speak of the technical aspect."**

In this situation the C.C. endorsed the historic decision of immediately starting preparations for an armed insurrection. This decision was opposed by only two members of the C.C., Zinoviev and Kamenev. This was not surprising, for it was the result of their opportunism and betrayal of the proletarian revolution. The C.C. rejected the arguments of these capitulators and issued a clear directive, which stated: "An armed insurrection is inevitable and has fully matured. The C.C. instructs all Party organisations to be guided by this and to examine and resolve all practical questions from this point of view."***

Thus, the Sixth Congress had shown that the forcible overthrow of the Provisional Government was inevitable and readied the proletariat for an armed insurrection, but now, in a situation when the revolutionary crisis had matured, the C.C. issued a directive ordering preparations for immediate action.

These preparations were started in an atmosphere of nation-wide revolutionary enthusiasm. In carrying out Lenin's instructions, the Party treated the insurrection as something requiring great skill and carefully prepared for it.

In these preparations and during the insurrection a key role was played by the Military Revolutionary Committee that was set up on October 12 by the Petrograd Soviet on the initiative of the Bolsheviks. It was an organ charged to lead the insurrection and had contact with the broadest sections of workers and soldiers. It was composed of representatives of the Petrograd Soviet and garrison, the Baltic Fleet, the Finland Regional Committee of Soviets, the Red Guards, the trade unions, and Party, military and other organisations. Through it the mass of workers and soldiers was drawn into the preparations for the insurrection.

---

* Lenin, *Collected Works,* Vol. 26, p. 24.
** *Ibid.,* pp. 188, 189.
*** *Protokoly Tsentralnogo Komiteta RSDRP(b)* (*Minutes of the Central Committee of the R.S.D.L.P.[B.]*), Moscow, 1958, p. 86.

Demonstration in Petrograd, July 1917

Revolutionary soldiers and Red Guards guard the Smolny
Institute, October 1917

An extended meeting of the Central Committee was held under Lenin's chairmanship on October 16. It was attended by representatives of the Petrograd Committee, the Military Organisation, the Petrograd Soviet, the trade unions, factory committees, the Petrograd District Party Committee and the railwaymen. The C.C. directive on the insurrection was endorsed. This meeting called upon "all organisations and all workers and soldiers to make all-sided, energetic prepartions for the armed insurrection".* Furthermore, the C.C. set up a Military Revolutionary Centre consisting of Yakov Sverdlov, Joseph Stalin, Felix Dzerzhinsky, Andrei Bubnov and Moses Uritsky, which became the leading Party nucleus of the Military Revolutionary Committee. After this meeting, on October 18, Zinoviev and Kamenev wrote an article for the semi-Menshevik newspaper *Novaya Zhizn*, in which they protested against the Central Committee decision on an armed insurrection. This was unparalleled treachery, a betrayal of the proletariat, which was preparing to seize power.

Lenin wrote to the C.C., denouncing this treachery and demanding Zinoviev's and Kamenev's expulsion from the Party. However, Stalin urged reconciliation with them.

The treachery of these two men inflicted enormous harm on the preparations, but it was now impossible to postpone the insurrection.

In Petrograd, the Red Guards, which had 23,000 armed workers, were brought up to combat readiness. Agitation was intensified in units of the Petrograd garrison and in the Baltic Fleet. The Military Revolutionary Committee sent its commissars to factories, regiments, naval barracks and warships. The preparations were directed by the C.C. and, personally, by Lenin, who guided the Party from his secret address.

Soon preparations were in full swing in other cities and industrial centres. The determination of the masses to seize power is strikingly illustrated by the number of district and gubernia congresses of Soviets as well as of the regional congresses of Soviets held in the Donbas, the Urals, the Volga Country, Siberia and other areas in October. These congresses demanded the transfer of power to the Soviets and made it plain that they were preparing for decisive battles.

Warned of the planned insurrection by Zinoviev and Kamenev, the Provisional Government began transferring loyal troops to Petrograd and reinforcing the guard around the Winter Palace and other government buildings. The counter-revolution was not limiting itself to defence. It planned to forestall the insurrection and crush the forces of the revolution.

---

* *Protokoly Tsentralnogo Komiteta RSDRP(b)* (*Minutes of the Central Committee of the R.S.D.L.P.[B.]*), Moscow, 1958, p. 104.

However, the balance of forces was on the side of the proletarian revolution. On October 22-23, the Military Revolutionary Committee drew up a concrete plan of insurrection, founded on Lenin's instructions on "a simultaneous offensive on Petrograd, as sudden and as rapid as possible, which must without fail be carried out from within and from without, from the working-class quarters and from Finland, from Revel and from Kronstadt".* It envisaged a combined offensive by the workers, military units and the fleet, which were the three principal revolutionary forces.

On a bleak day—Tuesday, October 24—the struggle entered the decisive stage.

At about 6 a.m., when the sullen dawn had only just broken, a unit of military cadets drove up to the offices of *Rabochy Put*, the Bolshevik Party organ, and produced a warrant authorising them to close the newspaper.** In an effort to control the situation and start an offensive itself, the Provisional Government ordered all the bridges to be raised and reinforced the guard at the Winter Palace with units of military cadets and "storm troops".

The government planned to deliver one of the main blows at Smolny, which the Bolsheviks had turned into the headquarters of the proletarian revolution.

The C.C. took retaliatory measures as soon as news was received that the counter-revolution had taken action. The Military Revolutionary Committee was ordered to drive the military cadets out of the *Rabochy Put* printshop and offices and ensure the safety of the newspaper's premises. The newspaper came off the press at 11 a.m. that same morning. Its editorial stated: "Power must pass into the hands of the Soviets of Workers', Soldiers' and Peasants' Deputies. A new government elected and replaceable by and responsible to the Soviets must be installed."

A report of the Military Revolutionary Committee on the new situation was read at a meeting of the Party Central Committee. Sverdlov, Dzerzhinsky, Bubnov and other C.C. members were placed in charge of key sectors and the C.C. issued a directive ordering the revolutionary forces to begin the insurrection.

The Military Revolutionary Committee prepared the Red Guards and revolutionary regiments for action. Revolutionary Petrograd went into motion. Composedly and fully determined to fight for the power of the Soviets to the victorious end, tens of thousands of Red Guardsmen and revolutionary soldiers and sailors rose to the attack. Representatives of factories, mills and military units arrived at Smolny. The revolutionary units summoned by the Military Revolutionary Committee began mustering in the vicinity.

---

* Lenin, *Collected Works*, Vol. 26, p. 180.
** After the July events *Pravda* was printed as the *Rabochy i Soldat*, *Proletary*, *Rabochy* and, lastly, *Rabochy Put*. It resumed publication under its own name on October 27.—*Ed.*

The forces of the revolution gradually gained control of the situation in the city. The initiative slipped out of the hands of the Provisional Government. Its hopes of receiving assistance from without the city proved to be futile. Through the radio station on the *Aurora*, the revolutionary cruiser that played an outstanding role in the insurrection, the Military Revolutionary Committee instructed all revolutionary organisations outside Petrograd to bar the way to the troops called out by the Provisional Government.

At the same time, in conformity with the plan for the insurrection, support was ensured for revolutionary Petrograd. Warships and units of sailors were hurriedly readied in Kronstadt for dispatch to Petrograd. A coded telegram, stating "Send regulations", was sent to the Central Committee of the Baltic Fleet in Helsingfors (Helsinki). This meant that it was time to move the revolutionary units of sailors and soldiers to Petrograd.

That day, October 24, Lenin was still in hiding. In the evening he wrote to the Central Committee, precisely stating its task: "The government is tottering. It must be *given the deathblow* at all costs."*

The Central Committee took all steps to expedite the insurrection. Red Guardsmen and revolutionary soldiers and sailors seized all the bridges across the Neva. They occupied first the Central Telegraph Office and then the Petrograd Telegraph Agency. A concentric offensive was started from the working-class districts towards the centre of the city. At the end of October 24, the Commander of the Petrograd District reported to General Headquarters in Mogilev: "The situation in Petrograd has become perilous. There is no street-fighting or disorder, but offices and railway stations are being methodically seized and people are being arrested. No orders [of the Provisional Government.—*Ed.*] are being obeyed. The military cadets are surrendering their posts without resistance, and the Cossacks, despite repeated orders, have not yet left their barracks. The Provisional Government is in danger of losing all its authority."

Lenin arrived at Smolny at around midnight and took over the direct leadership of the revolution. The news that Lenin was in Smolny quickly spread and gave the revolution added wings.

The offensive continued all night. By the morning of October 25, all the key positions—the railway stations, the power stations, the telephone exchange, the State Bank, and so forth—were in the hands of the revolution. The ring round the Provisional Government tightened. The latter had under its control only a small district in the centre of the city—the Winter Palace, the General Staff, the Mariinsky Palace and some other buildings.

The ministers feverishly took measures to send at least part of

---

* Lenin, *Collected Works*, Vol. 26, p. 235.

the garrison against the revolution. Kerensky dispatched several telegrams to General Headquarters and the Northern Front, asking them to send troops at once. But there was nothing the counter-revolutionary generals could do to help the government.

In the morning a car from the U.S. Embassy sped through the streets of Petrograd. It flew the U.S. flag and the Red Guards outposts let it drive out of the city. Kerensky was in it. The Entente representatives gave every assistance to the struggle against the revolution. They helped Kerensky to flee from Petrograd, hoping that he would be able to muster the counter-revolutionary forces and move them against the insurgents.

At 10 a.m., the Military Revolutionary Committee made public Lenin's historical address "To the Citizens of Russia!", in which it was announced that the Provisional Government had been overthrown. "The cause for which the people have fought," the address said, "namely, the immediate offer of a democratic peace, the abolition of the landed proprietorship, workers' control over production, and the establishment of Soviet power—this cause has been secured."*

The news that the Provisional Government had been overthrown spread throughout the country.

An emergency meeting of the Petrograd Soviet was held in the morning in Smolny's Assembly Hall. The workers' and soldiers' delegates gave Lenin an ovation when he appeared on the platform. When silence was restored, he began speaking:

"Comrades, the workers' and peasants' revolution, about the necessity of which the Bolsheviks have always spoken, has been accomplished.

"From now on, a new phase in the history of Russia begins, and this, the third Russian revolution, should in the end lead to the victory of socialism."**

The Petrograd Soviet greeted the victorious revolution and noted the solidarity, organisation, discipline and "complete unanimity, displayed by the masses in this unusually bloodless and unusually successful insurrection".

The culminating point of the insurrection was the storming of the Winter Palace and the arrest of the Provisional Government. By the evening of October 25, all the buildings in the centre of the city were occupied and the Winter Palace was surrounded. The ranks of the palace defenders grew steadily thinner, but the ousted government refused to surrender. The approaches to the huge brown palace were protected by barricades and covered by machine guns. The ministers expected to hold out until assistance, which Kerensky had hastened away to call, would

---

* Lenin, *Collected Works*, Vol. 26, p. 236.
** *Ibid.*, p. 239.

The Red Guards enter the Kremlin, 1917

Decree on Peace

Декретъ о мирѣ,

принятый единогласно на засѣданiи Все-
россiйскаго Съѣзда Совѣтовъ Рабочихъ,
Солдатскихъ и Крестьянскихъ Депутатовъ
26 октября 1917 г.

Soldiers and workers of Petrograd receiving the *Izvestia*, 1917

arrive. Moreover, they pinned their hopes on the Mensheviks and Socialist-Revolutionaries, who were fighting the insurrection side by side with the other counter-revolutionary forces.

However, the steel ring round the palace was steadily tightening. On instructions from the Party Central Committee, a triumvirate headed by Nikolai Podvoisky, Chairman of the Revolutionary Military Committee, was charged with directing the storming of the Winter Palace. The decision to storm the palace was taken when the ministers failed to reply to an ultimatum to capitulate. The cruiser *Aurora*, which had steamed in from Kronstadt with other warships, was anchored in the Neva, its guns trained on the Winter Palace. A blank shot from one of its six-inch guns gave the signal for the attack. The artillery of the Peter and Paul Fortress opened fire at the Winter Palace. On the night of October 25 the Winter Palace was taken by storm and at 2.10 a.m., October 26, the government was arrested.

October 25 (November 7) has gone down in history as the day the Great October Socialist Revolution triumphed. It ushered in a new era, the era of socialism and communism, in the history of Russia and the whole world.

The Second All-Russia Congress of Soviets of Workers' and Soldiers' Deputies opened at the Smolny Palace at 10.45 p.m. on October 25. Representing more than 400 Soviets, it was the organ of the revolutionary masses. A number of delegates from the Peasants' Soviets was also present. Of the 650 delegates at the Congress nearly 400 were Bolsheviks. At its first sitting the Congress debated the question of power. The Mensheviks and Right Socialist-Revolutionaries did all they could to save the Provisional Government. When, finally, their attempts failed they walked out of the Congress. An address "To Workers, Soldiers, and Peasants!", written by Lenin, was adopted by an overwhelming majority of votes. "Backed by the will of the vast majority of workers, soldiers and peasants," it said, "backed by the victorious uprising of the workers and the garrison which has taken place in Petrograd, the Congress takes power into its own hands. . . .

"The Congress decrees: all power in the localities shall pass to the Soviets of Workers', Soldiers' and Peasants' Deputies, which must guarantee genuine revolutionary order."*

The second and last sitting of the Congress was held in the evening of October 26. It adopted the historical decrees on Peace, on Land and on the formation of a Soviet Government. Thunderous applause greeted Lenin when he got up to speak.

"Now Lenin, gripping the edge of the reading stand, letting his little winking eyes travel over the crowd as he stood there waiting, apparently oblivious to the long-rolling ovation, which

---

* Lenin, *Collected Works*, Vol. 26, p. 247.

lasted several minutes. When it finished, he said simply, 'We shall now proceed to construct the socialist order!'

"Again that overwhelming human roar."*

Lenin's Decree on Peace, unanimously passed by the Congress, condemned imperialist, predatory wars. The Soviet Government proposed that all belligerent nations and their governments should at once begin negotiating a just, democratic peace. For its part, it declared, it was prepared to conclude peace without delay. The decree defined democratic peace as peace without annexations and without indemnities. It called upon the workers of Britain, France and Germany to take decisive action which would help "to conclude peace successfully, and at the same time emancipate the labouring and exploited masses of our population from all forms of slavery and all forms of exploitation."**

Lenin's Decree on Land, drawn up on the basis of 242 recommendations from the peasants themselves, likewise conformed with the interests of the masses. It was given wide publicity in the press. All landed estates were abolished without redemption. These estates, as well as land belonging to the royal family, the monasteries and the church together with all the implements, buildings and so on were turned over to the volost land committees and the uyezd Soviets of Peasants' Deputies. This far-reaching revolutionary act placed more than 150 million hectares of landed estates and other land into the hands of the peasants. The right of private landownership was abolished and the land was declared the property of the people. The nationalisation of land under the Decree on Land drew the working peasants over to the side of the Soviet government, played an immense role in strengthening the alliance between the workers and the working peasants and thereby helped to consolidate the proletarian revolution.

The Congress elected a new A.R.C.E.C., in which the leading role was played by the Bolsheviks. Lev Kamenev was elected chairman, but was soon succeeded by Yakov Sverdlov. The Congress concluded its sittings with the formation of a workers' and peasants' government—the Council of People's Commissars—headed by Lenin. The Bolsheviks in the new government included Anatoly Lunacharsky, V. Milyutin, Victor Nogin, Ivan Skvortsov (Stepanov), Joseph Stalin and Ivan Teodorovich.

After the October Revolution, Soviet rule was consolidated throughout Russia in struggle with the counter-revolution and its accomplices, the Mensheviks and Socialist-Revolutionaries. With the support of the Entente, the deposed exploiters started a civil war. Kerensky, who had escaped from Petrograd, assembled the counter-revolutionary forces and under General Krasnov these

---

* John Reed, *Ten Days That Shook the World*, New York, 1934, p. 126.
** Lenin, *Collected Works*, Vol. 26, p. 252.

forces marched on the capital. By October 28 Krasnov seized Gatchina and Tsarskoye Selo. On October 29, when this news reached them, the Mensheviks and Socialist-Revolutionaries provoked an anti-Soviet uprising in Petrograd, making the situation extremely critical.* But with the backing of the workers, soldiers and sailors, the Party C.C. and the Soviet Government ensured the rout of the counter-revolution. The uprising in the city was crushed. On October 30, the revolutionary troops put Krasnov's army to flight at the Pulkovo Heights. Soon afterwards Krasnov was captured and Kerensky went into hiding.

In the short span of time from October 1917 to February 1918, the socialist revolution swept triumphantly across the entire country, breaking down the resistance of the deposed exploiter classes.

The consolidation of Soviet rule in Moscow was an exceedingly important development. A major industrial and cultural centre, Moscow was called the country's second capital. Due to a number of reasons, the struggle in that city was more protracted than in Petrograd.

On the morning of October 25, when the news of the revolutionary uprising in Petrograd came through, the Moscow Committee of the Bolshevik Party called upon the working people to set up Soviets. The Red Guards and revolutionary soldiers occupied some of the key points in the city. A Military Revolutionary Committee was formed in the evening of the same day, but by that time the struggle in Moscow had entered the decisive stage. Besides, right until October 27 this committee included Mensheviks, who used every opportunity to disrupt its actions. Another negative factor was the opportunist vacillation of some of the leaders of the Moscow Bolshevik organisation.

The Military Revolutionary Committee's first step was to demand that the revolutionary forces be readied for combat without delay.

The first successes were achieved by the Bolshevik-led masses towards the morning of October 26, when they established virtual control over a number of districts in the city. But the counter-revolution was not idle either. It rallied its forces, from the Mensheviks and Socialist-Revolutionaries to the Cadets and monarchists,

---

* At this time the All-Russia Executive Committee of Railway Employees (A.R.E.C.R.E.), which was dominated by Socialist-Revolutionaries and Mensheviks, demanded in an ultimatum that the Council of People's Commissars set up a "homogenous socialist government" with the participation of Mensheviks and Socialist-Revolutionaries. The conciliators believed that this manoeuvre would offset the gains of the October Revolution. Their demand was supported by Kamenev, Zinoviev, Rykov and other opportunists and capitulators. When this act was scathingly censured by the Bolshevik C.C., the capitulators withdrew from the C.C. and the Council of People's Commissars, calculating that this step would precipitate a crisis in the government and Party. The defeat of the capitulators still further strengthened the Party's unity and solidarity.—*Ed.*

round the "Public Security Committee", which had been set up by the city Duma. To win time it started talks with the Military Revolutionary Committee on October 26. The latter agreed to withdraw the revolutionary soldiers from the Kremlin and also its guards from the post and telegraph office, a move which proved to be a great mistake.

On the evening of October 27, the counter-revolution went over to the offensive. On October 28, the military cadets captured the Kremlin and massacred the soldiers of the 56th Regiment stationed there.

On instructions from the Bolshevik Party, the Military Revolutionary Committee called upon the masses to take decisive action.

Red Guard units were rushed to Moscow from Ivanovo-Voznesensk, Shuya, Tula, Vladimir, Serpukhov and other towns. Lenin ordered several detachments of sailors and workers to be sent from Petrograd.

The decisive battles were fought on November 1-2. The revolutionary units dislodged the military cadets from the houses and streets. On November 2, they reached Red Square, and captured the Kremlin on the night of November 3. Led by the Bolsheviks, the masses fought heroically and defeated the counter-revolution. The "Public Security Committee" was dispersed and the authority of the Soviets was consolidated in the city.

In its struggle against Soviet rule, the counter-revolution banked greatly on the support of the army, primarily of the troops from the front line. Most of the support for the counter-revolution came from the reactionary section of the officer corps as well as from the Mensheviks and Socialist-Revolutionaries, who still retained their influence in army and front-line committees. But the events of the first week after the October armed insurrection showed that the soldiers were solidly behind the Soviet authorities. The counter-revolutionary plans collapsed first on the Northern Front, which was in direct proximity to Petrograd. Most of the troops of this front took the side of the Soviet authorities against the Kerensky-Krasnov anti-Soviet uprising.

Failing to win support on the Northern Front, the counter-revolution turned to the Western Front, and the Front Headquarters in Mogilev became the centre of another anti-Soviet conspiracy. It became the rallying point for enemies of Soviet power, one of them being the Right Socialist-Revolutionary leader Chernov, whom the reactionaries wanted to place at the head of an anti-Soviet government. But nothing came of this plan either. The uprising inspired by the counter-revolutionary Headquarters at Mogilev was foiled largely through the action of the soldiers of the Western Front, who actively supported the Soviet government.

The proletarian revolution thus triumphed first on the Northern and Western fronts, which were close to the country's most important industrial and revolutionary regions. On the South-Western and particularly on the Rumanian and Caucasian fronts, which were far from the centre, the struggle lasted longer. But even there, the overwhelming majority of the soldiers went over to the Soviet side by the end of November or in December.

Reassuring news of the consolidation of Soviet rule and of its first successes came from all parts of the country. In the central gubernias with their industrial and political centres and homogeneous, primarily Russian population, Soviet rule was quickly established. This was due to the leading role played in the revolution by the Russian working class. Soviet rule was established without bloodshed in the area around Moscow, in the Ivanovo-Voznesensk industrial district, in Vladimir, Yaroslavl, Pskov, Tula, Nizhny Novgorod and other towns and districts in Central Russia. In Voronezh, Saratov, Kaluga and Smolensk, the resistance of the counter-revolution was feeble and was quickly overcome.

Soviet rule rapidly spread over the Volga Country, the Urals, Siberia and the Far East.

The counter-revolution failed to entrench itself even in the Cossack regions, where the bastions of the reactionary forces were to be found. Within a few weeks the new Soviet power put down the uprising engineered by the Don Cossack leader Kaledin, whose forces had seized Rostov and Taganrog and were preparing to advance into the Donbas. Red Guard units were sent to the Don from Petrograd, Moscow and other regions. In January and February 1918, Kaledin's forces suffered a series of disastrous reverses. Rostov (end of February) and then Novocherkassk were liberated. Kaledin shot himself and on the Don power passed into the hands of the Don Military Revolutionary Committee headed by the Bolshevik Fyodor Podtelkov.

An attempt to organise an anti-Soviet insurrection headed by Orenburg Cossacks likewise collapsed. Ataman Dutov, who inspired the uprising and seized Orenburg, held out only until January 1918. The Dutov adventure was nipped in the bud by revolutionary sailors and soldiers from Petrograd and also by Red Guards from the Volga Country and the Urals. Orenburg was liberated on January 18, and the remnants of Dutov's gangs fled into the steppes.

The decrees on Peace and on Land as well as the first steps taken by the Soviet Government, which showed its close ties with the people, played a prominent role in helping to consolidate Soviet rule throughout the country. Lenin's nationalities policy, proclaimed as soon as Soviet power was instituted, was of tremendous significance to the non-Russian areas. On November 2, the Soviet Government adopted its historic Declaration of the Rights of the Peoples of Russia, which gave full equality to all the nationalities of Russia and guaranteed their right to self-determination up to secession. All national restrictions and privileges were abolished. The proletarian revolution laid a lasting foundation for the building up of a multi-national socialist state.

Battering down the resistance of the bourgeois-nationalist counter-revolution, the working people of the non-Russian regions joined in building the new way of life. The Soviets were consolidated in Byelorussia as early as the close of October. There the major role was played by the working people of Minsk, Gomel and Vitebsk and by the revolutionary soldiers of the Western Front. The Council of People's Commissars of the Western Region, headed by the Bolshevik Alexander Myasnikov, was set up in Byelorussia in November. Soviet rule triumphed also in unoccupied Baltic territory—in Estonia and Latvia.

In the Ukraine, fierce resistance was put up by the Central Rada, which took reprisals against the Kiev workers in early November. Almost the whole of the Ukraine came under its rule. Its bourgeois-nationalist leaders declared war on Soviet Russia and appealed to the imperialist powers for aid. The Donets Basin and Kharkov became the strong points of the struggle against the Rada. The First All-Ukraine Congress of Soviets, which proclaimed Soviet power in the Ukraine, was held in Kharkov in December. A Ukrainian Soviet Government was formed, and it included member of the C.C. R.S.D.L.P.(B.) Fyodor Sergeyev (Artyom), Yevgenia Bosh and Y. Kotsyubinsky. It was recognised by the Council of People's Commissars of Soviet Russia as the only legal government of the Ukraine. With fraternal assistance from the people of Russia, the Ukrainian revolutionary forces started an armed struggle against the Central Rada. Kiev was liberated on January 26, and soon afterwards Soviet rule was established throughout the Ukraine.

Soviet rule was also established in the Crimea and the North Caucasus. In Transcaucasia the bourgeois-nationalist counter-revolution retained its position for some time. Soviet rule was proclaimed in Baku on October 31, but in other regions of Transcaucasia the Musavatists, Dashnaks and Georgian Mensheviks, aided by foreign imperialists, made a dogged stand against the proletarian revolution.

In Central Asia and Kazakhstan the Soviet Government's address "To All Working Moslems of Russia and the East", published on November 20, was enthusiastically welcomed by the working people. The Soviet Government gave the Moslems the right of freely choosing their way of life. Tashkent became the centre of the revolutionary struggle of the peoples of Central Asia and Kazakhstan. An armed uprising by the working class there established Soviet rule on October 31. In mid-November, the Third Territory Congress of Soviets, held in Tashkent, proclaimed Soviet rule throughout the whole of Turkestan.

Showing the reasons for the successful establishment of Soviet rule in the vast expanses of Russia, Lenin pointed out that the Civil War, started by the counter-revolution, "gradually turned into a victorious triumphal march of the revolution as the masses of the people and the military units that were sent against us came over to the side of the Bolsheviks. We saw this in Petrograd, on the Gatchina front, where the Cossacks, whom Kerensky and Krasnov tried to lead against the Red capital, wavered; we saw this later in Moscow, in Orenburg and in the Ukraine. A wave of civil war swept over the whole of Russia, and everywhere we achieved victory with extraordinary ease precisely because the fruit had ripened, because the masses had already gone through the experience of collaboration with the bourgeoisie. Our slogan 'All Power to the Soviets', which the masses had tested in practice by long historical experience, had become part of their flesh and blood."[*]

The success of the Great October Socialist Revolution was a triumph of Marxism-Leninism. The Russian working class was the driving force of this revolution, coming forward as the leader of the people's struggle. The anti-popular bourgeois-landowner dictatorship would not have been overthrown if the proletariat had not had the millions of working peasants on its side as a faithful ally. The proletariat won the support of the working peasants and brought about the socialist revolution in alliance with the poorest sections of the peasantry.

The October Revolution triumphed because the masses were led by the steeled, militant, revolutionary Bolshevik Party. It was the soul and leader of the Russian proletariat. It created and strengthened the alliance between the working class and the peasants, and won the support of millions of people for the proletarian revolution. The Party directed various revolutionary movements towards the single objective of overthrowing imperialism. It united into a single revolutionary torrent the democratic movement for peace, the peasant democratic movement for land, the movement of the oppressed peoples for national equality and the socialist movement of the proletariat for the overthrow of the capitalists and the seizure of power by the people.

Accomplished by the masses themselves, who embarked upon a new life, the Great October Socialist Revolution was a genuinely popular upheaval.

Its triumph in Russia was the natural outcome of social development, particularly in the preceding 20 years.

It was an epoch-making triumph, for it laid the beginning for mankind's transition from capitalism to socialism and showed all nations the road to a new social system.

Lenin said that it had a dual international significance; firstly,

---

[*] Lenin, *Collected Works*, Vol. 27, p. 89.

in the broad sense, i.e., in the sense of its influence on the course of world history, and in the narrow sense, in the sense that its "repetition on an international scale"* was inevitable, that a socialist revolution in any country would inevitably be guided by some of the basic laws that governed the October Revolution in Russia.

Lenin, of course, had in mind not a mechanical repetition of the "Russian experience" or apish imitation of the tactics adopted by the Communists in Russia, but the inevitable manifestation of such phenomena of socialist revolution as the leadership given by the proletariat, and its vanguard—the Marxist-Leninist party—to the struggle of the masses for the triumph of the revolution and the establishment of the dictatorship of the proletariat; the alliance of the working class with the main mass of the peasants and urban working people; the abolition of national oppression; socialist transformation of industry and agriculture; an ideological and cultural revolution; solidarity between the triumphant proletariat and the working class of other countries, which is the principle underlying proletarian internationalism.

Such is the significance of the October Revolution in the narrow sense.

No other revolution has so profoundly influenced the course of world history. It awakened a popular revolutionary movement in all countries and in all continents. It gave free rein to the revolutionary initiative of the masses, who have risen to storm capitalism in many countries. The German and the Austro-Hungarian monarchies collapsed in the revolutionary conflagration that raged in the heart of Europe for more than five years, and were replaced by bourgeois republics.

Influenced by the October Revolution, the peoples of the colonies and dependent countries rose against imperialism and began to take an active part in the struggle to abolish the disgraceful colonial system.

The October Revolution brought organisation to the movement of the proletariat and other working masses: Communist Parties sprang up in many countries and their membership steadily increased; the trade unions were joined by ever larger numbers of working people; and the peace movement grew steadily stronger.

With the formation of the Soviet state, which proclaimed the great slogan of peace and implemented it in its relations with other peoples and countries, mankind found a reliable bulwark for its struggle against predatory wars, for peace and security.

In short, the October Revolution in Russia "shook the entire structure of world capitalism to its very foundations; the world split into two opposing systems".**

---

* Lenin, *Selected Works*, Vol. 3, p. 375.
** *The Road to Communism*, Moscow, p. 456.

Yakov Sverdlov

Felix Dzerzhinsky

Valerian Kuibyshev

Grigory Orjonikidze

Nikolai Shchors

Vasily Chapayev

Sergei Lazo

Such is the international significance of the October Revolution in the broad sense.

"We Shall Build a New World. . . ."

Having delivered the working people from oppression and exploitation, the October Revolution released inexhaustible creative forces and roused the people's energy in all branches of political, economic and cultural activity.

It fundamentally changed the position of all classes and sections of the population. The proletariat became the ruling class, leading the working masses of town and country. The Communist Party became the ruling political organisation of the world's first socialist state of workers and peasants.

The revolution placed the power into the hands of the Soviets, which became a state form of the dictatorship of the proletariat. Through them, under the leadership of the Communist Party, the people accomplished important revolutionary reforms within an incredibly short space of time. No vestige was left of the old bourgeois-landowner Russia. On its ruins, millions of workers and peasants began building a new, socialist state.

Colossal work was started. The old state apparatus was gradually superseded by a new machine. This work was constantly sabotaged by officials in the ministries and departments. The Communist Party placed workers and peasants at the helm of state. Fresh from the October battles, they enthusiastically got down to creating a new state apparatus. Sailors of the Baltic Fleet and workers of the Siemens-Schuckert plant in Petrograd went to work in the People's Commissariat for Foreign Affairs. Workers of the Putilov Plant helped to organise the People's Commissariat for Internal Affairs. The People's Commissariat for Education was set up with the active assistance of workers from Petrograd's Vyborg District.

In addition to the building up of a central state apparatus, colossal work went on on a local scale. On November 5, in an ardent speech to the workers and peasants, Lenin urged them on in this work:

"Comrade toilers! Remember that now *you yourselves* are at the helm of state. No one will help you if you yourselves do not unite and take into *your* hands *all affairs* of state. *Your* Soviets are from now on the organs of state authority, working bodies with full powers. . . .

"Strengthen them. Get on with the job yourselves, begin right at the bottom, do not wait for anyone."*

The Zemstvos, city Dumas and other bourgeois organs of power were abolished in the gubernias and uyezds and Soviet organs were

---

* Lenin, *Collected Works*, Vol. 26, p. 297.

set up in their stead. Large numbers of people were drawn into this work. Special departments to direct economic and cultural development were formed within the Soviets. Instructions on the rights and duties of the Soviets were published on December 24. These instructions set the pattern of the local Soviets and defined their rights and duties both to the central organs and to the electorate.

The power of the Soviets was consolidated in the villages and volosts. This was greatly furthered by the Extraordinary All-Russia Congress of Soviets of Peasants' Deputies, which sat in Petrograd in November. Most of the delegates gave their support to the "Left" Socialist-Revolutionaries* and the Bolsheviks. The Congress recognised Soviet rule and endorsed the decrees on Peace and on Land. The Central Executive Committee elected by it merged with A.R.C.E.C. of the Soviets of Workers' and Soldiers' Deputies. The Soviets of Workers' and Soldiers' Deputies were likewise amalgamated with the Soviets of Peasants' Deputies on a local level, a step resulting in the consolidation of the working-class leadership of the peasants in the interests of socialist construction.

Besides ending the rule of the capitalists and landowners, Soviet power abolished all the survivals of feudalism that had been burdening the people for many decades. On November 11, A.R.C.E.C. and the Council of People's Commissars promulgated a decree abolishing estates and civil ranks. The division of society into nobility, peasants, merchants, petty bourgeois and so forth, as well as all titles and ranks were annulled. Every person became a citizen of the Russian Soviet Republic. A new decree `On Civil Marriage, on Children and on Registers of Births, Marriages and Deaths was published. Women were given equal rights with men. On January 20, the Soviet Government announced that the church had been separated from the state and that the schools had been separated from the church.

The new world was born amid a relentless class struggle. By Civil War and anti-Soviet mutinies, the counter-revolution tried to throttle Soviet rule. The reactionaries mustered all their forces. Saboteurs in government offices, profiteers and gangs of hooligans and thugs were used in the struggle against the power of the workers and peasants. Entente representatives were active in

---

* The "Left" Socialist-Revolutionaries were a group within the Socialist-Revolutionary Party. At the close of 1917 this group became an independent party. To avoid losing all influence over the peasants, the Left Socialist-Revolutionaries formally, after long vacillation, subscribed to the policy of the Soviets. At the end of November 1917 their representatives were given portfolios in the Soviet Government (the people's commissariats for Agriculture, Justice and Posts and Telegraph). However, they were unreliable in their co-operation with Soviet rule. In the spring of 1918 they resigned from the government and shortly afterwards became active in the struggle against the Soviet state.—*Ed.*

organising this struggle. The Cadet Party became the heart and soul of all anti-Soviet conspiracies. The revolution took effective measures to defend its gains. The masses were roused to action against the enemies of the people. On November 28, the Council of People's Commissars passed the Decree on the Arrest of Leaders of the Civil War Against the Revolution, which proclaimed the Cadet Party an enemy of the people. Under this decree, which was drawn up by Lenin, all the Cadet leaders were subject to arrest and trial by revolutionary tribunals. At the close of October and early in November the leadership of the struggle against the counter-revolution was taken over by the Petrograd Military Revolutionary Committee. Early in December the Council of People's Commissars set up a special organ to combat enemies of Soviet rule, the All-Russia Extraordinary Commission for the Suppression of Counter-Revolution, Sabotage and Profiteering. The Party appointed the tested Bolshevik and Leninist Felix Dzerzhinsky to head this organ.

The militia organised by the Provisional Government was replaced by a workers' and peasants' militia, which protected revolutionary law and order and the security of Soviet citizens. The old bourgeois-landowner judiciary was supplanted by the people's courts, which became an instrument for the suppression of the exploiter classes and the consolidation of the Soviet state system.

In the first weeks after the Revolution the Red Guards and revolutionary military units became the bulwark of Soviet power. The old Army and Navy were democratised, and new armed forces were created at the same time that the old forces were demobilised. The Council of People's Commissars set up an All-Russian Collegium for the Organisation and Formation of a New Army. The collegium was headed by Nikolai Krylenko and Nikolai Podvoisky. On January 15, 1918, the Council of People's Commissars passed a decree forming the Workers' and Peasants' Red Army. On February 29, a decree on the formation of the Workers' and Peasants' Navy was published.

The building of the new life steadily gained momentum.

The country started building a new, socialist economy. This tremendous task would never have been fulfilled if strict accounting and control over production had not been introduced. On November 14, A.R.C.E.C. adopted Rules of Workers' Control, which were introduced at all enterprises employing workers. These rules embraced production, the purchase and sale of products and raw materials, and the financial activity of enterprises. Control was exercised by the workers of the given enterprise through factory committees, councils of elders and other elective organs. The All-Russia Council of Workers' Control was set up in Petrograd, and workers' control councils were formed at the local Soviets. The decisions of these councils were mandatory for owners of enterprises and could be overruled only by decision of higher workers' control organs.

Workers' control soon embraced thousands of factories, mines, trade, banking, agricultural and other enterprises. The control commissions enlisted the aid of tens and hundreds of thousands of workers. Far from restricting themselves to simply observing the work of enterprises, they made it their business to keep an eye on the work of the management and were active in passing decisions on all economic problems. These organs played an important role in curbing the capitalists and undermining their economic might. At the same time, they became a school of economic training for the working masses, and were a major preparatory step towards the socialist nationalisation of industry.

Lenin called the first months after the victory of the proletarian revolution a period of "attacks by Red Guards against capital". Soviet power did not repeat the mistake of the Paris Commune; it did not waste time taking the State Bank into its own hands. Control was instituted over private banks, and then, in mid-December, they were nationalised. Banking was declared a state monopoly, all private banks were merged with the State Bank and a single People's Bank of the Russian Republic was set up. At the close of January 1918, all the share capital of the former private banks was confiscated. This was followed by the publication of a decree annulling foreign and internal loans received by the tsarist and the Provisional governments.

The nationalisation of industry was started at the close of 1917 with individual large factories and mills. The capitalists kept sabotaging the government's measures in this direction and resisted workers' control in every way they could. In order to break the resistance of the capitalists, the workers took the management of factories and mills into their own hands.

Soon the government passed from the nationalisation of individual factories and mills to the nationalisation of entire industries. The sugar and oil industries were nationalised in May-June 1918, and this was followed by the nationalisation of transport, the merchant marine and foreign trade.

A Supreme Economic Council was formed on December 2, 1917, to direct the economy. Local economic councils were set up at the gubernia and uyezd Soviets.

The revolutionary economic reforms carried out during the first months of Soviet rule marked a radical break with capitalist relationships. That saved Russia from the economic disaster towards which capitalism had been leading her. After taking over the key positions in the economy, the Soviet government started building up a socialist economy.

Early in 1918 the counter-revolution made another attempt to depose Soviet rule. This attempt was linked up with the convocation of the Constituent Assembly. The elections to the Assembly were held in November 1917 under party lists drawn up prior to the October Revolution. A large portion of the people had not yet come to appreciate the significance of the socialist revolution and, naturally, the composition of the Assembly failed to reflect the new balance of class forces in the country. The majority of the seats were won by the Right Socialist-Revolutionaries. In spite of this, the Soviet Government decided to convene the Assembly, for it was necessary to show the people that it was nothing but a counter-revolutionary organisation.

Yakov Sverdlov, Chairman of A.R.C.E.C., opened the Constituent Assembly in the Grand Hall of the Taurida Palace on January 5. The Declaration of the Rights of the Working and Exploited People, drawn up by Lenin and endorsed by the A.R.C.E.C. on January 3, was submitted to the deputies. However, this document which gave legal force to the gains of the proletarian revolution, was rejected by the counter-revolutionary majority. When that happened the Bolsheviks walked out of the Taurida Palace and were followed by the Left Socialist-Revolutionaries. "The people from the nether world," as Lenin called the Socialist-Revolutionary-Menshevik deputies, started a fruitless debate, which ended late at night.

The counter-revolutionary majority in the Assembly showed its true colours at its very first sitting. On January 6, A.R.C.E.C. dissolved the Assembly quite painlessly. The only resistance came from a small group of bourgeois intellectuals, who tried to stage a "protest" demonstration in Petrograd but were quickly dispersed by Red Guards and revolutionary soldiers.

The next few days showed who was the real spokesman of the interests of the masses. The Third All-Russia Congress of Soviets of Workers' and Soldiers' Deputies was opened in Petrograd on January 10. Three days later the Third All-Russia Congress of Peasants' Deputies was convened. Its first act was to pass a decision to merge with the Third Congress of Workers' and Soldiers' Deputies.

The amalgamated Congress adopted the Declaration of the Rights of the Working and Exploited People. This constitutional act was later embodied in the first Soviet Constitution. The Declaration solemnly confirmed the gains of the proletarian revolution and formulated the basic principles and tasks of the Soviet state. "Russia," it said, "is proclaimed a Republic of Soviets of Workers', Soldiers' and Peasants' Deputies. All the power in the centre and on a local level belongs to these Soviets."

It stressed that the Soviet Republic was founded on a voluntary alliance of free nations as a federation of Soviet national republics.

It proclaimed that the fundamental task of the new society was to eradicate all forms of exploitation of man by man, build socialism and abolish classes.

Withdrawal from the Imperialist War

"The question of peace is a burning issue and the most painful question of the day," Lenin said when he started his report on peace at the historic sitting of the Second All-Russia Congress of Soviets on October 26.

The world war was in its fourth year. Millions of Englishmen, Frenchmen, Russians, Czechs, Austrians and Germans were dying or becoming maimed for the sake of objectives and interests alien to them, and millions of people behind the firing lines were losing their homes and their hopes for the future. Bourgeois parties all over Europe and America were daily appealing to the "patriotism" of the people, exhorting them to give all their strength and even their lives for the motherland. The socialist parties, whose task it was to protect the interests of the working people, had betrayed these interests by supporting the imperialist, anti-popular, predatory war along with the bourgeoisie.

The voice of the Bolshevik Party, the voice of Lenin, now became heard above this chorus of chauvinism and false patriotism. Speaking for all the world to hear, Lenin declared that the war, which had engulfed the whole world, had nothing in common with the interests of the peoples, that it had to be ended and that this could only be done by the working people themselves, who should take the problem of war and peace into their own hands.

In its Decree on Peace, the Soviet Government appealed to all countries to begin negotiations at once for the conclusion of a general armistice and peace. "The Government," the decree stated, "considers it the greatest of crimes against humanity to continue this war over the issue of how to divide among the strong and rich nations the weak nationalities they have conquered, and solemnly announces its determination immediately to sign terms of peace to stop this war on the terms indicated, which are equally just for all nationalities without exception."*

This first act of Soviet foreign policy expressed the idea of the need for peaceful coexistence between states with different systems. The proposal for instituting talks and signing a peace treaty was a practical expression of the possibility of peaceful coexistence between the Soviet state and the capitalist countries.

The Soviet Government announced that it rejected secret diplomacy by which vital foreign policy problems had been settled behind the peoples' backs. It followed this statement up with the publication of the secret treaties signed by the tsarist and the Provisional governments with the imperialist states.

---

* Lenin, *Collected Works*, Vol. 26, p. 250.

The People's Commissariat for Foreign Affairs was formed to take charge of foreign policy. Its staff—Petrograd workers and revolutionary sailors headed by the Bolshevik sailor Nikolai Markin—moved into the building of the former Ministry for Foreign Affairs. Markin and his assistants opened up the safes, enlisted the services of students to translate documents into the Russian language and selected nearly 100 treaties and agreements for publication. These documents were published in the course of November and December 1917 and revealed how the war was fomented. Lenin said that the whole world saw for the sake of what millions of people had perished, for the sake of what millions of people had been sacrificed.* The publication of these documents dealt bourgeois diplomacy a heavy blow.

As soon as the Soviet Government was formed it began an active struggle to terminate the war. On November 7, on behalf of the Council of People's Commissars, Lenin ordered General Dukhonin, Commander-in-Chief of the Russian Army, to begin armistice talks with the German Command. Dukhonin flatly refused to obey these orders and was relieved of his duties. On November 8, the People's Commissariat for Foreign Affairs sent a note to the governments of the belligerent states, proposing peace talks.** This note was handed to the ambassadors and envoys of these states, published in the Soviet press and repeatedly broadcast over the radio. Within a few days similar notes were sent to Sweden, Norway, Spain, Denmark and other neutral states.*** The Soviet Government asked these countries for mediation in getting the peace talks going. On three other occasions, on November 28, December 6 and January 30, the Soviet Government sent notes and statements to the governments of the U.S.A., Britain, France and other powers, proposing peace talks.

But not one of these notes was answered. After numerous meetings in their embassies, the ambassadors of Britain, the U.S.A., France, Italy and other countries in Russia decided to refrain from entering into relations with the Soviet Government or answering any Soviet peace appeals. They acted in accordance with instructions from their governments. U.S. Secretary of State Robert Lansing, for example, instructed his ambassador to leave all Soviet peace proposals unanswered.**** The British Assistant Secretary of State for Foreign Affairs Robert Cecil declared that the British Government had no intention of recognising the Lenin Government. The French Foreign Minister Stephan Pichon stated in the Chamber

---

* See Lenin, *Collected Works*, Vol. 30, p. 386.
** *Dokumenty vneshnei politiki SSSR* (*Documents Relating to the Foreign Policy of the U.S.S.R.*), Vol. 1, Moscow, 1957, pp. 16-17.
*** *Ibid.*, pp. 22-23.
**** *Papers Relating to the Foreign Relations of the United States. Russia*, Vol. 1, Washington, 1932, p. 254.

of Deputies that France would have no relations with the Soviet Government and would not sit down to peace talks.*

A similar decision was passed at the Inter-Allied Conference in Paris at the close of November 1917. The heads of government and ministers, representing the interests of the financial and industrial magnates of Britain, France, the U.S.A. and other countries, refused to have relations with the workers' and peasants' government of Russia, which had infringed upon the "sacred" right of private ownership; it did not suit them to agree to a democratic peace without annexations and indemnities, for the sake of which they were waging war.

Secret conferences and meetings were held in Washington, London and Paris, and it was becoming obvious that the Entente leaders were planning to isolate the Soviet Republic, to impose a blockade on her and, with the aid of internal counter-revolutionary forces, destroy the Soviet state and restore the old regime in Russia. On December 10, when Soviet peace proposals were coming from revolutionary Petrograd, Robert Lansing sent the U.S. President a memorandum** in which he pressed for financial and military aid to General Kaledin, who had mustered forces in the south of Russia for a campaign against the revolutionary government. President Wilson approved this memorandum and instructed Colonel Edward House, his special representative, to talk the matter over in London and Paris. Almost at the same time, on December 21-22, the British and French ministers agreed in Paris to divide Russia into British and French spheres of influence.*** Hundreds of U.S., British and French instructors, observers and members of missions went to the south, north and east of Russia; accounts running into millions were opened at banks in London, Washington and Paris for generals Kaledin, Kornilov, Krasnov, and the Transcaucasian and Ukrainian bourgeois nationalists, i.e., to everybody who fought against the Soviet government. British warships sailed for Archangel and Murmansk, and U.S. and Japanese warships appeared off Vladivostok.

Though rejected by the Entente governments, the Soviet peace proposals were supported by the working people and many progressive organisations in Europe, Asia and America. The events in Russia were distorted by the bourgeois press, but the decrees on Peace and Land and the Soviet peace proposals became known

_____

* R. D. Warth, *The Allies and the Russian Revolution*, Durchan, 1954, p. 209.

** *Papers Relating to the Foreign Relations of the United States. The Lansing Papers*, Vol. II, pp. 343-45.

*** *Ibid.*, Vol. 1, pp. 330-31; B. E. Stein, *Russki vopros na parizhskoi mirnoi konferentsii (1919-1920)* (*The Russian Question at the Paris Peace Conference* [1919-20]), Moscow, 1949, pp. 28-29.

and the working people began to express their sympathy for the Soviet government in no uncertain terms.

Rallies demonstrating solidarity with Soviet Russia were held in London, Manchester, Sheffield and other towns in Britain. A meeting of engineering workers, held on January 27, 1918, in London's Albert Hall, demanded that the British Government conclude an immediate armistice and begin talks on peace without annexations and indemnities. Early in 1918, pressed by the masses, the leadership of the British Independent Labour Party stated that peace must be reached.

In France, too, the masses demanded that an end be put to the war. In December 1917, the Congress of Trade Union Representatives passed a resolution calling for peace talks. "The peace formula of the Russian revolution is also the formula of the working class of France," the resolution stated. The demand for peace spread to the French Army, where disturbances broke out in 1917-18. The famous ten commandments of the French soldier were circulated in the firing lines. One of these commandments stated: "The war must be ended and peace without annexations and indemnities must be signed immediately, before winter sets in."

The Soviet peace proposals were approved by the working people in the U.S.A. as well; workers' meetings, at which solidarity was expressed with the Russian proletariat, were held in various parts of the country at the close of 1917 and beginning of 1918.

In Germany and Austria-Hungary even the bourgeois and Right socialist newspapers admitted that Lenin's Decree on Peace had a great attractive force. Powerful demonstrations demanding the acceptance of the Soviet peace proposals were held in November 1917 in Berlin, Hamburg and other cities. The revolutionary Spartacus Union had the Soviet Decree on Peace translated and printed in millions of copies. Scores of leaflets and proclamations were issued which demanded that the war be stopped at once and peace talks begun.

The working people of all countries and continents were demanding peace.

On November 14, 1917, Germany and her allies informed the Soviet Government that they were prepared to start peace talks. However, the objectives of the German imperialists had nothing in common with a democratic, just peace. They calculated that armistice and peace in the East would enable them to transfer their troops to the Western Front and inflict a decisive blow on the Entente countries. As regards Russia, Germany and her allies hoped to impose a predatory peace treaty on her and subordinate her economically and politically.

On the same day that the German agreement to begin peace talks came through, the Soviet Government once again contacted the Entente countries with the proposal to begin general talks. But no reply was received from London, Paris or Washington. This compelled the Council of People's Commissars to decide to enter into armistice talks with representatives of the German-Austrian bloc and, at the same time, to continue its efforts to secure the signing of a general peace.

In the second half of November the first Soviet delegation left for Brest-Litovsk, where the peace talks were to be held. They began on November 20. On one side were stand-offish German generals, representatives of the higher German military caste, and on the other—workers and peasants, delegates of revolutionary Russia. The Soviet delegation was headed by the Bolshevik Adolph Joffe. In addition to Bolsheviks, the delegation included representatives of the "Left" Socialist-Revolutionary Party, and several generals and officers of the old army, who had come over to the side of the revolution.

The Soviet delegation proposed a six months' armistice on all fronts; one of its terms was that no German troops should be transferred from the Eastern to the Western Front. On this point, the Council of People's Commissars had clearly and unequivocally stated: "In defending the interests of the Allied peoples at the talks, the Russian Government stipulated as one of the cardinal terms of the armistice that no armies should be transferred from the Eastern to the Western Front. The armistice neither can nor will help one group of militarists against another."

These talks resulted in an agreement on a cease-fire for 10 and then for 28 days. Guns fell silent along the entire Russo-German front, and millions of exhausted soldiers were given the hope that they would soon return home.

On December 9, after the armistice was signed, the Soviet delegation proposed a clear-cut programme for the conclusion of peace without annexations and indemnities. The German Foreign Secretary Richard von Kühlmann and General Max Hoffmann, who headed the German delegation, submitted peace terms to the Soviet delegation. These terms, under various pretexts, claimed more than 150,000 square kilometres of Russian territory. The Soviet delegation postponed the talks for ten days and returned to Petrograd. The Council of People's Commissars once more called upon the Entente countries to take part in the talks, but as in all other cases there was no answer.

The talks were resumed on December 27. The German delegation flatly refused to reconsider the question of German-occupied territories, underlying this point with threats and ultimatums.

The young Soviet state found itself in an extremely difficult position. The collapse of the army, the economic dislocation and the utter exhaustion of the people made it impossible for the Soviet Republic to continue the war. A respite had to be won at all costs to enable the country to build up the Red Army and Navy and rehabilitate the economy.

The onerous terms put forward by Germany aroused all the enemies of Soviet power to action. The Cadets, Mensheviks and Socialist-Revolutionaries shouted hysterically that the Bolsheviks "were selling" Russia to Germany. They called upon the people to show "patriotism" and fight for "mother Russia against Germany". This "activity" was obviously meant to push the Soviet Republic into war with Germany again so that German bayonets could be used to overthrow the Soviet Government.

The Entente countries likewise counted on destroying the Soviets with German assistance and then on dictating their terms to both Russia and Germany.

The situation was rendered all the more difficult by the fact that within the Bolshevik Party itself peace was opposed by a group of "Left" Communists headed by Nikolai Bukharin. They rejected the possibility of coming to an agreement with imperialism and demanded that a "revolutionary war" be declared on world imperialism. They were supported by Trotsky, who went to Brest-Litovsk as head of the Soviet peace delegation.

In this extraordinarily complex situation Lenin urged the acceptance of the German peace terms, ridiculing those who in principle rejected the possibility of signing agreements with capitalist countries. He said that peaceful coexistence between states with different social systems was possible and necessary, and that objective reality was compelling the Soviet Government to sign the peace treaty. One could pompously speak of the defence of the revolutionary motherland and of much else, he pointed out, but if there were no cannon or machine guns and if the soldiers were leaving the firing lines in their thousands there could be no question of repelling the onslaught of the German armies.

He felt the mood of the peasants in soldiers' greatcoats splendidly: he knew that they were tired of the war and wanted peace. Lenin's policy on this question was supported by the workers of Petrograd, Moscow, the Urals and the Donbas. The Soviet delegation was therefore instructed to stick to its proposals as long as possible, but to sign the peace treaty at once if the Germans presented an ultimatum. Trotsky disobeyed these instructions. On January 28, he informed the German delegation that Soviet Russia would not sign the peace treaty but would stop the war and demobilise her army.

The German Command took advantage of this. On February 18, firing was resumed and the German Army advanced towards Petrograd and Moscow.

The Central Committee of the Bolshevik Party and the Soviet Government appealed to the people to rise to the country's defence. The new revolutionary Red Army was formed of workers, working peasants and soldiers and sailors of the old army. The entire country was geared to defence requirements.

The Red Army held up the German advance towards Petrograd at Pskov and Narva. These fierce battles gave the Red Army its baptism of fire, and ever since then February 23 has been marked as Soviet Army Day.

Despite the heroic resistance put up by the defenders of the young Soviet Republic, the enemy continued his offensive. This was one of the most difficult periods in the life of the Soviet state, in the life of the Bolshevik Party.

The Party C.C. and the Council of People's Commissars met daily. Lenin infused waverers with confidence and severely criticised those who opposed the peace treaty.

His policy triumphed in this sharp struggle against the "Left" Communists. Despite the resistance of Bukharin and others, the Party C.C., the Council of People's Commissars and A.R.C.E.C. decided to accept the German peace terms. True, Germany now utilised the Soviet Republic's difficult position to add a series of territorial claims (in the Baltic and the Caucasus) and to impose an indemnity of 6,000 million rubles.

The peace treaty was signed at Brest-Litovsk on March 3, 1918. The Seventh Party Congress was opened in Petrograd three days later, on March 6. It endorsed Lenin's policy and the peace treaty.

The Fourth Extraordinary All-Russia Congress of Soviets, which was convened on March 14, ratified the treaty by a majority vote.

The Brest Peace terms were incredibly harsh. Soviet Russia lost the Baltic area, the Ukraine and part of Byelorussia and Transcaucasia. She undertook to pay a huge indemnity and to sign extremely unfavourable trade agreements. Yet the treaty gave her a vital respite.

The signing of this treaty was a triumph of the Leninist policy of peaceful coexistence. Despite the enormous difficulties, Soviet power gave the peoples of Russia the promised, long-awaited peace. All the efforts of the U.S., British and French leaders to hinder the signing of this peace collapsed.

The Brest Peace was of tremendous international significance, too, for by signing it Soviet Russia showed all the peoples the way out of the imperialist war.

World's First Socialist State

In the respite given it by the Brest Peace the Soviet Republic undertook the building of a new life, of a new, socialist society. This great creative effort was directed by the Bolshevik Party. At the Seventh Congress it changed its name to the Russian Communist Party (Bolsheviks). Explaining why the name Communist

Group of workers, who took part in the fighting to establish Soviet rule in Tashkent, 1917

John Reed

Group of workers, who took part in nationalising the Likino
Textile Mills, December 1917

Party was the only correct one, Lenin pointed out that "as we begin socialist reforms we must have a clear conception of the goal towards which these reforms are, in the final analysis, directed, that is, the creation of a communist society...."* At that time the Party had nearly 300,000 members, all of whom were tested Bolsheviks, leaders of the working people and foremost representatives of the working class.

In the previous year, in the spring of 1917, Lenin's famous *April Theses* set the Party the task of leading the people in the accomplishment of a socialist revolution. That task was now fulfilled.

New tasks faced the Communist Party in the spring of 1918. "We, the Bolshevik Party," Lenin wrote, "have *convinced* Russia. We have *won* Russia from the rich for the poor, from the exploiters for the working people. Now we must *administer* Russia."**

In mid-March the Central Committee of the Communist Party and the Soviet Government moved to Moscow, which became the capital of the Soviet state, the standard-bearer of the new epoch. In Moscow, in March-April 1918, Lenin wrote his outstanding *The Immediate Tasks of the Soviet Government,* in which he expounded a plan for creating a socialist economy and dealt with the key problems of economic, political and state development confronting the proletariat and its Party since the seizure of power. He declared that now the principal task of the proletariat and the poorest sections of the peasants led by it was "the positive or constructive work of setting up an extremely intricate and delicate system of new organisational relationships extending to the planned production and distribution of the goods required for the existence of tens of millions of people."*** In this work he set forth a programme of struggle for the building of socialist society, for the creation of new, socialist relations of production.

He emphasised that a socialist system that would be superior to the capitalist system could be built only if it had a higher labour productivity and labour organisation. He considered that labour productivity could be increased by building large-scale industry as a material basis of socialism, by ensuring a steady rise of the educational and cultural level of the people, by evolving a new production discipline and by inculcating a conscious socialist attitude to work.

The Immediate Tasks of the Soviet Government outlined concrete measures for improving socialist labour organisation: the introduction of the strictest accounting and control of production and distribution of commodities, the utmost promotion of socialist emulation, the implementation of the socialist principle of payment

---

* Lenin, *Collected Works*, Vol. 27, p. 127.
** *Ibid.*, p. 242.
*** *Ibid.*, p. 241.

for labour, the establishment of one-man management, the strengthening of labour discipline, the application of compulsion to idlers, the introduction of economy, and so forth.

Lenin's programme of socialist economic development was enthusiastically received by the people. Capitalism had led the country into an impasse. Surmounting the ruin and famine, the socialist revolution both saved the country from economic disaster and gave a powerful impetus for an unprecedented growth of the productive forces. As early as the spring of 1918, the country started extensive preparations for developing the power industry, the building of power stations, the development of natural resources and the promotion of technical progress.

The First All-Russia Congress of Economic Councils, held in May-June 1918, passed important decisions aimed at further promoting the country's productive forces. At the same time, it recommended the nationalisation of all industries. On June 28, the Council of People's Commissars promulgated a decree nationalising the major enterprises in all key branches of industry. More than 1,500 enterprises were nationalised by the close of August 1918. Only the small-scale industry and part of the medium-sized enterprises remained in the hands of private capital.

It was not easy to nationalise industry, but it was still harder to get the nationalised enterprises to operate efficiently, increase labour productivity and train skilled executives from among the workers. The October Revolution had fundamentally changed the position of the working class, turning it into the ruling class, which, together with other working people, owned all of the country's wealth, and laid the foundations for a new attitude to labour. Advanced workers began to realise that by working at socialist enterprises they were working for their own well-being, for the welfare of society.

In keeping with Lenin's instructions, the workers organised production and did their utmost to strengthen labour discipline. They drew up rules with a view to strengthening discipline and improving labour organisation.

The Soviet state embarked upon socialist economic construction under conditions of complete economic dislocation. But famine, which mounted in the spring and summer of 1918, made the difficulties still greater. This famine was due not only to the economic ruin but also to the savage class struggle that raged at the time in the countryside.

The kulaks refused to sell grain to the state, believing that by doing so they would strangle Soviet power.

To enable socialist construction to get under way it became necessary to consolidate Soviet rule in the countryside as well. This meant curbing the kulaks, who had risen against Soviet rule, rallying the poorest sections of the peasants, ensuring support of the middle peasant and thereby strengthening the alliance between the working class and the peasants. This task was part of the struggle for grain, because the solution of the food problem depended on whether Soviet power would be able to break the resistance of the kulaks and consolidate its influence over the main mass of the working peasants.

In the spring of 1918, the Communist Party and Soviet Government decided to send thousands of foremost workers to the villages to help the poor sections of the peasants curb the kulaks and organise the supply of grain for the towns. Leading workers of Petrograd, Moscow and other large industrial centres were appointed to the food detachments. By the autumn of 1918 there were nearly 20,000 workers in these detachments. They went to the villages armed with Lenin's slogan "The Struggle for Grain Is a Struggle for Socialism".

The poorest sections of the peasants fiercely combated the kulaks but they were still badly organised. On June 11, 1918, A.R.C.E.C. decreed the setting up of rural and volost Poor Peasants' Committees throughout the country. By November 1918, nearly 105,000 of these committees were functioning. They became the bulwarks of Soviet rule in the countryside. With their help the landed estates and the land belonging to kulaks were divided among the working peasants. The government confiscated 50,000,000 hectares of land, machines, draught animals, and primary processing industries from the kulaks. The Poor Peasants' Committees helped the peasants to work the newly received land, supplied them with seeds, implements and livestock, helped the families of Red Army men and took part in organising state farms, agricultural communes and collective farms. The committees did much to strengthen the rural and volost Soviets by purging them of kulak elements.

These measures dealt the kulaks a telling economic and political blow. The sending of workers to the villages and the setting up of Poor Peasants' Committees consolidated Soviet rule and played a decisive role in carrying through a socialist revolution in the countryside.

In surmounting all the difficulties confronting it, the young proletarian state grew steadily stronger. The Soviet state system was developed and basic reforms were carried out in the economy. The establishment of Soviet rule created the conditions necessary for starting a cultural revolution. The achievements of science, technology, art and literature, which had accumulated over the course of centuries, were now placed at the disposal of the people. The Soviet government advanced the slogan "Education for the People" and began to implement it in practice. Education became free and was conducted in the native language. A drive to abolish illiteracy among adults was started. Socialist construction was inconceivable without a tremendous cultural growth, without the all-sided satisfaction of the people's cultural needs.

On July 4, 1918, the Fifth All-Russia Congress of Workers', Peasants', Red Army men's and Cossack Deputies was opened at the Bolshoi Theatre in Moscow.

The report on the work of the Council of People's Commissars was delivered by Lenin, and Yakov Sverdlov reported on the work of A.R.C.E.C.

At this Congress the policy of the Soviet Government was opposed by the "Left" Socialist-Revolutionaries. A class struggle was raging in the countryside and the "Left" Socialist-Revolutionaries took the side of the kulaks against Soviet rule. At the Congress their faction demanded a change in the food policy and the disbandment of the Poor Peasants' Committees. However, despite this opposition, the policy of the Soviet Government was approved by the overwhelming majority of delegates.

Then the "Left" Socialist-Revolutionaries organised an anti-Soviet revolt in Moscow. On July 6, they assassinated the German Ambassador Mirbach, hoping that this would precipitate war with Germany. The same day, an armed insurrection broke out. The insurgents captured the Central Telegraph Office and sent out several false telegrams claiming that the "Left" Socialist-Revolutionaries had taken power.

With Lenin in command the Soviet Government took measures to suppress the uprising. The Central Telegraph Office was recaptured on the very next day, July 7. At dawn troops advanced towards the Trekhsvyatitelsky Lane, where the insurgents had their headquarters in the mansion that had belonged to the millionaire Morozov. Failing to win the support of the masses, the "Left" Socialist-Revolutionary leaders fled. At 4 p.m. on July 7, a statement was issued announcing that the insurrection had been quelled.

On July 10, the Congress passed a decision approving the first Soviet Constitution.

During the first few weeks after the October Revolution the need was felt to legalise the revolutionary gains of the people. With this purpose in view, the Soviet Government passed a series of constitutional acts, the most important of which was the Declaration of the Rights of the Working and Exploited People.

However, a Constitution had to be drawn up to define the organisation and structure of the organs of Soviet rule, the electoral system, and the rights and duties of citizens. In April 1918, A.R.C.E.C. set up a commission, headed by Yakov Sverdlov, to draw up a draft Constitution. A large contribution to the work of this commission was made by the Party Central Committee and by Lenin personally.

The Constitution of the R.S.F.S.R. legalised the dictatorship of the proletariat, the establishment of Soviet rule. At the same time, it embodied Lenin's nationalities policy. It proclaimed the full equality of nations and fraternal friendship between them. The Russian Republic was proclaimed a federation, i.e., a free union of free nations, adopting the title Russian Soviet Federative Socialist Republic.

The Constitution created firm grounds for the further development of the Soviet state system, served as a model for the constitutions of the other Soviet republics and exerted a tremendous revolutionary influence on the working class throughout the world.

The adoption of the Constitution marked the end of the first phase of revolutionary reforms that were started in October 1917. Only eight months had elapsed since the October Revolution had triumphed. But within that short span of time the socialist reforms carried out in the country showed the people the might of the Soviet system and its indisputable advantages.

Chapter Two

STRUGGLE OF THE SOVIET PEOPLE AGAINST FOREIGN INTERVENTION AND INTERNAL COUNTER-REVOLUTION (1918-20)

Attack by Interventionists

The international and internal counter-revolution did not reconcile itself to the emergence of the world's first socialist state. It mobilised its forces and unleashed civil war and intervention.

The respite won by the Soviet people at the cost of great sacrifice and privation was cut short.

The internal counter-revolution began its attacks against Soviet rule soon after the October Revolution, but these attacks were repulsed. It was obvious that alone, without foreign support, the Russian counter-revolution would be unable to fight a protracted civil war against the young Soviet Republic. Help came from the imperialists of the U.S.A., Britain, France, Japan and other countries.

The long and bloody Civil War in the U.S.S.R. was not a necessary consequence of the socialist revolution. It was sparked off by international imperialism.

Lenin noted that essentially speaking, the Civil War in Soviet Russia was brought about by world imperialism.

The objectives of the foreign military intervention and the internal counter-revolution were the overthrow of Soviet rule, the restoration of capitalism and the dismemberment and enslavement of the Soviet state.

The plan for this predatory attack on the Soviet Republic was drawn up by the Entente headed by the U.S.A. at the close of 1917 and beginning of 1918.

The Western imperialists delineated the spheres of military operations against Soviet Russia: the Ukraine, the Crimea and Bessarabia were to be occupied by France, the north of Russia, the Don, the Kuban and the Caucasus by Britain, the Far East and Siberia by the U.S.A. and Japan.

At first, the inspirers of the military intervention counted on smashing the Soviet Republic with Austro-German bayonets.

The Brest-Litovsk Peace, signed on March 3, upset the Entente's plans. The Entente powers refused to recognise the Brest Treaty and used it as a pretext for the military invasion of Russia. In March 1918, British, U.S. and French troops landed in Murmansk. Seizing Murmansk and then Archangel, the interventionists began preparations for an offensive in the direction of Petrograd and Moscow in order "to put an end to Bolshevism once and for all".

The Soviet Far East likewise became a theatre of military operations. The U.S. cruiser *Brooklyn*, the Japanese cruisers *Iwashi* and *Asahi* and the British cruiser *Suffolk* steamed into the port of Vladivostok at the close of 1917 and beginning of 1918. However, they did not at once begin an armed intervention. There was some delay because the imperialists had not agreed who would be the first to land troops. Britain and France wanted Japan to be the main force in the struggle against the Soviet Republic, but the U.S.A., while agreeing to this, was afraid that Japan would become the predominant power in the Far East and insisted that all the Allied states take part in the intervention. In the end it was agreed the intervention would be an inter-Allied affair and that Japan would be the first to land troops. Japanese troops were landed in Vladivostok on April 4, 1918, on the pretext that two Japanese citizens had been murdered. The murder had been engineered by Japanese agents. A British landing was made the same day. This was the signal for the whiteguard bands of Ataman Semenov in the Transbaikal area to begin an offensive against Soviet troops. In May and July Soviet troops led by the young and talented commander Sergei Lazo defeated the Semenov gangs and hurled them back to the Manchurian frontier. But the situation in Siberia and the Far East grew steadily graver. The Soviet Government called upon the people to organise resistance to the well-prepared imperialist intervention. A state of emergency was declared in Siberia and military revolutionary headquarters were set up throughout the area.

Initially the Entente imperialists confined their military operations to the outlying regions of Soviet Russia, but their objective was to destroy the proletarian republic from within. In May 1918, they inspired a counter-revolutionary uprising that involved the 40,000-strong Czechoslovak Corps and several thousand Russian whiteguards. This corps, consisting of former war prisoners, had been formed in Russia for the war against Germany. After the October Revolution the Soviet Government had given the corps permission to go to France via Siberia and the Far East, but the Entente counted on utilising it against Soviet rule. Part of the corps refused to take part in the anti-Soviet mutiny and joined the Red Army.

The mutiny of the Czechoslovak Corps was followed by kulak-Socialist-Revolutionary uprisings in the Volga Country, the Urals and Siberia. Soviet rule was overthrown in the affected regions, where the Socialist-Revolutionaries and Mensheviks formed their own "governments": the northern government in Archangel, the committee of Constituent Assembly members in Samara, the Siberian government in Omsk, and the Urals government in Yekaterinburg. In collaboration with the interventionists, the petty-bourgeois parties made preparations for establishing an open military dictatorship. The claimants to the "all-Russia overlordship" included Kolchak and Denikin.

The Entente imperialists rushed to seize the southern regions—the Northern Caucasus, Transcaucasia and Turkestan with their enormous natural wealth. This objective was furthered by material aid to the whiteguard generals Kornilov, Denikin and Alexeyev, who had formed a Volunteer Army on the Don.

Early in 1918 the British Command formed a combined force of British troops and Terek Cossacks on Iranian territory. This force was given the task of capturing Baku and occupying the territory around it.

In this region the British imperialists clashed with German and Turkish troops that had occupied Georgia and Armenia at the beginning of June 1918 and were preparing to seize Baku.

The summer of 1918 was a tragic period for Soviet rule in Baku: Turkish troops had come right up to the gates of the city, while the nationalist Socialist-Revolutionary-Menshevik counter-revolution reared its head in it. On July 25, 1918, the Dashnaks, Mensheviks and Socialist-Revolutionaries in the Baku Soviet decided to invite the British to enter the city. The Bolsheviks opposed this decision and appealed to the people to resist the enemy. But the forces were unequal. On July 31, 1918, Soviet rule in Baku ceased to exist. On the next day the Mensheviks, Socialist-Revolutionaries and Dashnaks formed a counter-revolutionary government: the Central Caspian Dictatorship. On August 4, 1918, British troops marched into Baku and remained in the city until September 25, when they were pushed out by the Turks.

The Transcaspian region was invaded by the British, who helped the local bourgeois-nationalist forces to overthrow Soviet rule and form a counter-revolutionary government.

From the Transcaspian region the British tried to break through into Turkestan, but were halted by Soviet troops. In their war against the Turkestan Republic the interventionists received considerable assistance from Ataman Dutov, who captured Orenburg and cut Turkestan off from the central regions.

Troops of the First Byelorussian Communist Detachment seen
just before leaving for the front, 1918

A regiment consisting of the poorest section of the peasants, 1918

The occupation of the Transcaspian region by the interventionists and whiteguards was marked by massacres of the civilian population and reprisals against Soviet and Party officials. In Baku they seized 26 commissars—B. Avakyan, M. Azizbekov, T. Amirov, A. Amiryan, M. Basin, A. Berg, P. Japaridze, I. Malygin, G. Petrov, I. Fioletov, S. Shahumyan, G. Korganov, and others —who represented Soviet power in the city. The commissars were shot on September 20, 1918, in the desert near the Caspian.

While the Entente imperialists were advancing from the east, north and south, the Austro-German troops occupied the Ukraine after the Brest Peace had been signed.

The bourgeois-nationalist Ukrainian Central Rada signed an agreement with the occupation forces, under which it undertook to supply Germany and Austria-Hungary with a large quantity of food and industrial raw material. After this agreement was signed, the Austro-German invaders found no further use for the Central Rada and disbanded it. On April 29, 1918, they nominated General P. Skoropadsky, a Ukrainian landowner, Hetman of the Ukraine, against the wishes of the Ukrainian people, who continued the war of liberation for their social and national rights under the leadership of the Communist Party and its underground organisations.

In violation of the Brest Treaty, the Austro-German troops invaded Transcaucasia, the Don region and the Crimea, supporting the tsarist generals Krasnov and Mamontov, who headed the counter-revolutionary section of the Don Cossacks. The invaders occupied the Baltic republics and part of Byelorussia.

Thus, in the first half of 1918, while still in a state of war with the Entente countries, the Austro-German imperialists joined them in the war against the Soviet Republic, creating a front that ran all the way from the Baltic Sea to the Caucasian mountains.

A reign of terror was established in occupied territory. There were massacres of the civilian population, and many prominent functionaries of the Communist Party and Soviet Government were killed.

Three-quarters of Soviet territory was in the hands of enemies. A ring of fronts surrounded the Soviet Republic, which was cut off from her main raw material, fuel and grain regions. An economic blockade was imposed by the imperialists, who planned to starve Soviet Russia into submission. Factories and mills stopped working. There was no fuel for transport or for the towns. Food was scarce. Typhoid and other epidemics broke out. These difficulties were intensified by the wavering of the middle peasants, who did not immediately appreciate the dangerous consequences of the invasion. Conspiracies, uprisings and acts of sabotage were organised in the country by the imperialists. The U.S., French and British ambassadors and consuls were in close touch with various counter-revolutionary organisations.

In the summer of 1918, Robert Lockhart, the acting British Consul-General in Moscow, Joseph Noulens, the French Ambassador, and David Francis, the U.S. Ambassador, in co-operation with counter-revolutionary terrorists, plotted the arrest of the Soviet Government and the assassination of Lenin. The Socialist-Revolutionaries instituted a reign of terror against Soviet and Party officials. In Petrograd they murdered V. Volodarsky, a prominent Party official, and on August 30, 1918, they made an attempt on Lenin's life. That same day Moses Uritsky, head of the local Extraordinary Commission for the Suppression of Counter-Revolution, was murdered in Petrograd. The people demanded stern punishment for the assassins. On September 2, 1918, A.R.C.E.C. discussed the attempt on Lenin's life and decided to carry out reprisals against the enemies of the revolution.

The events in Soviet Russia in 1918 showed the whole world the objectives of the internal counter-revolution headed by the capitalists, bankers, landowners, generals, Mensheviks, Right and Left Socialist-Revolutionaries, kulaks and bourgeois nationalists and the external counter-revolution represented by the Western imperialists. Their principal aim was to overthrow Soviet rule, restore the rule of the landowners and capitalists and enslave the workers and peasants.

Explaining to the workers and peasants of Russia the significance of the war that started at the end of July 1918, Lenin said: "We are now at war with British and French imperialism and with everything bourgeois and capitalist in Russia, with everyone endeavouring to frustrate the socialist revolution and embroil us in war. The situation is one where all the gains of the workers and peasants are at stake."*

To defend the Revolution, the Soviet Republic entered into mortal combat with the heavily armed forces of the intervention and internal counter-revolution.

The People Rise Against the Enemy

Led by the Communist Party and the Soviet Government, with Lenin at its head, the Soviet people rose to the patriotic struggle against the interventionists and whiteguards. The only way to save the Soviet Republic was to smash the ring of fire around it. This required a well-armed and well-supplied large, regular Red Army.

The Soviet Government tackled this task despite the terrible economic dislocation and the Civil War. The Red Army was formed

---

* Lenin, *Collected Works*, Vol. 28, p. 33.

first of volunteers and then of conscripts. The people themselves took an active part in this work. Much was done by the trade unions of Petrograd, Moscow, Ivanovo-Voznesensk, Tver and other industrial centres, and also by the Poor Peasants' Committees.

Motivated by proletarian internationalism, Czechs, Slovaks, Germans, Hungarians, Poles, Serbs, Croats and others joined the Red Army. In Moscow, Hungarian Communists led by Béla Kun and Tibor Szamuelly formed an international detachment. Similar detachments, regiments and brigades were formed in other towns and cities. Many of the men in them sacrificed their lives in the battles for the world's first state of workers and peasants. With the support of Party organisations, the okrug, gubernia, uyezd and volost military commissariats mobilised more than 800,000 men by the autumn of 1918.

Red Army commanders were promoted from among workers and peasants and former soldiers and officers. Many of them won undying fame. Among them were Vladimir Azin, Vasily Blücher, Semyon Budyonny, Kliment Voroshilov, Stepan Vostretsov, Ivan Kochubei, Grigory Kotovsky, Sergei Lazo, Alexander Parkhomenko, Vitaly Primakov, Ivan Fedko, Jan Fabricius, Vasily Chapayev, Nikolai Shchors, Alexander Yegorov, August Kork, Mikhail Tukhachevsky, Yeronim Uborevich, Mikhail Frunze, Robert Eideman, and Iona Yakir. A great contribution to the building up of the new army was made by cadres of the old army such as Vasily Altfater, Mikhail Bonch-Bruyevich, Joakim Vacetis, Dmitry Karbyshev, N. Krapivyansky, P. Lebedev, Fyodor Novitsky, A. Stankevich, Alexander Nikolayev, Sergei Kamenev, Boris Shaposhnikov, Vasily Shorin, and hundreds of others.

Foremost workers and tested Bolsheviks were sent to the army as military commissars. With the aid of Party cells they trained and educated soldiers and commanders, strengthened discipline, forestalled treachery and helped commanders who were devoted to the cause of the Revolution.

The Red Army was formed as a regular, mass army, into which workers and peasants of all nationalities of Russia were called up. Exploiter elements were not accepted. The detachments were merged into regiments and divisions, from which armies and fronts were shaped. The Eastern Front, then the most important, was formed in June 1918. The country's entire economy was reshaped under the slogan of "Everything for the Front, Everything for the Defeat of the Enemy!"

The policy of War Communism, adopted as a result of the Civil War, the intervention and the economic dislocation, played a leading role in the defeat of the Soviet Republic's enemies. Its principal objective was to supply the troops at the front and the workers behind the firing lines with everything necessary for victory. The Soviet Government went to the extreme measure of nationalising not only large-scale but also all the medium and part of the small-scale industries. This undermined the economic strength of the bourgeoisie. Free trade was forbidden: all food-stuffs and essential commodities were distributed to the population through consumer co-operatives.

All factories were switched over to war production. Defence requirements demanded the concentration of the workers' efforts on producing and repairing weapons, clothes and footwear for the Red Army.

Emphasis was laid on the production of small arms and ammunition. Most of the small arms and ammunition came from Tula, Simbirsk and Izhevsk, where workers from Petrograd were sent to reinforce the local manpower resources. They played a large role in increasing labour productivity. Arms output was stepped up considerably through the labour heroism of the workers and the efforts of Soviet and Party organisations. In 1919, the output of rifles drew up with the 1916 level.

The light industry supplied the Red Army with clothing.

It would have been impossible to defend the republic successfully without concentrating the grain reserves in the hands of the state. Under the conditions prevailing at the time the necessary amount of grain could be obtained only by strictly prohibiting its sale in the open market. All grain and fodder surpluses were procured from the peasants at fixed prices on the basis of the surplus food requisitioning decree promulgated on January 11, 1919. Food requisitioning was a major aspect of the War Communism policy, and the peasants accepted that policy because they did not want the landowners back. The working class formed a military and political alliance with the middle peasants, the purpose of which was to uphold the gains of the October Revolution and crush the invaders and whiteguards. This alliance had an economic foundation as well: the Soviet Government gave the peasants land, armed and supplied the army, organised the country's defence, while the peasants gave the Red Army grain, fodder and men. The working class, too, suffered great hardship.

The Soviet countryside changed in the course of the Civil War. There were now mostly middle peasants and the number of non-farming peasants or peasants without livestock diminished. The position of the kulaks was greatly undermined. Oppression by landowners and capitalists was abolished for all time.

Despite all the difficulties of the period of the intervention and Civil War, most of the peasants found themselves better off than under the tsar and the bourgeoisie.

Universal labour conscription was another aspect of War Communism. All classes, including the former propertied classes, were required to work. This enabled the workers to concentrate on the chief task, that of defending the country.

In the second half of 1918 the armies of the Eastern Front made headway against the interventionists and whiteguards. On September 10, they liberated Kazan. On September 12, the 1st Army, commanded by Mikhail Tukhachevsky, liberated Simbirsk. The whiteguards were ejected from Syzran and Samara, and this made the Volga waterway operational.

On November 7, 1918, the first anniversary of the October Revolution, the 2nd Army captured Izhevsk, a major war industry centre, and a week later it entered Votkinsk.

In mid-September 1918, units of a partisan army commanded by Vasily Blücher and consisting of South Urals workers broke out of the whiteguard encirclement in the region of Ufa. Fighting its way from Beloretsk to Iglino Station, 1,500 kilometres away, it routed whiteguard detachments and joined forces with the 3rd Army.

In August 1918, troops of the Tsaritsyn sector of the front repulsed Krasnov's first offensive against Tsaritsyn, and then beat back another onslaught that lasted from the latter half of September to the first half of October. The failure of these attempts put an end to the hopes the whiteguards in the south of Russia had of linking up with whiteguard units operating on the Eastern Front.

On September 11, 1918, the Revolutionary Military Council of the republic formed the Southern Front: the units operating in this sector formed part of the 8th, 9th and 10th armies. They fought bitter battles against troops commanded by Krasnov and Denikin, who were determined to break through into the central regions and capture Tsaritsyn.

The situation in the Northern Caucasus became critical. In July and August 1918, Denikin's Volunteer Army entered Tikhoretskaya, Yekaterinodar and Novorossiisk. The 16,000-strong Taman Army found itself cut off from other Soviet units. Commanded by the sailor and Bolshevik I. I. Matveyev, it fought its way from Novorossiisk via Tuapse to Armavir, where, in mid-September, it linked up with the North Caucasian Army, which had been reformed into the 11th Army. The latter was commanded by a Cossack officer and Socialist-Revolutionary named Sorokin, who proved to be a traitor. He tried to stir up an anti-Soviet mutiny in the North Caucasus.

Leaders of the Party and Soviet organisations in the North Caucasus fell victim to Sorokin's treachery. On October 8, Matveyev, hero of the Taman campaign, was shot on his orders.

The Sorokin adventure was crushed and Sorokin himself was shot. But the 11th Army found itself in a difficult position. It suffered a series of defeats at the hands of Denikin. It had no artillery shells, rifle ammunition, clothing or medicines. Disorganised and weary, it finally reached Astrakhan early in 1919.

The situation on the other fronts somewhat improved. On the Northern Front the advance of the interventionists on Kotlas and Vologda was halted.

By the autumn of 1918 the Red Army had become a large and efficient fighting machine. The middle peasants saw that the interventionists and whiteguards were out to restore the rule of the landowners and capitalists and went over to the side of the Soviet government. The change in the class balance of power in the countryside in favour of Soviet rule considerably strengthened the country's position. Thanks to the selfless efforts of the workers in the munitions industry ever larger quantities of weapons and ammunition began to be turned out.

The Soviet Republic found it possible to speed up the building of a large, regular Red Army.

On October 3, 1918, Lenin wrote to a joint session of A.R.C.E.C., the Moscow Soviet and trade union representatives that the republic required a large, regular army. "We had resolved," he wrote, "to have an army of 1,000,000 men by the spring; we now need an army of three million men. We can have it. *And we shall have it.*"*

In November 1918, the heroic Red Army was warmly greeted by the Sixth All-Russia Extraordinary Congress of Soviets, which appealed to the Entente powers to begin peace talks. But no reply was received.

Collapse of the Austro-German Occupation

Towards the autumn of 1918 the Soviet Republic's international position had changed substantially. The First World War ended in the West. Germany was in the grip of revolution and the Kaiser had been dethroned. On November 13, 1918, the Soviet Government repudiated the Brest Treaty and began an open war to drive the German occupation troops out of the Ukraine, the Crimea, Byelorussia and the Baltic area.

In Kiev, Poltava, Chernigov, Kherson, Yekaterinoslav and other gubernias the peasants had risen against the Austro-German occupation troops and the Hetman rule as early as the summer of 1918. They were joined by the workers in the towns and industrial centres of the Ukraine. This struggle was directed by the Ukrainian Communists who in July 1918 had formed the Communist Party of the Ukraine as part of the Russian Communist Party (Bolsheviks).

---

* Lenin, *On the International Working-Class and Communist Movement*, Moscow, p. 218.

70

On November 13, 1918, realising that the German occupation and the Hetman regime were nearing collapse, the Ukrainian bourgeois-nationalist parties formed a Directorate headed by Vladimir Vinnichenko and Simon Petlyura. When Hetman Skoropadsky fled to Germany, the Directorate seized power in the Ukraine with the sanction of the Germans and began organising counter-revolutionary detachments.

The Soviet Government in Russia went to the assistance of the Ukrainian workers and peasants, who had risen against the Austro-German occupation troops and the Directorate. The Ukrainian Front with Vladimir Antonov-Ovseyenko in command was formed on November 17, 1918. On November 29, 1918, the Ukrainian Soviet Republic was recreated and a Provisional Workers' and Peasants' Government formed. The Ukrainian Soviet Government appealed to the workers and peasants to intensify their struggle to drive out the occupation troops and the Directorate's bourgeois-nationalist detachments and restore Soviet rule in the Ukraine.

In Byelorussia, too, the working people redoubled their struggle against the occupation troops and the counter-revolutionary Rada in November and December 1918. The latter, aided by the Entente imperialists, tried in vain to remain in power. The Communists formed a Provisional Workers' and Peasants' Government on liberated Byelorussian territory on December 31, 1918.

On January 1, 1919, the new government proclaimed Byelorussia a Soviet Socialist Republic. The republic's Constitution was adopted in February 1919 by the Congress of Soviets of Byelorussia, which decided to begin talks on the establishment of federal ties with the R.S.F.S.R.

The Revolution triumphed over the interventionists in the Baltic area as well. In November 1918, led by Communists and aided by Soviet troops, the working people drove the Austro-German occupation troops out of a large part of Estonia. The Estonian Soviet Republic (Estonian Labour Commune) was proclaimed on November 29, 1918.

The working people of Latvia intensified their struggle against the Austro-German occupation forces in November and December 1918. A Provisional Soviet Government, which issued a manifesto proclaiming the creation of the Soviet Republic of Latvia, was formed on November 17, 1918. By January 1919, a considerable part of Latvia had been cleared of occupation troops and bourgeois nationalists.

In December 1918, Soviet rule was proclaimed in Lithuania as well.

The liberation war of the Ukrainian, Byelorussian and Baltic peoples, who were aided by the Russian people, thus led to the clearing of a considerable portion of the Ukraine, Byelorussia, Estonia, Latvia and Lithuania. The Russian Federation recognised the independence of the new Soviet republics, which, in their turn, sought to unite closer with Russia in the struggle against external enemies. The military and political alliance of the Soviet republics gradually took shape in the course of the struggle against the imperialists and the internal counter-revolution.

The Entente Steps Up Its Intervention

The defeat of the Austro-German bloc enabled the Entente to use more forces for its intervention in Russia. The Allied Command planned to continue military operations in the Soviet East, Northern Russia and the Caspain Sea area in the direction of the Volga and also to invade the Ukraine by way of Rumania and the Black Sea. Moreover, the Entente decided to use German troops to continue the occupation of the Ukraine, Byelorussia and parts of the Baltic area.

Nothing came of the plan to use German troops: the Ukrainian, Byelorussian and Baltic peoples expelled the Austro-German forces and their bourgeois-nationalist flunkeys.

In the south of the Ukraine the Entente planned to deal the main blow by seizing Odessa, Sevastopol and then Kiev, Kharkov, the Donets and the Krivoi Rog basins. Twelve French and Greek divisions were to be used in this operation. These divisions began landing in Odessa, Sevastopol and other ports in mid-November 1918, and soon the Entente had 130,000 troops in the south.

By agreement between the Directorate and the French Command in the south of the Ukraine, the Ukraine was recognised as a French Protectorate for "the entire period of the war against Bolshevism", while the French Command undertook to help form a 300,000-strong army under the leadership of Simon Petlyura.

Denikin and Krasnov hastened to establish contact with Entente representatives in the hope of receiving weapons, ammunition and other supplies for their armies.

By increasing aid to the Ukrainian nationalists and the armies of Ataman Krasnov and General Denikin, the Entente tried to unite these armies for joint military operations against Soviet rule in the south of Russia.

In the middle of November 1918, the Musavatist government of Azerbaijan requested General Thomson, commander of British troops in Transcaucasia to occupy Baku, which the Turkish troops had abandoned under the terms of the armistice. It servilely declared that such a step "would not violate the independence and territorial integrity of Azerbaijan".* The British general "grate-

---

* *Iz istorii grazhdanskoi voiny v SSSR (History of the Civil War in the U.S.S.R.),* Vol. 1, Moscow, 1960, p. 60.

fully" accepted the invitation from the traitors; in November British troops re-entered Baku. Britain counted on the support of the bourgeois-nationalist Musavatist, Dashnak and Menshevik parties to help her establish economic and political control over Transcaucasia.

The British occupation of the Caspian area and Transcaucasia gave effective assistance to the armies of Denikin and Krasnov.

In the north (in the Murmansk and Archangel areas) the strength of the interventionists was increased to 21,000 men in December 1918.

Estonian, Lithuanian and Latvian territory, where at the close of 1918 the bourgeoisie was still in power, was used by the Entente as springboards for intervention. Aid was increased to the bourgeois-nationalist bands fighting Soviet rule in the Baltic area. In January 1919, units of the Estonian bourgeois army, and Russian and Finnish whiteguards, pressed Soviet troops back across the Narva River. This turned Estonia into a springboard for an offensive on Petrograd. General Yudenich became head of the bourgeois North-Western "government" in Estonia. He appealed to the Entente powers to intensify the intervention against the Bolsheviks, using the Baltic area and Finland as the most suitable bridgeheads for an attack against Petrograd. "The major ports and towns of the Baltic provinces must be occupied by Entente troops," Yudenich wrote, "in order to strengthen law and order and enable the Russian forces to organise themselves for the struggle against the Bolsheviks."[*] Whiteguard units were formed in Estonia. Subsequently these units merged under Yudenich. The Entente furthermore counted on using Finnish troops.

The Entente was most active in the Soviet Far East and in Siberia, where it strove to unite all internal and foreign counter-revolutionary forces under a single command, utilising Admiral Kolchak for this purpose. With the aid of the Entente, Kolchak came to power on November 18, 1918, disbanding the Socialist-Revolutionary-Menshevik government and proclaiming himself "supreme ruler" of Russia. At the close of 1918, the U.S. Government supplied Kolchak with 200,000 rifles, 200,000 shells, a large number of cannon and machine guns and a great deal of other equipment. He received more than 100,000 rifles from Britain.[**] France's expenditures on these purposes came to 50,000,000 francs a month.

As a result of this aid, Kolchak was able to muster an army of 250,000 men by the end of 1918; nearly 200,000 foreign soldiers

---

[*] *Ibid.*, p. 77.
[**] See *Iz istorii grazhdanskoi voiny v SSSR (History of the Civil War in the U.S.S.R.)*, Vol. 3, Moscow, 1957, p. 334.

guarded Kolchak's rear, taking reprisals against workers and peasants. Soon the actual command of the interventionist troops and whiteguards in Siberia was taken over by the French general Janin and the British general Knox. They subordinated Kolchak to themselves. The Kolchak army, formed through the efforts of the Entente, became a grave danger to Soviet Russia.

By the end of 1918 the Entente had huge forces poised in the south, east, north and north-west for an offensive against Soviet Russia. But this offensive never materialised. In November 1918, the Central Committee of the Communist Party took energetic steps to strengthen the Southern Front, which now became the main theatre of military operations. The 8th and 9th armies operating on this front received considerable reinforcements with many Communists among them. Early in January 1919, these armies took the offensive against the White Cossack troops on the central sector of the Southern Front. In mid-February 1919, the success of this offensive enabled the 10th Army to inflict an overwhelming defeat on the whiteguards in the region of Tsaritsyn. Early in March 1919, Soviet troops reached the North Donets River, completely routing Krasnov's White Don Cossack army.

In the course of January and February 1919, troops of the Ukrainian Front, supported by Soviet partisans, engaged the interventionists and the Petlyura troops of the Directorate. In the beginning of January the 2nd Ukrainian Soviet Division drove Petlyura out of Kharkov and then out of Poltava and Yekaterinoslav. On February 1, it liberated Kremenchug. The 1st Ukrainian Division captured Chernigov and advanced on Kiev. Regiments commanded by Nikolai Shchors and Vasily Bozhenko defeated the Petlyura bands on the outskirts of Kiev and entered the city on February 5. The bourgeois-nationalist Directorate fled to Vinnitsa. The whole of the Ukraine on the left bank of the Don became Soviet.

The Ukrainian people were determined to liberate the rest of the Ukraine from Petlyura. Communist underground organisations intensified their work among the people and among the troops of the interventionists. In the south of the Ukraine these organisations were directed by the Odessa Committee headed by I. Smirnov, who was an outstanding organiser and staunch Communist. A group of French Communists led by Jeanne Labourbe was active among the interventionist troops. A Foreign Board, which conducted extensive agitation among foreign soldiers and sailors, was set up at the Odessa Party Committee. At the beginning of March, the interventionists arrested 11 members of the Board, including two of the leaders—Jeanne Labourbe and I. Smirnov. They were tortured and then shot. But that did not make the Communists give up agitation among the interventionist troops.

Cases of these troops refusing to fight became more and more frequent. In March 1919, the Ukrainian Soviet troops liberated Kherson and Nikolayev from the interventionists, and in April—Odessa, Simferopol and Sevastopol. In April 1919, influenced by the successful advance of Soviet troops and by revolutionary propaganda, the French squadron mutinied. French troops refused to attack Soviet units. The Government of France was compelled to withdraw its forces from the south of the Ukraine and from the Crimea. At the close of April 1919, these regions were cleared of the interventionists and whiteguards. Almost the whole of the Ukraine was liberated from the Petlyura troops of the Directorate, which had entrenched itself in Kamenets-Podolsk, retaining under its control only a small number of towns and villages.

The Soviet troops of the Eastern Front advanced successfully at the close of 1918 and beginning of 1919, liberating Ufa, Birsk, Orenburg, Uralsk and a considerable part of the Urals. That enabled Soviet Russia to establish contact with Turkestan.

The interventionists and whiteguards failed to link up their southern and eastern forces. The only success the Kolchak forces could boast of was scored on the northern sector of the Eastern Front. Striking at the Soviet 3rd Army they captured Perm at the close of 1918. But this was only a temporary success. Through the efforts of the Party Central Committee and Lenin personally the fighting efficiency of the 3rd Army was soon restored, and in January 1919 it stopped the Kolchak army and took the initiative into its hands, preventing Kolchak from linking up with interventionists operating in the north.

After the Soviet 6th Army had won a series of victories, anti-war sentiments began to spread among the interventionist troops on the Northern Front as well. The Entente failed to overthrow Soviet rule with its own forces; its troops proved to be unsuitable for intervention in Russia. Assessing the significance of this development, Lenin wrote: "The victory we won in compelling the evacuation of the British and French troops was the greatest of our victories over the Entente countries. We deprived them of their soldiers. Our response to the unlimited military and technical superiority of the Entente countries was to deprive them of it through the solidarity of the working people against the imperialist governments."[*]

Decisive Victories of the Red Army

Less than a year after the Austro-German bloc had forced a humiliating peace treaty on Russia, the countries of that bloc found themselves in the grip of revolution, which swept across

---

[*] Lenin, *Collected Works*, Vol. 30, p. 211.

Germany, Austria, Hungary, Bulgaria and Serbia. Now Anglo-U.S.-French imperialism played the role of hangman of the revolution not only in Russia but also in a number of other European countries.

Lenin said: "A whole number of countries are enveloped in the flames of workers' revolutions. In this respect our efforts and sacrifices have been justified. They were not adventures, as our enemies slanderously claimed, but an essential step towards world revolution, which had to be taken by the country that had been placed in the lead, despite its underdevelopment and backwardness."*

The Soviets that were set up in a number of European countries in the course of these revolutions won the support of the proletarian masses.

The Third Communist International was set up in a situation marked by an upsurge of revolutionary feeling in a number of countries, and a growth of the influence of Communist Parties and Left socialist organisations. Its First Congress was held in Moscow under Lenin's guidance early in March 1919. The Congress decisions stressed the international significance of the October Revolution and of the establishment of Soviet rule in Russia. It endorsed the platform of the Comintern and issued a Manifesto calling upon workers throughout the world to defend Soviet Russia in the struggle against foreign intervention.

The Eighth Congress of the Communist Party sat in Moscow on March 18-23, 1919. Yakov Sverdlov, an outstanding organiser of Soviet power, died on the eve of that Congress. His death was a heavy loss for the Party and the state. On a proposal moved by Lenin, A.R.C.E.C. elected Mikhail Kalinin as its Chairman.

The Party Congress adopted a new Party Programme, in which the tasks of building socialism were defined for the first time. Speaking of the international importance of the new Programme, Lenin declared: "Our programme will serve as extremely effective material for propaganda and agitation; it is a document which will lead the workers to say, 'Here are our comrades, our brothers; here our common cause is becoming reality.'"** On the basis of Lenin's report "On Work in the Countryside", the Congress passed a decision to switch from a policy of neutralising the middle peasants to a policy of forming a stable alliance with them and, in particular, with the poorest sections of the peasants, for the struggle against the kulaks. This decision played a tremendous role in securing victory over the interventionists and whiteguards and in promoting the building of socialism in the U.S.S.R.

---

* Lenin, *On the Foreign Policy of the Soviet State*, Moscow, p. 128.
** Lenin, *Collected Works*, Vol. 29, p. 222.

The Congress drew up a concrete programme for completing the build-up of the Red Army, improving the organisation of Party and political work in it, strengthening the link between the Party and the army and enhancing Party leadership in the military units.

1919 was the most difficult year in the history of the Soviet state. Towards the spring of that year the interventionists and whiteguards had an army of a million men poised for another offensive against the Soviet Republic.

The plan of joint invasion of Soviet Russia, that had been drawn up early in 1919 at the Paris Conference of the U.S., British and French heads of government, envisaged co-ordinated operations by all anti-Soviet forces. The Soviet Republic was forced to fight on six fronts.

The Kolchak army was to spearhead the attack. Kolchak now ruled a vast territory in the Urals, Siberia and the Far East and had the support of the bourgeoisie, the kulaks, the Cossack leaders and the semi-feudal nobility of the numerically small peoples. The Entente supplied his army with all kinds of weapons, for which he paid with the Russian gold seized by the whiteguards in Kazan.

The capitalist regime together with the laws and institutions of tsarist days was restored on territory occupied by the Kolchak army and a rigid military dictatorship was established.

The Kolchak offensive began on March 4, 1919, his army moving westward in a wide front extending from the forests of the Northern Urals to the southern Trans-Volga steppes. The Soviet 5th Army, which defended the approaches to the Volga, faced forces that were superior in numbers and had twice as much artillery. In March the whiteguards broke through the centre of the Eastern Front; they captured Votkinsk, Birsk, Ufa, Menzelinsk, Sterlitamak, Belebei, Bugulma and other towns. Kolchak's forces pressed forward towards the Volga to link up with Denikin, who was advancing from the south of Russia.

Bitter fighting raged throughout March.

Kolchak was supported by all the counter-revolutionary forces: General Denikin in the south, the White Poles in the west, General Yudenich on the approaches to Petrograd and, in the north, by General Miller's whiteguard army that was operating jointly with British, French and U.S. interventionist units. In mid-April 1919, Kolchak's units were only 85 kilometres away from Kazan and Samara and 100 kilometres away from Simbirsk. Any further advance of these units towards the Volga—in the region of Samara —would have threatened the right wing of the Eastern Front with encirclement. If, on the other hand, the Soviet troops retreated to the area west of the Volga, Kolchak would have made direct contact with Denikin, thus threatening the central regions of the Soviet Republic.

The enemy pushed back the Red Army on the Eastern, Northern, Southern, Western, Petrograd and Caucasian-Caspian fronts. The Soviet Republic had to draw upon all its resources to halt the enemy offensive, primarily the Kolchak offensive on the Eastern Front.

On April 12, *Pravda* published Lenin's *Theses of the C.C. R.C.P.(B.) in Connection with the Situation on the Eastern Front.* In these theses it was emphasised that the Eastern Front was the most important theatre of operations and that the task now was urgently to strengthen it, hurl Kolchak back from the Volga and liberate the Urals and Siberia. The Party Central Committee called on the people to work like real revolutionaries and rally to the country's defence.

In nine central gubernias of Russia five age groups were conscripted into the Red Army. Communists were mobilised everywhere. More than 60,000 foremost workers, all of them trade union members, over 15,000 Communists and upwards of 3,000 Y.C.L. members were sent as reinforcements to the Eastern Front. These reinforcements injected discipline and staunchness into the Red Army and fortified its confidence in victory.

The communist *subbotniks* (voluntary work after working hours) were a striking example of how the working class responded to the Party's and Government's appeal to the people to work in a communist way.

On April 12, 1919, the day on which the C.C. R.C.P.(B.) *Theses* were published, the first *subbotnik* was organised at the Moscow Marshalling Yard of the Moscow-Kazan Railway on the initiative of I. Burakov, fitter and chairman of a communist cell. The workers remained behind at the Marshalling Yard after working hours and, without remuneration, repaired three locomotives that were urgently needed to haul trains to the Eastern Front. The idea of holding these *subbotniks* quickly caught on and began to be practised throughout the republic.

Lenin called them a great beginning, a manifestation of the new, socialist attitude to work, the beginning of communism.

The Red Army began to be much better supplied as a result of the extensive organisational and political work of the Party and Government and the heroic labour of the Soviet people. The output of rifles, machine guns, ammunition, cannon shells and other war matériel was increased.

On instructions from the Party Central Committee and the Soviet Government, the Supreme Command planned a counter-offensive by the Red Army. The Eastern Front was divided into the Southern and Northern groups, the Kama River serving as the demarcation line between them.

The Southern group was to deal the main blow against Kolchak. Mikhail Frunze, an outstanding Soviet military leader, was put in command of the Southern group (1st, 4th, 5th and Turkestan armies), and Valerian Kuibyshev and Fyodor Novitsky, an officer of the old army, were appointed members of the group's Revolutionary Military Council. The Northern group (2nd and 3rd armies) was commanded by Vasily Shorin.

The Soviet counter-offensive was mounted on April 28, 1919. The Soviet troops dealt the enemy Western army a series of blows on its flanks and rear and pierced the Kolchak lines.

The Kolchak armies were utterly defeated in three successive battles: Buguruslan (April 28-May 13), Belebei (May 15-19) and Ufa (May 25-June 19).

In the Ufa operation the Soviet troops had to force the Belaya River along a front of 75 kilometres in face of heavy artillery, machine-gun and rifle fire. There were no fords worth mentioning. The 25th Division commanded by Vasily Chapayev (Commissar– Dmitry Furmanov) distinguished itself in these battles. Within three days (June 7-9, 1919) it annihilated the Kolchak shock battalions consisting solely of officers, and liberated Ufa.

The courage displayed by troops of the Southern group was highly appraised by the Soviet government. A Letter of Thanks was awarded to them by the Defence Council and many regiments were decorated with revolutionary Red Banners. In the space of two weeks, the Red Army completely defeated Kolchak's main forces, compelling them to go over to the defensive and then to retreat some 120-150 km. This placed the initiative on the Eastern Front firmly into the hands of the Red Army.

The successful Soviet offensive on the Eastern Front prepared the ground for Kolchak's final defeat and the liberation of the Urals and Siberia. Joakim Vacetis, the Supreme Commander, suggested suspending the offensive on the Eastern Front and transferring a considerable force to the Southern Front.

This plan was rejected by the Central Committee at its Plenary Meeting on July 3-4, 1919. The Party Central Committee and Soviet Government ordered the offensive to be continued; the objective was to prevent Kolchak from regrouping his forces and to liberate the Urals, whose industries were vital to the defence of the Soviet Republic.

In a telegram to the Revolutionary Military Council of the Eastern Front, Lenin said: "If we fail to capture the Urals before winter sets in, I consider the doom of the Revolution inevitable."[*] The offensive in the Urals, he declared, had to be stepped up and reinforcements sent to the troops operating in that area.

Acting on Lenin's instructions, the Red Army advanced rapidly eastward.

---

[*] Lenin, *Collected Works*, Vol. 35, "Telegram to the Revolutionary Military Council of the Eastern Front."

Yudenich, reinforced with counter-revolutionary units from Finland and Estonia, struck in the direction of Petrograd. This move was made by the Entente with the purpose of halting the Soviet offensive on the Eastern Front. The whiteguards had the support of a British squadron of 12 light cruisers, 20 destroyers, 12 submarines and other vessels. Moreover, their advance was paved by mutinies at three forts (Krasnaya Gorka, Seraya Loshad and Obruchev), which were engineered by Entente agents. Petrograd was directly endangered. Determined steps were taken by the Party Central Committee and the Soviet Government to strengthen the Petrograd Front. One of these steps was the transfer of troops from other fronts. The Petrograd workers rose to the defence of their city, the cradle of the Revolution. They fought shoulder to shoulder with the soldiers and sailors. At the close of July, the Yudenich troops were put to flight.

In the meantime, the danger from the south steadily increased. Denikin hurried to Kolchak's rescue. However, in the spring of 1919, he failed to link up with Kolchak on the Volga. This eliminated the threat of a joined attack on Moscow.

Hurled back from the Volga, Kolchak's armies withdrew eastward, suffering heavy casualties. By the beginning of August, the Red Army had completed the liberation of the Urals, thus increasing the Soviet Republic's defensive capacity. The Urals factories began supplying the Red Army with weapons as soon as the Kolchak forces were driven out.

On August 24, 1919, following the victory over Kolchak, Lenin addressed a letter to workers and peasants, formulating for them the principal lessons that the people had to learn in order to deal the enemy the final, crushing blow and avert a repetition of the calamities caused by Kolchak.

A powerful Red Army was needed; it could not fight without large state reserves of grain, and therefore the peasants had to loan the Soviet Government all their grain surpluses; there had to be strict revolutionary order. The experience of the political struggle in Russia showed that political parties had to be judged not by what they said but by what they did: the Mensheviks and Socialist-Revolutionaries called themselves socialists but in reality they were accomplices of the whiteguards and imperialists; the fifth and most important lesson, Lenin said, was that in order to defeat the enemy there had to be a firm alliance between the workers and the peasants. The Socialist-Revolutionaries and Mensheviks were frightening the peasants with the bogey of the dictatorship of the proletariat. The Kolchak regime in the Urals and Siberia had shown the peasants that they had to be on the side with the dictatorship of the proletariat; that was the major lesson taught by the Kolchak tyranny. "The workers' state," Lenin wrote, "is the only loyal friend helping the working people and the peasantry.

Lenin speaks at a parade of newly trained troops, May 25, 1919

Mikhail Tukhachevsky

Vasily Blücher

Ieronim Uborevich

Grigory Kotovsky

No leaning towards capital, an alliance of the working people to fight it, *workers' and peasants' power, Soviet power*–that is what the 'dictatorship of the working class' means *in practice*."*

Lenin's letter was instrumental in mobilising all the forces of the people for the defeat of Denikin's new offensive.

In the second half of 1919, the interventionists and whiteguards moved the centre of the struggle against the Soviet Republic to the south, pinning their hopes on Denikin. In the west and north-west Denikin was supported by the White Poles and Yudenich, in the east by the remnants of the Kolchak armies and in the north by General Miller. Winston Churchill boastfully announced that he had organised a "14-nation crusade" against the Soviet Republic, having in mind the U.S.A., Britain, France, Japan, Italy, Finland, Estonia, Latvia, Lithuania, Poland, the Ukraine, Georgia, Azerbaijan and Armenia. However, with the exception of Poland, the small countries that had been part of the tsarist empire, hung back from the war against Soviet Russia because Kolchak and Denikin had pursued a Great-Power policy, refusing to recognise their independence. The masses in these countries sympathised with the working people of Soviet Russia and were unwilling to fight them. Denikin's army was the principal assault force of this "crusade". In the summer and autumn of 1919, Denikin received from the U.S.A. more than 100,000 rifles, over 3,000,000 cartridges, 200,000 shells, over 600,000 pairs of boots, close to 200,000 greatcoats and large quantities of other supplies.** Churchill later admitted that Denikin received the bulk of British aid. Britain sent him at least 25,000 rifles, 200 pieces of artillery, 30 tanks and huge supplies of other weapons and ammunition. These supplies were shipped to Novorossiisk via the Dardanelles and the Black Sea. A few hundred British army officers and volunteers, acting as advisers, instructors and arms depot commanders, and several pilots helped to organise the Denikin armies.

The French turned over to Denikin a large quantity of Russian military property that had remained in France after the First World War; the governments of Rumania and Bulgaria likewise gave him a considerable part of the Russian military supplies that remained on their territory: over 300,000 rifles and 83,000,000 cartridges.

On May 19, 1919, the Denikin armies struck at the Soviet Southern Front near the southern boundaries of the Donbas. The Socialist-Revolutionary Grigoryev, who was one of Petlyura's commanders, led a mutiny behind the Soviet lines, seizing Yelisavetgrad, Yekaterinoslav, Kherson and Nikolayev. East of the

---

* Lenin, *Selected Works*, Vol. 3, p. 301.
** *Iz istorii grazhdanskoi voiny v SSSR (History of the Civil War in the U.S.S.R.)*, Vol. 4, Moscow, 1959, p. 196.

Dnieper, the Soviet rear echelons were attacked by anarchist and kulak gangs led by the adventurist Makhno; the Cossack uprising continued in the region of Veshenskaya Stanitsa.

At the close of May, Denikin forced the Soviet troops to retreat, and a month later he seized considerable territory in the Ukraine and the Donbas and reached a line running through Tsaritsyn-Balashov-Povorino-Novokhopersk-Belgorod-Alexandrovsk   and farther along the Dnieper. Denikin's large cavalry formations enabled him to manoeuvre and stab at the rear of the Red Army. Moreover, he had at his disposal a large body of officers. In fact, some of the units of his Volunteer Army consisted solely of officers. On July 3, he ordered an offensive directed at Moscow, with the aim of seizing the Soviet capital and putting an end to Soviet rule.

The situation at the fronts had again become unfavourable for the Red Army. It was, as Lenin said, "the most crucial moment of the socialist revolution". On July 9, 1919, the Central Committee sent a letter signed by Lenin to all Party members and working people. Headed "All for the Struggle Against Denikin!", it was a programme of measures for the defeat of the enemy.

Lenin wrote: "All the forces of the workers and peasants, all the forces of the Soviet Republic, must be harnessed to repulse Denikin's onslaught and to defeat him, without checking the Red Army's victorious advance into the Urals and Siberia. That is the *main task of the moment.*"*

In response to Lenin's call, the Party and Government stepped up their organisational and political work among the masses. The Southern Front was reinforced with Party and Government leaders and fresh units of the Red Army.

Vacetis, who had made a number of strategic blunders, was relieved of his duties as Supreme Commander on the recommendation of a Central Committee Plenary Meeting held on July 3-4, 1919. Sergei Kamenev, who had commanded the Eastern Front, became the new Supreme Commander. Pavel Lebedev was appointed Chief of Staff of the Revolutionary Military Council of the Republic. Mikhail Frunze was given command of the Eastern Front and Vladimir Yegoryev of the Southern Front.

Galina Okulova-Teodorovich, Andrei Bubnov, Valery Mezhlauk, Nikolai Anisimov and other leading Party workers were appointed to key Party and political posts on the Southern Front.

A plan for a counter-offensive against Denikin was drawn up in July 1919: under this plan the main attack force including the left-flank 9th and 10th armies was to strike in the direction of Novocherkassk from Kamyshin, Balashov and Tsaritsyn. This action was to be supported by the 8th, 13th and 14th armies.

---

* Lenin, *Selected Works*, Vol. 3, p. 260.

The plan conformed with the situation on the Southern Front and did not require extensive grouping or troop transfers.

In a single month, from August 15 to September 15, the Red Army dislodged the enemy from his positions, captured Valuiki, Kupyansk and Volchansk, approached to within 40 miles of Kharkov, and successfully advanced towards the middle reaches of the Don.

However, the Red Army did not have the forces with which to drive the offensive home. Denikin started a counter-offensive towards Kursk. In the region of Novokhopersk General Mamontov's cavalry corps broke through the front and drove a deep wedge into the Soviet lines. In August, Denikin seized Poltava and Sumy and advanced on Kiev. The Directorate's Petlyura troops captured Mogilev-Podolsky, Vinnitsa, Uman and Novgorod-Volynsky, and the White Poles entered Slutsk and Sarny. On August 31, Denikin's and Petlyura's forces marched into Kiev.

In September 1919, the Soviet Southern Front was divided into a new Southern Front commanded by Alexander Yegorov and the South-Eastern Front commanded by Vasily Shorin. The South-Eastern Front was assigned the task of smashing the enemy in the Don and Kuban regions and reaching Novocherkassk.

In the middle of September 1919, the situation on the Southern Front again became critical. Denikin seized the initiative and advanced towards the country's key centres. On September 12, 1919, he ordered another offensive in the direction of Moscow, assigning the capture of the Soviet capital to the Volunteer Army reinforced with Shkuro's and Mamontov's cavalry corps. Throughout the world the bourgeoisie rejoiced. The Don capitalists promised a reward of a million rubles to the first whiteguard regiment to enter Moscow.

The front held by the 8th and 13th Soviet armies was breached in the middle of September. On September 20, the whiteguards seized Kursk and in October they captured Voronezh and Orel. Tula, the Red Army's main arsenal, was threatened. Determined steps had to be taken to stop and destroy Denikin.

On Lenin's recommendation, the C.C. decided to reinforce the Southern Front with Party workers, rank-and-file Communists, Y.C.L. members and non-Party workers. Tula and its environs were fortified.

Additional reserves numbering nearly 50,000 men, including about 30,000 Communists and 10,000 Y.C.L. members, were sent to the Southern Front. The Red Army's political organs were strengthened. Joseph Stalin was appointed a member of the Southern Front's Revolutionary Military Council, and Vladimir Potemkin became the chief of its Political Department. Grigory Orjonikidze, Rozalia Zemlyachka, Vladimir Baryshnikov and other prominent Party leaders were transferred to the Southern Front.

On September 26, the Central Committee announced a Party Week for the admittance of foremost workers and peasants into the Party.

The threat hanging over the gains of October rallied the workers and peasants still closer round the Soviet Government. The people were solidly behind their army and nothing could stop them in the struggle against the counter-revolution. G. Okulova-Teodorovich, member of the 8th Army's Revolutionary Military Council, subsequently wrote of the battles against Denikin: "It was autumn. There were patches of frozen ground on the roads. Along the road were many corpses of horses that had died of exhaustion. They vividly accentuated the army's plight. Attacks alternated with retreats. The fighting was bitter. Our men's blood-stained toes were sticking out of their battered boots. I was told to go to a front-line regiment that consisted mainly of Petrograd workers. I was at a loss as to what to say to them. There was nothing I could promise. All I could do was to call upon them to show patience and heroism. I could not even tell them any comforting news about their families behind the firing lines....

"Yet, when I arrived I did not hear a single complaint. All I was asked was that the newspapers should be delivered more regularly. This small thing mirrored the amazing heroism of those days."

In the autumn of 1919, the situation on the Southern Front required a regrouping of Red Army forces to deal with the growing threat to Tula, Moscow and the adjoining regions.

On October 15, the Central Committee Politbureau ordered the Red Army to stand fast at Tula and Moscow and the approaches to them. It was planned to start a general offensive against Denikin in winter. A decision had been taken not to surrender Petrograd, and troops from other fronts were rushed to that city as reinforcements.

It was planned that the Red Army would start the main attack along the Kharkov-Donbas-Rostov-on-Don line.

An assault force was formed by the Soviet Command in the centre of the Southern Front to stop the enemy offensive in the most dangerous direction—towards Tula and Moscow—and enable the Red Army to start a counter-offensive. In the middle of October 1919, this force began its offensive. Sanguinary fighting raged near Orel. It marked the beginning of Denikin's defeat. The 14th Army likewise mounted an offensive. Orel was liberated on October 20. The Volunteer Army was forced to retreat.

On October 24, Denikin's units were defeated near Voronezh by Semyon Budyonny's Cavalry Corps, which soon afterwards was reformed into the 1st Cavalry Army, and by the 8th Army. In the liberation of Voronezh the Soviet troops were assisted by the town's workers and by the peasants of the outlying villages led by the local underground Party organisation.

Breaking the enemy's resistance, the Red Army advanced farther south. On December 12, 1919, it liberated Kharkov and on December 16, Kiev, capital of Soviet Ukraine. In January 1920, the Red Army captured Tsaritsyn, Novocherkassk and Rostov. The Soviet troops reached the Don and the Kuban, from where they continued their offensive, splitting Denikin's forces into two groups. One withdrew towards Odessa and the Crimea with the Southern Front, renamed the South-Western Front in January 1920, in pursuit. The main body, however, retreated to the North Caucasus. The South-Eastern Front, renamed the Caucasian Front in January 1920, pressed close on its heels. In February 1920, command of this front was taken over by Mikhail Tukhachevsky, and Grigory Orjonikidze was appointed member of the front's Revolutionary Military Council. In the heavy fighting in February and March 1920, the main forces of Denikin's armies were crushed and the remnants were pinned to the sea. Novorossiisk was liberated on March 27. In these battles the Red Army captured over 12,000 officers and 100,000 enlisted men, a large quantity of weapons and ammunition, and other trophies. Nothing remained of Denikin's armies. The survivors either fled abroad or went into hiding in the Crimea.

Defeat of Yudenich Near Petrograd

Yudenich's North-Western Army resumed its operations in the direction of Petrograd at a time when Denikin, flushed with success, was advancing towards Moscow. The enemy had considerable numerical superiority over the Soviet forces, which consisted of the 7th Army, the garrisons of several towns, and the Baltic Fleet. On September 28, 1919, supported by British tanks, Yudenich started his offensive.

The fighting reached its peak in October 1919. By October 20 the enemy had seized Yamburg, Krasnoye Syelo, Gatchina and Detskoye Syelo (now the town of Pushkin). Petrograd was threatened.

Lenin made an ardent appeal to the workers and Red Army men of Petrograd: "Fight to the last drop of blood, comrades. Hold fast to every inch of land, be firm to the end, victory is near! Victory will be ours!"*

Reinforcements were rushed to the Petrograd Front from the Northern Front and from Red Army reserves. Communists, Y.C.L. members and workers in the city were mobilised. On October 21,

---

* Lenin, *Collected Works*, Vol. 30, p. 69.

after receiving fresh reinforcements, the 7th Army took the offensive and in November, operating jointly with the 15th Army, defeated Yudenich, and drove the remnants of his forces back into Estonia, where they were disarmed by the Estonian authorities.

The Soviet victories over the main forces of the interventionists and whiteguards, above all over Denikin, sealed the doom of the whiteguard armies on the other fronts. In the East, Kolchak's army was living its last days.

Victory on Other Fronts. Partisan Warfare

The 3rd and 5th Soviet armies took the offensive in the region of the Tobol and Ishim rivers in the second half of October 1919. On November 14, the 27th Infantry Division entered Omsk, and on January 7, 1920, Red Army units in co-operation with partisans liberated Krasnoyarsk. That completed the defeat of Kolchak's army; its remnants fled farther east, while Kolchak himself was captured and shot in Irkutsk.

On the Northern Front the Red Army liberated Archangel on February 21 and Murmansk on March 13.

Partisans made a large contribution towards the defeat of the Kolchak and Denikin armies. Partisan units were formed in enemy-held territory by underground Party organisations. The Siberian Bureau of the C.C. R.C.P.(B.), headed by Filipp Goloshchekin, was set up in December 1919 to direct the underground Party organisations and partisan movement in Siberia. In its decision "On Siberian Partisan Detachments" on July 19, 1919, the C.C. R.C.P.(B.) set the task of centralising the leadership of the partisan movement and co-ordinating the operations of the partisans with those of the advancing Red Army. Large partisan units, some of which had up to 15,000-20,000 men, were active in Siberia.

The struggle of the working people in enemy-held territory in the south of Russia was directed by the Don Bureau of the R.C.P.(B.), which had been set up at the close of August 1918. In the summer of 1919, the Central Committee of the Ukrainian Communist Party organised a Bureau, headed by Stanislav Kosior, to operate behind the enemy lines. In the Ukraine the partisan forces were over 50,000 strong, and they helped the Red Army liberate a number of towns.

In the Caucasus the partisan movement was directed by the Caucasian Territory Committee of the R.C.P.(B.). An outstanding role in it was played by Filipp Makharadze and N. Gikalo.

The partisan movement sprang from the people's patriotism, from the military and political alliance between the working class and the peasants.

The alliance of the peoples of the Soviet republics took shape in the struggle against international and internal counter-revolution.

On July 1, 1919, the Russian Federation, the Ukraine and a number of other Soviet republics signed a treaty on the unification of the army command, the system of supplies for the Red Army and the railway administration. This amalgamation of the forces of the Soviet republics brought nearer the day of victory over the armies of the interventionists and whiteguards.

Breathing Spell

The beginning of 1920 brought the Soviet Republic a breathing spell: the interventionists had been driven out of a territory with a population of more than 50,000,000. Soviet rule was firmly established in the Urals, Siberia, the North Don, the Kuban, the Ukraine, Byelorussia, the Caucasus and a considerable part of Turkestan. Early in 1920, Britain, France and Italy were compelled to lift their economic blockade of Soviet Russia. Yet when the Soviet Government repeated its offer to begin peace talks, these powers made no reply. Soviet Russia achieved her first success in her struggle for peace in February 1920, when a peace treaty was signed with Estonia. This, Lenin said, opened a window on Europe for trade. Soon Latvia and Lithuania declared their desire to hold peace talks. That somewhat improved the international situation for Soviet Russia. But the threat of war still hung over her, compelling her to retain a 5,000,000-strong army while embarking upon economic rehabilitation. Temporary labour armies had to be formed from Red Army units.

With its main attention now concentrated on economic development, the Soviet Government reorganised the administration: in April 1920, the Council of Workers' and Peasants' Defence was reorganised into the Council of Labour and Defence to co-ordinate economic development with the country's defence.

The Ninth Congress of the Russian Communist Party (Bolsheviks), which sat at the close of March and the beginning of April 1920, endorsed the basic principles of the single economic plan, which envisaged an improvement of the country's transport system and the creation of the necessary reserves of grain, fuel and raw materials, to be followed by the development of the engineering industry and an increase of the output of consumer goods. The country's electrification was the foundation of this plan.

The Congress gave the trade unions the key task of drawing the masses into the work of rehabilitating and developing the country's economy.

Transport, the mines and factories were gradually brought back into working order, discipline was strengthened and labour productivity began to rise.

Defeat of the Last Interventionist Campaign

In the spring of 1920, the Soviet workers and peasants had to take up arms once more. This time the Entente planned using the armies of bourgeois Poland, ruled by the landowning class, and the whiteguard remnants in the Crimea commanded by Baron Wrangel. These armies were supplied with vast quantities of weapons, ammunition and other matériel. The Polish Government rejected the Soviet Russia's peace overtures and declared war on her.

On April 25, 1920, the Poles started an offensive in the direction of Kiev. The Soviet front was pierced and Zhitomir, Korosten, Kazatin and Kiev fell to the White Poles. The remnants of the whiteguard armies crawled out of the Crimea. Once again the Soviet Republic faced a serious threat. Once more the country was called upon to give everything for the front. A state of emergency was declared on May 11, 1920. Once again the entire industry was switched over to war production in order to ensure supplies for the Red Army. A Labour Front Week was held, during which the working day was lengthened by three hours. The output of arms and ammunition was substantially increased.

Once more Communists were mobilised: in May and June alone some 12,000 Communists were sent to the front.

The Red Army fought on two fronts: the Western and South-Western fronts. On the Western Front the Red Army launched an offensive in Byelorussia on May 14, in order to relieve the pressure on the troops of the South-Western Front. Although this offensive brought little success, it alleviated the situation on the South-Western Front. Semyon Budyonny's battle-hardened 1st Cavalry Army, which had nearly 18,000 men, 302 machine guns, 48 pieces of artillery, four armoured detachments, three air squadrons and four armoured trains, was transferred to the region of Uman on the South-Western Front from the environs of Maikop. Almost every fifth man in this army was a Communist.

The R.C.P.(B.) Central Committee's theses "The Polish Front and Our Tasks", which became the programme of battle against the enemy, were published on May 23, 1920. In them it was emphasised that the Soviet Republic was not infringing upon Poland's independence and sovereignty and that the Polish working people had to shape their own destiny.

Forming into a powerful fist, the 1st Cavalry Army attacked on June 5, breaching the Polish Front near Zhitomir and putting the Polish troops to flight. It liberated Zhitomir, Berdichev, Kiev and Vinnitsa. At the same time, the troops of the South-Western Front advanced rapidly towards the west.

The Western Front, commanded by Mikhail Tukhachevsky, likewise went over to the offensive on July 4. Towards the end of the month military operations were carried into Polish territory and

Mikhail Frunze, Kliment Voroshilov and Semyon Budyonny
planning the defeat of Wrangel, 1920

Troops of the First Cavalry Army, 1920

Petrograd Communists on the eve of their departure to the front against the White Poles

Voluntary work at the Kazan Railway Station, Moscow, May 10, 1919

approached Warsaw, the Polish capital. The appearance of the Red Army in Poland activated the revolutionary struggle of the Polish workers and peasants against bourgeois-landlord rule. A Provisional Revolutionary Committee of Poland, headed by Julian Marchlewski, was set up in Byelostok; more than 60 revolutionary committees, which instituted revolutionary reforms, sprang up in Poland's eastern regions. The workers of Byelostok formed a volunteer revolutionary regiment. The events in Poland were echoed in Western Europe.

In an effort to save the White Polish troops from utter defeat, the Entente pressed Soviet Russia to stop her military operations against Poland and Wrangel and offered to act as the mediator in talks. At the same time, it increased the stream of supplies for the White Polish army. When large reserves had been formed this army launched a counter-offensive on August 16 and dislodged the Soviet troops near Warsaw and Lvov. For a number of military, political and economic reasons the Red Army suffered a major setback near Warsaw. Economic dislocation prevented Soviet Russia from supplying the advancing troops with timely reserves, armaments and ammunition. The military command made a number of serious mistakes during the offensive against Warsaw: the positions won by the Soviet troops were not strengthened, the rear echelons lagged far behind and there was no co-ordination between the Western and South-Western fronts. One of the reasons for the failure of the offensive on Warsaw was opposition by the command of the South-Western Front (Yegorov, Stalin), to the transfer of the 12th, 14th and 1st cavalry armies to the Western Front.

The Red Army recovered from this defeat and prepared for a new offensive on bourgeois-landlord Poland, whose forces had by now been exhausted. The Pilsudski government agreed to the Soviet peace proposals. In October 1920, Poland signed a preliminary peace treaty with the Russian Federation and the Ukraine. That took the main force of the Entente's last crusade out of the game. Now the Soviet Republic could concentrate on destroying the Wrangel army, which was the Entente's "second arm".

Supplies poured in for this army. The Entente was still hoping to create a united Polish-Wrangel front.

In September, the Soviet Government formed the Southern Front, whose task was to deal Wrangel the death blow. Mikhail Frunze was put in command and Sergei Gusev and Béla Kun were appointed members of the Front Revolutionary Military Council. In addition to the 1st Cavalry Army, the Southern Front was reinforced with 8,000 Communists.

The Central Committee considered it necessary to liberate the Crimea before winter. Lenin briefed Frunze on the measures that the Party and Government were taking to ensure Wrangel's defeat.

For a whole month, from September 15 to October 15, the Soviet Southern Front fought fierce actions against Wrangel, who aimed at capturing the Donbas and breaking through to the region on the right bank of the Dnieper. His objective was to link up with Polish troops and upset the Soviet-Polish peace talks. But the fortunes of war were against him and he never achieved his goal.

However, the decisive battles against him were still to be fought. Frunze planned the rout of the whiteguard armies in Northern Tavria in order to prevent them from escaping to the Crimea. He ordered an offensive as soon as the 1st Cavalry Army was concentrated in the region of Berislav and Kakhovka.

The offensive was started on October 28. After three days of fighting the enemy was dislodged from his positions and forced to begin withdrawing to the Crimea. Budyonny's cavalry bore the main brunt of the enemy onslaught. "There was heavy fighting for three days," Semyon Budyonny recalls. "The enemy used armoured units and large cavalry and infantry forces. It was a fight to the death, for the enemy was determined to break through our lines at all costs." In these battles Wrangel's armies suffered huge casualties, but the bulk of them managed to break through to the Crimea and take cover behind powerful fortifications on the Perekop and Chongar isthmuses that had been built under the direction of foreign engineers. These fortifications were considered as impregnable as the Verdun Fortress. The Soviet troops could only enter the Crimea by taking them.

On the third anniversary of the October Revolution the 4th and 6th armies stormed the enemy's powerful defences and threw open the gates to the Crimea. The 1st and 2nd cavalry armies charged through these gates and pursued the retreating enemy.

The Crimea was cleared of whiteguards by November 17, and the Southern Front ceased to exist.

This rapid and decisive victory over the last of the Entente myrmidons was the result of a huge effort of all the forces of the Soviet Republic and of unparalleled heroism by its army. More than 40 formations were decorated with Orders and Red Banners. The divisions that had distinguished themselves in battle were given the name Sivash, Chongar and Perekop. Several thousand men and officers were awarded Orders and arms.

With the defeat of Wrangel the main forces of the counter-revolutionaries were routed.

Eighth All-Russia Congress of Soviets

The Eighth All-Russia Congress of Soviets opened in Moscow's Bolshoi Theatre at the close of December 1920.

The principal item on the agenda was the country's economic development. The interventionists and whiteguards had inflicted losses running into 50,000 million gold rubles on the Soviet Republic.

The Congress of Soviets, the highest organ of authority in the land, had to determine the ways and means of rehabilitating the country under the new conditions. Lenin moved the economic front to the foreground "as the basic and most important".

The drawing up of a single economic plan was one of the most important conditions for the successful rehabilitation of the Soviet economy. As has already been noted, early in 1920 the Ninth Party Congress defined the immediate economic tasks. Now the results of their fulfilment could be summed up. Transport was being restored under incredibly difficult conditions, and the country was straining every effort to increase the output and transportation of fuel, and was building up a reserve of foodstuffs.

With the experience of its first successes behind it, the Soviet Government now decided to draw up a long-term economic development plan to cover a period of several years. GOELRO* submitted to the Congress a scientific and fairly detailed plan of economic development.

The GOELRO plan envisaged doubling the industrial output as compared with 1913 and increasing power generation by 900 per cent. To reach this target the country had to build 30 large power stations operating on various kinds of fuel (the Dnieper, Volkhov, two Svir, Chirchik in Turkestan, Chusovaya in the Urals and others) in the course of 10 or 15 years.

Before the Congress was opened the Plan of the Electrification of the Russian Federation was published in book form and circulated among the delegates.

Lenin assessed the significance of the GOELRO plan in his famous formula: *"Communism is Soviet power plus the electrification of the whole country."***

On December 23, the eminent scientist Gleb Krzhizhanovsky, Chairman of the GOELRO Commission, read a report on the plan at the Congress, giving a picture of the future transformation of Russia.

The Congress endorsed the GOELRO plan, evaluating it as "the first step of a great economic undertaking". The Central Executive Committee and the Council of People's Commissars were instructed to complete the plan as quickly as possible and approve it. The Congress expressed the firm conviction that "all workers and working peasants would give all their strength and make every sacrifice to carry out the plan of the electrification of Russia at all costs and in face of all obstacles".

---

* In 1920, the State Commission for the Electrification of Russia, acting on Lenin's instructions, drew up a plan for the country's electrification.
** Lenin, *Collected Works*, Vol. 31, p. 516.

The Congress passed a special decision on heavy industry, in which it outlined measures for creating favourable conditions for building such an industry.

Agriculture, too, received great attention at the Congress. In view of the dislocation in agriculture, the Congress called upon the country to supply the peasants with implements, seeds and fertiliser and build repair shops and machine-hire and grain-cleaning stations.

The Congress made it obligatory for the peasants to sow their fields according to assignments from the government and to husband them correctly.

In its appeal "To All the Working People of Russia" the Congress congratulated the people on the great victory over the enemy and expressed gratitude to all those "who helped to win the victory by their sweat and blood, heavy labour and endurance, courage and self-sacrifice for the common cause".

Liberation of Outlying Regions

The defeat of the armies of Kolchak, Denikin, Yudenich, Wrangel and Poland, who were the principal forces of the counter-revolution, paved the way for the liberation of the outlying regions from the interventionists and whiteguards. The Russian proletariat came to the assistance of the non-Russian peoples in their liberation struggle. The military and political alliance of the Soviet republics, formed in mid-1919, was considerably strengthened.

In Central Asia the situation was extremely confused. At first Soviet rule was established only in Turkestan, which became an autonomous republic. Red Army detachments were formed of Russian and local workers and peasants, important agrarian reforms were carried out and all vestiges of the colonial regime were wiped out. At the close of 1919, the army of the Turkestan Front routed the Kolchak troops, linked up with units of the Red Army of the Turkestan Soviet Republic and restored direct communication between Turkestan, Kazakhstan and the R.S.F.S.R. Soviet Russia could now help the peoples of Central Asia, and Russian industry began to receive the cotton it needed.

The whiteguard and interventionist detachments operating in the Transcaspian area were annihilated in early 1920. This allowed destroying the main basmachi forces.

In Khoresm the people overthrew the khan and proclaimed a People's Republic on April 26, 1920.

Bordering on the Soviet Republic of Turkestan was the feudal Bukhara Emirate, where preparations were being made for an invasion of Soviet Turkestan. However, a popular uprising broke out against the emir in August 1900. Supported by the Red Army, this uprising ended in victory in September 1920: the emir was deposed and the Bukhara People's Soviet Republic was proclaimed. Subsequently, the people's republics of Khoresm and Bukhara became socialist republics.

The feudal despotism in Khoresm and Bukhara was overthrown under the leadership of the local Communist Parties.

Almost simultaneously Soviet power triumphed in Transcaucasia as well. There, too, the struggle was led by communist organisations. There was widespread dissatisfaction with the anti-popular regime of the Musavatists in Azerbaijan. On April 28, 1920, the Baku proletariat and the working people of the rest of Azerbaijan rose in revolt and appealed to Soviet Russia for assistance. The 11th Red Army, stationed on the frontier, entered Azerbaijan. Musavatist rule was broken. Soviet power was established in Azerbaijan, a prominent role being played in this by Grigory Orjonikidze, Sergei Kirov, Anastas Mikoyan and Nariman Najaf-ogly Narimanov.

In the autumn of 1920, the workers and peasants of Armenia rose against the Dashnak bourgeois-nationalist government. They were aided by the 11th Red Army. On November 29, 1920, Soviet rule was proclaimed in Armenia.

In February 1921, Soviet rule was established in Georgia, as well. The Menshevik government was overthrown by the people led by the Revolutionary Committee of Georgia, whose members included Filipp Makharadze, Mamiya Orakhelashvili and Shalva Eliava.

In the Far East the struggle dragged out. Kolchak's defeat and the vigorous partisan movement compelled the U.S.A., Britain and France to withdraw their troops in April 1920. The Japanese remained in the Far East, where they hindered the restoration of Soviet rule. To avoid war with Japan, the Central Committee of the R.C.P.(B.) and Soviet Government agreed to the creation of a "buffer" state in the Far East. In April 1920, a congress of the working people in Verkhneudinsk proclaimed the Far Eastern Republic, where a people's revolutionary government was set up. At the end of 1920, the people's revolutionary army, aided by partisans, drove the whiteguards out of almost the whole of the new republic.

However, the Japanese intervention continued. In 1921, with the support of the Japanese, the whiteguard remnants in Primorye Territory prepared for a fresh offensive. In Mongolia the Japanese formed a 10,000-strong army under Ungern. Its object was to invade the Transbaikal area and cut the Far Eastern Republic off from Soviet Russia. Red Army units and Mongolian revolutionary detachments led by the national hero Suhe-Bator, joined in the struggle against the whiteguards. Mongolia became a People's Republic.

In the summer of 1921, the whiteguards were defeated by the Red Army and the People's Army of Mongolia.

The whiteguard units on whom the Japanese pinned their hopes in the Soviet Far East were crushed by the People's Revolutionary Army in the battles of Volochayevsk and Spassk in 1922. The last of the whiteguards and interventionists were thrown into the sea on October 25, 1922. That put an end to the Civil War, and on November 14, 1922, the Far Eastern Republic merged with the Russian Federation.

Sources and Significance of the Victory

By defeating the interventionists and whiteguards the Soviet people inflicted a stinging military, moral and political defeat on world imperialism, and showed the great vitality of the Soviet state.

The key source of the Soviet Republic's strength and invincibility was its social and state system founded on a firm military and political alliance between the workers and working peasants, on friendship among the Soviet peoples.

In the Civil War, the military alliance between the workers and working peasants served as a basis for the creation of a large Red Army and a powerful partisan movement behind the enemy's lines.

An important role in securing victory was played by the Soviet Government's Leninist nationalities policy. It rallied the working people of all nationalities round the Russian proletariat and united them in the struggle against the interventionists and whiteguards, who were pursuing a policy of national oppression. Working people of many nationalities fought to establish Soviet rule, and defended it during the Civil War.

The Soviet people and the Red Army won because they fought a just, patriotic war in defence of the gains of the Great October Revolution, in defence of their socialist country.

The patriotism of Soviet people was a mighty source of the Soviet Republic's strength. It manifested itself in the mass heroism of troops at the firing lines and of workers in the rear.

Nearly 300,000 people joined the popular, patriotic partisan movement.

Victory over the interventionists and whiteguards was facilitated by Soviet foreign policy.

The Soviet Republic did its utmost to achieve peace, repeatedly offering peace to the Entente countries. Eight such offers were made in just the period from August 1, 1918, to February 1, 1919. But instead of replying the Entente continued fanning the Civil War.

In January 1919, the Soviet Government agreed to sit down to peace talks with the Entente at the conference on the Prince

Islands, being prepared to recognise the tsarist government's debts and to make territorial concessions.

Lenin received William Bullitt, an Entente representative, and had talks with him on peace terms. Lenin's proposals were communicated to the Entente powers, but the latter ignored them.

The Soviet Government's consistent struggle for peace and its policy of equality of big and small nations tremendously influenced the masses in foreign countries, won their sympathy for Soviet Russia and thereby undermined the anti-Soviet intervention.

Despite the betrayal by the Right socialist leaders, who slandered the Soviet Republic and actively supported the anti-Soviet intervention, the workers rose to defend Soviet Russia. Strikes, rallies and political demonstrations demanding the withdrawal of interventionist troops from Soviet territory and the establishment of friendly relations with Soviet Russia swept across Britain, France, Italy, the U.S.A., Japan and other countries. The workers organised Hands Off Soviet Russia Committees of Action.

Another manifestation of proletarian solidarity was the creation of international units of the Red Army. These units included tens of thousands of Hungarians, Chinese, Yugoslavs, Slovaks, Poles, Bulgarians, Rumanians, Germans, Koreans and Finns.

The chief and decisive condition for the victory of the Soviet Republic over the international and internal counter-revolution was the leadership of the Communist Party, of its Central Committee headed by Lenin. The Party's Central Committee was the fighting headquarters directing the republic's defence, the country's foreign and home policy, the building up of the Soviet Armed Forces and the management of the economy under wartime conditions.

The Party sent its best people into the Army and Navy. Nearly 50,000 Communists gave their lives for the cause of the revolution during the Civil War.

Thus, capitalism was defeated in its first open armed engagement with a socialist country. The Soviet Republic's victory promoted the growth of the international working-class and national liberation movements in the West and East and ensured the conditions for the successful building of socialism in this country.

Chapter Three

ECONOMIC REHABILITATION, FORMATION AND DEVELOPMENT OF THE U.S.S.R. (1921-25)

Internal Development of the Soviet State

The Soviet State After the War

The last battles died down. The war brought victory to the revolutionary people of the Soviet state. Discounting short breathing spells, this was the beginning of their first prolonged period of peace. They could now turn their attention to restoring the dislocated economy and complete the social and economic reforms that had been started in October 1917.

The Soviet state with a territory of over 21,300,000 square kilometres and a population of 132,000,000 was the largest country in the world.

Six Soviet republics—Russia, the Ukraine, Byelorussia, Georgia, Armenia and Azerbaijan—occupied a sixth of the globe's land surface. In contrast to the highly developed industrial states of the capitalist West, it was an agrarian country.

At the beginning of 1921, industrial output had dropped to 14.3 per cent of its pre-war figure. The fuel, iron and steel and engineering industries lay in ruin. The output of cotton fabrics had gone down almost 95 per cent, sugar 91.7 per cent, salt 71.5 per cent, matches 85.7 per cent, and so on. This was the result of four years of the imperialist war and three years of Civil War and foreign intervention.

The dislocation of transport crippled the economic links between various regions and between agriculture and industry. In the towns the people were suffering incredible hardship.

Agriculture, too, had suffered terribly. The area under grain and industrial crops had been reduced, the land was poorly cultivated, grain harvests had decreased and livestock-breeding had declined.

Various sectors had become intertwined in the country's economy: the *socialist* sector, covering all large-scale state industry, trade, transport, banks, co-operative enterprises, state and collective farms; the *small-commodity* sector, covering the peasant husbandry based on personal labour and linked up with the market only through the sale and purchase of goods; the *private capitalist* sector, consisting of kulak farms, using hired labour, owners of small factories, and private shop-keepers; the *patriarchal* sector, consisting of semi-natural peasant farms not linked up with the market; and *state capitalism*, which covered the lease of land, concessions, and controlled private enterprises.

The small-commodity sector predominated, but the leading role in developing the country's economy was played by the socialist sector, where the key branches of the economy were concentrated: large-scale industry, transport, foreign trade, finances, and state ownership of the land.

The principal classes in Soviet society were the workers and the peasants; the remnants of the former ruling exploiter classes —former landowners and capitalists and private merchants— formed an insignificant stratum. In the countryside the kulaks were the most numerous exploited class.

The classes had changed considerably during the war years. In those years the working class had accomplished an epoch-making feat: by ensuring the triumph of the socialist revolution it had become the ruling class, carried out radical socio-economic reforms and defended the country against the onslaught of international imperialism. It was now providing society with political leadership and actively helping to administer the country. But the greatest privations, difficulties and suffering had fallen to its lot. By the struggle that it waged it won the sympathy and support of all working people.

The number of workers in the large-scale industry continued to decrease, falling from 2,555,000 in 1913 to only 1,270,000 in 1921. The closing-down of factories and hunger had driven workers to the villages. When large-scale industry, the material basis of socialism and proletarian consciousness, began to decline, part of the workers displayed vacillation, hesitation, desperation and distrust, which was fanned by the counter-revolutionary propaganda of the Mensheviks and Socialist-Revolutionaries, the last ditch defenders of capitalism. This created a serious threat to the new Soviet system.

The peasants were the most numerous class of Soviet society, accounting for about 80 per cent of the population.

Far-reaching changes had taken place in the position and the thinking of the peasants during the war and the Revolution. They had been rid of landowner and capitalist oppression, of landowner-bourgeois rule, and were, to a large extent, freed from the influence of the church and religion. The ratio between the different sections of peasants—poor peasants, middle peasants and kulaks—had changed radically: prior to the Revolution the vast majority (about

65 per cent) of the peasants were poor, but now the middle-peasant group predominated, the number of poor peasants having diminished. The power of the kulaks had been broken, and the number of kulak farms had dropped to approximately one-third of the original number. The former exploiter classes—the landowners and the capitalists—had been completely expropriated. Between 1,500,000 and 2,000,000 landowners and capitalists, including their families, had emigrated, retaining their counter-revolutionary organisations with the purpose of strangling Soviet rule and restoring capitalism in Russia; some of the small landowners had remained in the countryside, receiving the right to the newly established quota of land.

The workers and peasants, forming, as we have already said, the main classes of Soviet society, had united in the military and political alliance that had taken shape during the Civil War. However, when the Civil War ended the military and political form of this alliance was no longer sufficient. The peasants began to voice their dissatisfaction with the compulsory deliveries of food. They demanded freedom to dispose of their surplus products at their own discretion, to exchange them for manufactured goods. This dissatisfaction was turned to account by the Cadets, Mensheviks and Socialist-Revolutionaries, who had lost influence during the Revolution, and also by the whiteguard leaders living abroad. They organised anti-Soviet kulak uprisings in Tambov Region, the Ukraine, on the Don and in Siberia. Some middle peasants became involved in these uprisings.

The enemies of Soviet rule changed their tactics. Inasmuch as the Soviets enjoyed the support of millions of people, they changed their slogan of "Down with the Soviets" to "Soviets Without Communists". The new tactics were, for example, responsible for the Kronstadt mutiny, which broke out on February 28, 1921, and threatened the gains of the Revolution because of that fortress' proximity to Petrograd. The mutineers were actively helped by the Western bourgeoisie. On March 18, 1921, the mutiny was put down by Red Army units commanded by Mikhail Tukhachevsky.

Among some of the workers, too, there was dissatisfaction with the War Communism policy.

In the spring of 1921, the situation in the country demanded a basic re-examination of the policy pursued by the Party and Government.

New Economic Policy

After having profoundly analysed the situation in the country in the spring of 1921, and taking the difficulties of the peasants into account, Lenin proposed revising the policy towards the peasants. Addressing Moscow metalworkers on February 4, 1921, he said:

"In the past winter the peasants found themselves in a desperate situation, and their dissatisfaction can be appreciated. Let us re-examine the attitude of the workers to the peasants."*

In this period Lenin received many peasant delegations from various gubernias and studied letters sent to central newspapers.

In March 1921, the Tenth Party Congress passed the decision to adopt a New Economic Policy.

The principles of this policy had been worked out by Lenin early in 1918 in his work *The Immediate Tasks of the Soviet Government*; in those days its implementation had been hindered by the intervention and the Civil War. But now the transition to the new policy was accomplished in a totally different situation and many questions of this transition were settled with due consideration for the experience of economic development that had been gained in 1918-20.

The first step towards the New Economic Policy was the replacement of the surplus requisitioning system by a tax in kind adding up to about half the value of such deliveries; peasants paid the tax according to the size of their plot of land, the number of people in the family, the harvest, and the property owned by them. The poorest peasants were accorded tax privileges, while the rich farms paid a higher tax.

Peasant households that had paid the tax could freely sell their surplus products in the market. The next step in the New Economic Policy was, therefore, to allow small-scale industry and peasants to sell their products freely. Private capital was permitted in this trade. That was one of the fundamental distinctions between the New Economic Policy and War Communism, when free trade was forbidden.

The new policy radically changed the position of the consumers' co-operative. In the period of War Communism it was subordinated to the People's Commissariat for Food and its functions were confined to distributing products and prime necessities among the population, its right to purchase farm output being restricted inasmuch as almost all surplus products had to be delivered to the state. Now the co-operative received the right to purchase all sorts of products and to trade in prime necessities in town and country. The state gave every encouragement to state and co-operative trade, the latter linking large-scale socialist industry with small-commodity peasant production. The state was interested in implementing this link through state and co-operative trade. That was why Lenin set Communists the task of learning to trade. The state was becoming a large wholesale dealer, primarily in manufactured goods.

The small enterprises that had not been nationalised during

---

* Lenin, *Collected Works*, Vol. 32, p. 110.

the war remained in the hands of their owners, while those that had been nationalised were leased to individuals or co-operatives. Concessions were leased in industry and for the development of natural resources. Concessions and leases were manifestations of state capitalism, i.e., capitalism permitted by the Soviet government on certain terms (contracts of lease or concession).

State capitalism, furthermore, embraced trade on commission, state-private joint-stock companies, and bourgeois co-operatives. The latter united small producers, helping the Soviet government to control them. Co-operative trade was much more useful and profitable than private enterprise because it helped to unite and organise the population and was "an enormous gain from the point of view of the subsequent transition from state capitalism to socialism".*

While permitting various forms of state capitalism and controlling it, the state used it to revive large-scale industry and to combat petty-bourgeois elements. State capitalism aided socialist development.

The transition to the New Economic Policy affected other aspects of the country's social and policial life. Food and raw materials that could be supplied by peasant economies were needed to restore large-scale industry. In order to satisfy the peasants' demand for manufactured goods, the state encouraged private and co-operative petty manufacturing and handicrafts industries. Large-scale industry, too, began manufacturing goods for the countryside. State enterprises were made to run on a self-supporting basis; the wage system was revised with the purpose of stimulating the workers' labour effort. The State Bank, the credit system and free financial operations were restored The New Economic Policy thus covered a large range of economic relations. Its main objective was to link socialist industry up with the peasant economy, for this was the only way to strengthen the alliance of the working class with the peasants for development in peacetime.

The New Economic Policy caused a certain revival of capitalism and a further intensification of the struggle between socialist and capitalist elements. Lenin said: "The whole question is: who will get there first. If the capitalists succeed in organising first—they will drive out the Communists and that will be the end of it. We must face up to the issue: who will come out on top?"**

With the large-scale industry, transport, banks, foreign trade and nationalised land in its hands, the Soviet government restricted and controlled the growth of capitalist elements and worked to promote the growth and consolidation of the socialist sector.

---

* Lenin, *Selected Works*, Vol. 3, p. 651.
** Lenin, *Collected Works*, Vol. 33, "The New Economic Policy and the Tasks of the Political Educational Department".

The New Economic Policy was thus a departure from War Communism. Showing the substance of this departure, Lenin said: "We know that in view of the desperate hunger and the present state of industry, we cannot hold all the positions we won in the period 1917-21. We have surrendered a number of them. But we can say that, *so far as making concessions to the capitalists is concerned, the retreat is now at an end.... We shall not retreat any further*; we shall set about deploying and regrouping our forces properly."*

Lenin's proposal for stopping the retreat was approved by the Eleventh Party Congress in March 1922, exactly a year after the New Economic Policy was started.

The purpose of the New Economic Policy, a special policy of the Soviet state, was thus to strengthen the economic alliance between the working class and the peasants, give all working people of town and country an incentive to develop the economy, and permit a certain measure of capitalism while keeping the command heights of the economy in the hands of the government; this policy was designed to give socialist elements the upper hand in the struggle against capitalist elements, destroy the exploiter classes, consolidate the Soviet state and promote the building of socialism.

From the historical point of view the significance of the New Economic Policy was that in alliance with the working peasants, the working class restored the country's productive forces, strengthened the state and built socialism. Its international significance is that the Russian experience will inevitably be repeated in any country where the working class is building or will build socialism in alliance with the peasants. At the Ninth All-Russia Congress of Soviets in December 1921, Lenin said: "The task that we are working on today, temporarily alone, seems a purely Russian task, but in fact it is a task that all socialists will be confronted with."** While strengthening the world's first workers' and peasants' state, the New Economic Policy influenced the world revolutionary movement and helped socialism to forge ahead in world competition with capitalism.

Obstacles to the New Economic Policy; the First Achievements

The turn from War Communism to the New Economic Policy involved considerable difficulties. It was accomplished under conditions where there was an acute food shortage in the industrial centres and a shortage of fuel, metal and raw materials for the factories and mills, and transport was dislocated. Many workers

---

* Lenin, *On the Foreign Policy of the Soviet State*, p. 389.
** Lenin, *Collected Works*, Vol. 33, "Ninth All-Russia Congress of Soviets".

did not understand why this turn was necessary, believing it was wrong to make such concessions to the peasants. Some Communists too could not appreciate the need for it.

Economic executives, the heads of co-operatives and trade union workers had to learn to work correctly under the new conditions, to ensure the profitability of enterprises, increase labour productivity, solve the food problem, conduct trade, expand local industries and step up commodity circulation.

The Communist Party used every means to explain the substance and importance of the New Economic Policy to the people: the central and local newspapers carried articles by leading Party propagandists; the articles and pamphlets on the New Economic Policy written by Lenin played an exceedingly important role. In April 1921, Lenin wrote a pamphlet entitled *The Tax in Kind,* in which he substantiated the objectives and significance of the new policy. The Tenth All-Russia Conference of the R.C.P.(B.), held in May 1921, was entirely devoted to the New Economic Policy. The Third Comintern Congress sat in the period from the end of June to the beginning of July 1921; at this Congress Lenin delivered a report on the tactics of the R.C.P.(B.), speaking at length about the New Economic Policy. In the Ukraine, Byelorussia and Transcaucasia the local Party organisations held congresses and conferences to discuss ways and means of implementing the new policy and spoke of the first steps that had been taken in that direction.

It was not easy to collect the tax in kind quickly and in time. Although it amounted to half the compulsory deliveries of surplus food, it was collected without any equivalent; the peasant farms had not yet recovered from the ruin caused by the war and by the crop failure that hit several gubernias in 1920. Profiteers undermined normal commodity exchange. Armed gangs of kulaks operated in the Ukraine and the western regions of Byelorussia, and basmachi were active in Central Asia. Secret enemies of the Soviet state, former landowners, capitalists, Mensheviks and Socialist-Revolutionaries hindered the struggle against kulak banditry, sowed distrust among the workers and let loose red tape in the Soviet state machine.

On top of everything the first year of the New Economic Policy coincided with a crop failure in a huge territory. The crop failure and the famine, Lenin wrote, were the aftermath "of Russia's backwardness and of seven years of war—the imperialist and then the Civil War".*

The Soviet Republic exerted a titanic effort to cope with the situation caused by the drought and the crop failure. To help

---

* Lenin, *On the International Working-Class and Communist Movement,* Moscow, p. 370.

the famine-stricken population A.R.C.E.C. set up an All-Russia Commission headed by Mikhail Kalinin.

On July 21, 1921, A.R.C.E.C. decreed the formation of an All-Russia Famine Relief Committee. This organisation was given authority to act in the country and abroad.

The Soviet Government appealed to the Soviet and world public for aid: on July 23, 1921, *Pravda* carried an appeal for famine relief.

On August 2, 1921, Lenin asked the international proletariat for assistance.

The country did all it could to relieve the famine: workers, office employees and Red Army men voluntarily deducted part of their pay and food rations, and the peasants collected food. Voluntary work days and collections of clothing, money and food for the famine relief fund were organised. Grain and seeds collected as food tax were sent to the famine-stricken areas. Part of the gold earmarked for the purchase of machinery abroad was used for the purchase of grain for the stricken areas.

The population, primarily children, were evacuated from these areas to Siberia, the Ukraine, Byelorussia and Central Russia, where the food situation was better.

An International Famine Relief Workers' Organisation was set up in August 1921 on the initiative of the Executive Committee of the Communist International. Workers' organisations collected money for the purchase of food and medicaments for the affected regions in Soviet Russia.

Workers from many countries and progressive Western writers, artists, cultural workers and scientists made their contribution. Anatole France donated the Noble Prize that he received in 1921 to the relief fund. Fridtjof Nansen, the Norwegian polar explorer, organised a collection of money and the purchase of food for Russia.

This assistance was highly appreciated by the Soviet people. The Ninth All-Russia Congress of Soviets, held in December 1921, put on record in its resolution that "despite the unemployment and difficult economic situation into which the systematic offensive of capitalism had forced the workers of a number of countries, the proletariat of Europe and America was generously aiding the famine-stricken population on the Volga...."* The Congress regarded this aid as an expression of true internationalist working-class solidarity.

In the U.S.A. various public organisations and individuals sponsored collections of donations to aid the population of Russia. At the close of 1921, the U.S. Government agreed to turn over to

---

* *Syezdy Sovetov v dokumentakh. 1917-1936* (*Congresses of Soviets in Documents, 1917-36*), Vol. I, Moscow, 1959, p. 166.

Russia $30,000,000 worth of food and seeds. The food and other donations were transported to Russia by the American Relief Administration on the terms specified in an agreement signed with the Soviet Government. The Soviet Government took into account the reactionary nature of A.R.A., that had been set up by American businessmen headed by Herbert Hoover with the purpose of selling old stocks of goods and strengthening the positions of U.S. imperialism in Europe.

Bringing food and donations to Russia, A.R.A. strove to distribute it among non-working elements, support counter-revolutionary forces and plant an espionage network. That forced the Soviet authorities to take steps to stop A.R.A.'s subversive activities and, finally, to turn down assistance from it.

The Soviet people surmounted the difficulties involved in the transition to the New Economic Policy and also the disaster caused by the 1921 drought and crop failure. The affected regions received considerable quantities of food and material aid. The spring sowing was successfully completed and there was even some enlargement of the area sown to crops. The food tax was collected in the unaffected areas. In the following year, 1922, after an excellent harvest, all consequences of the famine disappeared.

The transition to the tax in kind was welcomed by the peasants because it made their position easier. It enabled the peasant "to feel more secure and gave him a greater incentive to carry on his work".*

Resolutions approving the tax in kind were passed at congresses of Soviets and at non-Party conferences of peasants.

The entire country now turned its attention to restoring industry and transport and promoting agriculture.

Union of Equal Republics

In the life of the Soviet people the key political event was the creation at the close of 1922 of a union state, the Union of Soviet Socialist Republics. This event had been preceded by five years of extensive organisational and educational activity by the Communist Party, which consistently pursued the nationalities policy as mapped out by Lenin.

The resolution "On the Immediate Tasks of the Party in the Nationalities Question", adopted by the Tenth Party Congress, was an immense contribution to the formation of the U.S.S.R. It showed why the Soviet republics had to unite in a single state.

Soviet rule, rooted in the people themselves, drew the Soviet peoples together.

Another factor facilitating unification was that there was an

---

* Lenin, *Collected Works*, Vol. 33, "Ninth All-Russia Congress of Soviets".

economic division of labour between the different regions: industry in the centre of Russia supplied manufactured goods to the regions in the south-east and north, receiving raw materials in exchange—cotton, timber, flax; the southern regions were the main producers of oil, coal, iron ore and so forth.

The formation of the U.S.S.R. served the interests of all the Soviet peoples. All-sidedly developed productive forces were needed to enable socialism to triumph. Lenin's GOELRO plan envisaged the economic development of all the main regions.

Surrounded as they were by a hostile capitalist world, the Soviet republics could remain independent and sovereign states only by pooling their efforts in the military, diplomatic and foreign trade fields. The very first appearance of the Soviet republics on the international scene, at the Genoa Conference, showed them that they had to unite.

The experience accumulated by the socialist republics in co-operating with one another likewise helped them to unite.

The formation of the U.S.S.R., moreover, conformed with the interests of the international revolutionary movement. Soviet experience in all fields of state, economic and political activity was of immense value in promoting the national liberation struggle, particularly in the Eastern countries. Lenin declared that "tomorrow in world history will be just such a day when the peoples oppressed by imperialism will finally be aroused and waked and the decisive long, hard struggle for their liberation will begin".*

Lenin fathered the idea of uniting the independent Soviet republics into a single state, and the Communist Party organised their unification. In mid-1922 the Communist Parties of the non-Russian republics raised the question of establishing closer ties with the R.S.F.S.R.; soon afterwards unification became the objective of a popular movement, in the course of which it was proposed that the republics should pass from treaty relations to the creation of a single union state. The initiative came primarily from the Transcaucasian republics (Azerbaijan, Armenia and Georgia), which had in February 1922 merged together to form a federal union and later the Federative Transcaucasian Soviet Socialist Republic. Similar proposals were made by the peoples of the Ukraine and Byelorussia.

The C.C. R.C.P.(B.) set up a special commission headed by Joseph Stalin to study the question of uniting the Soviet republics. The commission included Alexander Myasnikov, Grigory Orjonikidze, Grigory Petrovsky and representatives from all the non-Russian republics. Soon Stalin drew up a project for uniting the republics, calling it an autonomisation plan; the Ukraine, Byelorussia, Armenia, Azerbaijan and Georgia would join the Russian

---

* Lenin, *The National Liberation Movement in the East*, Moscow, p. 312.

Federation as autonomous republics. Under this plan the supreme organs of power in the R.S.F.S.R. would become the supreme organs of power of the Union. Although Stalin's plan was approved by the Central Committees of the Communist Parties of Azerbaijan and Armenia, it was altogether erroneous, being a step back from the relations established between the republics.

Illness prevented Lenin from working on this question, but when he studied Stalin's plan and the resolutions of the Central Committees of some of the non-Russian Communist Parties he emphatically opposed them, regarding them as a belittlement of the rights of the Soviet republics and a threat to the friendship between their peoples. He proposed the creation of a Union of Soviet Socialist Republics through the voluntary merging of equal and independent Soviet republics.

Under Lenin's plan, the Russian Federation, the Ukraine, Byelorussia and the Transcaucasian Soviet Federative Socialist Republic would join in a union of *equal* republics. A Central Executive Committee of Soviets would be elected to administer the Union as an organ of power of *equal* republics.

Lenin's plan was accepted by the special commission of the C.C. On October 6, 1922, on the basis of this plan, a Plenary Meeting of the C.C. R.C.P.(B.) passed a resolution on the manner in which the independent Soviet republics should be united. It stated: "It is recognised that a treaty should be signed between the Ukraine, Byelorussia, the Federation of Transcaucasian Republics and the R.S.F.S.R. uniting them in a Union of Soviet Socialist Republics and leaving to each of them the right of freely seceding from the Union."

Mass meetings attended by industrial and office workers and peasants were held in the republics in the course of October and December 1922 to debate the question of unification. The vote was unanimous in favour of unification.

The Seventh All-Ukraine Congress of Soviets approved the formation of the U.S.S.R.

Decisions to form the Union were passed by the First Congress of Transcaucasian Soviets, the Fourth Congress of Soviets of Byelorussia and the Tenth All-Russia Congress of Soviets. Delegates were elected in the republics to a Constituent Congress of Soviets.

The First Congress of Soviets of the U.S.S.R. opened on December 30, 1922. It was attended by 2,215 delegates elected on the basis of proportional representation. The Russian delegation, 1,727 delegates, was the most numerous. The Ukrainian delegation consisted of 364 people. The Transcaucasian Federation was represented by 91 delegates, and Byelorussia by 33 delegates. Lenin, who was ill at the time, was elected honorary chairman of the Congress.

The Congress endorsed the Declaration and Treaty on the formation of the U.S.S.R. The declaration gave legislative force to Lenin's principles of organising a Union state: voluntary nature of the union and equality and fraternal co-operation of the Soviet peoples on the basis of proletarian internationalism. The opportunity to join the Union was left open to all existing and future Soviet republics. The treaty defined the procedure by which the Union could be joined, the right to freely secede from the Union, the procedure of forming the higher organs of state power and administration, and the terms of reference. The Congress elected a Central Executive Committee of the U.S.S.R. as the supreme organ of power in the interim between congresses.

At its first meeting the new Central Executive Committee elected a Presidium. It adopted Lenin's proposal that the C.E.C. should have four chairmen according to the number of republics in the Union: the newly elected chairmen were Mikhail Kalinin, Grigory Petrovsky, Alexander Chervyakov and Nariman Najaf-ogly Narimanov. In a speech closing the Congress, Kalinin said: "For thousands of years mankind's greatest brains have tried to formulate theoretical answers to the problem: which ways would give the peoples the possibility of living in friendship and fraternity without great suffering, without internecine struggle. The first stone in that direction is being laid today."*

Although Lenin was gravely ill while the Congress was in session he dictated his notes "The Question of Nationalities or 'Autonomisation'". He stressed that representatives of the Russian nation had to give the greatest attention to the interests of small nations; no injustice or wounding of national feelings was to be tolerated.

He outlined practical measures aimed at consolidating the new Union and removing all elements of Great-Power chauvinism from the Soviet state apparatus. In April 1923, the Twelfth Party Congress, acting on Lenin's recommendations, mapped out a programme of state organisation founded on equality of rights and duties of the Union republics. In the summer of 1923, the C.E.C. approved and gave effect to the Constitution of the U.S.S.R. A Union Government, the Council of People's Commissars with Lenin as its chairman, and other higher government institutions were set up.

In January 1924, the Second Congress of Soviets of the U.S.S.R. passed the final draft of the Constitution of the U.S.S.R., thus completing the formation of a single Union state as a Federation of Soviet Republics.

This truly democratic Constitution of the world's most progressive state consolidated the complete equality of peoples, their sovereignty, equal rights and duties to their state and the prin-

---

* M. I. Kalinin, *Statyi i rechi (1919-1935)* (*Articles and Speeches [1919-35]*), Moscow, 1936, p. 95.

ciple of democratic centralism. The voluntary nature of the Union was emphasised by the right accorded to each nation freely to secede from the Union and the free access to the Union by the existing or emerging socialist republics.

The Union's jurisdiction covered foreign policy, foreign trade, the armed forces and the means of communication; in all other questions the Union republics retained their sovereignty. The C.E.C. consisted of two equal chambers: the Soviet of the Union, which was elected at the congress by all the delegates to the congress, and the Soviet of Nationalities, which was elected from among representatives of the republics and national areas. This pattern of the supreme organ of state power ensured the active participation of the people of all nations and nationalities in the building of the new, socialist society.

The way the U.S.S.R. was formed showed its democratic, popular nature.

The epoch-making significance of the formation of the U.S.S.R. lay in the triumph of the principles of Lenin's nationalities policy—equality, fraternity and sovereignty of peoples.

The demarcation of the state territory of the socialist nations was given special attention by the Communist Party and Soviet Government. In 1924-26, Byelorussia was territorially doubled by the inclusion of Vitebsk, Gomel and Smolensk gubernias, where the population was predominantly Byelorussian. The Government of the R.S.F.S.R. transferred Ufa Gubernia to the Bashkirian Autonomous Republic, thereby uniting the West and East Bashkirians and doubling Bashkiria's territory and population.

A number of new autonomous republics and regions were formed in 1924-26 as a result of the successful development of the national statehood of the Soviet peoples. Thus, the Moldavian Autonomous Soviet Socialist Republic was formed within the Ukrainian Soviet Socialist Republic in October 1924.

New republics and regions were formed in the R.S.F.S.R. as well. The Buryat-Mongolian and Chuvash autonomous regions were made autonomous republics. The national statehood of the peoples of Georgia, Armenia and Azerbaijan was strengthened. The federal union of these peoples consolidated the fraternal relations between them. Each people was given the possibility of creating its own socialist state. The Abkhasian and Ajarian autonomous republics and the South Ossetian Autonomous Region took shape within Georgia. The Nakhichevan Autonomous Republic and the Nagorny Karabakh Autonomous Region were formed in Azerbaijan.

The national and territorial demarcation of Central Asia in 1924 was of great significance to the development of the Soviet multinational state.

In the past the peoples of Central Asia had been dismembered by the frontiers of feudal states. Three multinational states—the Turkestan Autonomous Soviet Socialist Republic and the Bukhara and Khoresm people's republics—were formed after the October Revolution. In these states there was an intermingling of Uzbeks, Turkmenians, Tajiks, Kazakhs and Kirghizes. For that reason, as early as 1920, Lenin requested the Turkestan Commission to draw up an ethnographical map of Turkestan to show Uzbekistan, Kirghizia and Turkmenia and elucidate the possibility of either merging or separating these three areas.

However, the conditions for demarcation matured only at the end of 1924, when by decision of their congresses of Soviets the Bukhara and Khoresm people's republics became socialist republics.

The Turkestan Central Executive Committee and the congresses of Soviets of the Khoresm and Bukhara republics passed the historic decisions to give the Uzbek, Kazakh and Turkmenian peoples the right to secede from these republics and form their own national republics.

Two new republics were formed as a result of the national and state demarcation of Central Asia. These were Turkmenia, with a predominantly Turkmenian population in the Transcaspian Region of Turkestan, the western regions of Bukhara and the southern regions of Khoresm, and Uzbekistan, which occupied the rest of the territory of Turkestan, Bukhara and Khoresm, where the population was predominantly Uzbek. The new Uzbek Soviet Socialist Republic embraced the Tajik Autonomous Republic. In 1925, the Third Congress of Soviets of the U.S.S.R. admitted the Turkmenian and Uzbek republics to the Union of Soviet Socialist Republics.

The national and territorial demarcation of Central Asia and the peaceful reunification of formerly dismembered national territories into independent republics were a major achievement of the Soviet nationalities policy. This achievement was due solely to the equality and friendship of peoples. The peoples of Central Asia were given a properly demarcated territory for their national states and the possibility to participate actively in Soviet state development.

The active participation of working people of all nationalities and nations in the country's political life, in the administration of the state, strengthened the Soviet Union and enabled it to restore its economy successfully.

Recovery in Agriculture

The New Economic Policy gave the productive forces of Soviet agriculture a powerful impetus for development, enabling it to reach the pre-war output level as early as the end of 1925.

The crop areas were almost as large as in the pre-war period, and grain output in 1925 amounted to over 73 million tons or approximately the quantity grown before the war. That was one of the principal successes of the country's economic rehabilitation. However, the crop yield was not stable. There were crop failures in 1921 and 1924.

The restoration of the livestock population, particularly of the cattle population, proceeded slowly. By the end of 1925 it was still below the 1916 level. However, the rate at which agriculture recovered in the U.S.S.R. was way ahead of its growth rate in many capitalist countries that had fought in the First World War.

This was, primarily, a result of the victory of the Revolution. Agrarian reforms were carried out after the interventionists and whiteguards were driven out: the peasants began to till more land, receiving it at the expense of the expropriated landowners and kulaks. Moreover, the Soviet victory in the Civil War made them confident that their new holdings were not temporary and gave them the incentive to improve and fertilise the land.

The nationalisation of land delivered the peasants from the need to purchase or lease it.

The New Economic Policy strengthened the link between the peasant farms and the market and stepped up their marketable value. That induced the peasants to make every effort to increase output.

The Soviet government popularised modern methods of farming and livestock-breeding by setting up model farms, agronomical stations, machine-hire and grain-cleaning stations, stud farms and pedigree stock-breeding farms.

The concern shown by the state to increase the crop yield, enlarge the crop areas and popularise agronomical knowledge, the aid given to the countryside, state seed loans and assistance at times of poor harvests stimulated the labour energy of the peasants.

For the first time in their long history the peasants saw that in return for taxes and other duties the state was helping them. This strengthened the economic alliance between the working class and the peasants.

The new agrarian laws were likewise instrumental in promoting agricultural development. A code of land laws, that regulated the use of land and gave the peasants the right to freely choose the manner in which to use land and privileges for collective farming, was passed in 1922 in the Russian Federation. Under the new laws the peasants could lease their land and hire labour. Codes of land laws were passed in other Soviet republics with due regard for local conditions.

Some state land, not being used for farming, was turned over to the peasants. That placed more land at their disposal.

The first attempts to mechanise agriculture were made during the period of economic rehabilitation. True, not many tractors were available, and on the small individual farms they were not always used efficiently.

Important social and economic changes were taking place in the countryside. The number of middle peasants steadily increased, some of them becoming prosperous kulak farmers, and the number of poor peasants decreased. This was due to assistance from the state, which helped the peasants acquire livestock and implements.

Lenin characterised the class pattern in the countryside after the Revolution as follows: "There are far more middle peasants now than before, antagonisms have been smoothed out, the land has been distributed for use far more equally, the kulak's position has been undermined and he has been in considerable measure expropriated. ... On the whole, however, statistics show absolutely definitely that there has been a levelling out, an equalisation in the village ... the peasantry in general has acquired the status of the middle peasant."*

These words were borne out by the data on the social composition in the Soviet countryside by the end of the rehabilitation period: the proletariat (farm labourers) and poorest section of the peasants comprised 35.6 per cent, the middle peasants 61.1 per cent and the kulaks 3.3 per cent of the gainfully employed population.

In the early period after the Revolution the stratification of the peasantry and the growth of the number of middle peasants was due largely to the nationalisation of the land and its distribution in accordance with the size of families: this considerably reduced the number of non-farming peasants and peasants with small plots of land. Subsequently, the property stratification of the peasants stemmed primarily not from the possession of land but from the distribution of the principal means of production (machinery, implements, draught animals) and from the development of commodity-money relations and trade.

Although some draught animals confiscated from the landed estates and kulak farms after the Revolution were turned over to the poorest peasants, and the peasants had more draught animals than before, by the end of the rehabilitation period 28.3 per cent of the farms had no horses and had to hire them from more prosperous peasants. The hiring out of draught animals and implements served the kulaks as a means of exploiting the poor and part of the middle peasants. The general rise of the prosperity of the peasant farms in the first years after the Revolution was accompanied by a growth of the number of kulak

---

* Lenin, *Alliance of the Working Class and the Peasantry*, p. 357.

farms: in the Russian Federation, for example, the number of farms leasing land increased from 3.6 to 7.2 per cent in 1924-26. The working peasants were exploited not only by the kulaks but also by usurers, wholesale buyers and private traders.

Through its financial and tax policy the Soviet government restricted the growth of capitalist elements in the countryside: the poorest sections of the peasants were exempted from taxes, the small farms were given a number of privileges, and the kulaks were made to pay a higher tax. However, the conditions for the growth of kulak elements obtained as long as petty-peasant economy existed.

Various co-operatives played an important role in the struggle against kulak domination. There were consumers' co-operatives supplying the villages with manufactured goods and purchasing farm produce, credit co-operatives to provide the peasants with cash loans, and the simplest types of producers' co-operatives (machine, seed-growing, grain-cleaning, land improvement). By joining these co-operatives the poor and middle peasants strengthened the position of socialism.

The state extended credits and a number of privileges to the co-operatives. By the end of the rehabilitation period the co-operatives covered about 6,600,000 peasant households and had an aggregate capital of 900 million rubles.

Although they were still few in number, the state and collective farms, which began to be set up as early as 1918-20, made progress. During the rehabilitation period they took only the first steps towards organising farming in a new way. Most of the collective farms were simply associations for the joint tilling of the land and very few of their means of production were socialised.

Thus there were two trends in the development of relations of production in the countryside during the period of rehabilitation: the petty-peasant economy gave rise to bourgeois relations, while the co-operatives and collective and state farms promoted the growth of socialist relations.

Individual peasant households continued to play the main role in farm production. However, the rehabilitation period made it clear that the possibilities of small farms were limited; they could not use even the simplest machines such as the double-share plough or the sower profitably. In the interests of the bulk of the working peasants it was imperative to go over from petty individual farming to large-scale, socialist farming.

Restoration of Large-Scale Industry. Labour Heroism of the Working Class

The prime objective of the Soviet government was to restore large-scale, particularly heavy, industry. Lenin said that "there is only one effective basis for the creation of a socialist society, namely, large-scale industry".* But its restoration required a Herculean effort because during the war the equipment had been badly worn, the number of skilled workers had decreased, and there was a shortage of food, fuel, metal and raw material. In 1921-22, when industry was going through a period of reorganisation to enable it to adapt itself to the new conditions, there was a low level of labour productivity at the factories and mills.

The working class, which had lost much of its strength in the seven years of war, famine and hardship, had to exert fresh selfless efforts to surmount these difficulties.

In 1921-22, the country concentrated on restoring the coal, oil, metalworking and iron and steel industries, and on bringing back the textile, sugar, tanning and other branches of light industry to their original levels. Workers were mobilised to restore the mines: thousands of Communists, demobilised from the army, and large numbers of Y.C.L. members were sent to work in the Donbas, where they exposed the hostile propaganda of the whiteguards, Socialist-Revolutionaries and Mensheviks who had gone into hiding.

In the Donbas the workers heroically surmounted all difficulties. Shock-work groups were formed at many mines where they substantially increased labour productivity. *Subbotniks* were organised.

The Donbas was aided by the entire country. Moscow and Petrograd sent skilled workers, equipment and gifts, the Kuban sent food, Azerbaijan fish and the Crimea fruit and tobacco.

Lenin closely watched the progress that was being made in the Donbas. On his insistence cutting machines were purchased abroad for the Donbas. In 1921, Felix Dzerzhinsky and Grigory Orjonikidze were sent to the Donbas to help the local Party organisations. As a result of the measures that were taken, the coal output began to grow: it rose from 5,500,000 tons in 1921 to 7,100,000 tons in 1922. Labour productivity also began to grow at the mines.

Rehabilitation was also started in the coal industry in the Urals and Siberia.

The oil industry was in pretty awful shape in 1921-22: many of the wells in the Baku and Grozny fields were idle, and the deposits were in danger of being flooded. The situation was saved by extensive government aid and the dedicated work of the oilmen.

The Communists inspired the labour upsurge at the oilfields, and the Y.C.L. and trade union organisations actively participated in the *subbotniks*.

---

* Lenin, *Collected Works*, Vol. 32, p. 408.

Lenin paid a lot of attention to bringing the oilfields back to full working capacity. Like the coal industry, the oil industry received priority in supplies. The Central Committee appointed Sergei Kirov to a key post in Azerbaijan. In the period 1921-25, he was First Secretary of the Central Committee of the Communist Party of Azerbaijan.

In 1922, in response to this concern by the government, the oilmen of Azerbaijan raised the oil output per worker to 35 per cent above the 1913 level.

In 1923, while progress was being made in restoring the coal and oil industries, it was found that the iron and steel industry was lagging behind. The Thirteenth Party Conference drew the attention of the entire Party to this fact.

It was important to restore the iron and steel industry in the Ukraine. The labour effort of the workers and the organisational work of the Party in the Ukraine resulted in the restoration of the Kramatorsk, Yuzovka, Yekaterinoslav, Yenakievo and other giant metalworking and metallurgical plants. The number of workers at these plants steadily increased and output grew monthly.

By 1923 there was an increase in the number of workers employed in industry, and the output of the large-scale industry reached 35 per cent of the pre-war level. These were the first signs that the country's economy was getting back on its feet.

However, in the autumn of 1923 state-owned heavy industry found itself confronted with serious difficulties in the sale of its products: due to high prices for manufactured goods and the low prices on foodstuffs, industry could not sell all its products in the market. This was due to both objective (the difference in the rate of growth of heavy industry and agriculture) and subjective reasons (attempts by economic organs to obtain profits to make up for losses sustained by industry during the first years of the New Economic Policy). The high prices for manufactured goods were the result of the lack of control over overheads and of shortcomings in planning sales and organising trade. Industry was unable to find a way to the peasant consumer with the result that its products remained in the storehouses. Factories found themselves unable to pay wages in time and this caused dissatisfaction among the workers.

The Communist Party and Soviet Government took urgent steps to overcome the economic difficulties: consumer goods prices were reduced and the prices of farm products were raised, wages were paid punctually, and a determined campaign was started to improve trade and oust profiteers. The peasants were given low-interest credits, and some grain was sold abroad.

These measures helped to alleviate economic difficulties, improve the material position of the workers and peasants and strengthen the alliance between them.

Notwithstanding these difficulties, Soviet industry was restored faster than in any capitalist country. For example, in France, where in 1920 industrial output reached 62 per cent of the 1913 level, it took six years to rehabilitate the industry despite the fact that she had reparations to draw upon. Soviet industry, on the other hand, was restored in approximately five years in spite of the terrible ruin wreaked on it by two wars. That showed the advantages of socialist economy over the capitalist economic system.

During the rehabilitation period some of the old plants, particularly machine-building plants, were reconstructed. The factories developed new lines of production such as tractors, diesel locomotives and powerful steam engines.

New building projects, particularly power stations, were started. Lenin attached decisive importance to electrification in the restoration of the country's ruined economy and in reorganising it along socialist lines. Lenin's plan of electrification, which was founded on the advantages of the Soviet system and on the creative potential of the Soviet people, was given a successful start.

In 1922, under the GOELRO plan, the Kashira (near Moscow) and Krasny Oktyabr (near Petrograd) district power stations were completed, seven other district power stations, including the Shterovka plant in the Donbas, were under construction, and preparations were made to build eight power stations in the Ukraine and a number of power stations in Transcaucasia and along the Volga. The Shatura Power Plant was commissioned in 1925, and the next year saw the completion of the Volkhov Hydropower Station, which for its day satisfied the latest world standards in technology. Smaller power stations were built in some villages.

Ivan Alexandrov, Genrikh Graftio, Alexander Vinter and many other scientists and engineers worked selflessly to build the country's first power stations. The GOELRO plan was so fantastically ambitious that it seemed a dream even to a bold thinker like H. G. Wells. In his *Russia in the Shadows* he wrote that "but their [of the projects.–*Ed.*] application to Russia is an altogether greater strain upon the constructive imagination".* But it took only 10-12 years to carry out this grandiose plan.

The rehabilitation of large-scale industry, the building of new plants and the reconstruction of some of the old factories gradually led to the skilled labour forces being built up again. Some 80-90 per cent of the old workers, who had left their work during the Civil War, had returned to industry and transport by 1925. Moreover, the ranks of skilled workers were reinforced by young workers and by peasants who came to the towns in search

---

* H. G. Wells, *Russia in the Shadows*, London, p. 135.

of a livelihood: petty farming could not employ all the manpower in the countryside.

By 1926 there were approximately as many workers in industry as before the Revolution, the urban population having risen to 26,900,000 as against 20,700,000 in 1920.

Assisted by the trade unions, the Soviet Government improved the material position of the workers. A major role in this was played by the Central Commission for the Improvement of the Living Conditions of Workers; branch commissions were set up in all the republics. These commissions did their utmost to improve the food supply, housing, public catering and so forth.

The health service too received a great deal of attention. By the end of the rehabilitation period four times more budget money was being spent on public health than before the Revolution: the number of hospitals was doubled and the number of pharmacies trebled. The former royal palaces in the Crimea, on the Black Sea coast of the Caucasus and around Moscow and Leningrad were turned into holiday resorts and health and holiday homes.

In all towns workers were moved from suburban districts, basements and temporary homes into houses formerly occupied by the bourgeoisie and the idle rich.

Housing construction was started in the towns and workers' centres in the Donbas and in the oilfields of Azerbaijan.

These and other measures improved the material position, housing and working conditions of the working people. An eight-hour working day was instituted, with shorter hours for juveniles. Women received the same pay as men. A pension scheme was introduced. Industrial and office workers were insured against disability and unemployment. The free medical services were substantially improved.

The workers began to show a greater interest in their work and in the country's political life thanks largely to the efforts of the trade unions, which Lenin regarded as a school of economic management, of communism.

In 1923 the main task in the fight against economic difficulties was that of increasing labour productivity and improving the organisation of production. These were the chief problems discussed at the time at production conferences, the first of which was convened in Petrograd in 1924 on the initiative of workers in the metallurgical industry. This initiative was emulated in Moscow, the Donbas, Tula and elsewhere, and soon production conferences became one of the main ways of drawing the workers into the management of industry. These production conferences were directed by the Communist Party through its primary cells.

Despite the efforts to better the situation, the difficulties were still great: there was a housing shortage because not all old housing had been restored and the scale of new construction was small. Unemployment rose frow 641,000 in 1923 to 1,240,000 in 1924.

The main causes of unemployment in 1921-25 were demobilisation from the army, surplus population in the villages, curtailment of handicraft industries, and so forth.

Determined steps were taken to combat unemployment, which in Soviet conditions was a temporary phenomenon. The workers knew that they were the masters of production and realised that their difficulties were temporary. An illustration of this was the greetings sent to the Soviet Government on the eve of the First Five-Year Plan by the workers of three large metalworking plants in Nizhny Novgorod. They wrote: "We have always wholeheartedly supported Soviet rule. We have not done that in vain. We see that the position of our working people's republic is improving and becoming stronger thanks to our solidarity, thanks to the firm alliance between the workers and peasants, thanks to the New Economic Policy.... We are the masters of industry and shall do everything we can to get production going and raise our material and cultural standards."[*]

Development of Trade. Strengthening of the Money System

The restoration of agriculture and industry served as a foundation for the development of trade. In view of the commodity-money relations existing in the country, trade was the main link between socialist industry and small-scale peasant production. Various forms of trade—state, co-operative and private—were promoted.

The socialist sector—the state and the co-operatives—played the leading role in wholesale trade. In 1922-23, the turnover of the socialist sector accounted for three-fourths of the entire wholesale trade. Three-fourths of the retail trade was handled by private capital. This was due to the millions of small producers, who were, under the New Economic Policy, allowed to sell their surplus products in the open market. In trade the socialist and capitalist elements were engaged in a bitter fight for markets. The state regulated the prices in the markets and made every effort to sustain the link between socialist industry and the peasant farms through co-operatives and state trade. This strengthened the economic alliance between the working class and the peasants and was one of the main objectives of the New Economic Policy.

The introduction of the New Economic Policy and the increased goods turnover in the market required an improvement of the monetary system, which was the key to restoring the economy and administering the country. A special decree, On the Financial

---

[*] *Metallist* No. 18, 1922, p. 59.

Policy, which indicated how to strengthen the Soviet financial system, was passed by the Eleventh Party Congress in March 1922. To achieve this objective it was of the utmost importance to step up labour productivity in industry and agriculture, increase the capacity of the markets and completely replace payment in kind by the circulation of money.

Famine and economic ruin had brought about a devaluation of money. There was widespread inflation.

A monetary reform and a stable currency were required to rid the markets of the deflated money that was flooding them. An important measure aimed at stabilising the currency was that the State Bank, established in 1921, was given the right to issue gold-backed banknotes.

Successful economic rehabilitation made it possible to carry out a monetary reform in 1922-24.

This reform was of vital economic and political importance; the stable currency enabled the country to ensure further economic progress, placed trade on a sound footing and established closer bonds between the socialist town and countryside. Restrictions were imposed on the growth of private capital, which was used chiefly to restore the small-scale industry and to promote the local turnover.

Small-scale industry, particularly artisan industry, was the foundation for the growth of private capital.

In large-scale industry, private capital ran only 17.2 per cent of the factories and employed 2.12 per cent of the workers, while its share of the total industrial product did not exceed 15 per cent.

State capitalism, whose main forms were the lease of land and concessions, hardly developed at all, because foreign capitalists were unwilling to deal with the Soviet state, and the successes scored in expanding socialist industry enabled the country to cancel all concessions.

With the commanding heights of the economy in its hands, the government directed and regulated economic development and strengthened and enlarged the socialist sector.

Social and Political Development

The New Economic Policy and the first successes in economic rehabilitation created favourable conditions for greater political activity by the masses. The Communist Party devoted great attention to promoting political activity by the masses and to rallying them round the working class.

The Communists were the heart and soul of the country's social and political life. They led the masses in the difficult work of rehabilitating the economy, directed the Soviets, trade unions and co-operatives, and organised all the political and economic campaigns. Prominent Party leaders headed the key sectors of the economy: Felix Dzerzhinsky was People's Commissar for Communications and later Chairman of the Supreme Economic Council; Leonid Krasin was People's Commissar for Foreign Trade; Grigory Orjonikidze devoted his energies to restoring the economy of the three Transcaucasian republics in his capacity of Secretary of the Transcaucasian Territory Party Committee; Sergei Kirov mobilised the Communists of Azerbaijan for the work of restoring the oil industry; Vlas Chubar directed the Donbas coal industry. Thousands of Communists, former commanders and commissars of the Red Army, became managers of factories and trusts and leaders of the masses on the labour front. In May 1924, the membership of the Communist Party increased from about 400,000 in 1923 to 860,000 chiefly through the influx of workers and peasants.

The Young Communist League was the Party's faithful assistant in all its undertakings. In a speech at the Third Y.C.L. Congress in October 1920, Lenin defined the programme of youth participation in the building of socialism and communism. Guided by Lenin's instructions, the Y.C.L. enthusiastically took a hand in restoring the economy and raising the people's cultural level. In the Donbas the Y.C.L., working under difficult conditions, helped to restore the mines destroyed by the whiteguards.

Around the big towns members of the Y.C.L. stocked firewood and built branch railway lines to transport it. On one of these jobs the Y.C.L. members were led by Nikolai Ostrovsky, secretary of the Y.C.L. cell at the workshops of the South-Western Railway. He subsequently wrote his famous books *How the Steel Was Tempered* and *Born of a Storm.* "It was an impossible task," he wrote, "but we built the line. The difficulties were incredible. Imagine, we worked for a week, and then the bandit Orlik destroyed everything in a few hours and fired at us every hour.... Yet we stuck to the job. We worked because each of us felt he was not alone, that he was a member of a large body, of the close-knit Y.C.L. family. The name Y.C.L. member carried obligations with it." In Azerbaijan, Y.C.L. members helped to restore oil wells and repair equipment. The picture was the same in all the towns, in all the industrial centres.

In the countryside, too, the Y.C.L. played an outstanding role. Its members helped to collect the food tax (which later was replaced by a single agricultural tax) and build schools and libraries. They took part in the work of the Soviets and co-operatives, in propagating advanced methods of tilling the soil and in the struggle against kulak bandits. In May 1922, the Y.C.L. united all children's organisations and laid the beginning for the Young Pioneer movement. The Navy was also helped by the Y.C.L., which gave it many noted commanders. In 1924, the Y.C.L. was named after Lenin.

On the political scene there were many domestic and external difficulties.

Capitalist elements took advantage of the New Economic Policy to intensify their fight against the new system. The main front of the class war was moved to the economic sphere.

While utilising private capital to rejuvenate the economy the Soviet government had to combat its attempts to control the peasant economy and by-pass Soviet laws for the purpose of profiteering.

Soviet state and trade union organisations defended the workers' interests in private industry and made employers observe Soviet laws on the eight-hour working day and on hygienic working conditions.

The subversive activity of enemies of Soviet rule included profiteering in goods in short supply, the secret buying up of foreign currency, the smuggling of gold out of the country, and trading in smuggled goods.

In the countryside the class struggle raged primarily around the measures the Soviet government was taking to assist the poor and middle peasants and to limit the kulaks' opportunities to exploit the peasants. The kulaks tried to infiltrate into Soviet organs of power in order to make use of the economic and political advantages that had been extended to the working peasants. They organised the assassination of Communists, Y.C.L. members, government and Party officials and rural correspondents of newspapers.

The press played an important role in the country's social and political life. A few months after the Revolution Lenin said that the task was "to convert the press from an organ mainly devoted to communicating the political news of the day into a serious organ for educating the mass of the population in economics".*

The Twelfth Party Congress passed a resolution emphasising the tremendous role of the Party press as a key means of propaganda and agitation and a means linking the Party up with the working class and peasants. The resolution underlined the need to train worker and rural correspondents.

A class struggle raged in the ideological field as well. The interests of the new bourgeoisie engendered in the period of the New Economic Policy were mirrored by supporters of the journal *Smena Vekh.*** Assessing the October Revolution as being of a

---

* Lenin, *Collected Works*, Vol. 27, p. 203.
** This trend took its name from a collection of articles published in 1921 in Prague under the general title of *Smena Vekh (Change of Epochs)* by N. Ustryalov, Y. Klyuchnikov and other white émigrés resident in Prague. A journal of the same name was published by white émigrés in Paris in 1921-22.

bourgeois nature they hoped that the New Economic Policy would be the means by which Soviet power would degenerate into the usual bourgeois rule. Prompted by this hope the ideologists of the new bourgeoisie began to co-operate with Soviet power in order to utilise it in an attempt to restore capitalism.

The Communist Party showed that the *Smena Vekh* adherents were out to restore capitalism, and defeated them ideologically.

The Mensheviks and Socialist-Revolutionaries found themselves in the same camp as the *Smena Vekh*. They too regarded the New Economic Policy as a step towards the restoration of private capitalist economy and decided to utilise the possibility of legally working in co-operatives, trade unions and other organisations in order to preach bourgeois ideology and the restoration of capitalism. In addition, as enemies of socialism, they continued their illegal counter-revolutionary activity in defence of capitalism. The subversive activity of the Socialist-Revolutionaries was brought to light at a trial in 1922.

Ideological weapons had to be placed in the hands of Party and government functionaries to enable them to carry on a successful struggle on the ideological front. This purpose was served by the publication of Lenin's works in 1900-25 and also the publication of the works of Marx and Engels, the founders of scientific communism. The latter works were published by the Marx-Engels Institute, which was opened in 1920. Marxist-Leninist theory was propagated by *Pod Znamenem Marksizma* (*Under the Banner of Marxism*), *Proletarskaya Revolutsia* (*Proletarian Revolution*) and other journals.

The Soviets played a special role in the country's political life, for they embodied the alliance between the workers and peasants and were the vehicle of proletarian leadership.

During the Civil War the Soviets were occupied with mobilising the war effort of the people, and when the country launched upon peaceful construction they directed the attention of the people to economic and political tasks and drew them into the administration of the state. To enable the Soviets to function more efficiently, measures were taken early in 1921 to improve their work. Sittings of Soviets at which local problems were examined and deputies reported on their work began to be held directly at factories. Much was done to improve the government apparatus by the People's Commissariat of Workers' and Peasant's Inspection, which was set up as early as February 1920. Its tasks included inspecting the state apparatus with the purpose of improving it, and weeding out bureaucracy and abuse of office.

Lenin devoted a great deal of time to improving the organisation and work of this People's Commissariat. In order to give it more efficient Party leadership and greater prestige, he suggested merging it with one of the higher Party organs—the Central Control

Commission—and thereby establish a single Party and government organ of control. These two bodies were merged by the Twelfth Party Congress in April 1923. The new organ, headed by Valerian Kuibyshev, a prominent Party leader and statesman, was instrumental in improving the structure of the state apparatus. It had close links with the masses, drawing many people into the work and teaching them the art of administration.

In many ways the efficiency of the Soviets was obstructed by their not having sufficient rights or their own budgets, on account of which many of them stood aloof from economic and cultural affairs and poorly fulfilled their role as organisers of the masses.

In December 1924 a special conference convened by the Presidium of the Central Executive Committee outlined a series of measures aimed at strengthening the local Soviets and their executive committees, and giving them greater rights, particularly in the sphere of the budget. The conference drew up the Rules of Town Soviets.

Subsequently, the Communist Party kept an eye on the work of the Soviets, enhancing their role as bodies directing the country's economic and cultural development.

In order to enable the Soviet state to develop it was of the utmost importance to improve legislation and strengthen revolutionary legality, which protected the rights won by the people in the October Socialist Revolution and guaranteed by the Constitution of the U.S.S.R. Moreover, with the transition to the New Economic Policy private capital had to be guaranteed the preservation of its property on the condition that Soviet laws were complied with.

The basic Soviet codes of law were drawn up in 1922 with the participation of representatives of the people. Besides the above-mentioned Land Code, these were the Code of Labour Laws, which legalised the eight-hour working day, annual paid leaves, labour protection (sanitary and technical), social insurance and the protection of the labour of women and juveniles. During the same period, the Civil and Criminal codes, and the Rules of Legal Procedure were adopted and the Procurator's Office was set up. These codes consolidated revolutionary law and order, protected the new system from encroachment by enemies and created a firm foundation for the economic activity of Soviet citizens.

Lenin's Behests

The Soviet state surmounted the economic dislocation and confidently moved ahead along the road of socialism. The economic upsurge that began in the country confirmed that the New Economic Policy had been a step in the right direction.

At a Plenary Meeting of the Moscow Soviet on November 20, 1922, Lenin said he was confident that the New Economic Policy would enable Russia to emerge as a socialist country. These prophetic words were enthusiastically received by the deputies of the Moscow Soviet.

But Lenin was already gravely ill. He was suffering from overstrain and from the consequences of the wound received in the assassination attempt. In May 1922, on the insistence of his doctors, he moved to Gorki, a countryside locality near Moscow. His health somewhat improved in June and he returned to Moscow in October of the same year, again immersing himself in work.

In December his health sharply deteriorated, and his doctors made him go to Gorki again. On December 16, there was a turn for the worse in his health, leaving him prostrate for a long time. Whenever there was some slight improvement he dictated articles and letters in which he expounded his ideas on the plans for the further development of the U.S.S.R. and on the fundamental tasks confronting the Party. The articles dictated by him in this period were: "Pages from a Diary", "On Co-operation", "Our Revolution", "How We Should Reorganise the Workers' and Peasants' Inspection" and "Better Fewer, But Better".

In these articles he completed elaborating the plan of building socialism in the U.S.S.R. This plan was based on the premise that the Soviet Union had all the prerequisites for completing the building of socialism even if the world socialist revolution were held up and in face of the hostile capitalist encirclement. To achieve socialism the Soviet Union had to create the appropriate material and technical basis and steadily follow the policy of socialist industrialisation. He wrote: "If we see to it that the working class retains its leadership of the peasantry, we shall be able, by exercising the greatest possible economy in the economic life of our state, to use every kopek we save to develop our large-scale machine industry, to develop electrification, the hydraulic extraction of peat, to finish the construction of Volkhov Power Station, etc.

"In this, and in this alone, lies our hope."*

The reorganisation of peasant farms along co-operative lines was one of the key elements of Lenin's plan. In his article "On Co-operation" he pointed out that co-operatives, first supply and marketing and then producers' co-operatives, were the simplest and most popular form of drawing the peasants into socialist construction.

To pave the way for socialism, scientific and cultural achievements must be made available to the broadest sections of the people. Lenin mapped out the ways of accomplishing a cultural revolution.

He regarded the Soviet state as the most important means of

---

* Lenin, *Selected Works*, Vol. 3, p. 842.

building socialism. Therefore, he said, socialist democracy had to be developed and improved to the utmost, the majority of the people had to be drawn into the administration of the country and the state had to be strengthened.

He considered the utmost strengthening of the alliance between the working class and the peasants and the friendship between peoples as one of the principal conditions for the successful building of socialism.

Furthermore, his programme envisaged ensuring external conditions for socialist construction. The inevitable result of the law of uneven economic and political development of countries in the epoch of imperialism is that the socialist revolution cannot triumph simultaneously in all countries. It began with victory in one country, Soviet Russia.

To be able to build socialism successfully, the Soviet state had to pursue a policy of peaceful coexistence with other, non-socialist countries, and establish business relations with them.

At the same time it had to hold aloft the banner of proletarian internationalism and aid the oppressed peoples in their struggle for liberation.

Lenin regarded the mighty revolutionary movement of the Eastern peoples as one of the sources of the victory of socialism on a world scale.

"Letter to the Congress",* "Granting Legislative Functions to the State Planning Commission", and "The Question of Nationalities or 'Autonomisation'", dictated in the period from the close of 1922 to the beginning of 1923, were among Lenin's last works.

In his "Letter to the Congress", written because of his concern for socialism in the U.S.S.R., Lenin suggested steps to strengthen the Party with the purpose of avoiding any possible split. One of these steps was to increase the number of C.C. members to 100. Lenin considered this was necessary in order to "raise the prestige of the Central Committee, to do a thorough job of improving our administrative machinery and to prevent conflicts between small sections of the C.C. from acquiring excessive importance for the future of the Party".**

He suggested enlarging the C.C. with rank-and-file workers, who "by attending all the meetings of the C.C. and all the sittings of the Politbureau, and by reading all the documents of the C.C., can comprise a cadre that would be loyal to the Soviet system and able, firstly, to impart stability to the C.C. itself and, secondly, really work on renewing and improving the apparatus".

---

* Lenin, *Selected Works*, Vol. 3, p. 791. Lenin considered it necessary to bring his "Letter to the Congress", better known as his *Behests*, to the notice of the next Party Congress.

** Lenin, *Problem of Building Socialism and Communism in the U.S.S.R.*, Moscow, p. 79.

Lenin wrote of the personal merits and demerits of some prominent members of the C.C., on whose relations with each other and proper utilisation the Party's unity and the prevention of a split largely depended.

Lenin mentioned Joseph Stalin as an important Party leader. He saw the latter's negative qualities as a leader, for example, his haste and inclination to use administrative methods in settling the nationalities question.

Characterising Stalin's shortcomings, Lenin wrote: "Comrade Stalin, having become General Secretary, has concentrated boundless authority in his hands, and I am not sure whether he will always be capable of using that authority with sufficient caution.... Stalin is too rude and this defect, although quite tolerable in our midst and in dealings among us Communists, becomes intolerable in a General Secretary. That is why I suggested that the comrades think about a way of removing Stalin from that post and appointing somebody else differing in all other respects from Comrade Stalin solely in the degree of being more tolerant, more loyal, more polite and more considerate to the comrades, less capricious, etc.*

Subsequent events showed how deep Lenin's insight was.

Lenin's letter was read to the delegates of the Thirteenth Party Congress. However, in view of Stalin's vigorous struggle against Trotskyism and his assurances that he would correct his shortcomings, the delegates voted in favour of leaving him in the office of General Secretary of the C.C.

The works written by Lenin illumined the road to communism in the U.S.S.R. and the prospects for the development of the entire human race for decades to come. They helped the Party to combat anti-Party Trotskyite elements, who as early as 1923 took advantage of the economic difficulties and of Lenin's illness to redouble their attacks against the Party line worked out by Lenin and prophesied that socialist construction was doomed to failure. The Trotskyites hurled slander on the Party. In violation of the Leninist principles of Party unity they demanded freedom for factions and groups. The Party unanimously rejected the fabrications of the Trotskyites. In January 1924, the Thirteenth Party Conference emphatically condemned Trotskyism, declaring that it was an "obvious *petty-bourgeois* deviation".

There was nation-wide concern for Lenin's health. His powerful constitution fought the illness, and during periods of improvement he strove to continue his work.

The whole people hoped Lenin would recover and rejoiced whenever the bulletin mentioned an improvement in his condition. However, this hope was not destined to be fulfilled. Lenin died at 6.50 a.m. on January 21, 1924. A serious illness, caused by

---

* *Ibid.*, pp. 81-82.

overstrain in work and struggle for the welfare of the people, cut short his life at the age of 53.

The government communication on Lenin's death stated: "He is no longer with us, but his cause remains unchanged. Expressing the will of the working masses, the Soviet Government continues the work of Vladimir Ilyich, moving farther along the path charted by him. Soviet power stands firmly at its post, guarding the gains of the proletarian Revolution."

On January 23, 1924, the coffin with Lenin's body was brought to the Hall of Columns of the House of Trade Unions in Moscow, where it lay in state for nearly a week.

The Second Congress of Soviets of the U.S.S.R. opened on January 26. The first sitting was dedicated to the memory of the great leader.

The Congress passed a decision to perpetuate the memory of Lenin and adopted an address to all working people of the world. It decreed that urgent steps be taken to publish selected works of Lenin in different languages as well as his collected works. Granting the wishes of the working people of Petrograd, the Congress decreed the renaming of Petrograd, cradle of the proletarian Revolution, into Leningrad.

In fulfilment of the will of the people, the Congress adopted a decision to preserve Lenin's body in a special Mausoleum in Red Square, near the Kremlin Wall beside the common graves of heroes of the October Socialist Revolution.

On January 27, the coffin with Lenin's body was taken to Red Square. The working people of Moscow and numerous delegations from all parts of the country filed past the coffin. At 4 p.m., with the air filled with the strains of a funeral march, the sound of thousands of factory whistles and the reverberation of artillery salvoes, the coffin was carried into the Mausoleum.

The working people of the U.S.S.R. and the whole world sorrowfully took leave of their teacher, best friend and champion.

In these days of mourning the Soviet people rallied round the Communist Party and displayed great fortitude, firmness and courage. After Lenin's death 240,000 men and women workers joined the Communist Party. That was the Lenin Enrolment into the Party. It showed that the working class was prepared to do everything to carry out Lenin's great ideas.

The Soviet economy had, in the main, been rehabilitated by 1926. In 1925, the socialist large-scale industry had reached 73 per cent of its pre-war output level. The number of workers in that industry rose to 2,451,600 or 90.8 per cent of the pre-war figure. The role of the socialist sector was enhanced: in 1925 it accounted for 96.1 per cent of the output of the large-scale industry and 81 per cent of the entire industrial product, if we include the output of small industries.

Agricultural production had reached 87 per cent of the pre-war level by 1925.

The material position of the population had improved.

Commodity turnover reached approximately 70 per cent of the pre-war level, half of it being accounted for by state and co-operative trade.

This general improvement was confirmation that the Soviet government had been right in starting the New Economic Policy.

At this stage the country's prospects for further development became the central issue. These had been formulated in Lenin's last works and in the decisions of Party congresses.

At the close of 1924, Trotsky made an attempt to steer the Party and country away from the socialist path and to undermine the Party's ideological foundation by replacing Leninism with theories of his own. This ignoble attempt was unanimously rejected by the whole Party.

Steadfastly progressing along the road mapped out by Lenin, the Communist Party at its Fouteenth Conference (April 1925) expressed confidence that it was possible to build socialism, although its triumph in the U.S.S.R. would not signify complete victory because the hostile capitalist encirclement was still aiming to restore capitalism in the Soviet Union. Victorious socialist revolutions in a number of countries were required as an iron-clad guarantee that such a restoration would not take place.

This conclusion was reaffirmed by the Fourteenth Party Congress in December 1925, which declared that the struggle for the triumph of socialism in the U.S.S.R. was the basic task before the Party. The Congress denounced the so-called New Opposition headed by Zinoviev and Kamenev, which, ideologically, had all the hallmarks of Trotskyism.

The Fourteenth Congress firmly took the line of socialist industrialisation as the only correct way of creating the material and technical basis of socialism. The successful economic rehabilitation, the creation of the U.S.S.R., the growth of its international prestige, the strengthening of the alliance between the workers and peasants on the basis of the New Economic Policy and the consolidation of the domestic situation enabled the Soviet people led by the Communist Party to enter a new stage of socialist construction.

The U.S.S.R. in the International Arena

First Successes of Soviet Foreign Policy

As early as during the Civil War and the foreign intervention Soviet Russia repeatedly offered to begin peace talks with the capitalist countries. But neither Britain, nor France nor any of the other countries replied to these proposals. Towards 1921, after the failure of the attempts to stifle Soviet rule with the aid of foreign troops and the internal counter-revolution, the situation had radically changed.

Despite this change the imperialists held on to their plans of restoring bourgeois rule in Russia. But there was no agreement as to the ways and means of achieving this goal. France's rulers still entertained the hope that further armed intervention would be successful and refused to establish any relations with the Soviets. In the British Government an influential group of Conservatives headed by Lord Curzon, then Foreign Secretary, questioned the advisability of economic and trade talks with Soviet Russia. Another group of British leaders, the Prime Minister David Lloyd George among them, had a different view of the situation and desired rapprochement with Soviet Russia. The following statement by Lloyd George is typical of this view: "We have failed to restore Russia by force. I believe that we shall be able to do it and save her by trade." By "saving" Russia he meant restoring bourgeois rule.

Despite all obstacles, the trend to establish normal relations with Soviet Russia mounted among different circles of the capitalist world.

At a meeting of A.R.C.E.C. on June 17, 1920, Georgi Chicherin, People's Commissar for Foreign Affairs, declared: "Our slogan of peaceful coexistence with other governments, no matter what they are, remains immutable. Events have brought us and other states round to the need to establish long-term relations between the workers' and peasants' government and the capitalist governments."*

Trade was one of the most realistic ways of establishing peaceful relations with the capitalist countries. Many capitalist countries wanted trade with Russia, and it was through trade that it was easiest of all to break the resistance of anti-Soviet elements. "There is," Lenin said, "a force that is greater than the desire, will or determination of any hostile government or class. That force is common world-wide economic relations, which compel them to take the road of rapprochement with us."**

The first major success of the Soviet policy of peaceful coexistence was the signing of a trade agreement with Britain in March 1921. This was the first de facto recognition of Soviet Russia by a leading capitalist country. The agreement was mutually advantageous. It enabled Russia to import vital machines and equipment. In the words of Lloyd George Britain was in 1920 a

---

* *Dokumenty vneshnei politiki SSSR* (*Documents on the Foreign Policy of the U.S.S.R.*), Vol. II, Moscow, 1958, p. 639.
** Lenin, *Collected Works*, Vol. 33, Ninth All-Russia Congress of Soviets".

shop that was winning new customers because its old clients had become bankrupt.

In establishing trade and political relations, Soviet Russia and Great Britain undertook to refrain from hostile acts and propaganda against each other.

Both the Soviet and British governments attached great significance to the agreement. Lenin said that "this agreement gives us a small window" on the capitalist world.

There was world-wide reaction to the Anglo-Soviet trade agreement. On March 19, 1921, the Italian Foreign Minister Count Carlo Sforza recommended trade talks with the Soviets. Similar recommendations were made in the German Reichstag and the French National Assembly.

A temporary trade agreement, similar to the Anglo-Soviet agreement, was signed between Soviet Russia and Germany on May 6, 1921.

Soon afterwards trade agreements were signed with Soviet Russia by Austria, Norway, Italy, Denmark, Czechoslovakia and other countries.

However, while signing these trade agreements the capitalist states refrained from establishing diplomatic relations with Soviet Russia. They wanted her to pay the debts of the tsarist and Provisional governments, cancel state monopoly over foreign trade and give capital free access to the country. Some countries, notably the U.S.A., categorically refused to have even trade relations with the Soviet Republic.

In a memorandum to the U.S. Congress and U.S. President Warren Harding on March 20, 1921, A.R.C.E.C. stated that Soviet Russia had no intention of interfering in U.S. affairs and only wanted to trade. The memorandum declared that Soviet Russia was prepared to send a delegation to the U.S. for talks. The reply sent on March 25 by U.S. Secretary of State Charles E. Hughes was a violation of all standards of international law and politics, it demanded a change of the regime in the Soviet Republic. Hughes wrote that only when the U.S. had convincing proof that the regime had been changed it would consider the question of trade relations.

However, many U.S. businessmen were much more far-sighted than their government and the Republican Party, which had then come to power. The U.S. Prodex Company, for example, already had extensive business dealings with Soviet Russia. Many other U.S. firms and companies had signed trade agreements with Soviet economic organisations, but the U.S. State Department tried to prevent them from being carried out.

Soviet foreign trade expanded despite the efforts of anti-Soviet forces, which refused to trade with Soviet Russia or grant her credits, in the belief that this would cause her economic collapse.

Soviet Russia confidently stepped into the world trade market.

Her policy of peaceful coexistence with capitalist states, a policy in conformity with the interests of the peoples of all countries, began to bear its first fruit.

Soviet Russia, Friend of the Peoples of the East

The year 1921 witnessed an important stage in the establishment of friendly relations between the Soviet Republic and Eastern countries. The October Revolution proclaimed the equality and freedom of the peoples, condemned colonial oppression and slavery and recognised the right of all peoples to political and economic independence.

As soon as the Soviet Republic was created the government began talks with the governments of Iran, Turkey, Afghanistan and China. This aroused apprehension in Britain and France over the fate of their colonies and they did their utmost to obstruct the Soviet talks with the Eastern countries. In particular, Britain was afraid of Soviet influence in Iran.

After the October Revolution, the Soviet Government annulled all unequal treaties concluded between Iran and tsarist Russia. Moreover, it withdrew Russian troops from Iran and recognised the country's independence and sovereignty.

In 1919, Britain, on the other hand, forced Iran to sign a treaty legalising British occupation of Persian territory and preserving the capitulations. London brought tremendous pressure to bear on the Shah, the Mejlis and Government of Iran. The bugbear of "Bolshevisation" was used on the Persians, and all sorts of promises were made to them with the sole object of maintaining the British hold on Iranian oil, on her natural resources and wealth, which occupied an important strategic place in the British colonial empire.

However, national forces came to power in Iran and first the government and then the Mejlis, under pressure from the national liberation movement, refused to ratify the Anglo-Iranian treaty of 1919.

Soviet foreign policy rendered effective assistance to the Iranian people in their struggle against inequality and their government's capitulations. Soviet-Iranian talks were started in Moscow in November 1920, and on February 26, 1921, they ended in the signing of a treaty. The Soviet Government reaffirmed its annulment of all the unequal treaties, conventions and agreements signed between tsarist Russia and Iran, annulled all Persian debts and returned to Iran concessions and property acquired by tsarist Russia. Of property alone, the Soviet Government turned over to Iran 582 million gold rubles worth.

This was the first equal treaty in Iran's history and it was highly appreciated by the progressive forces in that country. The Iranian newspaper *Rahnema* wrote: "A flash of blinding lightning that made a dazzling impression amid the dense gloom of Persian politics suddenly appeared from the north, from Soviet Russia, cutting through the darkness of our political horizon.... This bright light came from the north and its source is Moscow. This is from where it came to our dark spaces with driving force and at once brought radiance to our eyes."*

The general upsurge of the national liberation movement in the East spread to Afghanistan. The young and energetic Emir Ammanula-Khan came to power in that country in 1919. He opposed Britain's attempts to retain her colonial domination over Afghanistan and made every effort to establish friendly relations with the Soviet Republic. An Afghan delegation came to Moscow at the close of 1919, and, at the same time, a Soviet representative arrived in Kabul. The talks between the two countries proceeded successfully. At the close of 1920, Ammanula-Khan wrote to Lenin, saying that the Afghan people were friendly towards the Soviet Republic. He expressed satisfaction over the success of the Soviet-Afghan talks.

In reply to this message Lenin noted that the two countries, which wanted to see all the countries and peoples of the East independent, had common interests. The Soviet-Afghan Treaty was signed on February 28, 1921. Under this treaty both countries recognised each other's independence. Soviet Russia undertook to render Afghanistan material and cultural aid and to ensure the unhindered transit of goods purchased by Afghanistan. This paragraph of the treaty was of immense importance to Afghanistan, for it freed her trade of British control.

Soviet policy towards friendly Afghanistan was, furthermore, clearly set forth in the special instructions sent by Georgi Chicherin, People's Commissar for Foreign Affairs of the R.S.F.S.R., to the plenipotentiary representative of the R.S.F.S.R. in Afghanistan. He wrote: "We say to the Afghan Government: you have your system, we have ours; you have your ideals, we have ours; but we are bound to each other by our common striving to achieve the independence and sovereignty of our peoples."

British ruling circles made desperate attempts to hinder the friendly relations between Afghanistan and Soviet Russia. Dobbs, the British representative in Kabul, offered Ammanula-Khan 20,000 rifles, 20 field batteries and other arms, promising an annual subsidy of 4,000,000 rupees and the payment to Afghanistan of another 40,000,000 rupees in the course of 25 years. In return the British demanded the scrapping of the Soviet-Afghan Treaty,

---

* RSFSR, *Narodny komissariat inostrannykh del* (R.S.F.S.R., People's Commissariat for Foreign Affairs), 1921, No. 68, p. 38.

the expulsion of the Soviet Ambassador and the launching of a propaganda campaign against Soviet Russia.

This was an attempt to harness the peoples of Afghanistan to another colonial yoke. But the British political leaders were helpless to stop the collapse of the old colonial regimes in the Near and Middle East. In July 1921, Afghanistan rejected the claims of British imperialism and several months later signed a treaty under which Britain recognised her independence. The support from the Soviet Republic was thus an important factor in the struggle of the friendly Afghan people for freedom and independence.

The Soviet-Afghan Treaty, the first equal agreement in the history of Afghanistan, was a fresh manifestation of the Soviet Union's policy of establishing friendly relations with Eastern countries.

Another outcome of this policy was the signing in March 1921 of a treaty with Turkey, which was then fighting for her independence against British, French and Greek armed forces. Under this treaty, the Soviet Russia freed Turkey from her humiliating capitulations and inequality, and renounced all the special privileges that were enjoyed by tsarist Russia. The Soviet Government granted a loan of 10,000,000 gold rubles to Turkey, transferring the entire sum to her in 1921-22 despite the economic dislocation in Soviet Russia herself.

Mikhail Frunze, commander of Soviet troops in the Ukraine and the Crimea, arrived in Turkey at the close of December 1921, and on January 2, 1922, he signed in Ankara a Ukrainian-Turkish Treaty which still further cemented Soviet-Turkish relations.

In a conversation with S. Aralov, Soviet Ambassador to Turkey, Lenin said: "Your behaviour and actions must break the ice of hostility and win trust. It must be made clear to the Turkish people that there is an abyss between socialist Russia and tsarist Russia, that there is nothing in common between them.... Although things are difficult for us we shall give them not only moral support but also all the material aid we can."

Aid from Soviet Russia improved Turkey's international and domestic position and helped her to withstand the onslaught of the Entente and uphold her independence.

The progressive sections of the Turkish people welcomed the establishment of friendly relations with Soviet Russia, but among Turkey's rulers there were people who opposed Soviet-Turkish friendship. The British and French governments took advantage of this to try and drive a wedge between Soviet Russia and Turkey. A succession of British and French emissaries came to Turkey with that objective, but Kemal Atatürk firmly kept to his policy of friendly relations with Soviet Russia.

In April 1922, this outstanding Turkish statesman wrote to Lenin: "Friendship with Russia is lasting as it has been in the past, and is the cornerstone of the policy of the Government of the Grand National Assembly of Turkey. I believe that at present, more than ever before, our countries must unite their efforts against the new methods that the imperialist and capitalist states have begun to use. In our eyes the assistance that Russia has repeatedly rendered us acquires special importance."

Soviet Russia's aid to Turkey and other Eastern countries was free of political strings, while the colonial powers demanded economic and political privileges for every penny lent out by them. "We set great store by the Soviet people, your government and V. I. Lenin," Kemal Atatürk wrote, "for the fact that your aid is disinterested. You do not demand submission or any political commitments from us."

The Soviet Republic firmly championed Turkey's right to independence and defended her interests at international conferences. She pressed for Turkey's participation in the Genoa Conference against the wishes of the Great Powers. The Soviet Government spiritedly defended Turkey's interests at the Lausanne Conference (end of 1922) as well.

From the day of its birth the Soviet Republic strove for rapprochement with the Far Eastern countries, too.

An important role was played in the life of the Eastern peoples by the establishment of friendship between the R.S.F.S.R. and Mongolia. Set up in 1920, the People's Revolutionary Party headed the Mongolian people's struggle for independence. A people's government was formed in Mongolia after the defeat of the white-guard General Ungern in the summer of 1921. In October of the same year the new government sent a delegation led by Suhe-Bator to Moscow.

An agreement establishing friendly relations between Mongolia and the R.S.F.S.R. was signed on November 5, 1921. At the request of the Mongolian Government, Soviet troops remained temporarily in Mongolia to defend that country against attack by Japan.

Thus, as early as 1921 Soviet Russia had established friendly relations with a number of Eastern countries.

Soviet Russia at the Genoa Conference

The payment of tsarist Russia's debts was one of the terms on which the bourgeois states agreed to recognise Soviet Russia. In a note delivered on October 28, 1921, the Soviet Government informed the governments of Britain, France, Italy, Japan and the U.S.A. that it was prepared to normalise relations with all countries and agreed to recognise the "credit commitments to other states and their citizens undertaken by the tsarist government before 1914, provided favourable terms are granted to enable it to discharge these commitments".* Soviet Russia consented to this step on the sole condition that the Great Powers concluded peace with her and recognised the Soviet Government, and suggested an international conference with the purpose of settling mutual claims.

The Soviet note evoked a response throughout the world. In some countries, particularly in Britain, there was a growing demand for talks with the Soviet Government and for utilising Russia's economic resources to improve world economy. Lloyd George initiated a correspondence with the Soviet Government to discuss the proposed conference. The French Government, on the other hand, remained cool to the Soviet proposals. This exposed Anglo-French differences. However, like Britain, France had to take Germany's policy into consideration. The latter was demanding a re-examination or, at least, an easing of the Versailles terms, and calculating on using the Russian market to strengthen her position in Europe.

The Allied Supreme Council met at Cannes on January 6, 1922, and reached agreement on an international conference to examine questions concerning economic rehabilitation in Central and Eastern Europe and on inviting Germany and Russia to the conference. Genoa was selected as the venue.

On January 7, 1922, the Italian Government (as the host of the future conference) sent the Soviet Government and Lenin personally an invitation to attend the conference. Soviet Russia agreed to participate.

In the course of the preparations for the conference all progressive people in Europe and America hailed the first major foreign policy successes of the Soviet state and demanded that their governments put a halt to their anti-Soviet policy. The Communist Parties of the European countries were in the vanguard of the struggle to give the Soviet Republic equal rights with other countries at Genoa.

In the Soviet Republic itself the preparations for the conference were directed by Lenin. The Soviet Government's proposals on economic problems had the objective of establishing and broadening out Soviet relations with the capitalist countries. "We are going to Genoa," Lenin said, "for the practical purpose of expanding trade and of creating the most favourable conditions for its successful development on the widest scale."**

Moreover, the Soviet Government planned to present its views on key international issues and thereby weaken the anti-Soviet front and avert the danger of another intervention.

---

* *Dokumenty vneshnei politiki SSSR* (*Documents on the Foreign Policy of the U.S.S.R.*), Vol. IV, Moscow, 1961, p. 447.
** Lenin, *Selected Works*, Vol. 3, p. 726.

On January 27, 1922, an extraordinary meeting of A.R.C.E.C. approved the composition of the Soviet delegation to the conference. Lenin was to head the delegation and Chicherin, People's Commissar for Foreign Affairs, was to be his deputy. The members included Leonid Krasin, Maxim Litvinov, Vaclav Vorovsky, Adolph Joffe and Jan Rudzutak.

At a conference in Moscow in February 1922, representatives of the R.S.F.S.R., the Ukraine, Byelorussia, Azerbaijan, Armenia, Georgia, Bukhara, Khoresm and the Far Eastern Republic authorised the A.R.C.E.C. delegation to speak and conclude treaties and agreements on their behalf. The R.S.F.S.R. delegation was reinforced with representatives from the Ukraine, Azerbaijan, Georgia and Armenia.

The delegation was instructed by the Soviet Government to oppose interference in the internal affairs of the Soviet Republic and, at the same time, to show the maximum flexibility in defence of peace. In a note to Britain, France and Italy on March 15, the People's Commissariat for Foreign Affairs made it plain that the Soviet Government "would go to the conference at Genoa with the firm intention of initiating economic relations with all states mutually guaranteeing the inviolability of their internal political and economic organisation".*

In the Soviet Union attention was focussed on the preparations for the conference. Letters expressing apprehension for Lenin's safety at Genoa poured into the Party C.C., A.R.C.E.C., the Council of People's Commissars and newspapers and magazines in February and March 1922. Rank-and-file workers and Party, local government, trade union and other organisations wrote that they feared to entrust Lenin's life to bourgeois security forces.

Pressure of work and ill health prevented Lenin from going to the conference. The Soviet delegation was led by Chicherin.

The conference opened at the Palazzo San Giorgio on April 10, 1922. It was attended by delegates from 34 countries, including prominent leaders of the capitalist world: British Prime Minister David Lloyd George and Foreign Secretary Lord Curzon, French Foreign Minister Gean Louis Barthou, Reichschancellor Joseph Wirth and German Foreign Minister Walther Rathenau, Italian Premier Luigi Facta, and others. The U.S. appointed Richard W. Child, the American Ambassador to Italy, as its observer. Considerable interest was shown in the conference by financial and industrial circles.

The interest of all the delegates, guests and correspondents was focussed on the Soviet delegation. There was tense silence when

---

* *Dokumenty vneshnei politiki SSSR* (*Documents on the Foreign Policy of the U.S.S.R.*), Vol. V, Moscow, 1961, p. 155.

the floor was given to Chicherin. He read out a declaration, whose underlying idea was that the Soviet Republic could coexist peacefully with the capitalist powers. In this declaration it was stated that "in the present epoch, which makes possible the parallel existence of the old and the incipient, new social system, economic co-operation between states representing these two systems of ownership is an imperative necessity for universal economic restoration".*

Chicherin said that Soviet Russia wished to co-operate with all countries in Europe's economic construction and declared that the Russian delegation planned to submit a proposal for a general reduction of arms and to support any proposals aimed at lightening the burden of militarism on condition that the armies of all states were reduced and barbarous means of warfare were outlawed.

"We are prepared," Chicherin said in conclusion, "to take part in joint work in the interests of both Russia and the whole of Europe and for the sake of tens of millions of people experiencing unbearable privation and suffering as a result of economic dislocation, and to support all attempts to achieve at least a palliative improvement of world economy and to eliminate the threat of another war."**

Thus at Genoa the Soviet Republic set forth a programme of peace and disarmament. The conference showed that in Soviet Russia the working people of the whole world had an active champion of peace and universal prosperity, a champion against aggression and the arms race.

The Soviet peaceful proposals were rejected by the capitalist countries. French Foreign Minister Barthou took the floor after Chicherin and declared irritably: "As soon as the Russian delegation proposes that the First Commission examine this question [disarmament.—Ed.] it will be countered not only by the restraint and protest of the French delegation but also by its direct, categorical, final and determined opposition."

The Soviet programme was not accepted by the capitalist countries. A report drawn up in London by experts just before the conference was submitted to the Soviet delegation. It contained the capitalist countries' demands concerning rehabilitation in Russia and Europe and put forward a series of conditions under which foreign enterprises could contribute to "Russia's reconstruction". These conditions were that the Soviet Government should recognise all the financial commitments of the tsarist and Provisional governments and of all the former authorities in Russia.

---

* *Documenty Vneshnei politiki SSSR* (*Documents on the Foreign Policy of the U.S.S.R.*), Vol. V, Moscow, 1961, p. 78.
** *Ibid.*, p. 31.

To supervise the fulfilment of the Soviet Government's obligations the report envisaged setting up a Russian Debt Commission with the right to interfere in the work of Soviet financial bodies and to determine the utilisation of Soviet State Budget funds. The Soviet Government would be obliged to give foreigners residing in Soviet Russia special privileges that would enable them to interfere in the country's internal affairs. Lastly, the sponsors of the report demanded that Russia return nationalised enterprises to their former foreign owners.

The Soviet delegation could not accept these terms. In a memorandum on April 20 and a note on May 11, 1922, the Soviet delegation made it clear that the report ran counter to the resolution of the Cannes Conference and that what the capitalist powers were demanding was in fact the enslavement of Soviet Russia.

The course of events upset all the calculations and hopes of those who dreamed of directing Europe's destiny. The attempts of the British, French and Italians to create a united anti-Soviet front at the Genoa Conference collapsed. On the eve of the conference Soviet Russia had taken the step of proposing a treaty with Germany. The talks between the two countries were continued at Genoa and ended on April 16 with the signing of the Rapallo Soviet-German Treaty, under which the two countries renounced their claims for reparations arising from losses sustained during the war. Moreover, Germany renounced any claim to property that had been nationalised in Russia. The Soviet Republic and Germany agreed to extend their economic and trade relations on mutually favourable terms.

The signing of the Rapallo Treaty was a signal success of Soviet foreign policy: it demolished the Soviet Republic's diplomatic isolation by the imperialists and demonstrated that there was a real possibility of reaching agreement with Soviet Russia on the basis of mutual equality and advantage. The treaty was an example of peaceful coexistence between socialist and capitalist countries.

The Genoa Conference ended without adopting any decision. Its results showed that the foreign policy of the capitalist powers had reached a crisis and were, to all intents and purposes, a triumph for Soviet diplomacy. At its first international contact the Soviet Republic proved that it actively championed peace and disarmament and the establishment of broad trade and economic relations between states regardless of their social system.

Year of Diplomatic Recognition

The Soviet Union's domestic and international position grew stronger during the period of economic rehabilitation.

But early in 1923 its enemies organised a series of anti-Soviet campaigns in Europe, with the result that Soviet relations with Finland and the Baltic countries deteriorated. Russian counter-revolutionary forces remained active in some capitalist countries and were supported by the governments concerned.

Acts openly hostile to the U.S.S.R. were undertaken by Britain. On May 8, 1923, Lord Curzon, the British Foreign Secretary, used the death sentence meted out to one of the participants in an anti-Soviet conspiracy by a Moscow court as an excuse for sending an ultimatum to the Soviet Union. In this ultimatum he accused the Soviet Government of anti-British propaganda in Iran, India and Afghanistan and demanded that Soviet representatives be recalled from Iran and Afghanistan. Placing spies and saboteurs under his protection, Curzon demanded that the U.S.S.R. apologise for sentencing them, threatening to break off Anglo-Soviet relations if it did not do so.

The whiteguards who had found refuge in various parts of Europe reared their heads. The newspapers began a savage anti-Soviet campaign. On May 10, 1923, a whiteguard named Conradi assassinated Vaclav Vorovsky, the Soviet representative and a prominent diplomat, in Lausanne.

Curzon's ultimatum roused the indignation of the working people of the U.S.S.R. and the world.

Rallies and demonstrations protesting against the insolent demands of the British Government were held throughout the Soviet Union. The working people pledged themselves to the defence of the U.S.S.R. Another Hands Off Soviet Russia campaign was begun in the capitalist countries. This new attempt to isolate the U.S.S.R. failed as a result of action by progressive forces in all countries, and soon afterwards Lord Curzon was compelled to resign his post.

The elections to the British Parliament in December 1923 brought the Labour Party to power. The new government headed by Ramsay MacDonald was forced to change its policy towards the U.S.S.R. This was demanded by the working masses and many businessmen in Britain, who were interested in Anglo-Soviet trade. On February 2, 1924, the British Government informed the People's Commissariat for Foreign Affairs that Britain was extending de jure recognition to the Union of Soviet Socialist Republics.

In 1924, the Soviet Union was recognised by Italy, Norway, Austria, Greece and Sweden. Sino-Soviet relations were settled in May 1924 with the signing of an agreement. In the summer of 1924, diplomatic relations were established between the U.S.S.R. and Mexico.

Franco-Soviet relations improved, and in 1924 progressive forces in France forced Raymond Poincaré's reactionary administration to resign. The new Prime Minister, Edouard Herriot, informed

Moscow that France recognised the Soviet Government. The wave of recognition ended with the signing of a Soviet-Japanese agreement in January 1925. Thus, in the period 1921-25 the Soviet Union signed more than 40 treaties and agreements with capitalist countries.

That period was an important stage in the foreign policy of the Soviet Union. After withstanding the combined onslaught of international imperialism, the U.S.S.R. entered the world arena as a Great Power able to protect its socialist system and to help in strengthening peace.

Chapter Four

BUILDING OF SOCIALISM.
U.S.S.R. ON THE EVE OF WAR
(1926-41)

Socialist Industrialisation

Need for Industrialisation

Economic rehabilitation of the U.S.S.R. was completed at the close of 1925, and a new period of development, the period of the socialist reconstruction of the entire economy and the building of a modern industry, ensued.

The most acute problem facing the country now was the need for socialist industrialisation, i.e., the building up of large-scale socialist industry, primarily, heavy industry capable of manufacturing the latest types of machinery for factories and agriculture, and transforming the U.S.S.R. into an industrial country.

Industrialisation occupied the central place in Lenin's plan for socialist construction. In his theses on the tactics of the R.C.P.(B.) for the Third Comintern Congress in July 1921, he wrote: "A large-scale machine industry capable of reorganising agriculture as well can be the only material foundation of socialism." He developed this idea at the Fourth Comintern Congress in November 1922, when he said: "Salvation for Russia would be not only a good harvest on the peasant farms—that would not be enough—and not only a smooth-running light industry supplying the peasants with consumer goods—that too would not be enough; we must have a *heavy* industry as well.

"A heavy industry requires state subsidies. If we do not find them then as a civilised state—to say nothing of us as a socialist state—we shall have perished."[*] In line with Lenin's ideas, the Communist Party at its Fourteenth Congress in 1925 steered a course towards the country's socialist industrialisation.

For the U.S.S.R. this was a historical necessity, for on it depended the success of socialism in town and country, the preservation of the country's economic independence and the strengthening of its

---

[*] Lenin, *Collected Works*, Vol. 33, "Fourth Congress of the Communist International".

defence potential. Without the priority building of a heavy industry the country's age-old backwardness could not be rapidly surmounted. With the largest territory in the world, the third-largest population and colossal mineral wealth Russia was only fifth in the world and fourth in Europe for the volume of industrial output. Her output of coal was one-tenth of that of Britain, steel one-seventh of that of the U.S.A. and iron ore one-fifth of that of France. She had no automobile, tractor, engineering, aircraft, chemical, defence and other key industries.

Moreover, industrialisation was necessary to satisfy the demand of the millions of peasants for implements, machines, fertiliser and consumer goods. Small-scale production could be reorganised into large-scale socialist production and the productive forces enhanced only with the use of up-to-date machinery.

The only way to raise the living and cultural standards of the people was by developing heavy industry capable of advancing agricultural production, the light industry and the entire economy.

Another factor was that socialist industrialisation would create the basic prerequisites for victory in economic competition with capitalist countries. The Soviet Union could uphold its independence and emerge victorious in this competition only by industrialisation.

The U.S.S.R. had to build its industry without credits from the capitalist states. Back in 1922, when the Soviet Republic was rehabilitating her large-scale industry, Lenin said: "The economic history of the capitalist countries proves that in backward countries only long-term loans running into hundreds of millions of dollars or gold rubles can be the means of building a heavy industry. We have not had such loans and to this day we have received nothing."* That was the case not only during the rehabilitation period but also while the country was being industrialised along socialist lines; the Soviet Union could count only on its own resources. It had to keep expenditures down to a minimum, reduce its outlay on running the state apparatus, and economise on everything. This was the only way out of a difficult situation.

Many industries had to be set up from scratch. These included the defence industry. This work had to be rushed because of the external and internal conditions of the country's development. The Soviet Union lagged behind the developed capitalist countries and, being surrounded by hostile states, was compelled to bridge this gap as soon as possible. Otherwise it risked being strangled by the reactionary forces of imperialism.

The Soviet Union had the most advanced social system in the world but it rested on inadequate material and technical basis,

---

* Lenin, *Collected Works*, Vol. 33, "Fourth Congress of the Communist International."

an incongruity which could be eliminated only by swift industrialisation.

To develop her industry the country required skilled personnel, but most of the population was illiterate, a factor causing serious difficulties in training workers, technicians and engineers.

The Soviet Union did not have the time first to abolish illiteracy, train the necessary number of skilled personnel for industry and then embark upon socialist industrialisation. Everything had to be done simultaneously.

Industrialisation was fiercely resisted by capitalist elements, thus giving rise to additional difficulties. The class struggle in the country was reflected in the Communist Party: in the summer of 1926 the Trotsky and Zinoviev groups formed a bloc which vehemently attacked the policy of industrialisation. This bloc maintained that socialism could not be built in the U.S.S.R.

The struggle to implement Lenin's policy of socialist industrialisation against the opposition of the Trotsky-Zinoviev bloc and the national deviationists was headed by the Central Committee.

The Soviet Union started socialist industrialisation without having any experience to draw upon. Yet within a short space of time, without foreign aid, the U.S.S.R. built up a first-class large-scale industry and created the material and technical basis of socialism.

What enabled the U.S.S.R. to surmount these and many other difficulties? The principal source of success lay in the very nature of Soviet society, in the advantages of planned economic development and in the deep-rooted interest of the workers and peasants in industrialisation. Socialist ownership of large-scale industry and transport, the state monopoly on foreign trade and the promotion of state trade allowed the Soviet authorities to channel the profits from these branches of the economy into the development of socialist industry. The cancellation of the debts and loans of the tsarist and Provisional governments freed the country from paying 800-900 million rubles annually in the shape of interest rates and incomes to foreign capitalists; the peasants were delivered from the expense of purchasing land and the payment of rent and could give the state part of their means to further industrialisation, which they knew meant machines, fertiliser and consumer goods.

First Successes of Industrialisation

The industrialisation plan was drawn up in 1926 at the April Plenary Meeting of the C.C. C.P.S.U.(B.). The cardinal problem was to obtain the means for construction. One of the main sources of these means was accumulation in industry itself. In order to increase this accumulation determined steps had to be taken to rationalise production, reduce overheads, step up labour productivity and strengthen labour discipline. The success of these measures depended upon the workers themselves, on their conscious attitude to the country's problems, on efficient management.

The mobilisation of the country's resources yielded positive results: in 1926-27, the state invested nearly 1,000 million rubles in construction as against 800 million rubles in the previous year. It should be noted that in 1922 Lenin regarded it as a notable achievement that the country could invest 20 million gold rubles into the development of large-scale industry.

The steadily growing working class was the principal motive force in the industrialisation drive. In 1926 the large-scale industry employed over 2,000,000 workers, while in 1928 their number exceeded 3,000,000. Almost all the old skilled workers had returned to the restored factories and mines, and an influx began of new, untrained workers.

Workers came forward with suggestions on ways and means of reconstructing factories and improving machines, displayed a creative attitude to their work, mastered new technologies and worked and studied. Foremost men and women workers developed a new approach to work.

The main working-class cadres ensuring the country's industrialisation had been trained during the period of economic reconstruction.

In addition to veteran workers, who displayed a high sense of discipline, there were among the workers many people who came from the petty-bourgeois strata in the countryside and were only out to earn money to keep their farms going. They brought survivals of petty-bourgeois psychology and individualism to the factories. Among those who built the first industrial giants there were many former kulaks who were hostile to Soviet rule.

The selfless collective labour effort re-educated the people and gave them new values. The first builders of socialist industry were inspired by the grandeur of the task before them. People who had only recently been peasants likewise set examples of unprecedented productivity and real labour heroism.

The reconstruction of industry in fact signified a technical revolution. Suffice it to say that 44.2 per cent of the machine-tools at the engineering plants were installed in the period from 1929 to April 1932. Industry was supplied with modern equipment. At many factories reconstruction was so extensive that it really meant building new projects. At the Krasny Proletary Works in Moscow, for example, the old foundry and modelling and machine departments were pulled down and all the old equipment was dismantled. New buildings were erected for two machine and assembly departments, and steam hammers were installed in the forge. New machines, including powerful hoisting cranes, were installed.

The change was so drastic that veteran workers could hardly recognise the factory.

Machinery was modernised in a number of key industries: in the oil industry manual baling was replaced by compressors and pumps, wells were sunk with the aid of revolving bores and the electrification of the oilfields was started. Mechanisation spread to the coal industry, where in 1928 machines accounted for 15 per cent of the output. Hydraulic methods were introduced into the peat industry. In 1927-28, the iron and steel industry began to master the production of high-grade steels and rolled stock.

New building projects were started at the same time. In 1926-28, oil refineries were under construction at Baku, Grozny, Batumi and Tuapse and the Grozny-Tuapse and Baku-Batumi oil pipelines were laid.

Large-scale capital construction was launched in the Donets Basin. New mines were built and fitted with the latest equipment and the old mines were modernised. The mines in the Kuznetsk Basin were enlarged and reconstructed. The rising coal output enabled the U.S.S.R. not only to stop importing coal but also to begin to export it.

In 1928-29, more than 80 per cent of Soviet exports consisted of oil and timber products. For this reason side by side with the oil industry the timber and paper industry received great attention. The new projects included sawmills at Mtsensk, Onega, Ust-Luga and elsewhere, plywood mills at Kazan, Vitebsk and Bobruisk, and paper mills at Balakhna and Syask. Paper was needed to increase the output of books and the circulation of periodicals.

The new projects were planned with an eye to freeing the country from the necessity of importing manufactured goods that could be produced locally and increasing the export of such goods to obtain the currency with which to purchase plant for the factories under construction. The first changes took place in the geography of new construction: in Central Asia the first textile mills were built at Ashkhabad and Ferghana, and in the Transcaucasia at Kirovabad and Leninakan.

Thermal power stations were built at Chelyabinsk, Shterovka, Kizel and elsewhere.

The nearly 1,500-kilometre Turkestan-Siberia Railway (Turksib) was one of the major projects of the first years of industrialisation. It linked up the grain and timber regions of Siberia with the cotton regions of Central Asia. This railway helped to develop the economy of the Central Asian republics and abolish their economic and cultural backwardness.

Construction of the railway proceeded from two directions, from the north and south, and was completed in three years (1927-30) instead of the five originally planned. This was the result of the labour heroism of the 50,000 builders involved—Russians, Kazakhs, Kirghizes and other nationalities.

The building of the 558,000-kw Lenin Hydropower Station on the Dnieper, envisaged in Lenin's GOELRO plan, gave the Soviet Union valuable experience in the organisation of industrial construction. It solved the problem of cheap power for the industries on the Dnieper and in other areas in the Ukraine and also of navigation on the Dnieper. The building of the station was directed by Alexander Vinter and the project itself was drawn up under the direction of Academician Ivan Alexandrov. The foundation stone was laid on the 10th anniversary of the Revolution. All the republics contributed to the building of the station, the workers coming from all parts of the country: the Ukraine, Russia, Byelorussia and other republics. Eventually 26,000 workers were involved, and of that number approximately a third were young people, many of them members of the Y.C.L. For its giant contribution towards harnessing the mighty Dnieper the Y.C.L. was decorated with the Order of Lenin.

The project became a huge training centre. Alexander Vinter, who later became an academician, wrote: "We received what for those days was a considerable quantity of building machinery. We were short of people who could handle this machinery.... The workers, most of whom came from the countryside, had to be infected with enthusiasm. This was done primarily by the Party organisation at the project. The Communists and the Y.C.L. members, the latter keeping abreast of the former, were the cementing force that united the huge army of workers and ensured world records in labour productivity."

The builders set many examples of a selfless work and labour heroism. They established a new world record for the monthly quantity of concrete laid in the building of the dam, increasing it to 110,000 cubic metres.*

The Fourth Congress of Soviets of the U.S.S.R., held in April 1927, devoted much of its attention to the country's industrialisation. It heard a report on the state and prospects of industrial development delivered by Valerian Kuibyshev, Chairman of the Supreme Economic Council,** endorsed the government's industrialisation policy and instructed it to draw up a five-year economic development plan as soon as possible. Agriculture too received close attention, for its development was a key factor of industrialisation. At the Congress Mikhail Kalinin reported on the tasks of

---

* At the largest hydropower projects in the West the quantity of concrete laid monthly did not exceed 85,000 cubic metres.—*Ed.*

** Felix Dzerzhinsky died in July 1926 and Valerian Kuibyshev was appointed to take his place as Chairman of the Supreme Economic Council.—*Ed.*

　　　　　　　　145

agriculture. The Congress mapped out measures for increasing agricultural production and preparing the conditions for its reorganisation on socialist lines.

Ten Years After the Revolution

The large-scale industry was gathering momentum: in 1927 it increased output by 18 per cent as compared with the previous year; in the Western capitalist countries the annual rate of increase of industrial output averaged 4-5 per cent.

The main achievement, however, was that through the efforts of the Communist Party and the Soviet Government the people's attention was centred on fulfilling the tasks of industrialisation.

While the Party was mobilising the people for the country's industrialisation, the Trotsky-Zinoviev opposition persistently undermined all its work. In the autumn of 1926, members of this group tried to speak at meetings of some of the largest Party organisations, but the Communists refused to listen to them. Changing their tactics, they publicly admitted that they were wrong in pursuing factional activities but in secret continued their anti-Party struggle.

The Fifteenth Party Conference, held in October-November 1926, noted the increasing role that was being played by large-scale industry in the country's economy, in promoting agriculture and developing agricultural co-operatives. The Conference called upon the working class and the working peasants to push ahead with Lenin's plan of industrialisation.

This Conference considered the question of the Trotsky-Zinoviev bloc, which was obstructing the Party line on basic problems of socialist construction. Guided by Lenin's propositions on the possibility of building socialism in the U.S.S.R., the Party and the people were putting these propositions into effect. The Trotskyites, however, clung to their theory that without a victorious proletarian revolution in the West socialism could not triumph in one country. They claimed that the peasants could not be drawn into socialist construction and preached "super-industrialisation" by raising prices on manufactured goods and increasing the taxes paid by the peasants. This course was particularly dangerous because it could destroy the alliance between the working class and the peasantry and weaken the Soviet state.

The Trotsky bloc insisted on reviving factions and groups within the Party, aiming at a split in the unity of the Party ranks. In foreign policy they claimed there was no necessity for protecting the U.S.S.R. against attack by the imperialists and were prepared to stab Soviet power in the back in the event of an imperialist attack. Essentially, the object of their subversive activities was to restore capitalism in the U.S.S.R. The Fifteenth Party Conference condemned the Trotsky-Zinoviev bloc as a Menshevik deviation in the Party and gave them a serious warning. But that did not stop them. They continued using every difficulty in the country to attack the Party and try to cripple its unity. In October 1927 a Plenary Meeting of the Central Committee and the Central Control Commission expelled Trotsky and Zinoviev from the C.C. for their factional struggle against the Party and for undermining its unity. In the course of the discussion started by the C.C. shortly before the Fifteenth Party Congress less than one per cent of the membership voted for the Trotsky-Zinoviev opposition. The entire Party rallied to the Leninist policy, censuring the opposition. The people unanimously supported the Party. This was strikingly shown on the 10th anniversary of the October Socialist Revolution.

The end of the first decade of Soviet rule was celebrated with rejoicing, with achievements in all spheres of socialist construction. An anniversary meeting of the Central Executive Committee of Soviets was held in Leningrad on October 15-20. While this meeting was in session there was a demonstration in Palace Square in support of socialist industrialisation. The meeting adopted a Manifesto to the Working People of the U.S.S.R. and the Whole World, which stated that within the next few years the working day would be shortened from eight to seven hours, the allocations for building schools and homes would be increased, small peasant farms would be exempt from the agricultural tax and other measures would be taken to improve the standard of living. These decisions were in line with the interests of the people and evoked nation-wide satisfaction.

The first decade of Soviet rule witnessed a growth of the labour and political activity of the people. The Party Central Committee announced an enrolment of workers into the Party. More than 108,000 working people joined the Party in this enrolment, which still further strengthened the Party's link with the masses and enhanced the leading role played by the working class in socialist construction.

The building of socialism in the U.S.S.R. acquired world-wide significance.

Many foreign workers' delegations came to the Soviet Union for the celebration of the 10th anniversary of the October Revolution.

A World Congress of Friends of the Soviet Union, attended by 1,000 delegates from 30 countries, opened in Moscow on November 10, 1927. It called upon the working people of all capitalist countries to defend the gains of the October Socialist Revolution.

The Soviet Union's successful advance along the road to socialist industrialisation caused alarm in the capitalist camp. In 1927, reactionary bourgeois circles in the West redoubled their efforts to disrupt the peaceful economic development in the U.S.S.R. and aggravate the international situation. Capitalist elements in the country also went into action. This onslaught by external and internal counter-revolutionary forces was one of the reasons for the Trotsky-Zinoviev anti-Party bloc becoming active.

During a working people's demonstration under Party slogans in honour of the 10th anniversary of the October Revolution, groups of Trotskyites led by Trotsky, Zinoviev and Kamenev broke Soviet laws by demonstrating in the streets of Moscow and Leningrad with anti-Party and anti-Soviet slogans. These renegades only won the contempt of the people. In October 1927, a joint Plenary Meeting of the Central Committee and Central Control Commission expelled Trotsky and Zinoviev from the Party and removed a number of opposition members from the Central Committee and the Central Control Commission.

Further Industrialisation

Having started an accelerated development of socialist industry, the Communist Party steadfastly kept it in the centre of its attention. It drew up a detailed programme of industrialisation, improved the methods of managing construction and readjusted the work of mass organisations.

In the history of the Soviet people's struggle for industrialisation, an important place is occupied by the Fifteenth Party Congress which sat on December 2-19, 1927. It summed up the results of the first two years of industrialisation and considered the question of drawing up the First Five-Year Plan of economic development. The basic tasks of this plan were formulated in the report read by Gleb Krzhizhanovsky and in the speeches of Valerian Kuibyshev and other delegates. These tasks included ensuring socialist industry, primarily heavy industry, with a rapid rate of development, promoting an upsurge of all branches of the national economy, enlarging the socialist sector and ousting capitalist elements, increasing the country's defence potential and improving the standard of living. The Congress set the Soviet people the task of collectivising agriculture on the basis of Lenin's co-operative plan.

In its decisions the Congress defined what had to be done to prepare for a new stage of socialist construction, for the advance of socialism in all spheres of the country's life. A major condition for the success of this advance was unity of the Party.

The Congress examined the question of the Trotsky-Zinoviev opposition, which undermined that unity, and approved Trotsky's and Zinoviev's expulsion from the Party. Recognising affiliation to the Trotsky opposition as incompatible with membership in the

Party, the Congress expelled active members of this group from the Party.

At the new stage of socialist construction, in the period of economic reconstruction, a bigger role was played by mass organisations: Soviets, trade unions and the Y.C. L. Their work was reorganised under the slogan of "Facing Production". The activation of the Soviets, begun at the end of the period of rehabilitation, continued.

Much was done to improve the work of the state apparatus, reduce its size and lower the cost of its upkeep, and to weed out bureaucracy. In this field an important role was played by the Central Control Commission–Workers' and Peasants' Inspection. Noting the work of the C.C.C.–W.P.I. in activating and strengthening the Soviets, the Fifteenth Party Congress recorded that this was only "the beginning of a historical period, whose task is gradually to draw the entire working population into the administration of the state and thereby completely eradicate bureaucracy".* The Central Control Commission enlisted the assistance of large numbers of people. At factories the Workers' and Peasants' Inspection was helped by trade union committees and production meetings and conferences.

The trade unions, as the largest organisations of the working class, helped to educate young workers, rationalise production, strengthen discipline and increase labour productivity.

The Y.C.L. initiated new ways by which young workers could participate in the industrialisation drive. It too contributed towards reducing production costs, rationalising production and maintaining order and discipline. In 1926, Y.C.L. members at the Krasny Treugolnik Plant in Leningrad formed the first shock-work team that employed advanced methods of work. In 1927, when the success of this initiative became evident, shock-work teams were formed at other enterprises in Leningrad and also in Moscow, Tver, the Urals and the Donbas.

The management of industrial enterprises was improved as the transition to industrialisation took place: up to then the main function of management had been concentrated in the hands of the trusts, which had charge of all the means and personnel in the enterprises under them, but now the basic rights were transferred to the factory or plant director. He was vested with all authority to deal with the enterprise's means and personnel. This reform, carried out in 1927, became possible only after Soviet economic executives, who combined the experience of political and economic leadership, had been trained.

---

* KPSS v resolyutsiyakh... (C.P.S.U. in Resolutions...), Part II, Moscow, 1954, p. 443.

The First Five-Year Plan of economic development (1928-32) was the decisive stage in the history of the Soviet Union's industrialisation.

This plan was drawn up by the Party with the assistance of leading scientists and broad sections of the people. Some of the old scientists and engineers did not believe that it was possible to carry out such a vast programme of construction in so short a period as five years. The Right deviationists headed by Rykov, Bukharin and Tomsky came out against the five-year plan's main targets, which envisaged rapid rates of industrialisation.

They also objected to the socialist reform of the countryside, arguing that state and collective farms were not necessary and that the small peasant farm should be the basis of agriculture. Bukharin advanced the theory that the kulak would grow into socialism through the co-operatives. At a Plenary Meeting in November 1928 the C.C. noted that the Right, frankly opportunist deviation found expression in "attempts to hold up the further building of large-scale industry and reduce its rate of growth, in a disparaging or negative attitude to collective and state farms, in belittling or glossing over the class struggle, particularly the struggle against the kulaks, in bureaucratic disregard to the requirements of the people, in underestimating the struggle against bureaucracy, in minimising the threat of war".*

The Plenary Meeting made it plain that the Right deviation was the chief danger: a triumph of the views of this deviation would inevitably have brought about the restoration of capitalism. The exposure of the Right deviation and its subsequent complete ideological and organisational defeat ensured the drawing up of the First Five-Year Plan and its successful fulfilment.

The five-year programme was a major success of Soviet planning: from the GOELRO plan, from the plans of rapidly expanding individual branches of industry and transport, from annual control figures of economic development, the Soviet Union passed to a plan covering five years, which specified in detail the relationships between branches of the economy and took the outlay of material and labour resources and the development of industry in the different republics into account.

The overall target of the First Five-Year Plan was to modernise industry, turn the Soviet Union from an agrarian into a powerful industrial country that would be economically independent of the capitalist states, and strengthen its defence potential.

The socio-economic relations in the country had to be changed,

---

* *KPSS v resolyutsiyakh...* (*C.P.S.U. in Resolutions...*), Part II, Moscow, 1954, p. 539.

industry and agriculture had to be developed on a single social-ist foundation, and a considerable proportion of small peasant farms had to be merged into socialist, collective farms. It was planned to draw some 4-5 million peasant farms into collective farms and enlarge their crop area to 17.5 per cent of the total crop area in the country. It was planned to improve the standard of living, introduce universal elementary education, and so forth.

This was a truly stupendous plan. The allocations for new construction alone amounted to 64,500 million rubles. Only 5,200 million rubles had been invested in industrial construction during the preceding five years. The plan envisaged 1,500 new factories, including such giants as the iron and steel works in Magnitogorsk, the Kuzbas and Zaporozhye, the tractor factories at Stalingrad, Kharkov and Chelyabinsk, the Urals and Novo-Kramatorsk engineering plants, the farm machines plant at Rostov, the auto works at Moscow and Gorky, and the chemical plants at Bobrikovo and Berezniki. Their size is seen from the fact that 50-60 projects swallowed nearly half of the investments.

The plan was greeted enthusiastically by the whole country. It was discussed at national conferences of branches of the economy convened in Moscow, at the Eighth Congress of Trade Unions of the U.S.S.R. and at meetings of workers directly at factories and state farms. It was approved by the Sixteenth Party Conference (April 1929) and the Fifth All-Union Congress of Soviets (May 1929).

The Soviet people regarded the First Five-Year Plan as a matter vitally concerning them and ensured its fulfilment by their selfless labour.

The entire country was turned into a vast building site, inspiring millions of people to give their best. This labour upsurge found expression in a mass socialist emulation movement.

In response to an appeal by the Communist Party the socialist emulation movement was joined by the workers and employees of factories, mills, mines and building projects. The movement took the form of emulation between shock teams. Young people initiated a movement aimed at tightening up discipline, reducing costs and improving the quality of output. This initiative was caught up in the Donbas, Moscow, Leningrad, the Urals and Siberia, where the workers began to conclude socialist emulation agreements.

Mikhail Putin, one of the initiators of this movement at the Krasny Vyborzhets Plant in Leningrad, wrote: "I had read Lenin's article 'How to Organise Emulation', in which he said that the victorious proletariat counterposes socialist emulation to capitalist competition.

"During a lunch break I told my team-mates about this article. They asked me to read it to them. . . .

"Lenin's burning words about emulation found a deep response among the workers. The plant was ready for it because it was still working inefficiently.

"I suggested that we organise an emulation movement so that we would not have shirkers, late-comers or spoilage, so that everybody would work conscientiously and constantly overfulfil his assignment.

"My suggestion was taken up.... By the time the lunch break ended we had decided to start that movement."

Socialist emulation soon became a mass movement.

The Magnitogorsk and Kuznetsk iron and steel plants were among the large projects of the First Five-Year Plan in the Soviet East. The builders, mostly young people, Y.C.L. members, worked in subzero temperatures and snowstorms. A large contribution was made by veteran workers, men who had fought in the Civil War and helped to restore factories in 1921-25. Despite the difficulties, they built coke batteries, blast-furnaces and some of the world's largest mines in record time. The first blast-furnace at Magnitogorsk became operational on January 31, 1932. Six months later the Y.C.L. members commissioned the second blast-furnace. The entire project was completed in two years.

The Kuznetsk Iron and Steel Works with an annual output of 3,000,000 tons of metal, making it one of the biggest plants of its kind in the world, was also built rapidly. The project, ordered by the Soviet Government, was drawn up by the U.S. Freyn Engineering Corporation. It took the builders nearly a thousand days, under the rigid conditions of the Siberian winter and with inadequate machinery, to build this modern giant plant.

Ivan Bardin, the noted metallurgist, who was one of the project's heads, wrote:

"People streamed to us from all parts of the country. In addition to Russians and Ukrainians there were Kazakhs and Kirghizes. These formerly illiterate people who had never seen a real factory in their lives performed incredible exploits. Instead of their quota of 150 mixes, the concrete-mixers produced 408.... The rivetters drove 266 rivets home during a shift instead of their quota of 105. The navvies sometimes fulfilled ten quotas during a single shift. Y.C.L. members braved temperatures of −50°C to continue rivetting at a great height. Bricklayers each laid up to 15 tons of refractory brick during a shift.

"Nothing, neither snowstorms nor rain, could dampen the labour enthusiasm of the builders."

The first Siberian metal was produced on April 3, 1932.

The Magnitogorsk and Kuznetsk iron and steel plants formed the backbone of the Soviet Union's second, Eastern, coal and metallurgical base. A movement to fulfil the five-year plan ahead of

Lenin in conversation with H. G. Wells

Members of the former GOELRO Commission: Professor
K. Krug, Academician G. Krzhizhanovsky, Professor
B. Ugryumov and engineers R. Ferman, N. Vashkov and
M. Smirnov, 1940

Shatura Power Station, 1924

Foremost workers at the Dnieper Hydropower Station
project, 1932

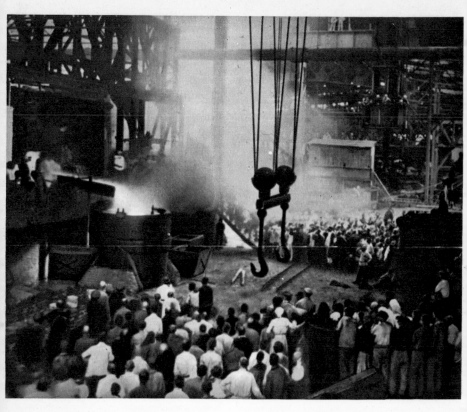

First steel smelt from an open-hearth furnace, 1922

schedule was started in different parts of the country. "The Five-Year Plan in Four Years" became the slogan of the entire nation.

At the close of 1929, the First All-Union Congress of Shock Teams summed up the results of the socialist emulation movement in the first year of the five-year plan period. The movement embraced over 900,000 industrial and office workers and engineers. The assignments of the first year were overfulfilled.

Further notable successes were scored towards the summer of 1930: in the first two years of the five-year plan period the large-scale industry increased its output by 63 per cent. It was the first time in the country's history that the industrial sector rose above the agricultural sector in annual statistics. The Soviet Union was indeed becoming an industrial power.

Socialism started a nation-wide offensive against capitalist elements. The bulk of the peasants began joining collective farms and that created the conditions for getting rid of the kulaks, the last surviving capitalist class in the country.

Under these conditions the Sixteenth Party Congress, which sparked off the full-scale offensive of socialism, sat from June 26 to July 13, 1930.

The Soviet Union had overtaken the capitalist countries in the rate of industrial development but lagged behind them in the level of output, occupying fifth place in the world for the output of steel, sixth place for the output of pig iron and coal and ninth place for the output of electric power. In particular, economic development was held up by the slow progress of the iron and steel industry. The Sixteenth Congress, therefore, decided to accelerate the rate of industrial development, with emphasis on the metallurgical industry. Higher targets were set for the output of tractors, automobiles, non-ferrous metals and farm machines. The Congress drew the attention of the Party and the entire people to the development and reconstruction of transport, which was not coping with the heavier traffic. It was planned to build powerful, modern steam engines in 1931 and improve the building of railways.

As the Congress noted, the successes scored in industrialisation were due to the labour and political activity of the working class. More than 2,000,000 workers had joined the socialist emulation movement, and of these about a million were members of shock teams.

The Congress set the trade unions the task of promoting the socialist emulation movement, organising business-like, useful production conferences and improving the training of personnel.

Successful socialist construction enhanced the role of planning. To improve this field of activity Valerian Kuibyshev was appointed Chairman of the State Planning Commission and Grigory Orjonikidze was put in charge of the Supreme Economic Council. In

1932 that body was split into three people's commissariats—heavy industry, light industry and timber industry, which were headed by G. Orjonikidze, I. Lyubimov and S. Lobov respectively.

A People's Commissariat for Supplies, headed by Anastas Mikoyan, was set up.

Many new difficulties arose while the First Five-Year Plan was still being fulfilled. For example, new machinery required better training facilities for workers, most of whom were new to factory work.

The difficulties encountered in developing new machinery are best illustrated on the example of the Donbas. Although by 1930 labour productivity at the mines had surpassed its pre-war level, the Donbas fell short of its plan assignment. Labour mechanisation was held up by the shortage of cutters, mechanical picks, electric locomotives and other equipment. Labour flux was another serious obstacle: it hindered the training of workers in the use of machines, reduced productivity, and so forth. In 1931, the Council of People's Commissars, the C.C. C.P.S.U.(B.) and the Supreme Economic Council set miners the task of mechanising all the basic mining operations. The Y.C.L. sent 36,000 members to the Donbas. Of that number 10,000 were trained as machine operators. Nikita Izotov, a Gorlovka miner, undertook to train young workers in advanced methods of mining. His example was followed by many other miners and by the close of the five-year plan period the Izotov movement had tens of thousands of followers.

The Y.C.L. organisation in the Donbas played an outstanding role in helping young workers to learn to handle modern machinery, and many of the miners trained by it won nation-wide renown. For its services in helping to step up the coal output the Donbas Y.C.L. organisation was decorated with the Order of Lenin.

Through the efforts of the Soviet Government and the Party and thanks to the heroic labour of the workers the Donbas was enabled to catch up with the plan. In 1932, it produced 45 million tons of the country's total coal output of 64,400,000 tons.

The mastering of foreign technology, particularly the mass production method, did not come easy. The Dzerzhinsky Tractor Plant in Stalingrad (now Volgograd) was commissioned in June 1930, but failed to fulfil its programme for both 1930 and 1931. That caused serious alarm.

Grigory Orjonikidze arrived at the plant on April 24, 1931, studied the situation and helped the management to draw up a realistic production programme and map out ways of removing flagrant shortcomings in labour organisation. A *Pravda* team of correspondents headed by Alexander Kosarev, Secretary of the C.C. Y.C.L., worked at the plant for a long time. The situation improved and on April 20, 1932, the plant began working at its planned capacity, turning out 144 tractors a day. The experience of this plant was taken into account at the Kharkov Tractor Plant, which reached its planned capacity much more swiftly.

New machinery was thus mastered and skilled workers trained while the five-year plan was being fulfilled. Facilities for training workers and apprentices were set up at the largest factories. A technical examination was instituted for workers and employees. The workers learned to operate machinery. The country built, studied and grew.

Extensive use was made of the achievements of world science and technology: machinery and machine-tools were imported, Soviet workers and specialists were sent for training abroad and foreign workers and specialists were invited to the U.S.S.R. to teach Soviet workers to operate new equipment. The Soviet Government placed contracts with foreign firms to draw up projects for the reconstruction of old factories and the building of new plants.

On the whole, the utilisation of foreign machinery played a positive role. Many foreign workers and engineers, including F. Winter, M. Winter (who worked on the Dnieper hydropower scheme), Leon E. Swidjean and W. Murphy made a notable contribution to the building of socialism in the U.S.S.R. and were decorated with Soviet Orders.

But some of the foreign specialists who came to the U.S.S.R. were insufficiently qualified or were hostile to the Soviet system. Many foreign firms did not cope with the contract assignments. For example, engineers from the American Freyn Corporation drew up the project for the Kuznetsk Iron and Steel Works, but were unable to direct the realisation of the project. They acted only as consultants.

The American Mackee Company signed a contract for blueprints for the Magnitogorsk Iron and Steel Works but failed to cope with the task with the result that the contract was cancelled and the project drawn up by Soviet engineers.

Results of the First Five-Year Plan in Industry

The First Five-Year Plan was completed by the close of 1932, in four years and three months. That was the most notable event in the history of those years. Even the bourgeois press could not pass it over in silence. The U.S. magazine *Nation* wrote in November 1932: "The four years of the five-year plan have witnessed truly remarkable developments.... Russia is working with wartime intensity on the positive task of building the physical and social molds of a new life. The face of the country is being changed literally beyond recognition."

Soviet achievements were also admitted by the British magazine *Forward*: "Russia is building up a new society on what are, generally speaking, fundamentally sound lines. To do this it is taking risks, it is working enthusiastically with an energy that has never been seen in the world before... it has tremendous difficulties to contend with, difficulties inseparable from this attempt to build up socialism in a vast, underdeveloped country isolated from the rest of the world."

Indeed, the Soviet Union carried out a vast building programme without foreign economic aid. In the course of the five-year plan it built 1,500 industrial enterprises, around which sprang up towns with a numerous population. Such were Magnitogorsk, Kuznetsk, Khibinogorsk, Komsomolsk-on-Amur and many other towns.

The First Five-Year Plan gave the economy a large material and technical basis, which enabled it, during the Second Five-Year Plan, to complete the technical modernisation of all branches of the economy. The industrial product increased by 170 per cent as compared with 1913, while its share in the country's economy rose from 48 to 70 per cent. In total industrial output the U.S.S.R. outstripped Britain, France and Germany to occupy first place in Europe and second place in the world.

In 1928-32, the U.S.S.R. imported 17,300 million rubles' worth of equipment, mostly capital goods. In 1932, the import of machinery diminished drastically. The task of turning the U.S.S.R. from an importer of machines and equipment to a country manufacturing them, first set by the Fourteenth Party Congress, was now being successfully carried out. In the course of the five-year plan the output of the engineering industry rose by 300 per cent over the 1928 level, while the output of farm machines increased by 450 per cent.

New industries—tractor, automobile, aircraft, chemicals, engineering and munitions—were built, while the iron and steel industry doubled its output.

Lenin's famous plan of electrification was carried out in the course of the First Five-Year Plan period. Its targets were passed by 1931: district power stations' output exceeded 2,000,000 kw as against the 1,500,000 kw called for by the plan.

Successful electrification and the building up of an engineering industry made it possible to step up the mechanisation of the basic branches of the economy. When the five-year plan was started only 15 per cent of work in the coal industry was mechanised, but towards the end of the five-year plan mechanisation covered more than 63 per cent of the work. The picture was the same in all the key industries: the Soviet Union was accomplishing a complete technical revolution.

One outstanding result of the First Five-Year Plan was the growth of the working class from 11,600,000 in 1928 to 22,900,000 in 1932. The share of industrial workers rose to one-third of the gainfully employed population. Almost all the workers were employed in socialist industry, which turned out 99.3 per cent of the industrial output; private capital accounted for only 0.7 per cent. The question of "Who will beat whom" in industry had been finally and irrevocably decided in favour of socialism.

Profound changes took place among the working class: its members acquired greater political knowledge and higher technical qualifications: large numbers of seasonal workers learned trades and became skilled workers. A number of arduous trades involving manual labour, particularly in the mines, disappeared.

The national composition of the working class changed as well: the building of new plants in Central Asia, Transcaucasia and the non-Russian republics in the Russian Federation accelerated the rise of a local working class.

Aided by modern machinery Soviet workers increased labour productivity in industry as a whole by 41 per cent and in heavy industry by 53.1 per cent. For the rate of growth of labour productivity the U.S.S.R. overtook the leading capitalist countries, thus giving further proof of the advantages of socialism over capitalism.

By 1930, as a result of the rapid growth of the industrial working class and the reorganisation that had been begun in the countryside, unemployment, the bugbear of workers in capitalist countries, had been wiped out. For the first time in human history the working class became confident of the morrow, of always having employment. The right to work was guaranteed to every Soviet citizen.

The abolition of unemployment was an epoch-making triumph of Soviet society.

In 1932, the leading capitalist countries had huge armies of unemployed: in the U.S.A. the number of unemployed reached 11,500,000, in Germany 5,600,000 and in Britain 2,300,000.

The successes of socialist industrialisation brought their first tangible results in improved standards of living. In the course of the five-year plan period wages rose by 103.6 per cent, topping the plan target by 44 per cent.

More than 4,000 million rubles were invested in urban housing. Many workers' families were moved from temporary dwellings to modern apartment buildings.

The shortest working day in the world was instituted in the U.S.S.R.: in the early 1930s more than 80 per cent of the factories went over to a seven-hour working day, while in industries involving work of a dangerous nature and for miners working below the surface the working day was shortened to six hours.

The state made every effort to organise more facilities for recreation, to improve free medical assistance, social insurance and the pension scheme, and promote public education. In the course of the five-year plan the allocations for social insurance were increased by more than 300 per cent, for public health by over 200 per cent, for education by 500 per cent, for scholarship grants by 1,300 per cent, and so forth.

In 1931, the Communist Party passed a decision to improve municipal economy throughout the country and, in particular, to reconstruct Moscow and make it a model for all big towns in the country. Under the plan approved by the Party in 1931, construction was started on an underground railway in Moscow, many of the capital's streets and squares were replanned, and the building of the Moskva-Volga Canal was begun. A plan for the reconstruction of Leningrad was approved, and extensive work was started on building housing and everyday services in other towns.

However, on account of the rapid growth of the urban population there was a shortage of modern housing. Great difficulties were encountered in supplying the towns with food. During the First Five-Year Plan period bread and other food were rationed. However, these were temporary difficulties; rationing was ended at the close of 1932. Noteworthy improvements were introduced in everyday services, medical assistance and public health.

First steps towards industrialisation were taken in the Central Asian Republics, Kazakhstan and the Transcaucasian Republics. Power stations, cotton and silk mills, and heavy and food industries were built in Central Asia. Mines were built in the Karaganda Basin of Kazakhstan. Other major projects included a ferrous metallurgical plant at Ridderovo, a lead plant at Chimkent and a chemical plant at Aktyubinsk. In Azerbaijan the oil industry was reconstructed, and coal and cotton industries were founded in Georgia and Armenia. Wood-working plants were built in the Komi Autonomous Republic.

The Ukrainian and Byelorussian republics were conspicuously successful in developing their industry.

The Ukraine invested 9,400 million rubles in economic development in the course of four years of the five-year plan. This enabled her fundamentally to reconstruct her key industrial regions and start the building of new projects. The Donbas began to produce almost twice as much coal annually as in 1913.

Byelorussia became an industrial republic during the First Five-Year Plan. She enlarged her power-generating facilities and built new industries: fuel, engineering and chemical. In the central regions industrial output doubled during the First Five-Year Plan, but in the non-Russian republics it increased by 250 per cent. This was a significant triumph of the Leninist nationalities policy aimed at surmounting the economic backwardness of the former oppressed peoples.

The successful fulfilment of the First Five-Year Plan had tremendous repercussions throughout the world. The U.S.S.R. strengthened its economic might and independence, becoming a major force in international life. Its defence potential was also increased.

Delegations from almost all countries in the world visited the Soviet Union during the five-year plan period. They saw for themselves that the working masses could administer the country without landowners and capitalists, that the new, socialist system had indisputable advantages. There were no economic crises or unemployment, an intrinsic part of capitalism, and the people were guaranteed a steadily rising standard of living.

Once an agrarian country, the U.S.S.R. became an industrial power during the First Five-Year Plan. Industrial development continued during the second and third pre-war five-year plans. By accomplishing the country's industrialisation, the working class and entire Soviet people performed a great exploit. Economically, the U.S.S.R. became completely independent of the capitalist world.

Revolutionary Changes in the Countryside

Preparations for Collectivisation

For long centuries the peasants had lived in the same old way, farming on a small scale and each depending on himself for his welfare. True, there were occasions when the peasants came to the assistance of a fellow-villager in the building of a house, threshing corn or harvesting grain. Prior to the Revolution there also were agricultural co-operatives, but these engaged chiefly in supply and marketing. But neither peasant mutual aid nor rural co-operatives could bring the pre-revolution countryside to socialism, because the basic implements and means of production were privately owned and power was in the hands of the landowners and capitalists. The Great October Socialist Revolution and the deep-going reforms instituted by it—the confiscation of the landed estates and nationalisation and redistribution of land, implements and draught animals—were needed to enable the countryside to overcome its backwardness and to deliver it from the domination of landowners, kulaks and usurers, from the rule of private capital.

But even after the Revolution the countryside remained a sea of small peasant farms among which the socialist communities—co-operatives, communes and state farms—were like tiny islands.

The ways of reorganising the small peasant economy into large-scale socialist enterprises had been mapped long before the Revolution by Marx and Engels and then by Lenin. Their purpose had not been to destroy or expropriate the property of the small peasant, to deprive him of his means of subsistence. "When we are in possession of state power," Engels wrote, "we shall not even think of forcibly expropriating the small peasants (regardless of whether with or without compensation), as we shall have to do in the case of the big landowners. Our task relative to the small peasant consists, in the first place, in effecting a transition of his private enterprise and private possession to co-operative ones, not forcibly but by dint of example and the proffer of socialist assistance for this purpose."*

After the Communist Party, headed by Lenin, came to power it it did not set itself the task of immediately reorganising the small peasant farms. The Party knew that collectivisation would save the peasant from the disadvantages of small-scale farming and serve to uplift agriculture, combat the kulaks and free the peasants from exploitation. But the peasants did not realise that. "We were well aware," Lenin wrote, "that the peasants live rooted to the soil. The peasants fear innovations, they cling tenaciously to old habits. We knew that the peasants would come to believe in the benefits of any particular measure only when their own intelligence led them to understand and appreciate these benefits."**

It took twelve years after the Revolution to create the prerequisites for the collectivisation of agriculture.

The main prerequisite was the establishment of Soviet power and the creation of a new social system founded on the nationalisation of the banks, large-scale industry, trade, transport and land. This gave rise to new laws governing the development of small-scale peasant farming. Small peasant economies have the same features as capitalist economies, for large, kulak farms grow out of them. Soviet rule made it possible to regulate the class stratification in the countryside, restrict the growth of kulak farms and raise the economies of the poorest section of the peasants to the status of middle peasant farms. The middle peasant became the central figure of the Soviet countryside. For the first time in history small peasant farms were given the possibility of joining in the building of socialism through co-operatives.

Prior to collectivisation there had been a struggle between two trends: the capitalist trend which was the consequence of the development of the petty-peasant economy, and the socialist trend that stemmed from the development of co-operatives. Soviet power did its utmost to restrict the former tendency and encourage the latter. That prepared the ground for a fundamental reorganisation of petty-peasant farming.

The Soviet Government kept the peasant farms supplied with basic farm implements—ploughs, harrows, seeders and threshers—and in 1928-29 it began to supply them with tractors and other modern machines. However, not all the small peasant farms could

---

* Marx, Engels, *Selected Works*, Vol. II, p. 433.
** Lenin, *Alliance of the Working Class and the Peasantry*, Moscow, p. 241.

Ploughing virgin land at the Hammer and Sickle State Farm, 1932

Spring sowing at an individual peasant farm, 1927

Peasants joining a collective farm, 1929

Team of workers repair farm implements at the Tverskaya
Pravda Collective Farm, 1929

Workers leaving for Central Asia to help peasants, 1930

First tractors made at the Chelyabinsk Tractor Works

afford to purchase these machines and implements. In order to buy them the peasants united in associations. Co-operative and state enterprises set up hire stations and fleets of tractors to help agriculture.

The available farm implements were distributed very unevenly. Most of them were in the hands of the middle peasants. A considerable number of the poorest farms had no implements at all or experienced an acute shortage of them. Moreover, a considerable portion of the means of production was concentrated at the kulak farms. The poor and small middle-peasant farms had to hire draught animals and implements from the kulaks on onerous terms or lease part of their land allotments to them. Collectivisation was the only way out for these farms.

The main difficulty of the early period of collectivisation was that there was a shortage of technical resources—tractors, harvester combines and other machines for large-scale collective farming. In 1928, the U.S.S.R. had 27,000 tractors, and in 1929 their number rose to 35,000.

The fundamentally new feature in the utilisation of tractors and other farm machines was that it was linked up with the organisation of collective farms. An illustration of this is the help given by the Shevchenko State Farm, in the Ukraine, to the peasants in the surrounding villages. In 1927, the land of these peasants was ploughed by tractors from the state farm with the result that they harvested a larger crop than their neighbours.

The outcome of this assistance was that the peasants decided to work their land collectively by using the tractor fleet belonging to the state farm. This experiment led to the setting up of machine-and-tractor fleets and then machine-and-tractor stations that served the collective farms.*

The technical reconstruction of agriculture proceeded simultaneously with the organisation and consolidation of the collective farms.

Steps were taken by the Soviet Government to accelerate the enlargement of the farm machine industry. The Stalingrad Tractor Plant with an output capacity of 50,000 tractors a year was completed in 1930; in 1931, the Kharkov Tractor Plant was built and construction was in full swing on a tractor plant in Chelyabinsk; the Rostov Farm Machines Plant was commissioned in 1930 and the harvester machines plant at Zaporozhye began putting out

---

* Machine-and-tractor stations were state-run enterprises which concluded agreements with the collective farms under which they ploughed the land and harvested and transported the crops. The collective farms paid for these services in kind and in cash. The machines were operated by personnel permanently employed by the machine-and-tractor stations and also by collective farmers temporarily assigned to this work during the field-work and harvesting season.—Ed.

harvester-combines. In 1932, agriculture was served by 148,000 tractors with a total capacity of 2,200,000 hp and by 14,000 lorries.

The number of machine-and-tractor stations rose from one in 1928 to 360 in 1930 and to 2,446 by the end of the First Five-Year Plan period.

These stations were prominent in promoting collectivisation. By setting them up the Soviet Government freed the collective farms from the large expense of purchasing tractors, harvester-combines and other machines and helped them to stand on their own feet.

A consistent policy of strengthening the alliance between the working class and the peasants was the prerequisite for the rise of the collective-farm system in the Soviet Union. Consolidation of this alliance was furthered by the fact that the peasants were drawn into the development of the Soviet state, by state aid to the peasants, and by the organisation of co-operatives in the countryside. This alliance was also strengthened in the struggle against the kulaks, who in their opposition to socialist construction kept disrupting the Soviet government's efforts to raise the peasants' living standards.

More than ever the kulaks intensified their anti-Soviet activities in 1928 when the country faced an acute food shortage. The small peasant farms were unable to meet the grain requirements which had increased on account of the growth of the urban population, while the kulaks who had considerable grain surpluses refused to sell them to the state, thus threatening to leave the towns and the army without food and hold up industrialisation.

Much was done by the Communist Party to alleviate the grain shortage: the grain purchasing system was improved and more consumer goods were sent to the countryside in exchange for food. The kulaks were made to pay taxes and were prosecuted for food profiteering. The 1928 kulak sabotage was broken and the grain delivery plan was fulfilled.

The Soviet government pushed ahead with the development of collective and state farms. Rapid industrialisation made this an urgent task because small-scale farming could not meet the growing demand for raw materials for industry and for bread for the population and the army. The expansion of the socialist economy of the towns was held up by the backwardness of agriculture. The only solution was to go over from small peasant holdings to large-scale, socialist farming.

Lenin's famous co-operative plan defined how to reorganise agriculture. Drawing upon this plan the Fifteenth Party Congress (end of 1927) stated that collectivisation was the Party's principal task in the countryside. The broad co-operation movement prepared the peasants for transition to collective farming.

By setting up various types of co-operatives—from the simplest supply and sales co-operatives to the highest forms of production co-operatives (artels, communes and associations for the joint tilling of the land), the Soviet government taught the peasants to farm collectively. Through the co-operatives the government established direct contact with the peasant farms and concluded agreements with them for the delivery of farm produce and regulated their development.

Nearly 70 per cent of all peasant households joined the cooperation movement in 1929-30.

The first communes and artels, which showed the peasants the advantages of collective farming, played an important part in preparing the ground for collectivisation: their crop yields were higher, their livestock and machines were better looked after, and their members had higher living and cultural standards. The peasants from the surrounding villages arranged tours of the first communes and artels, displaying a heightened interest in the new life.

Bulk of the Peasants Join Collective Farms

Peasant co-operation in production began to grow into a movement, embracing both the poor and middle peasants, to set up collective farms. The turn of the bulk of the working peasants to collective farming was the decisive stage in the fulfilment of the first part of Lenin's co-operative plan.

This movement started in the second half of 1929: the number of peasant households in collective farms rose from 1,000,000 on July 1 to 2,000,000 on October 1 and to 4,700,000 towards the end of December 1929. In other words, within six months the number of households in the collective farms rose by almost 400 per cent, comprising nearly 20 per cent of the total number of peasant households in the U.S.S.R.

Collectivisation proceeded at an extremely fast rate in the main grain regions: it embraced 67.9 per cent of the peasant households in the Lower Volga area, 35-37 per cent in the North Caucasus and about 30 per cent along the Middle Volga.

This voluntary, mass movement to unite in collective farms showed that a radical change had taken place in the minds of the peasants, who had seen the practical advantages of large-scale socialist farming over small, individual holdings. Entire villages, districts and even regions joined the movement to set up collective farms.

At a Plenary Meeting in November 1929, the C.C. C.P.S.U.(B.) examined the results of collectivisation and its further tasks, noting that "these outstanding successes of the collective-farm movement are the direct outcome of the consistent implementation of the Party's general line". The Plenary Meeting declared that "a *new and historic stage* of the socialist transformation of agriculture is beginning"* and instructed all organisations to concentrate not on the pursuit after high indices but on the qualitative side of collectivisation, on strengthening the collective farms, implementing the Leninist principle of giving the collective farmers material incentives with the object of making their work on the collective farms more productive, on creating socialised assets as the basis of collective-farm development, and so on.

The Party condemned the Right opportunist suggestion that industrialisation and the socialist transformation of agriculture should be slowed down.

The Plenary Meeting decided to begin the accelerated building of the technical basis for collectivisation and to set up a People's Commissariat for Agriculture to direct the collective and state farms.

A commission to summarise the experience of nation-wide collectivisation and settle the practical problems of implementing it was set up in December 1929 at the request of local Party organisations. Its proposals were embodied in a resolution on the speed of collectivisation and what measures should be taken by the state to help the development of collective farms. This resolution, passed by the C.C. C.P.S.U.(B.) on January 5, 1930, was a concrete plan for collectivisation.

Provision was made for building more tractor plants and for increasing credits to collective farms. It was emphasised that under no circumstances should the peasants be coerced into joining collective farms. The Party Central Committee warned all local organisations against "ordering" the collective-farm movement from above. Lastly, the approximate schedule for collectivisation was established in the C.C. decision for different parts of the country.

Liquidation of the Kulaks as a Class

Successful collectivisation on a mass scale raised the question of the destiny of the kulak farms in a new way. Prior to collectivisation the Soviet government had pursued a policy of restricting them.

As a result of this policy, some kulaks stopped using hired labour and leasing land, becoming middle peasants. The number of kulak farms diminished from about 15 per cent in 1918 to approximately 4-5 per cent (1,100,000 households) in 1928. However, the kulaks remained the last and most numerous exploiter class with considerable means of production. They played a substantial role in the output of marketable grain. In 1927 they sold the state 20 per cent of all its marketable grain.

---

* KPSS v resolyutsiyakh... (C.P.S.U. in Resolutions...), Part II, Moscow, 1954, pp. 643, 645.

When mass collectivisation was started, they stepped up their struggle against the collective farms, instituting a reign of terror against the Soviet authorities and leaders of the collective-farm movement. In the Ukraine, for example, 290 acts of terrorism, were registered at the end of 1928 and in 1929. A counter-revolutionary organisation of kulaks and ex-officers, who were plotting an armed uprising, was uncovered in the Khoper District, the Lower Volga, in 1929. The kulaks set fire to collective-farm buildings and spread malicious rumours about the collective farms.

The peasants who joined collective farms themselves demanded that no kulaks be admitted as members.

Mass collectivisation thus brought to the fore the question of liquidating the kulaks as a class.

Why was the Soviet government able to pass from restricting the kulaks to liquidating them as a class only in 1929-30? The explanation is that by that time the balance of class forces in the country had changed in favour of socialism. The growth of the socialist sector in industry was accompanied by an increase of the urban population, and of the working class, the main, leading force in the struggle for socialism. At the same time, the mass movement for collectivisation brought the bulk of the peasants, particularly the middle peasants, to the collective farms, which became the mainstay of Soviet rule in the countryside. All this enabled the government to proceed with liquidating the kulaks as a class.

Another factor that made this policy feasible was the growth of collective- and state-farm production. Already in 1929 the collective and state farms gave the country 2,080,000 tons of marketable grain, i.e., a larger quantity than was sold by the kulaks, while in 1930 they planned to increase their sales to the state to over 6,400,000 tons, making it possible to get along without the kulaks.

In the acute inner-Party struggle of that period the Right opportunist theory of the peaceful growth of the kulaks into socialism was exposed and defeated. Events showed that the kulaks were hostile to collectivisation.

The new policy was framed in the above-mentioned resolution of the Party C.C. of January 5, 1930, and in the resolution of the Central Executive Committee and Council of People's Commissars of February 1, 1930 "On Measures to Consolidate the Socialist Reorganisation of Agriculture in Areas Entirely Embraced by Collectivisation and on the Struggle Against the Kulaks".

The substance of this policy was first and foremost to deprive the kulaks of their productive sources of subsistence. They were deprived of the right to the free use of land, implements and means of production and of the right to lease land and to hire labour.

In areas where there was total collectivisation the transfer of land to the collective farms closed the door to the growth of kulak holdings. When the poorest sections of the peasants began joining collective farms en masse the kulaks were deprived of the opportunity of growing rich by exploiting hired labour. The dispossessing of the kulaks of the means of production was not a mere administrative measure. It took the form of a public campaign in which the Soviet authorities and the peasants who had joined collective farms participated. The question of dispossessing individual kulaks was debated beforehand at meetings of poor peasants and at general meetings of peasants in the villages.

The kulaks and their families were moved to new localities where they were given the chance of working productively. Some of them moved to towns or other districts, where they were given employment at factories or state farms. Those that worked conscientiously received all the rights of citizens. But determined steps were taken against those who continued their anti-Soviet struggle by engaging in subversive activities and sabotage.

In the course of two years (1930-32) 240,757 kulak families—approximately one per cent of the peasant households or about a quarter of the kulak households—were moved out of the areas which had been collectivised.

Total collectivisation and the liquidation of the kulaks as a class came to be radical revolutionary turning point in the relations of production in the countryside.

This revolutionary change could not have been effected without the participation of the masses themselves. Collectivisation was carried out by the peasants, urban workers, the rural intelligentsia, the Soviets and numerous mass organisations. A leading role was played by the workers of Moscow, Leningrad, Ivanovo-Voznesensk, Kharkov, Dnepropetrovsk and other major industrial centres.

The new collective farms required chairmen, team-leaders, agronomists, experts in land exploitation, bookkeepers and other trained personnel. These people were trained at higher and secondary agricultural educational institutions, at short-term courses and at large collective and state farms, where they could study advanced methods of organising labour and utilising machines.

Taking into consideration the features of the initial stage of collective-farm development, the C.C. C.P.S.U.(B.), at its Plenary Meeting in November 1929, decided to send industrial workers to the collective farms and machine-and-tractor stations. For this purpose in early 1930 trade union and Party organisations selected 25,000 industrial workers with sufficient organisational and political experience. They were the foremost representatives of the working class, profoundly devoted to the Party and Soviet Government, with experience of the class struggle and of proletarian collectivism and organisation. Of these 25,000 workers 89 per cent were veteran workers, and about 70 per cent were Communists.

They arrived in the villages in February and March 1930 when mass collectivisation was at its height. Most of them were appointed to the management of the new collective farms, chiefly as chairmen of the boards. M. Ivanov, a Moscow worker, headed the Kuibyshev Collective Farm, Ryazan Region, V. Lyukshin became chairman of the Druzhba Collective Farm, Moscow Region, I. Buyanov managed the Vladimir Ilyich Collective Farm, Moscow Region, and the Dnepropetrovsk metalworker G. Litovchenko became chairman of the largest collective farm in Genichesk District, Kherson Region. Many of the 25,000 workers won distinction as heads of collective farms and were made Heroes of Socialist Labour.

The epic story of these workers is wonderfully told in Mikhail Sholokhov's *Virgin Soil Upturned.*

The peasants themselves promoted many outstanding organisers from among their midst. This, too, testified to the vitality and strength of the new, collective-farm system created under the leadership of the Communist Party.

Working-class assistance was not limited to the dispatch of 25,000 workers. Factories sent teams to repair farm machines, help with the sowing and carry on educational work. Industrial workers initiated socialist emulation between rural districts and factories.

A large contribution towards the socialist transformation of the countryside was made by the rural intelligentsia, particularly by teachers. In the eyes of the peasants the village teacher was the most authoritative representative of the intelligentsia and everybody heeded his voice.

The Red Army too assisted the countryside: not less than 100,000 demobilised officers and men were trained for practical work at the collective farms as tractor-operators, drivers, accountants and team-leaders.

The poorest section of the peasants and the farm labourers played an important role in collectivisation. Early in 1930 the Russian Federation alone had 24,000 poor peasant and farm labourer groups that united nearly a quarter of a million people. These groups existed in all organisations: on collective-farm boards, in rural Soviets and co-operatives.

The development of the collective farms confronted the rural Soviets with new tasks, one of which was to organise new collective farms. On January 25, 1930, with the aim of improving the work of rural Soviets, the Central Executive Committee passed a resolution "On the Tasks of the Soviets in Collectivisation", which made provision for new elections to the Soviets in districts completely covered by collectivisation. The aim was to promote capable organisers of the collective-farm movement to the leadership of the Soviets. In the period when collective farms were being set up throughout the Soviet Union, the Communist Party and Soviet government gave the countryside day-to-day assistance.

Difficulties and Errors in the Development of Collective Farms

The collective-farm movement expanded rapidly in January and February 1930, when more than 10 million peasant households joined collective farms. However, the initial period of collective-farm development witnessed considerable difficulties, errors and distortions of the Party line.

The main difficulty was that in this very period the capitalist countries tried to organise another intervention against the Soviet Union. An anti-Soviet campaign in defence of the kulaks prepared public opinion in the West for this provocation. This incited the kulaks to oppose collectivisation. Influenced by malicious tales spread by the kulaks, the peasants began slaughtering their livestock, greatly reducing the livestock population. This had a disastrous effect on the future development of livestock-breeding. The kulaks had the support of several underground bourgeois counter-revolutionary organisations. In the period of mass collectivisation state security bodies discovered anti-Soviet organisations in transport and in some industries. The leading role among them was played by the so-called Industrial Party. It was linked up with former Russian capitalists living abroad, who had formed a Trade Industrial Committee. This committee and the Industrial Party, which were in contact with the intelligence services of the capitalist countries, plotted another anti-Soviet intervention.

The Labour Peasant Party, headed by kulak ideologists named Kondratyev and Chayanov, was associated with the Industrial Party. Members of the former party infiltrated the People's Commissariat for Agriculture as specialists and tried to disrupt the financing of the collective farms, muddle sowing plans and plant homesteads with the purpose of preserving the kulaks as a class.

In 1931, the security forces also brought to light an anti-Soviet Menshevik organisation that called itself the Allied Bureau. It was headed by a Menshevik named Sukhanov. Its members had entrenched themselves in the Supreme Economic Council, the State Planning Commission, the Central Co-operative Union and the State Bank, where they made every effort to confuse planning and disorganise production. The class struggle spread from the countryside to the towns and was sustained from abroad.

The criminal activities of the various counter-revolutionary organisations were cut short by the Soviet courts with the approval of the entire Soviet people.

The absence of private land ownership was one of the key factors that made the transition to the establishment of collective farms relatively painless.

However, collectivisation was a difficult undertaking because it involved the rearrangement of the way of life of many millions of peasants who had no experience of large-scale collective farming.

The difficulties in the promotion of collective farming were made all the greater by the major errors that were committed in the process of collectivisation. Lenin had repeatedly warned the Party that there should be no haste, ordering or pressure in the question of switching the small peasant households to collective farming. He stressed that force with regard to the middle peasants was a crime.

Stalin disregarded Lenin's advice and in a number of cases acted hastily and brought pressure to bear on local Party organisations in the question of collectivisation. On December 27, 1929, speaking at a conference of Marxists in the countryside, he said that collectivisation was proceeding with relative ease. Stalin underestimated the peasant's attachment to his small holding and his small-proprietor habits.

Signs that the Party line in the question of collectivisation was being violated and that the peasants were being subjected to ordering and pressure became evident as early as the end of 1929. Stalin, Molotov and other members of the Political Bureau were informed of this at a Plenary Meeting of the C.C. in November 1929 but failed to take the proper steps. On top of that, after the Plenary Meeting the central Party and Soviet press began printing articles urging a faster rate of collectivisation. In particular, *Pravda* ran an editorial which said that collectivisation of 75 per cent of the peasant households by the spring of 1930 was not the limit.

The forced rate of collectivisation upset the schedule that had been drawn up in the C.C. resolution of January 5, 1930.

In Moscow Region, for example, the authorities decided to complete collectivisation in 1930 despite the fact that they had more than three years at their disposal. The collective farms hastily set up in this way without careful preparations soon collapsed.

Thus, the violation of the schedule of collectivisation as a result of the forced pace was the first error. An error accompanying it was that the voluntary nature of membership in collective farms was disregarded. Instead of patiently explaining the government's policy to the hesitating middle peasants, the latter were forced to join the collective farms and some were even dispossessed. Another gross error was the violation of the Party's resolutions on collectivisation, where it was said that the artel would be the main type of collective farm. Communes with socialised herds of sheep, goats and pigs, poultry and dwellings began to be set up in various parts of the country.

As a whole, the errors in collectivisation in early 1930 were an infraction of the Leninist policy towards the peasants. They seriously endangered the very idea of collectivisation and threat-ened the alliance between the working class and the peasants. Distortions of the Party line caused discontent among the peasants, who in some places resisted collectivisation.

The whole Party had to make a tremendous effort to rectify the errors and distortions in the collective-farm movement.

Steps were taken to this end by the Party Central Committee. In a special resolution on February 20, 1930, on collectivisation in the Transcaucasian and Central Asian republics and in the non-Russian areas of the R.S.F.S.R., the Central Committee warned the local authorities against applying the forms and methods of collectivisation that had been used in regions that were more prepared for the establishment of collective farms. The Central Committee instructed the local Party organisations to concen-trate on preparations for collectivisation and to take the national and economic features of the various regions into account.

The Model Rules of the Agricultural Artel were amended in February 1930 and published on March 2. On the same day *Pravda* published Stalin's article "Dizzy with Success", written at the request of the C.C. Political Bureau.

The article emphasised that coercion was impermissible in col-lectivisation. This was favourably received by the peasants and calmed the bulk of them, but could not stop some from leaving the collective farms.

On the other hand, Stalin gave a one-sided explanation of the reasons for the errors and distortions of the Party's policy. He blamed local Party workers for these errors, groundlessly accus-ing them of being "dizzy with success".

At the same time, carried away by the success of collectivisa-tion, Stalin and Molotov urged local Party workers to accelerate the rate of collectivisation. Up until February 1930 they did nothing to stop the distortions of the Party line. Stanislav Kosior, a Ukranian leader and a member of the C.C. Political Bureau said that success had turned the heads of all sections of the Party and government apparatus, including the leadership in the centre.

In an important decree On the Struggle Against Distortions of the Party Line in Collective-Farm Development, adopted on March 14, 1930, the Central Committee instructed Party organisa-tions to stop the practice of forcing peasants to join collective farms and, at the same time, to proceed with collectivisation along voluntary lines. Party and local government officials were given the task of strengthening the collective farms organisationally and economically.

The errors were rectified and dissatisfaction among the peasants ceased.

The government gave the new collective farms a number of privileges and considerable help in organising production, thus consolidating the successes of collectivisation. By July 1, 1930 the country had 86,000 collective farms, which united 6,000,000 or about 24 per cent of all the peasant households. The enemy's attempts to frustrate mass collectivisation came to nothing.

The supply of machines to the villages played a substantial role in strengthening the collective-farm system. During the First Five-Year Plan period agriculture was supplied with 120,000 tractors totalling 1,900,000 hp and 1,600 million rubles' worth of other farm machines. Towards the end of 1932 there were about 2,500 machine-and-tractor stations serving the collective farms.

In that period the state machine-and-tractor stations were the most efficient form of utilising farm machinery. Concentration of machinery at these stations enabled the state to render considerable production aid to the collective farms, promote their development and teach the collective farmers a new, socialist attitude to work and new ways of organising farming.

Historic Importance of Collectivisation

The collective-farm system was firmly consolidated throughout the country by the end of the First Five-Year Plan period, when collectivisation was, in the main, completed in the principal grain areas: the Middle and Lower Volga, the North Caucasus, the Ukraine and the Crimea, where from 68 to 90 per cent of the peasant households were organised into collective farms. On a nation-wide scale the collective farms united 61.5 per cent of the peasant households and nearly 70 per cent of the crop area owned by the peasants. The five-year plan period witnessed the setting up of 211,000 collective farms and also the organisation of 5,000 state farms on disused land. In 1933, the collective and state farms delivered to the state more than 16,000,000 tons of grain, accounting for the bulk of the country's farm output.

A revolutionary change had taken place in the countryside: private peasant ownership of the implements and means of production was transformed into public ownership, while the small peasant economy was replaced by large-scale farming. That was a major step towards building the foundations of socialism in the U.S.S.R.

As is stated in the Programme of the C.P.S.U., adopted at the Twenty-Second Party Congress, the "introduction in the Soviet countryside of large-scale socialist farming meant *a great* *revolution in economic relations, in the entire way of life of the peasantry.* Collectivisation for ever delivered the countryside from kulak bondage, from class differentiation, ruin and poverty. The real solution of the eternal peasant question was provided by the Lenin co-operative plan".*

While continuing with its policy of drawing peasants into collective farms, the government now laid stress on strengthening the collective and state farms organisationally and economically, for not all the new collective and state farms were properly organised. Because of that there was even a drop in the total output of farm products, particularly of grain and animal products, in the early period of collectivisation. Many of the new farms operated at a loss. The Communist Party did not conceal these shortcomings.

New production relations and other new elements were engendered in face of tremendous difficulties. The new collective farmers were still in the grip of private-ownership mentality. Nobody had any experience of collective labour, and the collective-farm leaders knew nothing about managing large enterprises. There was petty-bourgeois levelling in the distribution of the social product. That deprived the collective farmers of the incentive to promote socialised farming and raise labour productivity. Hostile elements wormed themselves into the collective farms and undermined them from within.

Under these conditions the collective and state farms could not be expected to grow stronger straightaway. The collective farmers acquired experience in the struggle against difficulties and found the right way of organising labour by introducing work-days with payment by piece-rate. The work-day covered a definite volume of work, in which account was taken of the type of work. The incomes of the collective farms were distributed in kind or in cash against work-days at the end of the year, and the value of the work-day was determined depending on the income received by the collective farm as a whole. The more efficiently a collective farm was run the larger was the payment in kind and in cash per work-day. The Sixth Congress of Soviets of the U.S.S.R., which sat in March 1931, recommended that all collective farms should use the work-day as a measure of social labour and distribution, while in June 1931 a Plenary Meeting of the C.C. C.P.S.U.(B.) suggested transferring all work to a piece-rate, evaluating work and distributing incomes by work-days. This innovation was welcomed by the collective farmers. All collective farms went over to work-days in 1931.

An important role in organising labour at the collective farms was played by production teams, which were given definite plots

---

* *The Road to Communism*, Moscow, p. 458.

172

of land, draught animals and machines. Payment against work-days depended on the results of the work of the team.

In 1933 compulsory grain deliveries to the state at fixed prices were instituted for the collective farms; the delivery quota was determined on the basis of per hectare of crop area. Surplus grain could be sold in the open market.

To stop subversive activities by the kulaks and other hostile elements against collective-farm property, the Central Executive Committee and Council of People's Commissars passed a decree (on August 7, 1932) protecting socialist property. Like the property of the state, collective-farm property was declared sacred and inviolable. Stern punishment was meted out to people who encroached upon this property.

I the Kula had liquid

The political departments set up in January 1933 at the machine-and-tractor stations and state farms were prominent in strengthening the state and collective farms organisationally and economically.

At that difficult period for the collective farms the Communist Party and Soviet Government set about strengthening the Party leadership of the collective farms and raising the living standard of the collective farmers.

The attention of the All-Union Congress of Foremost Collective Farmers, held in February 1933, was focussed on that task. That Congress played an important role in promoting the political activity of the collective farmers.

Within a short space of time the political departments at the machine-and-tractor stations had done much to strengthen the new collective-farm system and help to organise labour at the collective farms more efficiently. This work bore fruit as early as the close of 1934, and a Plenary Meeting of the C.C. C.P.S.U.(B.), held in November of that year, passed a decision to reorganise the machine-and-tractor station political departments into ordinary Party bodies, which were merged with district Party committees. In 1935, the Second All-Union Congress of Foremost Collective Farmers drew up the Rules of the Agricultural Artel, which generalised the experience of collective-farm development. Founded on democratic principles of farming, the Rules opened the road to a further consolidation of the collective-farm system.

* * *

The successful fulfilment of the First Five-Year Plan radically changed the alignment of class forces in the country. A result of the decisive triumph of collectivisation was that agriculture and industry began to develop on a uniform, socialist foundation. A closer bond was forged between the working class and the collective-farm peasantry, which became the mainstay of Soviet rule in the countryside. Private ownership was abolished in industry and agriculture, and small commodity production was relegated to the background.

Socialist industrialisation created the material basis for the new, socialist society and led to the disappearance of capitalist elements in industry, while total collectivisation and the liquidation of the last exploiter class—the kulaks—completed the building of the economic foundation of socialism.

In the resolutions adopted by the Seventeenth Party Conference, it was stated that the "building of the foundation of socialism in the U.S.S.R. signified that the Leninist question of 'who will beat whom' has been decided against capitalism in favour of socialism finally and irrevocably both in town and country".

This economic victory and the signal successes in cultural development enabled the Soviet Union to complete the reconstruction of its economy and, in the main, build socialism during the Second Five-Year Plan period (1933-37).

U.S.S.R.—the First Country Where Socialism Triumphed

Second Five-Year Plan and Its Results. Victory of Socialism

Having surmounted enormous difficulties and fulfilled the First Five-Year Plan, the Soviet peoples built the foundation for socialist society, and during the Second Five-Year Plan period they completed, in the main, the building of socialism.

The Second Five-Year Plan was endorsed by the Seventeenth Party Congress early in 1934. It had far-reaching economic and political objectives: the building of over 4,500 new industrial enterprises, the commissioning of new plants that had been re-equipped during the First Five-Year Plan period, a considerable increase in the volume of industrial output, the complete technical reconstruction of the economy, a substantial rise in the standard of living and cultural level of the people, the completion of collectivisation, increase in the level of mechanisation in agriculture and strengthening the machine-and-tractor stations and collective and state farms organisationally and economically.

In the political field the main tasks were to eradicate all capitalist elements and causes giving rise to class differences and the exploitation of man by man, and eradicate capitalist survivals in the economy and in people's minds.

The struggle to fulfil the Second Five-Year Plan had a number of features of its own. First and foremost, there was considerably more machinery in industry and transport thanks to the commissioning of many new enterprises. In the coal industry, for example, mechanisation of cutting rose from 16.5 per cent in 1928 to 65.4 per cent in 1932 and to almost 90 per cent at the end of

1937. The railways were supplied with powerful new locomotives and new means of communication and signalling. New locomotive and railway carriage building plants were placed in operation.

At the beginning of the Second Five-Year Plan period the machine-and-tractor stations had a total of 75,000 tractors, which served approximately half of the collective-farm crop area.

The power generating facilities were enlarged: the main targets of the GOELRO plan were greatly surpassed by 1935. The output of power was doubled in the course of the five-year plan, exceeding 26,000 million kwh* in 1935. The engineering industry made rapid headway: mammoth plants like the Urals and Novo-Kramatorsk engineering works became operational during the Second Five-Year Plan period. The iron and steel industry brought the Urals and Kuznetsk plants up to their full output capacity and built new giant factories at Krivoi Rog, Novo-Lipetsk and Novo-Tula.

The large and developing material and technical base provided new conditions for the development of socialist society.

During the first two years of the Second Five-Year Plan the Soviet Union produced almost as large a quantity of machine-tools, machines and new equipment as during the First Five-Year Plan: the task of completing the technical reconstruction of the entire economy was being successfully carried out.

The production relations that were firmly established in the economy gave rise to new incentives for work and for raising labour productivity.

Parallel with material incentives deep roots were sunk by a new, communist attitude to work as a source of multiplying social wealth and enhancing the might of the Soviet state.

The availability of new technical means brought to the forefront the task of teaching the *masses* of the workers, peasants and all working people to handle them. The Communist Party put forward the motto "Cadres Decide Everything". This was a call to learn to operate the new machinery created during the period of industrialisation. The response to this call was that in all branches of the economy a movement was started for raising labour productivity and for revising technical quotas that no longer conformed with the new working conditions.

In industry and transport the army of shock workers grew to 5,000,000. The socialist emulation movement for revising the existing technical quotas and mastering new machinery became known as the Stakhanov movement, which was started in the Donbas.

On August 31, 1935, a young miner named Alexei Stakhanov cut 102 tons of coal with a mechanical pick in a single shift,

---

* In 1913 Russia's power output totalled 2,000 million kwh.—*Ed.*

exceeding the existing quota by 1,300 per cent. This remarkable achievement was not accidental. Following Stakhanov's example miners and workers in other industries achieved higher output quotas after they had correctly organised their work cycle and mastered new machinery. They included Pyotr Krivonos in the railway, Alexei Busygin in the automobile industry, N. Smetanin in the footwear industry, Yevdokia and Maria Vinogradova in the textile industry, and Maria Demchenko, Praskovya Angelina and Y. Borin in agriculture.

The Communist Party and Soviet Government gave the initiators of the new movement every encouragement. An All-Union Conference of Stakhanovite workers was held in the Kremlin in November 1935 with the participation of leaders of the Party and Government. Workers from different branches of industry told the conference how they had achieved a high level of labour productivity.

This new development was analysed at a Plenary Meeting of the C.C. C.P.S.U.(B.) in December 1935. The Stakhanovite movement, the Plenary Meeting pointed out, meant that labour was being organised in a new way, that technological processes were being rationalised. The movement was ensuring a rapid rise of labour productivity and a considerable growth of wages. It was raising the cultural and technical level of the working class, breaking the old technical quotas and, in some cases, surpassing the labour productivity in the leading capitalist countries.

The movement mirrored the new features of Soviet people, namely their concern for social welfare and their striving to make their personal achievements available to all workers.

As a result of the Stakhanov movement labour productivity in the course of the Second Five-Year Plan rose by 82 per cent instead of by 63 per cent as envisaged by the plan. Thanks to this, the Second Five-Year Plan, like the first, was fulfilled in four years and three months.

The results of the Second Five-Year Plan were truly remarkable: industrial output increased by more than 100 per cent as compared with 1932 and by almost 500 per cent as compared with 1913. A total of 4,500 industrial enterprises were commissioned; in 1937 the new factories accounted for 80 per cent of the Soviet industrial product.

By this time collectivisation had been nearly completed, resulting in the setting up of 243,500 collective farms which united 93 per cent of the peasant households. The collective farms had grown stronger organisationally and economically.

At the close of the Second Five-Year Plan the farms had 456,000 tractors, 128,000 harvester-combines and 146,000 lorries. Output increased. The crop area was enlarged by 30 million hectares as compared with 1913.

Fulfilment of the Second Five-Year Plan made it possible sharply to improve the standard of living: the national income rose to 96,300 million rubles as against 21,000 million rubles in 1913, the level of consumption doubled and the wages fund increased by more than 100 per cent. Important successes were scored in cultural development.

The Second Five-Year Plan was marked by an enormous rise in economic and cultural standards. What were backward outlying regions of the Russian Empire became advanced socialist republics with highly developed industries, agriculture and culture. Thanks to the Soviet system the peoples of Central Asia, Kazakhstan and some other regions were able to build socialism without having had to go through the tormenting process of capitalist development. Socialist nations consisting of two friendly classes— workers and peasants—united by common economic and political interests and aspirations took final shape towards the end of the Second Five-Year Plan period.

Significant social and economic changes took place in Soviet society.

Towards the close of the Second Five-Year Plan period socialism triumphed in industry, trade and agriculture, becoming the all-embracing system of economy. All other systems either perished or were absorbed by the socialist system. Socialist ownership in its two forms—state (public) and collective-farm-co-operative— became the economic foundation of Soviet society, covering 98.7 per cent of the production assets.

Basic changes took place in the class structure of Soviet society. The exploiter classes existing when the building of socialism was begun had been eradicated and the reasons giving rise to exploitation and class distinctions had disappeared; 94.1 per cent of the able-bodied population were employed in the socialist economy.

The working class and the collective-farm peasantry became the main classes of Soviet society. Only about 6 per cent of the population were individual peasants or artisans.

These classes, too, underwent fundamental changes. A new, Soviet working class came into being, freed from exploitation and from uncertainty about the future, from poverty and unemployment, and standing at the helm of society. The new, collective-farm peasantry was rid of all forms of exploitation and took part in building socialism, in the administration of the state. A new intelligentsia emerged from among the working class and the peasantry.

These far-reaching changes led to the gradual ironing out of class distinctions. The alliance between the working class and the peasants grew stronger than ever, and there was firm moral and political unity in Soviet society.

The triumph of socialism united all the peoples of the U.S.S.R.

and consolidated their friendship and co-operation. The outlying regions rapidly overcame their former economic and cultural backwardness and reached the level of advanced countries.

The triumph of socialism brought about a noteworthy improvement in the standard of living. The shortest working day in the world had been instituted, consumer goods prices were systematically reduced and the allocations for free medical services and the building of health and holiday homes and spas were steadily increased. Every Soviet citizen had the opportunity to learn a speciality, study free of charge in a secondary school or institution of higher learning and to develop his talents.

Socialism was built by the end of the Second Five-Year Plan period. That ended the transition period from capitalism to socialism. The objective of the New Economic Policy, that of ensuring the triumph of socialism, had been secured.

This was an epoch-making feat on the part of the Soviet people. Socialism triumphed in the U.S.S.R. mainly through the heroic labour of the Soviet people and through the advantages of the new socialist system, which is free of exploitation of man by man. The planned development of the economy delivered it from crises of overproduction and the accompanying unemployment.

The triumph of socialism was ensured by the correct leadership given by the Communist Party, which organised and inspired all the victories of socialism.

This triumph of the Soviet people was of immense international significance. The Soviet economy developed rapidly and living standards rose steadily; in the capitalist countries there were periodical crises of overproduction and millions of people lost their jobs, while huge stocks of food were destroyed. Working people throughout the world saw that workers and peasants could build a new society and administer a country without capitalists and landowners.

Progressive people in all countries expressed their admiration for the triumph of socialism in the U.S.S.R. Belgian workers wrote: "In the course of the 20 years of its existence the Soviet Union has given the world more than the preceding 20 centuries of civilisation."

The triumph of socialism enhanced the Soviet Union's significance as the bulwark of the international working class in the struggle for democracy, against the onslaught of fascism, reaction and the preparations for another world war.

New Constitution of the U.S.S.R.

The triumph of socialism was recorded in the new Constitution of the U.S.S.R. There had been two previous constitutions: the Constitution of the R.S.F.S.R. adopted in 1918 and the 1924

Constitution of the U.S.S.R. They were more democratic than any constitution that had ever existed in a class society, for they enfranchised all the working people and put the power in their hands. True, they justifiably deprived exploiter elements of electoral rights. Suffrage had been unequal due to the different representation quotas in the Soviets for the towns and villages, while the elections themselves required several stages.

Lenin had repeatedly declared that the exploiter classes were disfranchised solely because of their savage resistance to the new system and that in future the slight inequality in the voting rights between workers and peasants would be abolished.

The time had now come when it became possible to lift all limitations to Soviet, socialist democracy.

A decision to draft a new Constitution was passed at the Seventh All-Union Congress of Soviets in 1935. In 1936, it was published in the press for nation-wide discussion.

Nearly half of the adult population took part in the discussion.

The new Constitution was adopted in November 1936 by the Eighth Extraordinary Congress of Soviets of the U.S.S.R. in Moscow.

It recorded the triumph of socialism and provided the foundation for broad socialist democracy, stating that a socialist economic system and ownership of the means of production were the economic basis of the Soviet Union, while the Soviets of Working People's Deputies were its political foundation. It removed the remaining restrictions in elections to the Soviets, replaced multi-stage elections by direct elections and established the election of all Soviets on the basis of universal, equal and direct suffrage by secret ballot. Citizens of the U.S.S.R. received equal rights to elect and be elected to the Soviets.

The new Constitution guaranteed citizens the right to work, rest and leisure, education, and maintenance in old age and in case of sickness or disability. At the same time, it charged citizens with important duties: the observance of labour discipline, honest attitude to civic duty, strict observance of the country's laws, respect for the rules of the socialist community, and safeguarding and strengthening of socialist ownership.

The adoption of the new Constitution was accompanied by a change in the national-state system of the U.S.S.R.: two autonomous republics—Kazakhstan and Kirghizia—which had grown economically, politically and culturally during the five-year plan periods, were made Union republics.

The Transcaucasian Federation, which had completed its historic mission, was abolished. Three Union republics—Armenia, Azerbaijan and Georgia—were formed in its place. The number of republics in the U.S.S.R. rose from seven to 11. That was a fresh triumph of the Leninist nationalities policy.

The further democratisation of the Soviet social and state system enhanced and strengthened the social foundation of the dictatorship of the proletariat. The Constitution recorded the leading position of the Communist Party in Soviet society.

Such were the basic principles underlying the new Constitution. Its adoption was of historic importance.

Elections to the Supreme Soviet of the U.S.S.R. were held on December 12, 1937. The Communist Party advanced the idea of forming a bloc with non-Party people at the elections.

The election campaign coincided with the 20th anniversary of Soviet rule and was a review of the successes of socialist construction in those years. The elections were held in an atmosphere marked by heightened political activity by the masses: out of 94 million electors, 91 million or 96.8 per cent went to the polls. Of these, 90 million or 98 per cent voted for the candidates of the bloc of Communists and non-Party people.

The supreme organ of power in the U.S.S.R. thus rested on the support of the majority of the people.

Of the deputies in the Soviet of the Union 45.3 per cent were workers, 23.7 peasants and 31 per cent employees and intellectuals; in the Soviet of Nationalities 38 per cent were workers, 34 per cent peasants and 28 per cent employees and intellectuals. Of the 1,143 deputies in both chambers 870 were Communists and 273 non-Party people. Twenty-nine nations and nationalities were represented in the Soviet of the Union and 54 nations and nationalities in the Soviet of Nationalities. This composition mirrored the moral and political unity of the people.

At its first session in January 1938 the Supreme Soviet elected the Presidium of the Supreme Soviet and the Soviet Government. Mikhail Kalinin became President of the Presidium. New constitutions were drawn up in the Union and Autonomous republics after the Constitution of the U.S.S.R. was adopted. Elections to the Supreme Soviets of the Union and Autonomous republics were held in June 1938 and to the local Soviets in the following year on the basis of these constitutions.

Stalin Personality Cult

In the U.S.S.R. socialism was built under complex, difficult conditions. In the period of transition from capitalism to socialism there were within the country elements who were hostile to the Soviet system—kulaks, the bourgeoisie that emerged during the period of the New Economic Policy, and remnants of the former ruling landowner and bourgeois classes who were eager to restore capitalism.

A class struggle continued to rage in the country, at times taking acute forms.

In the building of socialism Soviet power rested on the alliance between the working class and the peasants. Within this alliance there were some contradictions, for as long as the small peasant households were not reorganised into collective farms there was always the danger that this alliance would be weakened and capitalism revived. The working class and its Party had to pursue an able policy aimed at consolidating the alliance between the two classes.

The international situation, too, was complex: the imperialists utilised every domestic difficulty in the Soviet Union to harm the country. This required iron-clad discipline, unceasing vigilance and the strictest centralisation.

The internal and external conditions under which socialism was built inevitably affected the development of certain democratic forms of leadership in the Party and the state and placed restriction on democracy. The Party and the people regarded these restrictions as temporary.

Stalin, who was General Secretary, and other members of the C.C. actively combated the Trotskyites, Right opportunists and national deviationists. They safeguarded the Party line and repelled the sallies of imperialist reaction against the U.S.S.R. In this struggle Stalin won high esteem and popularity in the U.S.S.R. and abroad.

Soon, however, all the achievements of the Soviet people began to be attributed to him. The cult of his personality had taken shape by the time the Seventeenth Party Congress was convened in 1934. At the Congress he was excessively lauded for his services to the Party and country. For the first time in the Party's history a Congress failed to adopt an extended resolution on the report of the Central Committee, confining itself to a decision to take the conclusions and propositions in the report read by Stalin as a guide.

By that time Stalin had come to believe that he was infallible and begun departing more and more from the Leninist standards and principles of Party life, violating the principle of collective leadership and abusing his position. The negative features of his personality—incivility, disloyalty to leading Party workers, intolerance of criticism, administration by injunction—came to the fore. The joint Central Control Commission—Workers' and Peasants' Inspection, which prevented him from concentrating unlimited power in his hands, was abolished on his suggestion.

On December 1, 1934, Sergei Kirov, one of the most popular Party leaders, Secretary of the C.C. and the Leningrad Regional Party Committee, and member of the Political Bureau, was assassinated in the Smolny Institute in Leningrad. His murder, not all the circumstances of which have been brought to light to this day, was used as a pretext for mass reprisals, first against former opposition members and then against honest people who were devoted to the Party and the Soviet system but were disagreeable to Stalin, against leading Party and government cadres and against rank-and-file Communist and non-Party people.

At a Plenary Meeting of the C.C. C.P.S.U.(B.) in February-March 1937, Stalin propounded the harmful and erroneous thesis that the class struggle would grow as the U.S.S.R. advanced towards socialism. This thesis was wrong first and foremost because the class struggle had reached its zenith in the period of socialist construction when the issue of "who will beat whom" was in the balance. With the triumph of socialism in the U.S.S.R. the class struggle shifted to the international arena; in the Soviet Union the people had united round the Communist Party. In practice Stalin's thesis was used as a pretext for mass repressions against Party and government leaders.

Flagrantly infringing upon socialist legality Stalin removed Party control over the People's Commissariat for Internal Affairs, placing it under his own control and personally selecting the leading cadres for its various bodies. On Stalin's instructions Yezhov was appointed People's Commissar for Internal Affairs and in that post he destroyed many people who were devoted to the Party. After Yezhov was removed, Stalin gave the post of People's Commissar for Internal Affairs to Beria, who subsequently committed the most heinous crimes against the Party and the people.

Pavel Postyshev and G. Kaminsky, who protested against Stalin's arbitrary rule, were the first to fall victim to the repressions started under the personality cult. Soon afterwards the repressions were spread to include Stanislav Kosior, Robert Eikhe, Vlas Chubar, Andrei Bubnov, Nikolai Krylenko, Jan Rudzutak, Vasily Blücher, Alexander Yegorov, Mikhail Tukhachevsky, Iona Yakir, Ieronim Uborevich, A. Korkh, Robert Eideman, and many other prominent Party, government and military leaders. Many Red Army commanders and political workers were jailed or exiled. Grigory Orjonikidze, Jan Gamarnik, N. Skrypnik and other prominent leaders of the Party and Government could not carry on their work in this situation of arbitrary rule and illegality and committed suicide. Many veteran Communists were removed from active government and Party work.

This illegality came to light only after Stalin's death and the exposure of the adventurer Beria, for the people had been made to believe that the measures taken against so-called "enemies of the people" had been correct. It was not until after Stalin's death that it became known that the arbitrary rule and illegality were Stalin's work and that Molotov, Kaganovich and Malenkov had also had a hand in it. Other conditions were required for justice to triumph. In the period of the Stalin personality cult the fact that the people had faith in Stalin made it difficult to struggle against illegality and arbitrary rule. Any acts against him were not supported by the people and were regarded as acts against socialist construction.

The personality cult period was marked by suspicion and distrust, violations of socialist legality, and infringement upon the Leninist standards of Party life and the principles of collective leadership.

Dogmatism and pedantry dominated the ideological scene. Theory was divorced from practice and Stalin's role in the history of the Party was exalted. The *Short Course of the History of the C.P.S.U.(B.)*, put out in 1938, was permeated with the spirit of the personality cult and distorted many events in the history of the Party.

The Stalin personality cult and its negative consequences seriously harmed the socialist state and weakened its leading organs. However, the cult could neither change the nature of Soviet society nor stop its onward development.

U.S.S.R. on the Eve of War

The Soviet Union was completing the building of socialism and entering the period of gradual transition to communism. It was at the time the only socialist country in the world and was completely encircled by hostile capitalist states.

Under these conditions the triumph of socialism could not be regarded as final. The Soviet Union was not guaranteed against armed intervention or against the danger of a capitalist restoration with the aid of international reaction. The capitalist countries were far ahead of the U.S.S.R. in both the economic and military field. The Soviet Union constantly had to build up its defence potential and improve its armed forces for the defence of its frontiers.

In March 1939, the Eighteenth Party Congress adopted the Third Five-Year Plan, which called for a further growth of the country's industrial might: by the end of 1942 industrial output had to increase by approximately 100 per cent over the 1937 level. It was planned to increase agricultural output by more than 50 per cent, further strengthen the collective-farm system, improve standards of living and make better use of the wealth of the country's eastern regions.

This plan got off to a successful start: nearly 3,000 new industrial enterprises were commissioned in the course of three years; by mid-1941 the Soviet industrial product had reached 86 per cent of the level planned for the end of 1942.

A mass socialist emulation movement to fulfil the plan was started. New names gained prominence. Steelworkers achieved outstanding results. At the Ilyich Plant in Mariupol, the Ukraine, foremost workers began producing 15 tons of steel per square metre of hearth bottom instead of the usual four or five tons. This revolution in the technology of steelmaking was started by a young worker named Makar Mazai.

Nation-wide fame was won by A. Semivolos, a miner at the Krivoi Rog iron-ore basin. Innovators came to the fore in transport, and in many industries. As a result of socialist emulation labour productivity increased by almost 40 per cent during the two years of the five-year plan.

But the clouds of war were gathering. The Soviet Union had to accelerate the rate of growth of its industrial might. In June 1940, on the insistence of industrial and office workers the Soviet Union went over to an eight-hour working day and a six-day working week. Steps were taken to heighten labour discipline at factories and offices. That, too, helped to increase output during the pre-war years.

An important role was played by the measures taken to ensure industry with skilled labour. A system of state labour reserves embracing factory and trade schools was set up. These schools annually trained from 800,000 to 1,000,000 workers.

Thanks to the selfless efforts of industrial, office and other workers Soviet industry scored fresh successes on the eve of the war.

Agriculture too made progress. Its fleet of machines was enlarged. Motors accounted for nearly 80 per cent of its power; 70-80 per cent of the ploughing was done by tractors and 40 per cent of the harvesting by harvester-combines.

More innovators appeared in agriculture. The collective-farm peasants displayed genuine patriotism. In 1938, a woman tractor-driver named Praskovya Angelina appealed to women to become tractor-drivers; nearly 200,000 women responded to her appeal and learned to operate tractors and harvester-combines.

In 1940, the grain output exceeded the 1913 level. However, requirements had soared and the grain problem still remained to be solved when war broke out.

In the pre-war years the U.S.S.R. was one of the most powerful states in the world; in the course of the three pre-war five-year plans the country had built and placed in operation 9,000 industrial enterprises. The industrial product had grown by 1,100 per cent as compared with 1913, bringing the U.S.S.R. into first place in Europe and second place in the world for the volume of industrial output.

Instead of an ocean of small peasant farms there now were large socialist enterprises—collective and state farms—using the most up-to-date machinery.

Sergei Kirov

Mikhail Kalinin

Ivan Bardin (who became an academician in 1932) seen here in his capacity of Chief Engineer of the Kuznetsk Metallurgical Project

Kuznetsk Iron and Steel Works under construction, 1931

Nikita Izotov, a leading
Donbas miner

Assembling cars at the Gorky
Auto Works, 1931

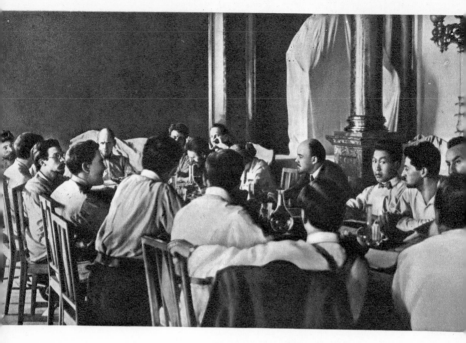

Lenin with representatives of Eastern peoples

The cultural revolution produced skilled cadres for the economy, all fields of political and cultural life, and the armed forces.

A powerful military and economic potential was created. In 1940, the U.S.S.R. produced 15 million tons of pig iron, more than 18 million tons of steel, 166 million tons of coal, 31 million tons of oil and nearly 3,000,000 tons of cotton. That was far above the 1913 level.

By 1941, the U.S.S.R. had a population of 193 million, of whom more than 60 million lived in towns and workers' townships. The entire people were united round the Communist Party and Soviet Government, their moral and political unity becoming the motive force of the development of Soviet society.

Friendship among nations played a tremendous role in the life of the country. The triumph of socialism brought genuine prosperity to the Soviet republics. In the friendly family of equal nations the leading role was played by the Russian people: in 1937, the Russian Federation had about 80 per cent of the metal-working industry, two-thirds of the power generating facilities, two-thirds of the fleet of tractors and harvester-combines and 70 per cent of the crop area. The Russian people rendered the fraternal peoples considerable assistance in economic and cultural development.

Enormous progress was made by the Ukraine, which had become an industrial and collective-farm republic during the five-year plans. In 1937, her industrial output was as great as that of the whole of Russia in 1913. She produced a quarter of the country's electric power, had about a fifth of the country's fleet of tractors and harvester-combines and almost a fifth of the grain crop area and nearly two-thirds of the area sown to sugar beet.

Byelorussia, which had been a backward area, became a developed republic during the five-year plans. Her industrial output more than doubled and her crop area was considerably enlarged. Her industries accounted for almost 80 per cent of her economy.

Giant strides had been made in promoting the economic and cultural growth of Kazakhstan and the Central Asian and Transcaucasian republics. Kazakhstan began producing ferrous metals, coal and oil. Large industrial centres sprang up in the deserts. A local working class emerged. During the Second Five-Year Plan the people of Kazakhstan passed from nomad economy to settled farming.

Uzbekistan supplied the bulk of the cotton for the Soviet textile industry; 380 industrial enterprises were built in the republic during the first two five-year plans.

Major successes were scored by the other Central Asian republics—Turkmenia, Tajikistan and Kirghizia—and by the Transcaucasian republics—Armenia, Azerbaijan and Georgia.

New republics were formed: the Karelo-Finnish Republic, Moldavia, Lithuania, Latvia and Estonia. The Karelo-Finnish S.S.R. was formed in March 1940 on the territory of the Karelian Autonomous Soviet Socialist Republic and part of the regions that went over to the U.S.S.R. under the Soviet-Finnish Treaty of 1940.* Three republics—Lithuania, Latvia and Estonia—were formed as a result of the people's victory over the reactionary regimes in those countries and the proclamation of Soviet rule.

The working class and toiling peasantry of the Baltic republics remembered that in 1918-19 their power was forcibly overthrown with the aid of troops from the imperialist countries. For more than 20 years the more politically-conscious and courageous representatives of the workers and peasants, united in Communist Parties, carried on 'an open and underground struggle for the restoration of Soviet rule. In June 1940, thousands of people demonstrated in Riga, Tallinn, Kaunas and Vilnius. The workers released political prisoners, set up armed detachments and occupied government buildings. There was spontaneous fraternisation with Red Army troops, stationed there by agreement between the U.S.S.R. and the governments of those countries. Left-wing organisations set up popular governments headed by well-known progressive leaders. The people's front was victorious in all three Baltic states.

In the new situation parliamentary elections were held in Estonia, Latvia and Lithuania in July. All three parliaments unanimously proclaimed Soviet rule and adopted decisions to join the U.S.S.R.

The destiny of Bessarabia, forcibly seized from Soviet Russia by Rumania in 1918 was settled in June 1940. The Soviet Government secured the restoration of justice peacefully: the Rumanian Government agreed to return Bessarabia and transfer Northern Bukovina, inhabited mainly by Ukrainians, to the Soviet Union.

The working people of Bessarabia and the Moldavian Autonomous Republic, Moldavians by nationality, unanimously decided to unite in a single national state. Northern Bukovina and some regions of Bessarabia, inhabited chiefly by Ukrainians, were included in the Ukraine.

In August 1940, the Seventh Session of the Supreme Soviet of the U.S.S.R. passed a law forming the Union Moldavian Republic. It also considered the declarations of representatives of the Lithuanian, Latvian and Estonian Soviet republics and admitted these republics to the U.S.S.R. This opened new vistas for the peoples of these republics.

---

* In July 1956, the Karelo-Finnish S.S.R. was transformed into the Karelian Autonomous Soviet Socialist Republic and became part of the Russian Federation.—*Ed.*

The enlargement of the Soviet Union strengthened its economic and defence potential.

The family of Soviet peoples now consisted of 16 Union republics. The new, socialist nations united in a powerful state. Friendship between them became the source of the Soviet Union's stability and the motive force of its development.

Such was the situation in the U.S.S.R. before war broke out. The successes in industrialisation, collectivisation and cultural development prepared the material and spiritual forces for the repulsion of any aggressor.

The growing war threat made the Soviet Government give greater attention to the war industry. Defence expenditures in general and the allocations for the production of armaments in particular were substantially increased. This made it possible to accelerate the development of the defence industry. A prominent role in organising that industry was played, among others, by Vasily Vakhrushev, Nikolai Voznesensky, B. Vannikov, P. Goremykin, A. Yefremov, Ivan Tevosyan and D. Ustinov.

The creation and expansion of the material basis of the aircraft and tank industries were of key significance in strengthening the Soviet Union's defence potential. The Red Army received new types of aircraft and KV and T-34 tanks, which were much superior to the tanks abroad.

Although a modern defence industry had been created during the pre-war five-year plans, its potentialities for the mass production of weapons and ammunition were poorly utilised.

On account of the Stalin cult the production of new types of armaments proceeded very slowly. G. Kulik, L. Mekhlis and Y. Shchadenko who headed the People's Commissariat for Defence and the General Staff knew little about the armaments of the potential enemy's armies or of their own army and failed to appreciate the need for equipping the Soviet Army with the latest types of weapons. Kulik, for example, who was Deputy People's Commissar for Defence, considered submachine guns a weapon for policemen. Acting on unverified information that German tanks had been re-equipped with more powerful cannon, he persuaded Stalin and Zhdanov to order the cessation of the production of 45 and 76mm tank and anti-tank guns and their replacement with 107mm guns. B. Vannikov, People's Commissar for Armaments, protested against this unwise decision, for which he was removed from his post and arrested. A similar fate overtook B. Shavyrin, chief designer of mortars. When war broke out the nature of these acts became particularly glaring: the production of new weapons had not been started and none of the old types were being produced. For that reason the Soviet Army found itself acutely short of weapons at the beginning of the war.

Struggle for Peace

Abortive Attempts to Form a United Anti-Soviet Front

The international situation was tense in 1926-32 when the Soviet Union proceeded with socialist industrialisation and agricultural reforms. After the serious economic and political setbacks in the early 1920s, the capitalist countries entered a period of partial and temporary stability. It was an extremely precarious stability and led to a further exacerbation of all the contradictions of the capitalist system and an intensification of the struggle between the leading capitalist countries, particularly between Britain and the U.S.A. which was making things difficult for Britain in the world market.

The Soviet Union was occupied with peaceful construction and worked perseveringly to establish trade relations with the capitalist countries, strengthen friendship with the Eastern countries, avert war and achieve a reduction of armaments and universal disarmament. This foreign policy enhanced the Soviet Union's international prestige and was a major factor in international relations. Influential circles in the capitalist West could not reconcile themselves to this. With the British ruling circles acting as their spearhead they tried to stiffen their anti-Soviet policy, believing that that would give them a way out of their serious economic and political difficulties.

The British Conservative Government (Prime Minister Stanley Baldwin; Foreign Secretary Austen Chamberlain) launched a virulent anti-Soviet campaign, in which many ministers and MPs took part. In 1927, *The Morning Post* wrote that it would be useful to sever diplomatic relations with the Soviet Union and throw a sanitary cordon around it. The same idea was advanced by the *Empire Review*, which wrote: "Europe, faced with the grave problem of its economic future, cannot hesitate. She must set about the downfall of the Soviets."

Stanley Baldwin and Austen Chamberlain were in favour of breaking off diplomatic relations with the Soviet Union.

In February 1927, following in the footsteps of his predecessor, Lord Curzon, Austen Chamberlain sent a note to the Soviet Government, in which he made the preposterous charge that the Soviet Union was conducting anti-British propaganda and violating the Anglo-Soviet trade agreement, and threatened to break off Anglo-Soviet diplomatic and trade relations.

In its reply the Soviet Government rejected the accusations of the British Government as completely unfounded, and said that it continued to favour peaceful relations with Britain and other countries.

In the meantime reactionary forces in Britain and some other countries hastened to take advantage of the Chamberlain note to touch off a new wave of anti-Soviet actions. The offices of the Soviet Co-operative Society for Trade with Britain and the Soviet Trade Mission were raided on May 12 of the same year. The raid was carried out with the knowledge and approval of the British Government.

The actions of the British Government harmed primarily Britain's political and economic prestige. Even some representatives of the British ruling circles, to say nothing of the British working people, censured the British authorities for these actions.

The Soviet Government strongly protested against the actions of the British Government, and the Conservative Government retaliated by annulling the 1921 trade agreement and breaking off diplomatic relations with the Soviet Union.

British political circles believed that this step would help isolate the U.S.S.R. and organise a new anti-Soviet bloc. The hostile acts of the British authorities were only a link in a chain of anti-Soviet provocations. On June 7, 1927 a Russian whiteguard named B. Kaverda assassinated P. Voikov, the Soviet Ambassador to Poland, in Warsaw. The architects of this heinous crime hoped to stir up a Soviet-Polish conflict and involve the U.S.S.R. in war. But nothing came of this diabolical plot.

In April 1927, political circles in Britain and the U.S.A. tried to provoke a military conflict between the Soviet Union and China. Police and troops broke into the Soviet Embassy in Peking, arrested members of the staff and searched and ransacked the premises. This provocation was instigated by representatives of the Western powers, a fact which was confirmed by the Chinese charge d'affaires in the U.S.S.R. in his reply to the Soviet protest note. He stated quite clearly that the action of the Chinese military authorities and police had been pre-arranged with Western diplomats.

On this occasion, too, the Soviet Government showed restrain and did not allow itself to be drawn into a military conflict.

The British Government broke off relations with the U.S.S.R. believing that its example would be followed by other countries, primarily by Germany and France. That was a miscalculation, for although some German diplomats wanted the relations with the U.S.S.R. to deteriorate, the German bourgeoisie as a whole preferred to develop economic relations with the Soviet Union in order to strengthen their political position in Europe.

France, too, did not follow the British initiative. Although the French Government took a series of anti-Soviet steps, the economic relations between France and the U.S.S.R. continued to develop. French industrialists utilised the situation to sign a number of agreements with the Soviet Union.

After stemming the anti-Soviet wave of 1927, the Soviet Union continued strengthening its relations with the capitalist countries. As early as 1925 the Soviet Government offered to sign a non-aggression and neutrality pact with a number of countries. In 1925-27 such pacts were signed with Turkey, Germany, Lithuania, Afghanistan, Iran and other countries.

International Conference. Kellogg-Briand Pact

In May 1927 the Soviet Union took part in an international economic conference, at which the Soviet delegation submitted detailed proposals founded on the idea of peaceful coexistence between states with different social systems.

The Soviet proposals provided for the annulment of all military debts and payments, the withdrawal of troops from colonies, the recognition of the right of all peoples to political and economic self-determination, the cessation of the military intervention in China, the lifting of the political and economic boycott of the U.S.S.R., the setting up of relations based on peaceful coexistence between the two systems and, lastly, effective and complete disarmament.

This Soviet programme of peace and disarmament pursued the aim of improving the economic situation and was supported by the working people of all countries. However, the stand of the delegates of the capitalist countries did not permit the economic conference to achieve any positive results.

A major Soviet foreign policy triumph was the disruption of the plans to isolate the U.S.S.R. and the Soviet Government's subscription to the Kellogg-Briand Pact. In April 1927, the French Foreign Minister Aristide Briand offered to conclude with the U.S.A. a bilateral treaty for the renunciation of war. The U.S. Secretary of State Frank B. Kellogg suggested that it should be developed into a multilateral pact. In August 1928, after negotiations, the pact was signed by the U.S.A., Britain, France, Germany, Italy, Japan, Czechoslovakia, Poland and other countries. Some countries joined the pact with reservations that allowed them to use force under certain circumstances. One of the reservations made by Britain, for example, concerned "governments that have not been recognised by everybody" (an obvious reference to the U.S.S.R.).

For almost a year the negotiations on the signing of the pact went on behind the back of the Soviet Union.

The Soviet Government exposed the Western attempts to spearhead the Kellogg-Briand Pact against the U.S.S.R. and declared its preparedness to take part in the talks, provided it was sent an official invitation.

On August 27, 1927, the U.S.S.R. was invited to subscribe to the pact. Four days later the People's Commissariat for Foreign

Affairs replied that the Soviet Government would sign the pact inasmuch as it imposed certain obligations on the powers and gave the Soviet Government a further opportunity of raising before the signatories the question of disarmament, whose settlement was the only guarantee against war.

The capitalist countries once more saw that their attempt to solve key international issues without the U.S.S.R. were unrealistic.

Failure of Further Anti-Soviet Intrigues

In 1929, the capitalist world was shaken by an unprecedented economic crisis. The ruling classes in the West tried to lay the blame for the grave consequences of that crisis on the U.S.S.R. The Soviet Union was accused of having precipitated the crisis by dumping.* There were demands for boycotting Soviet exports and for organising a crusade against the U.S.S.R. This had the sole purpose of distracting the attention of the people from the contradictions of capitalism that had come to the fore during the crisis.

The 1929-32 crisis and its consequences were so catastrophic that it became obvious to every unbiased observer that its roots were in the economic and political system of the capitalist countries.

In the summer of 1929, a few months before the crisis broke out, ruling circles in the U.S.A., Japan, Britain and France made another attempt to provoke a Sino-Soviet clash and involve the U.S.S.R. in war in the Far East. On May 27, 1929, bandits attacked the Soviet consulate in Harbin, and on July 10, Chinese militarists tried to seize the Chinese Eastern Railway, which was administered jointly by the U.S.S.R. and China. Members of the Soviet staff were imprisoned and beaten, and a number of Soviet offices were raided. In September and October 1929, detachments of Chinese militarists and Russian whiteguards invaded Soviet territory. The Special Far Eastern Army commanded by Vasily Blücher drove them out of Soviet territory and forced the Chinese Government to sue for peace.

The Sino-Soviet conflict was settled in December 1929, and the situation on the Chinese Eastern Railway was normalised. During the conflict the imperialist powers headed by the U.S.A. alleged that the U.S.S.R. had violated the terms of the Kellogg-Briand Pact. The Soviet Government punctured this imperialist interference in Sino-Soviet relations and emphasised that Soviet troops on the Chinese Eastern Railway had acted in self-defence,

---

* The absurdity of this accusation is shown by the simple fact that in those years the Soviet export did not account for even two per cent of the world trade.—Ed.

while troops of the imperialist powers were in China in order to tighten their stranglehold on that country.

The Soviet Union's successful fulfilment of its First Five-Year Plan and the economic and political interests of the ruling classes of the capitalist countries compelled the latter to seek an improvement of relations with the U.S.S.R. Diplomatic relations between the U.S.S.R. and Britain were restored in October 1929, and a Franco-Soviet non-aggression pact was signed and various treaties and agreements concluded with Britain, Iran, Latvia, Estonia, Finland, Italy, Turkey and Afghanistan in 1932.

The Soviet Union's international prestige steadily grew, and its trade and economic relations with the capitalist states expanded. The attempts of the reactionaries to weaken the U.S.S.R. and form an anti-Soviet coalition failed ignominiously.

Struggle for Disarmament

In 1927-32, the U.S.S.R. started a vigorous campaign for general disarmament. Those years witnessed an intensification of the arms race in which the leading role was played by Britain, the U.S.A. and France.

In the capitalist countries the working masses opposed the arms race, for they were aware that it was bringing nearer the threat of another war. In order to distract their attention, the ruling circles of Britain, France and other countries had, as early as 1925, proposed convening a conference on a reduction and restriction of arms under the auspices of the League of Nations. A Preparatory Commission, set up for that purpose, met in 1926 and during the succeeding years. The question of preparing for the conference was discussed at sittings of the League of Nations itself.

But the problem of disarmament, a key issue which worried millions of people, was drowned in a sea of debates, which were used as screens to continue the arms race.

The arrival of the Soviet delegation in Geneva on November 30 for participation in the work of the Preparatory Commission brought a fresh breeze into this musty atmosphere. The Western diplomats found their inactivity threatened with exposure. The French newspaper *Echo de Paris* wrote: "The arrival of the Soviet delegation in Geneva held out the danger of further compromising the already shaken prestige of the League of Nations."

A declaration on behalf of the Soviet Union was read at the very first sitting of the Preparatory Commission by Maxim Litvinov, who headed the Soviet delegation. The proposals in it were: the disbandment of all land, naval and air forces of all countries, the destruction of weapons and ammunition, the promulgation of laws forbidding military service, the closure of munitions plants,

192

the cessation of allocations for military purposes, and so forth. In making these proposals the Soviet delegation declared that it "was prepared to participate in each and every discussion of the problem of disarmament inasmuch as practical, realistic steps aimed at disarmament would be suggested".

In the West the working people and their organisations welcomed the Soviet initiative and demanded that their governments accept the Soviet proposals. But the delegations of the capitalist countries turned a deaf ear to public opinion and declined the Soviet draft on the grounds that the Preparatory Commission was supposed to examine not complete but only partial and gradual disarmament.

At a sitting of the commission in March 1928 Soviet diplomats submitted a draft convention on a partial arms cut, envisaging a gradual decrease of land, air and naval forces and of stockpiles of arms and ammunition, the complete destruction of chemical means of warfare, a reduction of military budgets, and the setting up of a Standing International Inspection Commission to inspect and control partial and gradual disarmament.

The U.S.S.R. insisted on the acceptance of the disarmament convention, but the Western powers did not desire disarmament and did everything to bury the Soviet draft in endless discussions in the commission.

Not daring to reject the Soviet draft, the Preparatory Commission included it in its general report for examination at the next conference.

In 1930-32, the international situation was full of sinister signs. Japanese aggression gave rise to a seat of war in the Far East, nazism was gaining ground in Germany and the arms race was in full swing in other countries. That held out the threat of another world war. Anti-Soviet forces again became active in a number of countries in 1932.

On February 2, 1932, in that tense atmosphere, the World Conference on the Reduction and Restriction of Armaments opened in Geneva.

It revealed the deep-going contradictions between the capitalist countries. France submitted the Tardieu Plan of setting up international armed forces under the aegis of the League of Nations. The object of this plan was to consolidate France's supremacy in Europe and safeguard her against the strengthening of Germany.

The German delegation sought to secure an annulment of the restrictions imposed on Germany by the Versailles Treaty and demanded that either she be allowed to increase the strength of her armed forces or that the Versailles Treaty restrictions be spread to other countries.

The British wanted to satisfy Germany's demands and give France some sort of guarantee, but on the whole they were out to obstruct the strengthening of both these countries. The U.S. delegates proposed "quality disarmament", i.e., the outlawing of tanks, artillery and so forth. In short, all this meant that in reality each country sought to undermine the military might of other states and preserve her own armed forces.

Soviet diplomats submitted a draft that could have served as the foundation for agreement. On February 11, 1932, Maxim Litvinov declared that the Soviet Government had unequivocally condemned war as an instrument of national policy, opposed all indemnities and territorial annexations and the oppression of some nations by others, and proclaimed the slogan of self-determination of nations.

He said that the Tardieu and other plans were leading the conference away from a realistic settlement of the disarmament problem and proposed the adoption of a convention on complete disarmament, once more submitting the Soviet plan of a partial arms reduction as the first stage of complete disarmament.

The Soviet proposals were received with understanding in many bourgeois circles in the West. Turkey supported the Soviet plan. Though the plan was torpedoed by the U.S., British, French, Japanese and other delegations, this opposition could not prevent the Soviet delegation from winning a moral victory.

In addition to failing to reach agreement, the conference, in effect, sanctioned Germany's demand to increase her armaments and buried the plans for real disarmament. The ominous clouds of war steadily covered the horizon. The war threat could be averted only by the collective effort of all peace-loving forces.

The War Threat Grows

The end of the world economic crisis coincided with serious political changes in Europe: on January 30, 1933, the nazis came to power in Germany, the largest European bourgeois power. Their leader Hitler became Chancellor of the German Empire. He had long been known for his preaching of revenge, of the forcible revision of the Versailles Treaty. After Hitler and his gang seized power, the relatively small Reichswehr became the nucleus of a rapidly growing German army. The actions of the nazi government in the international arena—the annulment of military restrictions imposed by the Versailles Treaty and the military occupation of the Rhine—showed that danger was hanging over the European countries.

Moreover, the international situation deteriorated still further by fascist Italy's attack on Ethiopia in October 1935. In the summer of 1936, the German nazis and Italian fascists began a joint intervention in Spain. At the same time, they formed the Rome-Berlin axis, which became a tripartite military and political agreement when the Anti-Comintern Pact was signed by Berlin and Tokyo shortly afterwards.

The aggressive acts of the fascist powers affected the vital interests of the British and French bourgeoisie. Any connivance at these acts threatened their countries with disaster.

This was appreciated by the more far-sighted politicians in the West, and they correctly assessed the Soviet Union as a force capable of giving a rebuff to the aggressors.

Early in 1936 Edouard Herriot declared: "They tell me that after all they are Bolsheviks. I reply that that does not concern me. As a son of the French revolution I am happy when I see a people bent upon social progress, and I consider it my duty to help that people to establish co-operation for common aims."

Franklin D. Roosevelt too appreciated the role played in the world by the Soviet Union, and one of his major acts as U.S. President was to establish normal diplomatic relations with it (November 1933).

But the anti-Soviet-minded politicians, who were prepared to make any concession to the fascist powers provided these concessions drew nearer the longed-for German crusade against the East, prevailed among the ruling circles of the so-called democratic countries. Pierre Laval and Pierre Flandin in France, Neville Chamberlain and Lord Halifax in Britain, and a considerable number of U.S. congressmen and high government officials sought to channel nazi aggression against the Soviet Union. Aggressors were encouraged in the Far East as well, where in 1937 Japan renewed military operations against China.

From time to time, despite the serious contradictions, which mounted with the extension of fascist aggression, the leaders of the "democratic" and fascist powers tried to find a common platform, to reach agreement (the Four Power Pact between Italy, Germany, Britain and France in 1933, and Stresa Front—consisting of Britain, France and Italy—and the Anglo-German agreement of 1935). The U.S.S.R. faced the constant threat of the emergence of an anti-Soviet bloc of imperialist powers.

Struggle of the U.S.S.R. for a Collective Rebuff to Aggressors

At the International Disarmament Conference, exactly a week after Hitler became Reichschancellor, the Soviet delegation submitted a proposal for defining aggression. The Soviet Union proposed considering a country an aggressor if it committed one of the following acts:

1. Declared war on any state.

2. Invaded the territory of another state, even without declaring war.

3. Attacked the territory, ships or aircraft of another state by its land, naval or air forces even without declaring war.

4. Blockaded the coast or ports of another state.

5. Supported armed gangs, formed on its own territory, in the invasion of the territory of another state, or, despite the demands of the state being invaded, refused to take every measure to deprive the above gangs of all assistance or patronage.*

One of the articles of the Soviet draft stated that neither the political, economic or cultural backwardness of any people, nor civil war, disorders, strikes, or any other conditions of a country's internal situation can serve as justification for an attack. The purport of this draft was to deprive any potential aggressor of the possibility of utilising a false pretext or argument to justify his actions, and also automatically to invoke sanctions against aggression.

This clear and exact definition of aggression was welcome in many countries. On February 7, 1933, the *New York Herald Tribune* wrote that the Soviet draft may some day "be the basis of an organised world's definition of aggression". The convention on defining aggression could have served as the foundation for the setting up of a system of collective security against fascist attack. However, only the small countries responded officially to the Soviet Union's proposals. Not one of the Great Powers agreed to take part in the convention. In July 1933, the convention was signed by the Soviet Union, Estonia, Latvia, Poland, Rumania, Turkey, Iran, Afghanistan, Czechoslovakia, Yugoslavia and Lithuania (later it was signed by Finland).

In 1934, the Soviet Union wholeheartedly supported Jean Louis Barthou's idea of an Eastern Pact or Eastern Locarno and invited Germany, Poland, the three Baltic states, Finland and Czechoslovakia to sign a treaty on mutual guarantees of the frontiers in Eastern Europe. The plan was that France should be the guarantor of the Eastern Pact while the Soviet Union one of the guarantors of the Locarno Pact. That same year the Soviet Union was invited to join the League of Nations. The Soviet Government accepted that invitation and the U.S.S.R. became a member of the League on September 18, 1934. The international significance of this event was emphasised by the fact that two aggressive states— Germany and Japan—had withdrawn from the League in 1933.

Barthou was murdered by nazi agents on October 9, 1934, while the negotiations on the Eastern Pact were in progress. Laval, who

---

* *Sbornik deistvuyushchikh dogovorov, soglashenii i konventsii zaklyuchennykh s inostrannymi gosudarstvami* (*Operating Treaties, Agreements and Conventions Signed with Foreign States*), Moscow, 1935, Issue VIII, p. 28.

succeeded him as French Foreign Minister, hesitated to come out at once against the Eastern Pact and the policy of rapprochement with the Soviet Union, which was popular in France. He was compelled to continue the talks with the Soviet Government, initiated by Barthou, on a mutual assistance pact. That pact was signed on May 2, 1935. Reinforced by the Soviet-Czechoslovak Treaty of May 16, 1935, it was planned as a serious obstacle to aggression.*

But behind the scenes the new French Foreign Minister began to undermine the treaty; soon the projected Eastern Pact was buried through the joint efforts of the French and British governments.**

When the fascist states went over to overt acts of aggression and Ethiopia was turned into a battlefield, the Soviet Union sharply censured Italy's aggression and demanded that repressive sanctions be invoked against her in accordance with Article 18 of the League of Nations Charter. A decision to apply the sanctions was passed by the League of Nations Assembly. But Britain and France, the two major colonial powers, had no sympathy for the struggle of the Ethiopian people. They hoped that Italian imperialism's claims would be satisfied at Ethiopia's expense and that agreement would be reached with Italy on a broad range of problems. In December 1935, Britain and France conspired to support Italy against Ethiopia. The sanctions were disrupted, and the seizure of Ethiopia was completed by the summer of 1936.

During the Italian-Ethiopian war, the Soviet Union made the proposal that any country attacking a member of the League of Nations should automatically be considered to be in a state of war with the other members of the League. If that proposal had been accepted, it would have meant the establishment of a powerful system of collective security. The countries that did not want war were many times more powerful than Germany, Italy and

---

* Article 2, which obligated either one of the signatories immediately to come to the assistance of the other if it were attacked by a third European power, was the key instrument of the Franco-Soviet Treaty.

The text of the treaty between the U.S.S.R. and Czechoslovakia was almost identical with that of the Franco-Soviet Treaty. However, there was an important reservation in the protocol on the signing of the treaty with Czechoslovakia, namely, that the signatories agreed to assist each other if France came to the assistance of the victim of aggression.—Ed.

** Public opinion made Laval sign the Franco-Soviet treaty on mutual assistance, but he was its main opponent and tried to prevent its ratification. The Paris Ordre wrote in February 1936: "It is indeed painful to see in the Senate lobby former Foreign Minister Laval, who is now opposing the treaty he had himself signed." Despite the efforts of the extreme reactionaries, the treaty was ratified on February 27, 1936, by 353 votes against 164 in the Chamber of Deputies, and on March 12 by 233 votes against 52 in the Senate.—Ed.

Japan. But the U.S.A., Britain and France did not support the U.S.S.R. They began to encourage the aggressors more and more openly. As early as 1935, the U.S. Congress passed a Neutrality Bill which outlawed the export of arms to belligerent countries. Formally, this law placed the aggressor and the victim on an equal footing, and that made it advantageous to a well-armed aggressor.

The fifth column became active in the democratic bourgeois countries, particularly in France. A small but extremely influential minority, enjoying the support of part of the big bourgeoisie, urged rapprochement with Hitler Germany and giving her a "free hand in the East". Entering into polemics with this group, the prominent French bourgeois journalist Emile Buret wrote in June 1936: "I simply cannot understand what you are aiming at. You evidently want an alliance with Germany, which would signify an end to France's historical role. We must now make our choice: either to cede to the German cannibal and agree to the role of a miserable fellow-traveller, or to resist him by uniting all the threatened peoples."*

In the meantime, Germany, Italy and Japan methodically went ahead with their plans. One act of aggression followed another. The Soviet Union was the only country openly to urge resistance and collective action in defence of the victims of aggression.

From the first to the last day of the fascist uprising in Spain, the Soviet Union sided with the democratic forces and gave the lawful government of Republican Spain moral and political support. The Soviet Government had to reckon with the policy of "non-interference" proclaimed by France and other powers, but in contrast to the initiators of that policy the Soviet Union demanded the effective cessation of the intervention in Spain and that all countries honestly honour their commitments. As soon as it became clear that the London International Committee for Non-Interference in Spanish Affairs was only a screen for the fascist aggressors, the Soviet Union began rendering direct assistance to the Republican Government.

Soviet tanks and aircraft appeared on the battlefields of China as well. More than 100 Soviet volunteer airmen died defending the freedom and independence of the Chinese people. At the same time, the Soviet Union did not relax its efforts to unite all peace-loving forces for a rebuff to aggression in the Far East. In March 1936, the Soviet Union signed a treaty of mutual assistance with the Mongolian People's Republic, and in August 1937, a treaty on non-aggression with China. The latter treaty, signed with China when she was being attacked by Japan, was a serious demonstration of the Soviet Union's sympathy for the victim of

_____
* Ordre, June 27, 1936.

the Japanese militarists. In 1938 and 1939, the Soviet Union granted China loans totalling $250,000,000.

After Japan had seized Manchuria in 1931, the Soviet Union was time and again forced to give a rebuff to Japanese invaders crossing the Soviet frontiers. In 1938-39, the Red Army had to engage Japanese troops in battles on a larger scale. In July 1938, Japanese troops crossed the Soviet frontier in the region of Lake Hasan but were driven back by units of the Red Army. In May 1939, a large Japanese army invaded the Mongolian People's Republic. In fulfilment of the Soviet-Mongolian Treaty, the Soviet Government at once went to Mongolia's assistance. Jointly with the Mongolian People's Army, the Red Army surrounded picked Japanese units and destroyed them towards the close of August. The scale of the fighting may be gauged from the fact that in the air battles the Japanese lost 660 aircraft.

After the forced *Anschluss* in Austria in March 1938, the Soviet Union proposed the immediate convocation of an international conference to adopt the necessary measures against the further spread of aggression.

Betrayal at Munich

Instead of stopping the aggressors the French, British and U.S. ruling circles went out of their way to give them moral, political and material assistance. In November 1937 Lord Halifax visited Hitler. The British visitor made it plain to the nazi dictator that Britain would not hinder Germany's advance in Eastern Europe.

The Western powers supplied the aggressors with strategic materials. In October 1936, nazi Minister of National Economy Hjalmar Schacht signed a new agreement with France on the delivery to Germany of more than 3,500 million marks' worth of iron ore annually. In the period 1933-38, Germany's bauxite imports increased by 400 per cent, enabling German monopolies to become the world's biggest producers of aluminium. The U.S.A. and Britain sold Japan iron ore, petroleum and other raw materials. The U.S.A. played the leading role in providing the aggressors with money. U.S. investments in German enterprises (excluding loans) reached the sum of $1,000 million on the eve of the Second World War. The shrewd politicians in London, Paris and Washington could not fail to see that their anti-communism was serving the nazis. But they were counting on provoking a clash between the nazis and the Soviet Union. That short-sighted policy manifested itself most strongly in 1938-39 during the Czechoslovak crisis.

When Czechoslovakia was threatened with German invasion the Soviet Union announced that it was prepared to fulfil its obli-gation under the 1935 treaty, i.e., come to her assistance provided France, too, assisted Czechoslovakia. The Soviet Government insisted on an emergency conference of the Chiefs of the General Staffs of the U.S.S.R., France and Czechoslovakia. Moreover, in September the Czechoslovak Government was on two occasions informed that the Soviet Union was prepared to assist Czechoslovakia even if France failed to do so.

France declined all of the Soviet Union's proposals. The Government of Czechoslovakia, on account of the pressure being brought to bear on it by Anglo-French diplomacy, adopted a defeatist position, hesitating to mobilise the army and people and accept military assistance from the Soviet Union.

On September 29, the British Prime Minister Neville Chamberlain, the French Premier Daladier and the chief of the Italian fascists Benito Mussolini arrived in Munich for talks with Hitler. There Czechoslovakia's fate was sealed in a matter of a few hours: she was ordered to turn the Sudeten region over to the nazis.

On September 30, that shameful deal was clinched by a bilateral Anglo-German declaration, which was, to all intents and purposes, a non-aggression pact. Two months later, on December 6, a similar declaration was signed by the nazis and the French Government.

Thus "Western democracy" evolutionised from the 1933-34 plans of collective security in Eastern Europe to open co-operation with aggressors. The British and French leaders considered that Hitler's crusade on the East was a matter of the immediate future. Robert Coulondre, the French Ambassador in Berlin, reported to his government on December 15, 1938: "German dynamism will not stop before any difficulties and German military circles are already speaking of a jaunt all the way to the Caucasus and Baku."

A week before the Munich agreement was signed, the newspaper *Pravda* warned Britain and France that their policy was fraught with danger not only to the cause of peace but also to themselves, "because it constantly whets the nazi appetites".

On March 15, 1939, the nazis occupied the whole of Czechoslovakia. On March 21, they demanded that Poland transfer Danzig to Germany. On the next day, German troops entered the Lithuanian region of Klaipeda. At the close of March, the almost three-year-long heroic struggle of the Spanish people ended in Franco's victory. A few days after that Mussolini's fascists seized Albania.

What were Britain and France doing all that time? They were still counting on Hitler moving to the East.

However, the seizure of Czechoslovakia and fresh acts of aggression by the nazis created serious difficulties for the British and French men of Munich. Mass indignation was aroused in Britain and France by the actions of the nazi invaders in the spring of 1939. These actions showed the people what the "peace" that Chamberlain and Daladier had brought from Munich was worth. Public opinion demanded resistance to aggression. The British bourgeoisie began to realise that Hitler might deceive his Munich partners and move westward.

In mid-April 1939, the governments of Chamberlain and Daladier approached the Soviet Government with the proposal that Poland and Rumania should be given guarantees against German aggression.

1939 Moscow Talks. Outbreak of the Second World War

Despite the bitter experience of the preceding years the Soviet Government decided to make another attempt to create a front of peace-loving forces and on April 17 proposed beginning talks on the conclusion of a tripartite pact of mutual assistance. The Soviet proposals envisaged guaranteeing the independence of all the states bordering on the Soviet Union from the Baltic to the Black Sea. Under pressure of public opinion in their own countries the British and French governments had to agree to negotiations.

From the very outset of the talks Britain and France tried to place the Soviet Union in an unequal position. They hoped to utilise Soviet assistance in case Hitler attacked the West but had no desire to commit themselves in the event the nazis decided to turn to the East (in particular, they gave no guarantees to the Baltic countries, thereby opening a wide corridor to the Soviet frontiers for the German army).

On July 23, the Soviet Government suggested that the military representatives of the three powers should meet in Moscow and work out concrete ways of co-ordinating military action. Britain and France agreed to sent military missions, but behind the scenes British diplomacy had already initiated talks with Germany on the settlement of disputed issues through the division of spheres of influence between the two countries.*

Documents exposing these perfidious actions of the British Government became known many years later, but the real position of the Western powers could be seen already then, in the summer of 1939. Although the situation required urgent measures, London and Paris did not hurry. Nineteen days passed from the moment the Soviet Government proposed military talks

---

* Robert Hudson, then British Chairman of the Board of Trade, had talks in London with Wohltat, Goering's economic adviser, on July 20, 1939. The nazi emissary also had talks with Horace Wilson, Chamberlain's chief diplomatic adviser. In these talks the British offered to conclude a non-aggression pact with Germany, demarcate spheres of influence, guarantee Germany's participation in the exploitation of colonies, and so forth. Chamberlain informed the British Parliament on July 24, 1939, that Hudson and Wilson had conducted negotiations on the granting of a £500,000,000-£1,000,000,000 loan to Germany.—*Ed.*

before the British and French military missions arrived in Moscow. When they finally came (on August 11), it turned out that the British mission was not authorised to conduct negotiations. The Soviet military delegation included Kliment Voroshilov, People's Commissar for Defence, Boris Shaposhnikov, Chief of the General Staff, and other top military leaders. The British and French missions, on the other hand, were headed by secondary military chiefs, as though emphasising the deprecatory attitude of the two governments to the Moscow talks.

The Soviet Union did not have common frontiers with Germany and consequently it could play the most effective role in resisting nazi aggression only if Britain's and France's allies—Poland and Rumania—permitted Soviet troops to pass across their territory.

But neither the British nor the French did anything to induce the Polish and Rumanian governments to give the Soviet Union the required permission.

The talks were deliberately sabotaged and protracted by the British and French missions. The Soviet Government had every reason to fear another Munich, this time directly spearheaded against the Soviet Union.

In Europe war could break out any day; in the Far East (Mongolia) Soviet troops were already locked in battle with the Japanese army. There was the danger that within weeks or even days the Soviet Union would be involved in war on two fronts. Nobody would come to its assistance. It was therefore the duty of the Soviet Government to deliver the country from that danger.

It was exactly at that time that the German Government, fearing that its military and economic potential was not sufficient to crush the Soviet Union, proposed signing a non-aggression pact with the U.S.S.R. When it finally became obvious that in the four-month-long talks the British and French were reluctant to form an honest alliance with the U.S.S.R. the Soviet Government agreed to Germany's proposals. The Soviet-German non-aggression pact was signed on August 23, 1939. That checkmated the policy of the men of Munich. Germany did not attack the Soviet Union at the time. In mid-September the Soviet Union settled the conflict with Japan and obtained a respite and the possibility to prepare for the inevitable clash with nazism.

For the Soviet Government the treaty with nazi Germany was not a desired solution, but in face of the policy pursued by Britain and France it was the only way out of the dangerous situation at the end of the summer of 1939.

On September 1, 1939, Hitler Germany started the Second World War by invading Poland. The governments of Britain and France could no longer stand aloof: public opinion in their countries demanded that the aggressor be given a determined rebuff.

The position of these countries as Great Powers and the future of their vast colonial empires were at stake. There could be no further retreat. On September 3, Britain and France declared war on Germany.

U.S.S.R. Strengthens Its Western Frontiers

Despite the heroic resistance of the Polish Army, the nazis rapidly advanced eastward. The Polish bourgeois-landowner state collapsed. The Soviet Government resolutely came forward in defence of the Ukrainian, Byelorussian and Polish population of the eastern part of the country. On September 17, Soviet troops crossed the Soviet-Polish frontier and within a matter of days reached a line running approximately along the Curzon Line,* thus placing a limit on the movement of nazi troops to the east. The liberated areas united with Soviet Ukraine and Soviet Byelorussia into single states of the Ukrainian and Byelorussian peoples.

By advancing 200-300 kilometres westward, the Red Army moved away the strategic lines from which the nazi army could begin an offensive against key centres of the Soviet Union.

With the war conflagration enveloping almost the whole of Europe, the Soviet Government had to take urgent steps to strengthen the defences along its entire western frontier. There were many weak spots in these defences. The leaders of Estonia, Latvia and Lithuania and also of Finland adopted a sharply anti-Soviet stand; the Finnish Government, in particular, began building fortifications along the Soviet frontier, 32 kilometres away from Leningrad.

The Soviet Government offered a mutual assistance pact to the three Baltic countries. These pacts were signed at the close of September and early in October. Under the treaty with Lithuania, the Soviet Union turned over to that country its ancient capital Vilnius and Vilnius Region which had been captured by Polish troops in 1920.

Talks were started with Finland in October on the initiative of the Soviet Union. The Soviet Government proposed moving the frontier between the two countries on the Karelian Isthmus 20-30 kilometres into Finland in exchange for double that territory in Soviet Karelia. However, whipped up by promises from the Great Powers, Finland's leaders rejected all the Soviet proposals. The rupture in the talks was accompanied by an anti-Soviet propaganda campaign in Finland. The relations between the two countries deteriorated rapidly, and on November 30, the Finnish Government officially declared war on the Soviet Union.

---

* Proposed Eastern frontier of Poland recognised by the Entente on suggestions from lord Curzon.—Ed.

·In this period the deep-rooted hostility of the British and French governments for the Soviet Union came to the fore again. On their initiative, the League of Nations, which had never expelled any real aggressor, quickly expelled the Soviet Union, which had shown that it was a tested champion of peace and collective security. Britain and Germany, whose armies were inactive on the Western Front, suddenly livened up in connection with the Soviet-Finnish conflict. They sent Finland 280 war planes, 686 pieces of artillery, hundreds of thousands of shells, etc. A large Anglo-French expeditionary corps was scheduled to leave for Finland in mid-March. Twelve days after the conflict started, the U.S. Government granted Finland a large loan. On December 30, 1939, the *New York Times* forecast that the Soviet-Finnish war could lead to the creation of a united front against the Soviet Union.

But all these plans were not destined to be fulfilled. On March 1, 1940, the Red Army breached the powerful Finnish fortifications and began to win operational space. The road to Helsinki was open. But the Soviet Government did not take advantage of its military successes to occupy Finland or impose onerous peace terms on her. Under the treaty signed on March 12, 1940, the frontiers were moved only a small distance into Finland—on the Karelian Isthmus and in some other regions, thereby giving greater security to Leningrad, Murmansk and the Murmansk Railway. On Hanko Peninsula, at the entrance to the Gulf of Finland, the Soviet Union was enabled to build a naval base. The territory involved was leased to the Soviet Union for 30 years at an annual rate of 8,000,000 Finnish marks.

In the meantime, the situation in Europe changed rapidly. In April 1940, the nazi army occupied Denmark and Norway. Sweden was threatened. On April 13, in a special memorandum to Werner Schulenburg, the German Ambassador in Moscow, the Soviet Government stated that it was against any violation of Sweden's neutrality. Not wishing to exacerbate her relations with the Soviet Union at the time, Germany was compelled to take that warning into consideration.

On May 10, German troops invaded the Netherlands, Belgium and Luxemburg. Within a few days they occupied these countries, by-passing the French Maginot Line, and reached the coast of the English Channel on May 21. On June 10, four days before the fall of Paris, fascist Italy entered the war on the side of Germany. A Great Power, France, was crushed and forced to capitulate in the course of only five weeks. The remnants of the British Expeditionary Force saved themselves in flight. The nazi occupation spread over almost the whole of Central and Western Europe. Towards the summer of 1940, the German and Italian armies controlled a territory with a population of nearly 220 million. The resources of the occupied countries were used to bolster the German military machine.

The Soviet Government further strengthened the country's defences when the threat of nazi aggression eastward sharply increased with France's defeat and the imminent collapse of the Allied front in Western Europe.

The situation in the three Baltic countries caused serious alarm. Despite the treaties of mutual assistance with the Soviet Union, the governments of these small republics established closer contact with nazi Germany. In the summer of 1940, the Lithuanian Government asked the nazis to move German troops into the Baltic area at once.

In mid-June, the Soviet Government demanded that Estonia, Latvia and Lithuania form governments that could and would be ready to fulfil the mutual assistance pacts. The three governments accepted the Soviet demands; the ruling circles in those countries thought they could replace some individuals in their governments and let matters stand. But the masses actively joined in the struggle. They established Soviet rule and joined the U.S.S.R.

The destiny of Bessarabia, which had been forcibly wrested from the Soviet Union in 1918, was settled. The Soviet Government secured the restoration of justice peaceably. The establishment of Soviet rule in the Baltic and Bessarabia greatly enhanced the safety of the Soviet Union's western frontiers.

In the summer of 1940, Hitler signed a directive authorising preparations for the invasion of the U.S.S.R. The fascist powers consolidated their forces by signing a tripartite pact in Berlin in mid-September. The secret articles of this pact provided for the abolition of the Soviet state and its partition between Germany, Italy and Japan, the signatories to that pact.

Despite all the efforts of the Soviet Government to prevent a further extension of the war in Europe, the nazi aggression spread swiftly. In October 1940, nazi troops entered Rumania and then Bulgaria. Large German forces occupied Yugoslavia, invaded Greece and reached her southern coast after furious fighting. That placed almost the whole of continental Europe, except the Soviet Union and a number of small countries, into the hands of the nazis and their allies. The forces released in the Balkans were transferred to the frontiers of the Soviet Union.

A major success of Soviet foreign policy during these months was the signing of a neutrality pact with Japan (April 1941). This pact strengthened the Soviet defences in the Far East and foiled the plans for a simultaneous invasion of the U.S.S.R. from the west and east. The Soviet Government did not want war and tried to avert it.

But in the summer of 1941 war was already on the threshold of the Soviet Union.

Chapter Five

THE GREAT PATRIOTIC WAR
OF THE SOVIET UNION
(1941-45)

Nazi Germany Attacks the U.S.S.R.

The war begun in Western Europe came inexorably closer to the borders of the Soviet Union. There was ample evidence that Germany was preparing to attack the U.S.S.R. Hitler's diplomats were hastily forging an anti-Soviet war bloc. In the autumn of 1940 and the spring of 1941 the nazis concluded military treaties with Rumania, Bulgaria, Hungary and Finland, and a "friendship pact" with Turkey. In East Prussia, in areas seized from Poland, in Rumania, Hungary and Finland, the Germans built fortifications, airfields, depots and fuel stores, and improved and widened roads leading to the Soviet frontier. Goebbels's propaganda machine clamoured for 'Lebensraum' in the East.

Endless trainloads of nazi troops and arms rolled from France and the west of Germany to the borders of the Soviet Union.

Warnings of the imminent attack were also sounded through diplomatic channels. A communication came from the U.S. Government in January 1941, and another from the British Government on April 19.

In view of the looming danger, the Soviet Government took measures to buttress the country's war potential. It worked out a plan to convert industry to military production, transferred some of its armed forces from the Far East to the central and western regions, and began to build fortifications on the western border. The numerical strength of the Soviet Armed Forces was substantially increased and the rearming of troops with new weapons was begun.

But these measures were inadequate and belated. The conversion of industry to war production, for example, was scheduled to begin in the latter half of 1941 and in 1942.

The plan worked out by the German General Staff for the attack on the U.S.S.R., known as Operation Barbarossa, envisaged a blitzkrieg. Hitler's strategists, heartened by the success of the blitz campaigns of 1939 and 1940 in Western Europe, expected to crush the Soviet Union in some six to eight weeks, or at most by the autumn of 1941. The nazis were certain in their vain belief that the Red Army was weak, the Soviet system unstable, and the alliance of the working class and the peasants, like the friendship of the peoples of the U.S.S.R., unreliable. In view of the pre-war policy of France, Britain and the United States, the German rulers hoped that the Soviet Union would be politically isolated and that Britain and the United States would launch out against the U.S.S.R.

The nazi High Command expected to seize the most important Soviet industrial and political centres, such as Moscow, Leningrad, the Donets Basin and the Caucasus, in next to no time and thereby break down Soviet resistance.

Armed and equipped with the latest weapons, well trained, steeled by two years of war, the nazi army was a powerful adversary. In the spring of 1941 it consisted of over 200 divisions, of which 153 were massed along the Soviet border, supported by another 37 Finnish, Rumanian and Hungarian divisions. The bulk of the nazi divisions had had two years of combat experience in the West. Besides, Germany had at its disposal the material resources and the manpower of conquered Western Europe. The nazi Command deployed its troops along the western frontier of the U.S.S.R. in one strategic echelon, the objective being to gain the initiative in the border fighting at one powerful stroke.

The peoples of the Soviet Union were in deadly peril. The Soviet border was covered from the Barents to the Black Sea by troops of the Special Leningrad, Baltic, Western, Kiev and Odessa military districts. They were expected to stem the enemy onslaught and give the Soviet Command time to mobilise and deploy the main strength of the Red Army. Numerically, the Soviet troops along the border were outnumbered two to one. They were a match for the enemy in arms, especially tanks and airplanes, but most of their weapons were obsolete, while replacement with new models had only just begun. The Red Army was positioned in a balanced line, with the main forces stationed 150 to 500 kilometres from the border.

The effectives of many of the Soviet formations had been conscripted shortly before the nazi attack and had not yet been sufficiently trained.

The groundless persecutions of the Red Army's most experienced officers between 1936 and 1939 also had a very adverse effect on its fighting capacity.

The country's poor preparedness was due to grave errors of judgement made by Stalin in evaluating the general strategic situation and in his estimates of the probable time the war would break out. Stalin dismissed information coming in from various quarters about Germany's preparing to attack the U.S.S.R. as a provocation

Stalin never believed that war would come to him.

devised by the foreign press to create trouble between the U.S.S.R. and Germany. A week before the war, the Soviet press published a TASS statement describing as groundless the rumours of an impending war between the U.S.S.R. and Germany. The troops of the western military districts received no orders to move to the border, and were not even alerted. They followed a peacetime routine, and the initial assault of the fascist troops took them completely by surprise. The enemy's numerical superiority and the surprise element contributed greatly to the early success of the German forces, and put the Red Army in an extremely difficult position.

Sunday, June 22, 1941, has gone down in world history as the beginning of an unequalled and criminal tragedy. Early in the morning of that day, without so much as a declaration of war, the nazis and the armed forces of their satellites invaded the U.S.S.R. Only then did the German Ambassador in Moscow, Werner Schulenburg, inform the People's Commissar for Foreign Affairs that Germany considered itself at war with the Union of Soviet Socialist Republics. In so doing, he presented no charges against the Soviet Government to justify the German invasion.

This was the beginning of the Great Patriotic War which the Soviet Union fought for nearly four years, or, more precisely, for 1,418 days and nights.

Fascist Germany's attack on the U.S.S.R. ushered in a new stage of the Second World War. Initially it had been an imperialist war between the capitalist powers for the redivision of the world and for spheres of influence. But when whole peoples joined in the struggle against German and Italian fascism in Europe and Japanese militarism in Asia, it became a just war of liberation. The involvement of the Soviet Union added to the liberative character of the Second World War. The fight of the peoples of the U.S.S.R. against the nazi invaders combined with the struggle of the peoples of other countries for freedom and independence, democracy and socialism.

As for nazi Germany, it was waging a totally unjust war, as aggressive and predatory as the substance of fascism itself.

Operations began with massive German air raids on towns, ports, airfields, railway junctions and other military targets in the Soviet border areas. Artillery, tanks and motorised infantry attacked the Soviet border posts. The border troops, enormously outnumbered, fought tenaciously to their dying breath, their last bullet and hand grenade. Yet they could not stem the onsweep of enemy armour.

Hastily, cover troops took up positions in the border zones where fortifications had not yet been completed. The course of events could not have been more unfavourable for the Red Army. The nazi troops launched their offensive along a vast frontage stretching from the Barents to the Black Sea.

Moscow scene, autumn 1941

Leningrad during the siege, 1941

The Peterhof Palace near Leningrad destroyed by nazi troops, 1944

In the north, German and Finnish troops incorporated in Army Group Norway advanced on Murmansk and Kandalaksha. But this was a secondary operation. The main blow was struck in three central strategic directions against Moscow, Leningrad and Kiev, where the nazi Command had massed most of its forces under generals who had carried out the lightning assault on France—Fieldmarshal Wilhelm Ritter von Leeb in command of the northern army group, Fieldmarshal Fedor von Bock of the central army group, and Fieldmarshal Gerd von Rundstedt of the southern army group.

Army Group North advanced from East Prussia on Leningrad along the Baltic coast, Army Group Centre from north-east of Warsaw on Minsk, Smolensk and Moscow, and Army Group South from Lyublin on Zhitomir, Kiev and, subsequently, the Donets Basin.

The enemy armies were opposed by formations of the Baltic, Western and Kiev military districts, which were converted with other border commands on the first day of the war into the North-Western Front, the Western Front and the South-Western Front. A Northern Front was soon formed, to defend the territory from Leningrad to Murmansk, and a Southern Front, too, which deployed its troops along the Prut River. The nation's armed forces were headed by the Headquarters of the High Command formed by decision of the Soviet Government on June 23, 1941, which was later changed into the Headquarters of the Supreme Command

Hitler hoped that his surprise attack would knock out the Red Army, and, to be sure, Stalin's errors of judgement, and his outright mistakes, went a long way to further his designs. In the first few hours of the war the fascist air force reduced 66 airfields to uselessness in the border regions, destroyed 1,200 Soviet aircraft on the ground and in the air, and won air supremacy. Striking swiftly deep into the country, the nazis seized a large number of airfields. The troops of the Western Front lost all their artillery depots with more than 2,000 waggon loads of munition. The Germans also captured more than 3,000 tanks and nearly 2,000 guns, which tilted the scales still more in their favour.

Red Army units engaged the enemy at different times in a haphazard manner, lacking contact with front headquarters and deprived of the necessary leadership and co-ordination. Isolated from each other, they suffered defeat after defeat.

In the first few days of the war powerful thrusts by the German strike forces breached the Soviet border defences, overpowered the Soviet cover troops, and advanced deeper into Soviet territory.

Troops of Army Group North, consisting of the 16th and 18th armies and the 4th Panzer Group lunged into the Baltic states from East Prussia. Their objective was to cut off the troops of the North-Western Front stationed in the Baltic states, and to destroy them. After this, they were to thrust at Leningrad and Kronstadt, seize the Soviet naval bases in that area and make contact with Finnish troops north and south of Lake Ladoga. Hitler attached cardinal importance to the offensive along the Baltic seaboard, and even established his personal headquarters in East Prussia, near the Lithuanian border.

The troops of the Soviet North-Western Front, consisting of the 8th and 11th armies under Colonel-General F. Kuznetsov, tried to stem the enemy advance, but their effort was in vain. By July 10, German forward units reached Pärnu, Tartu, Pskov and Opochka. Save for part of Estonia and the city of Tallinn, the territory of the Soviet Baltic republics was lost to the enemy.

It should be noted, however, that Hitler's plan of enveloping and destroying the Red Army in that area was dashed, and so was his hope of seizing the Baltic Fleet. The Baltic Fleet changed its base, moving first to Tallinn, and then breaking through to Kronstadt and Leningrad.

The situation in the centre was still graver. As in the Baltic area, the nazi Command there was intent on encircling and destroying the Red Army troops defending the borders of Soviet Byelorussia. In pursuing this plan, the Germans concentrated strong and mobile forces on the flanks of the Western Front with orders to advance in converging directions. They mounted the offensive on the right flank with the 9th Army and 3rd Panzer Group from Suvalki against Grodno, and then in a south-easterly direction detouring Byelostok. The nazi 4th Army and 2nd Panzer Group advanced to meet them from the south via Brest and somewhat to the north of the Bug River.

The Soviet Western Front, commanded early in the war by General D. Pavlov, consisted of three armies: the 3rd Army neighbouring on the North-Western Front, the 4th Army adjoining the South-Western Front, and the 10th Army occupying the Byelostok bulge in the centre. After the enemy crushed the 11th Army, the 3rd Army was compelled to withdraw fighting towards Grodno to avoid encirclement, and then south-east of that city.

On the left flank, the Germans left part of their forces to besiege the Brest Fortress and mounted a rapid advance north-eastward. On June 28, the two enemy army groups made contact in the Minsk area, cutting off avenues of retreat for eleven relatively battleworthy Soviet divisions. Only a few units of these eleven divisions managed to break out of the German encirclement after heavy fighting and join the main forces. Many units withdrew into the dense Byelorussian forests and joined the local partisan detachments, but a still bigger section was taken prisoner by the fascists.

To sum up, by July 10, enemy troops in the centre of the country advanced to a line from Polotsk through Vitebsk, Orsha and Mogilev to Zhlobin.

To bolster the defences in the centre, the Western Front was quickly reinforced by High Command Reserves, and Marshal of the Soviet Union Semen Timoshenko was put in command of the front.

On the southern flank of the Soviet-German front the enemy was faced by the South-Western Front under Colonel-General M. Kirponos and the Southern Front under General of the Army I. Tyulenev. The two fronts consisted of six armies.

The nazi Army Group South, which consisted of three German armies, one panzer group, two Rumanian armies and one Hungarian army corps, struck out from the Lyublin-Zamostye area towards Dubno, Novograd-Volynsky and Zhitomir at the right flank of the South-Western Front. Making the most of his numerical superiority, the enemy broke through the Soviet defences and threatened to envelop the main Soviet force in that area. So the Supreme Command decided to withdraw its troops to the fortified lines along the former state border. By July 10 the withdrawal was completed and the troops dug in along the line Novograd-Volynsky, Zhitomir, Berdichev, Proskurov and Kamenets-Podolsk.

The German army had thus won the battle in the frontier area. But the fighting showed that the nazi leaders and their generals could not have been more wrong when they thought the Red Army was weak. The Soviet troops fought the enemy tooth and nail. Even when encircled, they did not, to the surprise of the German generals, hoist the white flag and surrender. The small garrison of the border fortress at Brest, for example, fought on for a month. The enemy entered it only after all of its defenders were put out of action.

Gunners fired at enemy tanks at close range and when their supply of shells ran out, they hurled hand grenades and incendiary bottles at them, engaging the panzers in unequal combat. Airmen rammed enemy planes in mid-air. Members of the armed forces performed countless deeds of valour. Take the exploit of the air crew of N. Gastello, A. Burdenyuk, G. Skorobogaty and A. Kalinin, whose names will go down in history for their unexampled courage. When their plane was hit and burst into flames during a sortie on July 26, Captain Gastello steered it into a column of enemy tanks and fuel-carriers. Dozens of lorries and fuel-carriers and a few enemy tanks were set aflame when the plane exploded.

Taking advantage of their temporary superiority, the nazi troops by early July 1941 had overrun Lithuania, a considerable part of Latvia, and the western regions of Byelorussia and the Ukraine. Their drive into Soviet territory continued. They strained every sinew to reach the country's nerve centres. The Soviet troops rolled back under the continuous pressure of superior enemy forces.

When they started the war, the nazi leaders banked on an assumed instability in the Soviet rear and a possible split among the socialist nations. They scoffed at the moral and political unity of the Soviet people. But they could not have been more wrong.

The peoples of the Soviet Union responded eagerly to the call of the Communist Party and rose to the defence of their socialist homeland. Before the war was a few days old hundreds of thousands of Soviet men and women had volunteered for the army. A powerful popular militia, 35 divisions strong, was formed in Moscow, Leningrad, Kiev and other cities.

Far from shaking the unity of the Soviet peoples, the surprise enemy assault only added vigour to it.

It was clear from the first day of the war how deeply the German strategists had erred by banking on internal weaknesses.

The Communist Party, which had headed the people in peace-time socialist construction, now led the nation in the fight for its survival and independence, against fascist enslavement. The Central Committee of the Party told the people about the full extent of the danger facing the socialist homeland and defined the aims and the character of the war.

All Party organisations were put on a wartime footing by order of the Party Central Committee. Party work was conducted under the slogan, "Everything for the Front, Everything for Victory". Very soon this slogan became the guiding motive of everything the Soviet people did in the four long years of the war.

The Soviet Government appeal to the people on the first day of the war and the directive of the Council of People's Commissars and of the C.C. C.P.S.U.(B.) to Party and government organisations in the frontier regions, dated June 29, 1941, supplemented and developed by Stalin's speech on July 3, defined the main tasks facing the Party and the people. "The purpose of the nazi attack," said the directive, "is to destroy the Soviet system, seize Soviet land, enslave the peoples of the Soviet Union, plunder our country, take our bread and oil, and restore the power of the landowners and capitalists. . . . The war imposed on us by fascist Germany is a matter of life and death for the Soviet state, and will decide whether the people of the Soviet Union are to remain free or fall captive."

The directive urged the nation to shake off its peacetime mood and to devote all its vigour to strengthening the Red Army and fighting the enemy. Here is what it said about the tasks of the Soviet people in the occupied territories:

"Partisan detachments, on horseback and on foot, and subversive groups must be organised in enemy-occupied areas to harrass the enemy troops, to conduct partisan warfare, to blow up bridges and roads, to cut telephone and telegraph lines, to set fire to forests, warehouses and transports. The position of the enemy and his accomplices in occupied areas must be made intolerable. They must be pursued and destroyed at every point, and all their measures must be sabotaged and thwarted."

The ideas set out in these Party documents guided the Soviet people in their war effort on the front and in the Soviet rear.

The Red Army had to be reinforced with Communists and members of the Young Communist League. The Party Central Committee issued an order for the mobilisation of Communists to improve political work in the army. By the end of 1941, the Armed Forces had 1,300,000 Communists, nearly half the Party membership. Communists fought with selfless courage and total disregard for their lives. In just the first year of the war 400,000 of them laid down their lives in battle. The young people fought heroically.

When the war broke out, the Soviet Government issued a series of orders to convert the country to a wartime footing.

On June 22, the Presidium of the Supreme Soviet of the U.S.S.R. ordered the mobilisation of reservists born in 1905-1918 in the territory of 14 military districts. Millions of Soviet men from 23 to 36 were called up to the army and dispatched to military formations. Manpower was marshalled to replace them in production.

On June 30, the Presidium of the Supreme Soviet of the U.S.S.R., the C.C. of the Party and the Council of People's Commissars jointly decided to form an extraordinary wartime body, the State Defence Committee, to be headed by Stalin, which was invested with supreme military and political powers. The exigencies of war called to life other political organisations. A Council for Evacuation was formed under the Council of People's Commissars to supervise the evacuation of the population and of property. A Committee for the Registration and Distribution of Manpower was established to ensure fuller and more effective use of the labour force.

The Soviet Information Bureau was founded in the early days of the war to report on the hostilities. In all spheres of life, at the front and in the rear, in political and ideological affairs, the Party thus rallied forces to repel the aggressor.

It assigned its finest sons to the most important and crucial sectors of the front and rear, to underground work and to promote the partisan movement behind the enemy lines. The efforts of central and local Party and government organisations turned the country into a tightly knit military camp.

The summer months of 1941 were the most trying for the Soviet Union. The army was in retreat, abandoning region after region and town after town. An endless stream of troop trains moved eastward, evacuating workers and equipment, stocks of grain, cattle, farm machinery, etc. The roads and railway junctions were crowded with refugees. Towns and villages, and factories, too, stood in flames behind the enemy lines.

The nazi invasion impelled the conversion of the country's economy to a wartime footing. This was a challenge of no mean proportions.

Factories which had produced peacetime goods had to be urgently converted to war production. Tractor works were hastily refitted to manufacture tanks, and iron and steel mills produced new types of alloys for armour, while farming machinery plants manufactured mortars. It was a task of prime urgency to organise co-operation between the factories, to supply the key plants with semi-manufactures and instruments essential for the production of military equipment.

The army and the urban population required a vast amount of food, and the war industry needed raw materials. All this had to be supplied by the farms.

The peasants had to harvest the crops and transport them from threatened areas. At many points, the collective farmers harvested under enemy fire and turned the crops over to government procurement agencies for shipment to the country's eastern areas. Cattle and farm machinery were shipped east, too, and the peasants abandoned their villages.

The rapid enemy advance did untold harm to agriculture in the western areas.

Food and other consumer goods were rationed in order to marshal all food and raw materials for wartime needs. The entire able-bodied population worked at the factories, the collective farms and the state farms.

The wartime conversion of the economy was made more difficult by the forced evacuation of industrial enterprises from war-imperilled areas deep into the country. An immense number of factories was removed to the country's east from the Ukraine, Byelorussia, Latvia, Lithuania, Estonia, the Karelo-Finnish and Moldavian republics, and the western areas of the R.S.F.S.R. The biggest factories of Moscow, Leningrad, Kharkov, Odessa and other Soviet industrial centres were put on wheels. Most of them were evacuated to the Urals, Siberia and the Central Asian republics. All in all, as many as 1,523 industrial enterprises were removed to safe regions during the first three months of the war.

The evacuation proceeded round the clock, often under shell fire and air bombardment. The vast undertaking taxed the railways to the utmost, but the country's railway workers performed miracles of devotion and coped with their task.

The factories and their personnel were really in a sorry plight when they arrived at their new sites. More often than not there were no industrial premises for the equipment they had brought with them, and no housing for the workers. And they had to contend with a disastrous shortage of fuel and electric power. But the workers, technicians and engineers did wonders to surmount all these difficulties and put the enterprises back into operation in short order. The restarting of the evacuated factories occupied an average of 6 to 8 weeks.

All in all, the conversion of industry to war production was accomplished in 3 to 4 months, and the conversion of the rest of the economy in less than a year. This was an economic feat, unparalleled in world history.

In the latter half of 1941 the country's economy was at its lowest. Some factories had been lost to the enemy, while others had not yet been restarted after evacuation. Aggregate industrial output dropped to less than half from June to November. But the decline ceased in December, and production began to mount steadily.

The numerical strength of factory and office workers decreased considerably by the end of 1941. This was due to the enemy occupation of vast territories, and to army conscription. Women, juveniles and elderly people came to the factories. They were taught labour skills hastily, and worked selflessly for victory.

The conversion of the Soviet Union into a close-knit military camp and the phenomenal rate at which the economy was reshaped along wartime lines laid the foundation for ultimate victory.

Emergence of the Anti-Hitler Coalition

Hitler and his henchmen hoped to forge a united imperialist front against the Soviet Union. But the course of events dashed his hopes. On June 22, 1941, Winston Churchill, the head of the British Government, though reiterating his aversion for the Soviet Union, hastened to declare Britain's resolve to fight side by side with it. An identical declaration came from U.S. President Franklin Delano Roosevelt on June 24. Lively negotiations ensued between the U.S.S.R., the U.S.A. and Great Britain throughout the summer of 1941, culminating in a series of agreements. At a conference in Moscow from September 29 to October 1, Soviet, American and British spokesmen worked out a plan for Anglo-American shipments of arms, equipment and food supplies to the Soviet Union. The Soviet Union, for its part, undertook to supply *really* the United States and Britain with strategic raw materials.

The major capitalist powers joined hands with the socialist state against a grouping of imperialist countries related to them by their class nature. This was due to the contradictions that prevailed in the capitalist world and that had grown doubly acute during the war. Far-sighted British and American statesmen were aware of the danger that Germany would be to them if it succeeded in capturing the resources of the Soviet Union. Alliance with the U.S.S.R. was distinctly profitable to Britain and the United States.

The more reactionary imperialist groups in the U.S.A. and Britain, it is true, were far from eager to cut short the nazi aggression. They wanted the war to sap the strength of the Soviet Union as much as of Germany. This notion was formulated baldly and cynically by Senator Harry Truman, later the President of the U.S.A. When he learned of Germany's attack on the Soviet Union, he said:

"If we see that Germany is winning we ought to help Russia and if Russia is winning we ought to help Germany and that way let them kill as many as possible."

But the general public in America, Britain, France and other countries looked favourably upon alliance with the Soviet Union. Their sympathies were with its people and they demanded that their countries help and support the U.S.S.R.

The governments of the United States, Britain and other countries had to reckon with public opinion on this score. Thus, thanks to the judicious Soviet foreign policy and the will of the nations, an anti-Hitler coalition emerged in the world by the end of 1941. It consisted of the Soviet Union, Britain and the United States, and had the support of the peoples of nazi-occupied Poland, Czechoslovakia, Yugoslavia, Belgium, Holland, Norway, etc. China, locked in mortal combat with imperialist Japan, and the British dominions and a number of other countries joined the coalition in due course.

The contradictions that prevailed between the capitalist countries had thus acted in favour of the Soviet state in its deadly battle against fascism. Germany and her allies had to face an alliance of freedom-loving peoples, determined to stand their ground to the end for freedom and independence.

The First Nazi Defeat. Blitzkrieg Fails

The retreat of the Red Army in the north-west in the autumn of 1941 brought the nazi troops to the gates of Leningrad and they blockaded that Soviet port city. Leningrad's population at the time exceeded 2,500,000, the majority being women, children and elderly people. Leningrad's communications with the rest of the country were cut, only a narrow route remaining across Lake Ladoga. The city's food and fuel supplies were negligible. After capturing Leningrad's suburbs, the German 18th Army shelled the city day and night, while nazi planes showered it with thousands of explosive and incendiary bombs. Blocks of dwellings were engulfed in flames.

But no matter how hard the fascists tried, they failed to advance any farther than Leningrad's outskirts. The troops of the Leningrad Front,* the seamen of the Baltic Fleet and the civilian population turned Leningrad into a fortress, swearing they would sooner die than let the enemy enter the birthplace of the proletarian revolution. The city's Communists, whose pre-war strength topped 153,500, were the heart and soul of the resistance. The Leningrad Party organisation was headed by A. Zhdanov, A. Kuznetsov and Y. Kapustin. More than 70 per cent of Leningrad's Communists and 90 per cent of its Y.C.L. members took part in the fighting.

In their drive towards Moscow, the nazis captured Smolensk and advanced on the capital, fighting bitterly for every inch of ground. After seizing a considerable part of the Ukraine, German troops also drew close to the gates of Kiev, Odessa and other important cities.

The nazi High Command attached immense importance to the capture of Kiev, the capital of the Soviet Ukraine, hoping to envelop and annihilate the main forces of the Southern and South-Western fronts, and then move on against Moscow.

The battle for Kiev lasted 83 days. The city's population took arms and joined the troops of the South-Western Front in the trenches.

The heroic defence of Kiev held up the German offensive against Moscow. Enemy casualties in the battle for Kiev exceeded 100,000 officers and men killed and wounded. The nazis also lost many tanks and other weapons. But in the end they drove through the flanks of the Soviet South-Western Front, enveloped its main force, and compelled it to abandon Kiev on September 19.

The defence of Odessa, which lasted 69 days, had a strong strategic and political impact. The port city was defended by ground forces, the navy and its own population. The enemy suffered heavy losses. But the city was abandoned on orders of the command due to the deterioration of the strategic situation in the Southern Ukraine. Odessa's heroic defenders were removed to Sevastopol, where another long-drawn-out siege began on November 3. After capturing Odessa, the nazi troops mounted an offensive for possession of the Crimean Peninsula and imperilled the Donets Basin.

But whatever successes the invaders scored, they were a mere shadow of what they had expected.

Red Army resistance grew more and more tenacious, while the nazi advance slackened. The German divisions suffered heavy losses and were forced to mark time, and eventually dig in in the

---

* On August 23, 1941, the Northern Front was divided into the Karelian and Leningrad fronts.—*Ed.*

muddy autumn soil, nipped here and there by early frosts. Behind the German lines Soviet patriots began partisan operations.

By the end of September 1941, the nazis were nowhere near the objectives envisaged for that date in the Barbarossa Plan. The resistance of the Soviet people and the Red Army stiffened. All the peoples of the U.S.S.R. had risen to defend the socialist homeland. Latvians, Estonians, Lithuanians, Uzbeks, Turkmen, Kirghizes, Kazakhs and the peoples of the Caucasus and Siberia fought the enemy shoulder to shoulder with the Russian, Ukrainian and Byelorussian peoples.

Dreading the collapse of the blitzkrieg, the Wehrmacht High Command attempted to save the day by concentrating all its efforts on one strategic blow against Moscow. Added prominence was given to the Soviet capital in its plans. The nazis hoped that on losing the capital the Soviet Union would be compelled to surrender. Army Group Centre, advancing on Moscow, was strongly reinforced with reserve troops and formations moved in from other sectors of the Soviet-German front. The enemy massed something like 80 divisions, including 14 panzer and eight motorised divisions, against the Western, Reserve and Bryansk fronts, which were drawn up to defend Moscow. This nazi force amounted to more than one-third of the infantry and nearly two-thirds of the armoured and motorised divisions operating on the Soviet-German front. The nazis had superior strength and more weapons—40 per cent more guns and mortars, and 160 per cent more aircraft.

The German Command intended to seize Moscow with three strike groups. Two of them were to outflank the capital from north and south and cut it off from the rear, while the centrally placed third group would strike directly at Moscow through Gzhatsk.

The battle for Moscow began on September 30, when the southern enemy group mounted an offensive against Orel, Tula and Kashira, engaging the troops of the Bryansk Front. The central and northern groups joined in the offensive on October 2.

Superior strength enabled the enemy to breach the Soviet defences, compelling the Red Army troops to retreat. The nazis captured Kalinin, Bryansk, Orel and Vyazma, approached the outskirts of Tula and entered Moscow Region. In the capital a state of siege was proclaimed. The Communist Party and the Soviet Government were determined to hold the city at any price. Hundreds of thousands of Muscovites helped build fortifications. Barricades were erected in the streets of Moscow as the capital prepared for possible street fighting.

The Moscow Party organisation played a prominent part in the defence of the capital. More than 360,000 Communists and Y.C.L. members in Moscow and Moscow Region joined the army as volunteers.

Heavy fighting broke out at the distant approaches to Moscow. The enemy strained all his energies, disregarding the casualties.

At the close of October the nazi offensive on Moscow petered out and came to a standstill. The front ran from Kalinin through Volokolamsk, Naro-Fominsk and Alexin to Tula. But the general situation on the Soviet-German front continued to deteriorate. In the north-west the enemy crossed the Volkhov River and reached Tikhvin. The Wehrmacht's aim was to come into contact with the Finnish troops between Lake Ladoga and Lake Onega, close the ring around Leningrad and bring its heroic defenders to their knees.

In the south, enemy troops drove into the Donets Basin and developed their offensive towards the Caucasus. They captured Rostov and in the Crimea laid siege to Sevastopol, the base of the Black Sea Fleet.

For the Soviet Union this was the most precarious period of the war. The country had lost territory producing before the war 63 per cent of the nation's coal, 68 per cent of the pig iron, 58 per cent of the steel, 60 per cent of the aluminium, 38 per cent of the grain, 85 per cent of the sugar, etc. The burden of supplies fell squarely on the Urals, Siberia, the Soviet Far East and the Central Asian republics. The army was short of weapons and ammunition.

Certain that they would win the war and go unpunished, the nazi occupation forces subjected the Soviet population in the occupied territories to unheard-of hardships. They destroyed and pillaged towns and villages, and tore down cultural and research institutions. Concentration camps were set up throughout the length and breadth of nazi-occupied territory, where Soviet people were put on starvation rations, killed in gas chambers, and infected with contagious diseases. And when Germany began experiencing a shortage of manpower, Soviet people were shipped away en masse to do forced labour in Germany.

The Japanese imperialists waited impatiently for the nazis to capture the Soviet capital before attacking the U.S.S.R. in the East.

Moscow had to be held at all costs. The Supreme Command massed troops from military areas in the rear, such as Siberia, the Volga area, and Central Asia. Three new armies were formed in a short time. Gradually, numerical and weapons superiority tipped in favour of the Red Army, a fact which, as was later learned, the German Command did not even suspect.

In the decisive stage of the battle for Moscow, the Red Army mounted its first major offensive operation in the Tikhvin area and at the southern tip of the Soviet-German front, in the region of Rostov-on-Don. The Soviet troops smashed the enemy there, recaptured the city and compelled the nazis to beat a hasty retreat. The victories at Tikhvin and Rostov-on-Don were of inestimable help to the defenders of Moscow, preventing the German Command from transferring troops there from other sectors.

The second nazi "general offensive" on Moscow began in the latter half of November 1941. Fifty-one divisions, including 20 panzer and motorised divisions, were flung into action. The operational plan was the same—to start a pincer movement on Moscow from north and south with a large tank force and to breach the Western Front in the centre. The German central group attacked on November 15, and the flanking attacks began three days later.

Bitter fighting ensued once more along the vast line from Kalinin to Tula. The Soviet troops fought to their last drop of blood for every inch of soil. A handful of soldiers and officers—Russians, Ukrainians, Kazakhs and Kirghizes—of General Ivan Panfilov's division was attacked by a company of nazi submachine gunners and 50 nazi tanks at the Dubosekovo railway siding near Volokolamsk. "Russia is large, but there is nowhere we can retreat. Behind us lies Moscow," said V. Klochkov-Diev, the political instructor who took charge of the battle. His words sounded like a pledge. The men did not flinch in face of the enemy and nearly all of them perished.

The Tula workers took up arms and fought like lions for their city. Hundreds of partisan detachments struck at the enemy behind the lines.

The nazi troops suffered very heavy losses, and their advance towards Moscow was slow. But in the north-west they were no more than 30 to 40 kilometres from the city limits.

The Germans believed that their victory was a foregone conclusion.

Yet at that hour the Red Army mounted a counter-offensive with the aim of repulsing the Army Group Centre. It began on December 5, launched by troops of the Kalinin Front under General Ivan Konev. Troops of the Western and South-Western fronts, commanded respectively by General Georgi Zhukov and Marshal Semen Timoshenko, assumed the offensive on December 6. All along the 800-kilometre line fighting was resumed with renewed vehemence. For the first time in the war, the fascist army turned tail. In panicky flight, the Germans abandoned their arms, weapons, cars and lorries, and thousands of dead, wounded and frostbitten officers and men in the snow.

The Soviet troops crushed the fascist attack groups on the flanks and recaptured Kalinin, Yelets and Kaluga. In January 1942, the Soviet counter-offensive at the approaches to Moscow developed into a general Red Army offensive, with the Soviet troops rolling forward as much as 400 kilometres at some points, clearing all of Moscow and Tula regions and recapturing dozens of towns and hundreds of villages in the adjoining regions.

The defeat of the nazi troops at Moscow and the Red Army winter offensive, generally, was of immense military and political importance. For the first time, the axis armies suffered a bad defeat. The notion of their being unbeatable burst like a bubble and the blitzkrieg collapsed. It assumed the nature of a war of attrition. Japan did not risk attacking the U.S.S.R. The anti-fascist struggle in occupied countries gained in intensity.

The rout of the German troops in the Moscow battle raised the morale of the Soviet people and gave them fresh confidence in ultimate victory.

By the beginning of 1942, a powerful anti-Hitler coalition emerged consisting of 26 countries, whose manpower and material resources considerably exceeded the resources of Germany and her allies. But the main burden of the war still lay on the Soviet Union. The British and United States governments declined to open a second front in Europe, and confined themselves to operations in Africa and the Pacific Ocean. This enabled Germany and her allies to rush considerable new forces to the Soviet-German front. In the summer and autumn of 1942, the enemy operating against the Soviet Army increased his strength to 237 divisions and, ultimately, to 266 divisions, of which 193 were German. In the meantime, only 4 German and 11 Italian divisions were engaged against the British troops in Northern Africa.

The situation on the Soviet-German front was still extremely tense. Though they were flung back 120 kilometres from Moscow, the nazis dug in and still presented a very real danger to the capital. In the north-west the enemy kept up the siege of Leningrad.

In the south, the nazis seized Kerch Peninsula in May 1942 and continued the assault on Sevastopol in the Crimea. The Soviet troops there were in a desperate plight. The port was cut off from the rear by land, and ammunition and food supply lines were precarious. In early July, the Supreme Command ordered the heroic defenders of Sevastopol to abandon the hero city after 250 days of bitter fighting.

Transport, industry and farming were strained to the extreme. There were shortages of metal, coal, electric power, oil, raw materials, food and manpower. People worked day and night at the factories, mines, oilfields, collective and state farms.

The Battle on the Volga

The German 1942 summer offensive had the objective of smashing the Red Army, capturing the key industrial and raw material areas of the Soviet Union, and achieving a final victory in the East.

The nazi Command massed its main force of 90 divisions on the southern end of the Soviet-German front with the design of seizing the Caucasian oil supplies and reaching the bank of the Volga. But the enemy group in the central sector, in the proximity of Moscow, still consisted of 70 divisions.

The Soviet Supreme Command knew that the enemy had concentrated a strong force in the south, but thought it more probable that the nazis would reopen their drive for Moscow. This was a strategically wrong deduction drawn by Stalin, and caused fresh losses in the south.

In May and June 1942, the Soviet troops attempted a large-scale offensive in the Ukraine, driving for Kharkov, but it failed. The Soviet reverse at Kharkov and in the Crimea tipped the scales in favour of the enemy still more decisively on the southern wing of the Soviet-German front.

The enemy offensive began on June 28. Eight armies—five German, one Rumanian, one Italian and one Hungarian—all of them part of Army Group South—took part in it. They seized the initiative and mounted operations all along a line from Orel to Taganrog. At first, they struck a fierce blow at Kursk and Voronezh, and succeeded in breaching the battle lines of the Bryansk and South-Western fronts, reaching the outskirts of Voronezh on July 7 and 8. But the Soviet troops fought tenaciously and managed to stem the enemy advance at this point, repulsing all further nazi attempts to move forward.

So the axis armies veered towards the Caucasus and Stalingrad (now Volgograd).

Between June 28 and July 24, 1942, the enemy advanced 150 to 400 kilometres, capturing the fertile land on the right bank of the Don and the eastern industrial areas of the Donets Basin. An enemy task force reached the big curve of the Don, captured Rostov and crossed the river, threatening the Caucasus. In the middle of July, stubborn and heavy fighting began at the distant approaches to Stalingrad.

The city's Party organisation marshalled the population to build fortifications. At the factories, workers laboured day and night making and repairing arms and manufacturing ammunition, which was instantly sent to the front lines. However, under the pressure of superior strength the Soviet troops were compelled to retreat. By mid-September the nazis had reached the Volga and the fighting shifted to the outskirts of Stalingrad. In the south, they captured Krasnodar, Stavropol and Maikop, and drove towards the vital oilfields in the Caucasus.

Due to the setbacks suffered in the summer of 1942 the Soviet Union was again put in a difficult position. The enemy was in possesion of territory where 45 per cent of the country's population had lived before the war, and which accounted for 33 per cent of the country's aggregate industrial output and 47 per cent of its arable.

The battle on the Volga and the battle for the Caucasus gained in intensity. But in the south the furious enemy onslaught petered out in the foothills of the western section of the Caucasus, the passes in the central part of the Caucasus and along the Terek River in the Mozdok area.

The fighting on the Volga, however, was furious and costly. Communists and Y.C.L. members, factory workers, railwaymen, rivermen and students rose to the defence of Stalingrad. Their volunteer units were incorporated in the regular army and fought heroically for every inch of land. The city became a battleground. Factories were continuously shelled by enemy guns and enemy planes bombed them from the air. Yet the workers continued to repair battle-damaged tanks and to build new ones, which drove out of the factory yard straight into battle.

Bitter fighting raged also at other points of the vast Soviet-German front. In August and September the Soviet troops of the Western and Kalinin fronts took the offensive at Rzhev and Vyazma, while the troops of the Leningrad and Volkhov fronts attacked at Sinyavino. This prevented the German Command from transferring forces from these sectors to the Volga. The Soviet Supreme Command assigned the 62nd and 64th armies, which were part of its strategic reserve, to defend the outskirts of Stalingrad. A Stalingrad Front was established under the command of General Andrei Yeremenko. Nikita Khrushchov was appointed member of its Military Council. Strong defences were raised around the city. But the situation was critical all the same. On August 25, 1942, a state of siege was declared in Stalingrad.

On September 12, the 62nd Army under General Chuikov and part of the 64th Army under General Shumilov were assigned to defend Stalingrad. On the morning of September 13, troops of the nazi 6th Army began the assault on the city. Street fighting of unparalleled intensity began. The heroic defenders of the city fought tooth and nail for every street and every house. A small group of Soviet soldiers under Sergeant Y. Pavlov, for example, held a 4-storeyed building for two months. Their daring and bravery turned it into an invulnerable bastion.

The city was enveloped in smoke and ravaged by fire. The Soviet troops clung to a narrow strip of land along the Volga. The Volga flotilla delivered supplies to the western bank of the river under heavy shell fire. Units of General A. Rodimtsev's 13th Division, Colonel I. Lyudnikov's 138th Division, and Colonel S. Gorokhov's, General N. Batyuk's, General A. Sarayev's and General L. Gurtiev's troops, and Lieut.-Col. Batrakov's marines covered themselves with glory in the street fighting.

The defenders made the enemy pay heavily for every inch of ground. By mid-November 1942, the nazis were compelled to assume the defensive.

The defensive stage of the Volga battle marked the end of the first period of the Soviet-German war. The following period opened with a Soviet counter-offensive between the Volga and the Don and saw the tide turn in favour of the Soviet Union.

The ground for this turning of the tide had been laid by the economy. By the close of 1942 the Soviet munitions industries were in full swing and growing rapidly. Factories that had produced consumer goods became arms manufacturers. The big plants evacuated from the western areas to the east of the country resumed operations. New factories, new power stations, new open-hearth furnaces and new mines appeared in the Urals, in Siberia, the Central Asian republics and the Soviet Far East. Extraction of ore and other minerals increased considerably. The country's industrial geography changed in a phenomenally short time.

The rapid growth of war industries enabled the Soviet Army to be re-equipped with the latest types of weapons—first-class tanks, new types of aircraft, cannon, mortars, and submachine guns. No longer did the army have to contend with shortages of arms and ammunition.

The operational and tactical skill of the Soviet troops improved. Soviet generals and officers learned to direct battles involving large numbers of tanks, guns and planes. They learned to co-ordinate the various services. The soldiers gained in military prowess. The Soviet Army was, at this time, already superior to the nazi army in all respects.

At the close of 1942 Soviet troops mounted a counter-offensive between the Volga and the Don. When still fighting defensive battles, the Soviet Army Command had begun massing large forces with large amounts of artillery, armour and aircraft, and on November 19, troops of the South-Western (General Nikolai Vatutin) and Don (General Konstantin Rokossovsky) fronts breached enemy defences north-west of the city. The following day, troops of the Stalingrad Front (General Andrei Yeremenko) launched an attack and broke the enemy lines south of Stalingrad. Motorised columns of the three Soviet fronts converged and enveloped a large number of enemy divisions in an immense pocket between the Volga and the Don. On November 23, after four days of fighting, the troops of the South-Western and Stalingrad fronts made contact near Sovietsky Village and closed the ring round the nazi troops in the city and its environs. Twenty-two enemy divisions numbering more than 330,000 officers and men were trapped. To avoid needless bloodshed, the Soviet Command called on them to surrender, but their commanding officer, General Fieldmarshal von Paulus, turned down the offer on Hitler's orders,

Partisans in Byelorussia, 194

Members of the Y.C.L. in Yaroslavl turn over fighter planes,
bought on their own money, to pilots, 1941

Stalingrad in ruins, 1942

Fieldmarshal Paulus, captured
by Soviet troops in the base-
ment of a department store
on his way to Soviet Army
Headquarters with members
of his staff, 1943

despite his hopeless situation. So, tense fighting ensued to wipe out the surrounded forces. The 51st and 2nd armies under General Rodion Malinovsky warded off a large-scale enemy attempt at Kotelnikovo to come to the aid of the invested nazi army in Stalingrad.

While the troops of the Don and Stalingrad fronts drove wedges into the pocket and pulled the noose tight, troops of the Voronezh and South-Western fronts mounted a fresh attack and reached the rear of the nazi army operating in the big bend of the Don, pinning it down, and preventing it from going to the aid of Paulus and his divisions.

On February 2, 1943, the fighting along the Volga ceased. Paulus's Army Group was no more. One hundred and forty-seven thousand enemy officers and men were picked up and buried in the city and its environs. Ninety-one thousand men, including General Fieldmarshal Paulus and 24 generals, were taken prisoner. The Soviet troops came into possession of a vast stock of German armaments.

The Soviet victory on the Volga showed the world that the highly touted nazi war machine had begun to crumble. Germany entered a period of deep crisis, while its allies, Japan and Turkey, abandoned the idea of declaring war on the U.S.S.R. In Italy, Rumania and Hungary public discontent with the nazis mounted steadily. The morale of the German people, too, was impaired.

The peoples in the occupied countries of Western Europe heaved a sigh of relief. Their faith in the ultimate downfall of fascism grew stronger. They fought more intensively against the German invaders.

The historic battle on the Volga swung the tide in the Second World War. The Red Army seized the initiative and did not relinquish it until final victory was achieved.

The Turning of the Tide

On a vast front stretching from Velikiye Luki to the Caucasus the Soviet troops struck crushing blows at the German-fascist invaders, liberating towns and villages, and millions of Soviet men and women from the nazis. This marked the beginning of the massive expulsion of nazi invaders from Soviet soil.

Leningrad was relieved in January 1943. Troops of the Leningrad (General Leonid Govorov) and Volkhov (General Kirill Meretskov) fronts mounted an offensive south of Lake Ladoga on January 12 and recaptured Petrokrepost (Schlisselburg) after a week of heavy fighting. They cleared enough territory to re-establish railway connections with Leningrad, thus breaking the blockade.

When the winter offensive was over the German troops had been flung back 600-700 kilometres west of the Volga and the Caucasian mountain range. Such militarily important cities as Kursk, Rzhev, Vyazma, Gzhatsk, Velikiye Luki and Demyansk were liberated.

The vast territory cleared by the Soviet troops was of great economic and strategic importance.

In the recaptured areas the Soviet soldiers came upon evidence of dastardly nazi crimes–demolished and ravaged cities, gutted and depopulated villages, ruthlessly exterminated war prisoners and civilians, ravished and ruined club-houses, museums, schools and hospitals, and defiled monuments of history and culture.

The whole Soviet people joined in the rehabilitation of the liberated regions.

The partisan movement in enemy-occupied areas grew rapidly. This testified to the popular character of the Soviet-German war. By the end of the second year of the war, Soviet partisans behind the enemy lines had killed more than 300,000 nazi officers and men, derailed at least 3,000 trains and blown up 825 nazi depots. They also destroyed many tanks, aircraft and other enemy arms. The names of M. Guryanov, S. Solntsev, Zoya Kosmodemyanskaya, Alexander Chekalin, Liza Chaikina and many other partisans and members of the underground were inscribed with glory in the annals of the war.

As from May 1942, the partisan fighting was put under the guidance of a Central Partisan Headquarters and the relevant head-quarters operating with the Military Councils of the various fronts.

The Soviet winter offensive put the nazi troops in a precarious position, especially on the southern wing of the Soviet-German front. But the absence of a second front in Europe enabled the German Command to transfer reserves from Western Europe to the eastern front, to regroup its troops and to stabilise the front line for some time. The enemy even mounted a counter-offensive, half-hearted though it was, in the Ukraine left of the Dnieper and in the Donets Basin. In March 1943, the nazis recaptured Kharkov, which had only shortly before been liberated by Soviet troops.

The friendship of the Slav peoples gained strength in the common fight against Hitlerism. The first Czechoslovak military unit, the nucleus of the People's Liberation Army of Czechoslovakia, had its baptism of fire in the battle for Kharkov in March 1943 in the proximity of Sokolovo.

By the end of March 1943, the Soviet troops assumed the defensive for a short time. Both combatants were preparing for the summer fighting. The Soviet Supreme Command learned that a "total" mobilisation was under way in Germany and that Hitler was preparing a large-scale offensive to avenge his winter's defeat.

It was not known where the nazis would strike. But Soviet experts made a careful study of all nazi possibilities and decided that an enemy offensive at the Kursk Bulge was the most likely. At that point, between Orel and Belgorod, troops of the Central and Voronezh fronts had thrust westward considerably, creating a bulge in the battle line. Enemy troops hugged the flanks of the Soviet troops. Very soon scouts turned in information backing the experts' opinion. A formidable and deep belt of fortifications was built, with a stress on anti-tank defences, because the Soviet Command had learned that the nazis intended to use their new heavy tanks—the Tiger and Panther and the self-propelled Ferdinand guns. Large strategic reserves were concentrated in the Soviet fortified belt, giving the Soviet troops in the Kursk Bulge a numerical advantage. The stage was thus set for an offensive action to follow a tenacious defence designed to exhaust Hitler's troops.

In the early morning of July 5, 1943, the Wehrmacht made an assault on the Soviet fortifications. The Soviet soldiers in the Kursk Bulge fought tenaciously for every inch of land, accounting for thousands of enemy officers and men. Hundreds of Panthers, Tigers, Ferdinands and other armour were put out of action. At the price of tremendous casualties, the German troops finally managed to drive a wedge 9 to 15 kilometres deep towards Orel and Kursk, and 15 to 35 kilometres deep in the direction of Belgorod and Kursk. But that was all they could do. The German offensive collapsed.

On July 12, 1943, troops of the Western and Bryansk fronts, followed by troops of the Central Front on July 15 and troops of the Voronezh and Stepnoi fronts on August 3, assumed the counter-offensive. Crushing stubborn enemy resistance, the Soviet troops captured Orel and Belgorod on August 5. Moscow fired its first gun salute to mark the occasion. Salutes were fired after this to mark every major victory of the Soviet Army.

The Kursk Bulge victory sealed the fate of the nazis in the Second World War. It ushered in a big Red Army summer offensive. The offensive proceeded along a frontage some 2,000-km long stretching from Nevel to the Sea of Azov. In three months' fighting Soviet troops advanced 400 to 450 kilometres at some points, liberating Smolensk, Yelnya, Roslavl, Bryansk, Gomel, Kharkov, Poltava, Kremenchug, Zaporozhye, Melitopol, Dnepropetrovsk, Dneprodzerzhinsk, and many other cities. Kiev, the capital of the Soviet Ukraine, was freed on November 6, 1943.

The Soviet troops reached the bank of the Dnieper along a wide frontage. The German Command thought its positions there impregnable. But the Soviet troops, impelled by an irresistible enthusiasm, gave the enemy no time to dig in. They lunged across the river and consolidated their bridgeheads on its right bank. For this operation about 2,000 Soviet officers and men were awarded the title of Hero of the Soviet Union, while many thousands were decorated with Orders and medals.

North-east of Mogilev the Tadeush Kostyushko First Polish Division fought its first engagement for Lenino as a unit of the Western Front. The division was formed in the Soviet Union and was the nucleus of what later became the Army of the People's Republic of Poland.

By November 7, the national holiday of the U.S.S.R., the Red Army had liberated nearly two-thirds of the territory occupied by the enemy. More than 100 German divisions were smashed in the summer and autumn fighting of 1943. In the latter half of 1943 and the beginning of 1944, the partisan movement behind the enemy lines reached its peak. More than 350,000 partisans were active in nazi-occupied areas. Partisan-controlled regions appeared. Partisan detachments under Sidor Kovpak, Vasily Kozlov, M. Naumov, Alexei Fyodorov, S. Rudnev, A. Saburov and many others struck terror into the German occupation troops.

Soviet youth took an active part in the partisan struggle and the underground Party groups. The Young Communist League inscribed glorious chapters into the chronicle of the Soviet-German war. The underground youth organisation in Krasnodon was a model of devotion and heroism. It had a membership of 100 young men and women, and called itself the Young Guard. Its most prominent members were Ivan Turkenich (Commander), Victor Tretyakevich (Commissar), Oleg Koshevoi, Ivan Zemnukhov, Sergei Tyulenin, Ulyana Gromova and Lyubov Shevtsova, whose memory is dear to the grateful nation. The Young Guard circulated anti-fascist leaflets, conducted sabotage, etc. Ultimately the Gestapo arrested them, and they were put to a slow and painful death.

Organisations like the one in Krasnodon operated nearly in all occupied areas, almost all the large towns and cities.

As the nazis retreated westward they left behind a scorched earth and drove the local population away to Germany. To avoid fascist slavery, Soviet people escaped to the woods, where they joined the partisan units. The position of the invaders was made untenable.

People in industry, farming and other pursuits spared neither strength nor effort to speed the victory. The patriotic movement of collecting funds for the war effort spread far and wide. People gave up their savings to purchase tanks, aircraft and artillery.

In 1943, industry, agriculture and transport made further important advances. The population evacuated to war-free areas began to return to territory cleared of the invaders. Life came back to scorched and ravaged lands, to war-demolished towns and villages. Factories rose from their ruins, and flooded mines were drained and put back into operation. The rehabilitation effort was immense.

On August 21, 1943, the Council of People's Commissars and the Party's Central Committee passed a decision on Urgent Measures for the Economic Rehabilitation of Districts Liberated from German Occupation. Republics, territories and regions that had not been overrun sent assistance to the war-ravaged areas.

The Soviet Union's military and economic achievements added to its international prestige. In 1942 and 1943 Australia, Cuba, Colombia, Bolivia, Canada, the Netherlands, Mexico, Uruguay and Luxembourg established diplomatic relations with it.

In the meantime, the situation in nazi Germany continued to deteriorate. The Axis began to crumble. In July 1943, an Anglo-American landing was made in Sicily, followed in the latter half of August by a landing on the Italian Peninsula. Benito Mussolini, the fascist dictator, was deposed on July 25 and a government headed by Pietro Badoglio came to power. For a time, it attempted to continue the war, but the sweeping anti-fascist movement organised by the Italian Communists, the effects of the Red Army pounding and the Anglo-American forces, compelled it to surrender. On October 13, 1943, Italy declared war on Germany. Anti-fascist sentiment ran high in Rumania, Hungary and Finland. A powerful national liberation movement swept across Poland, Czechoslovakia, Albania, Yugoslavia, France and the other nazi-occupied countries.

In the circumstances, the nazis saw their only salvation in protracting the war and concluding a separate peace with the Western countries.

Hitler's plan had to be thwarted. A conference of the Foreign Ministers of the Soviet Union, United States and Great Britain convened in Moscow from October 19 to 30, 1943, and adopted a declaration pledging that the war would continue until Germany's complete and unconditional surrender. It also outlined the principles governing post-war arrangements. At the same time, the heads of the Allied governments signed a declaration that the nazis would be brought to justice for atrocities and ill deeds. Severe retribution was promised to war criminals.

From November 28 to December 1, 1943, a summit conference was held in Teheran, at which the three Allied Powers reached an understanding on the conduct of war and post-war co-operation.

The British and U.S. governments undertook to land in northern and southern France not later than May 1, 1944, and open a second front in Europe in earnest.

This dashed fascist Germany's hope of splitting the anti-Hitler coalition. The Great Patriotic War, and the Second World War as a whole, entered a new period, in which the enemy was crushed and the war victoriously concluded.

The German nation saw in 1944 with dark forebodings, although fascist propaganda tried to infuse cheer with shrieking reports about a new weapon that would reverse the fortunes of war and about an imminent clash between the Allies.

The Soviet-German front was still the main theatre of the war. Of Germany's 315 divisions and 10 brigades, as many as 198 divisions and six brigades, or 70 per cent, were deployed on the Soviet-German front in the beginning of 1944. Besides which, Germany's minions had 38 divisions and 18 brigades in Soviet territory. The Anglo-American forces in Italy, meanwhile, faced no more than 19 divisions and one brigade, or a mere six per cent of Germany's ground forces, and despite the imminent Allied invasion from the British Isles, the German Command kept as few as 64 divisions and one brigade, or just 20 per cent of its ground strength in France, Holland, Belgium and Norway.

The Soviet Army victories and the liberation of the key Soviet industrial and agricultural areas in 1943 gave the Soviet troops numerical and technical superiority. This enabled the Soviet Supreme Command to plan the final liberation of the country from the German-fascist invaders in 1944. Successive strategic operations were projected on the northern and southern wings of the Soviet-German front, to be followed by an offensive in Byelorussia against the main enemy force.

The offensive began at the close of December 1943 on the southern wing against the nazi Army Group South and Army Group A with the objective of clearing the still occupied regions of the Ukraine. In this action the Soviet troops engaged a huge enemy force of 106 divisions and two motorised brigades, including 12 divisions in the Crimea.

The assault was begun by troops of the First Ukrainian Front on December 24, 1943.* They smashed the enemy force in the Zhitomir-Berdichev area and two German armies faced the threat of envelopment.

In January 1944, the Soviet offensive spread to the northern wing of the front.

Three Soviet fronts—Leningrad, Volkhov and Second Baltic—mounted an attack with the support of the Baltic Fleet against the nazi Army Group North on January 14, 1944. They breached the heavily and deeply fortified enemy defences around Leningrad and Novgorod in a matter of a few days, and drove the nazis

---

* The various fronts were renamed in October 1943. The Central Front was renamed Byelorussian Front, the Kalinin Front the First Baltic Front, the Baltic Front the Second Baltic Front, and the Voronezh, Steppe, South-Western and Southern fronts were renamed First, Second, Third and Fourth Ukrainian fronts respectively.—*Ed.*

westward. On January 20, they recaptured the ancient Russian city of Novgorod, and on January 27, a gun salute was fired to mark the end of the 870-days-old enemy blockade of Leningrad. By the beginning of March Soviet forces had regained the Leningrad and part of the Kalinin regions, clearing them of the enemy, and entered Estonia.

In the meantime, 10 enemy divisions and one enemy brigade were cut off in the Korsun-Shevchenkovskaya area on the right bank of the Dnieper. By mid-February the invested nazi group was wiped out. The rest of February, and in March and April, troops of the four Ukrainian fronts battled through the spring mud to prosecute their offensive along a large front. They broke through the enemy defences and pressed forward without giving the nazis a chance to organise their defences, trapping the retreating German troops in large and small pockets, wiping out manpower and matériel. Steadily, the Soviet Army came nearer the western border of the U.S.S.R. The spring 1944 offensive liberated all of the Ukraine west of the Dnieper, the large industrial centres of Krivoi Rog, Nikopol and Nikolayev, and the port of Odessa. Soviet troops entered Moldavia, arrived at the border of Czechoslovakia, and crossed the frontier into Rumania. On April 8, 1944, operating jointly with the Black Sea Fleet, troops of the Fourth Ukrainian Front and the Separate Maritime Army crushed through the strong enemy fortifications across Perekop Isthmus and Kerch Peninsula, took Sevastopol by storm, flung the remnants of the German 17th Army into the sea, and by May 12 cleared the Crimean Peninsula.

The Soviet winter and spring offensive of 1944 culminated in a crushing nazi defeat. The enemy was driven back 150 to 300 kilometres from Leningrad and Novgorod and as much as 600 to 700 kilometres in the southern sector of the Soviet-German front. The Soviet troops reached the Soviet frontier along a frontage of more than 400 kilometres.

At this point the Red Army prepared to carry the war beyond the Soviet frontier and liberate the European peoples languishing under the nazi yoke.

It now became eminently clear that the Red Army was able alone to bring fascist Germany to its knees. So the governments of the United States and Britain at last hastened to open the second front. The situation was extremely favourable, for the main strength of the German-fascist army had been deployed to the Soviet-German front, and only a negligible German force remained in occupied France, while the Resistance movement in Europe had gained tremendous momentum.

On June 6, 1944, Anglo-American troops made a landing in Normandy in the north of France. After two years of procrastination the second front in Europe had at long last become a reality.

From that day on the Soviet Army and the Anglo-American forces gained the opportunity for co-ordinating their operations on a strategic level. Yet, even though the second front now existed, the brunt of the fighting was borne by the Soviet Union as before.

In the latter half of 1944 the Red Army offensive was intensified. Devastating blows were struck now here, now there along the vast Soviet-German front. The German Command reeled under the pounding, wondering where its quickly melting reserves were needed most.

On June 10, 1944, a resolute attack was mounted against the German and Finnish troops with the object of liberating Soviet Karelia and putting Finland out of the war. Co-ordinating their operations with the Baltic Fleet, troops of the Leningrad Front breached the strongly fortified deep enemy defences across the Karelian Isthmus and took Vyborg (Viipuri) by storm on June 20. After the fall of Vyborg troops of the Karelian Front launched an offensive in southern Karelia in a drive for Petrozavodsk and Svir. Defeated Finland signed an armistice with the Soviet Union in September 1944, and joined in the war against nazi Germany on October 1.

The nazi generals applied themselves to determining in advance where the Soviet troops would aim their main blow in the summer of 1944. It was later learned that the German intelligence service had deduced erroneously that the offensive would be launched in the Western Ukraine by the First Ukrainian Front. Large panzer units were rushed there. But the Soviet Army attacked in Byelorussia, aiming its blow against Army Group Centre, the largest strategic enemy force, with the objective of smashing it and liberating Byelorussia.

Four Soviet fronts, supported by the Dnieper flotilla and a large partisan force, kept up the offensive through June and July 1944 along an immense frontage from Polotsk to the Pripyat River. They cut the enemy army group into several sections and pounded it into pulp. Thirty enemy divisions were wiped out at Vitebsk, Minsk and Bobruisk. The nazis lost 540 thousand officers and men. The Soviet troops advanced 500 kilometres, freed Byelorussia, part of Lithuania, including Vilnius, the capital, crossed the Niemen and reached the frontier of East Prussia.

When the offensive in Byelorussia ended, troops of the First Ukrainian Front made a thrust at Lvov and Rava-Russkaya against Army Group Northern Ukraine. There, too, in July and August, the German forces suffered a painful defeat. The enemy was flung out of the Western Ukraine and the south-eastern regions of Poland. Soviet units made a power crossing of the Vistula and captured a large zone west of Sandomierz.

In the meantime, the Anglo-American forces advanced rapidly in north-western France. The noose round nazi Germany tightened.

The nazi generals saw their only hope in a compact with the Americans and British. As a preliminary, they had to remove Hitler. After Hitler's assassination, Allen Dulles, head of the U.S. intelligence service, was to have established contact with the German military opposition and helped it set up a German government capable of signing an armistice with the West and concentrating its war effort entirely against the Soviet Union. But the attempt on Hitler's life, made on July 20, 1944, failed, and wholesale reprisals followed.

By this time Germany's economy had begun to totter. The nazis were hard put to it to keep Rumania on their side, because they needed her oil, and to retain control of the resources of the other Balkan states. This is the reason why Hitler rejected the idea of withdrawing Army Group Southern Ukraine, which covered the path to the Balkans, despite its desperate situation after the rout of Army Group Northern Ukraine.

The assault on the German forces in the south began on August 20, 1944. After a three-day offensive, the troops of the Second and Third Ukrainian fronts surrounded 22 German divisions and several separate units and formations south-west of Kishinev. A part of the Soviet forces was left behind to mop up the invested enemy, while the rest continued their advance into Rumania. On August 29, the mopping-up operation was completed.

The Rumanian Tudor Vladimirescu Division, formed on Soviet territory in 1943 of volunteer Rumanian war prisoners took part in the battles for the liberation of Rumania. The Vladimirescu Division became the nucleus of the Armed Forces of the People's Republic of Rumania.

The approach of the Soviet Army gave impetus to a revolutionary movement in Rumania. The Rumanians, who had languished for years under the pro-nazi Antonescu dictatorship took up arms to fight for their freedom. On August 23, an anti-fascist uprising headed by Rumanian Communists broke out in Bucharest. The people overthrew Antonescu's government and replaced it with a new, more democratic cabinet. On August 24, the new government announced Rumania's withdrawal from the war on Germany's side, and declared war on Germany on the following day.

The Soviet troops continued their rapid advance and entered Bucharest, the capital of Rumania, on August 31, 1944. In the meantime, ships of the Black Sea Fleet landed troops in Sulin, Tulcea and Constantsa, and steamed into the mouth of the Danube. Twenty-two Rumanian divisions fought alongside the Red Army for their country's liberation.

The rout of the fascist troops in Rumania sparked a strongly revolutionary anti-fascist movement in neighbouring Bulgaria. Yet the pro-fascist Bogrianov government there defied the will of the nation and continued to help nazi Germany. The Soviet troops had no choice but to cross the border into Bulgaria. The population welcomed the Soviet soldiers enthusiastically. A nation-wide uprising against the reactionary government broke out on September 9. The insurrectionists formed a Fatherland Front government headed by the Communist Party of Bulgaria. Soon, the new government declared war on Germany and Hungary.

In the autumn of 1944, the troops of the Ukrainian fronts continued their offensive with the object of liberating Czechoslovakia, Hungary and Yugoslavia, and wiping out the enemy in the southern sector of the Soviet-German front. The Red Army campaign of liberation merged with the far-flung popular liberation movements in Central and South-East Europe. In Slovakia the partisan movement grew into a nation-wide uprising by the end of August. The German Command sent a large force to suppress it. But Soviet troops came to the aid of the patriots. Jointly with the Czechoslovak Corps, troops of the First Ukrainian Front crashed through the enemy defences in the Carpathians (at the Dukla Pass) and entered Czechoslovakia.

On October 20, troops of the Third Ukrainian Front, jointly with the Yugoslav People's Liberation Army, entered Belgrade, the capital of Yugoslavia.

The Axis crumbled under the Soviet pounding. Hungary was now the only remaining ally of Germany. The Szálasy clique, which clung to power with the help of German bayonets, still maintained its alliance with Germany. So the Soviet Supreme Command assigned the Second and Third Ukrainian fronts to put Hungary out of the war. At the end of October 1944, a Soviet force mounted an attack in the direction of Budapest. After ferocious battles, troops of the Second and Third Ukrainian fronts forced the Danube with the support of the Danube flotilla and closed the ring round the 180,000-strong enemy force ensconced in the Hungarian capital on December 24. The liberated Hungarian people formed a Provisional National Government, which declared war on fascist Germany on December 28.

The developments on the northern wing of the Soviet-German front were just as spectacular. After crushing Army Group Centre, the Soviet forces reached the border of East Prussia. But a large enemy force, Army Group North, was still operative along the Baltic seaboard. The German Command attached considerable importance to it and assigned it to maintain German supremacy on the Baltic Sea, secure shipments of iron ore from Sweden, pin down the Soviet troops in its area and hinder a Red Army offensive through the centre.

The Soviet Command weighed the existing situation and decided to cut off the German force from East Prussia by striking towards Riga.

The Riga offensive was opened on September 14, 1944, by the three Baltic fronts. The Leningrad Front, supported by the Baltic Fleet, advanced north of Narva on Tallinn. Its objective was to liberate Estonia. Within a month the nazi forces in the Baltic were crushed in hard-fought battles. Thirty German divisions had their backs to the sea on the peninsula between Tukums and Liepaja. National military units of the Baltic republics, the Estonian and Latvian rifle corps, and the Lithuanian rifle division took part in the liberation of the Soviet Baltic states.

In the extreme north, troops of the Karelian and Northern fronts mounted an attack towards Petsamo on October 7, 1944. By November 1 they cleared Petsamo Region of German forces and entered Norway.

The succession of Red Army offensives cleared the territory of the Soviet Union of occupation troops. Latvia was the only Soviet territory where badly mauled and demoralised enemy divisions still resisted.

The state border of the Soviet Union was restored entirely from the Barents to the Black Sea. The Soviet Army carried the fighting into the adjoining countries in pursuance of its mission of liberation.

The same year also witnessed stirring accomplishments in the Soviet rear. Iron and steel production rose by a third over the previous year's, coal production by 31 per cent, and the output of the engineering industry by 30 per cent. The collective and state farms stepped up production of food and industrial crops.

The country put its heart into the job of restoring the economy of the liberated areas.

Reactionaries in the United States and Britain had hoped the Soviet Union would be bled white before the end of the war. But their expectations were dashed. The U.S.S.R. emerged from the war a mighty power.

Writhing between the hammer and the anvil of the two European fronts, Germany faced inevitable surrender. As before, the main enemy forces were engaged on the Soviet-German front. A host of 204 nazi divisions operated there, while less than 70 confronted the Anglo-American troops.

In January 1945 the Red Army was poised to strike the final blows. The Soviet Command planned to smash enemy concentrations in East Prussia with two of its fronts, crush the nazi force between the Vistula and Oder with three fronts, liberate Poland and lay open the road to Berlin. The troops on the southern wing were to mop up the Axis forces still clinging to Budapest and to set the stage for an assault on Vienna.

The offensive was planned to begin on January 20, 1945. But an unforeseen development compelled the Soviet Command to bring the date forward. On December 16, 1944, the Wehrmacht

235

launched an attack on the Anglo-American troops in the Ardennes, wrought confusion in their lines and set out in pursuit. According to Guderian this was meant "to win time and dash hopes of a full Allied victory, to make the Allies withdraw their demand of unconditional surrender and induce them to conclude a negotiated peace."*

Winston Churchill asked the Soviet Government for urgent help. Responding to his plea, the Soviet Command launched the offensive on January 12, although the weather was unfavourable for artillery and air action.

The biggest winter offensive of the war was launched by the Red Army along a 1,200-kilometre front stretching from East Prussia to the Carpathians. The German strategists had to move troops from west to east hastily. This relieved the Anglo-American troops in the Ardennes, and soon they were able to reassume the offensive. Thus, Hitler failed in his attempt to demonstrate strength to the British and Americans, and thereby to induce them to conclude a separate peace.

In January, troops of the Second and Third Byelorussian fronts, supported by the Baltic Fleet, pierced the strongly fortified enemy belt in East Prussia, cut off Army Group Centre and chopped it up into several isolated segments. Ivan Chernyakhovsky, one of the finest Soviet generals, who was in command of the Third Byelorussian Front, was killed on February 18 when inspecting the battle area where the invested enemy troops in East Prussia were being mopped up.

After smashing the central enemy concentration in Byelorussia the Soviet forces crossed the border into Poland. The beginning of the campaign to liberate Poland coincided with a tragic event in her history. The population of Warsaw staged an armed uprising against the German garrison on August 1, 1944. This move, inspired by a group of political adventurists with the object of seizing power, came as a total surprise for the Soviet Command. Fatigued by the two months' offensive, the Soviet troops were not ready at the time to force the Vistula and liberate Warsaw. Doomed to failure before it ever began, the uprising was brutally crushed by the nazis.

In mid-January 1945, troops of the First Byelorussian and First Ukrainian fronts mounted an assault from bridgeheads on the western bank of the Vistula at Magaushev, Pulawy, and Sandomierz. Farther south, the right wing of the Fourth Ukrainian Front also assumed the offensive. Bitter fighting raged on the western bank of the Vistula for six days and nights. The German troops resisted desperately. But the Soviet assault pulverised the nazi defences and drove the enemy westward. Warsaw was liberated on January

---

* Heinz Guderian, *Erinnerungen eines Soldaten*, Heidelberg, 1951, S. 344.

17, 1945. The First Polish Army acquitted itself splendidly in the fighting for the Polish capital.

The nazis deployed troops from other sectors of the front in a frantic attempt to stem the advance of the First Byelorussian and First Ukrainian fronts. Some thirty divisions and more than 300 other units were involved in a gigantic reshuffle. But the enemy failed to form intermediary defence belts. Driving forward day and night, the Soviet troops arrived at the end of January on the bank of the Oder, the last strategic defensive barrier of nazi Germany. The offensive carried them across the river at some points, and they succeeded in establishing some bridgeheads.

In the southern sector of the Soviet-German front the Soviet Army repulsed a series of German counter-attacks in Hungary, mopped up the remaining units of the Budapest garrison and was poised for an offensive on Vienna.

In the meantime, the Anglo-American-Canadian troops in the West prepared for an offensive with the object of reaching the Rhine and then capturing the industrial Ruhr area.

Yet it was the Armed Forces of the Soviet Union that bore the brunt of the fighting against Hitler Germany and her allies and that inflicted the decisive defeat on the nazis in the final stage of the war. Germany faced certain surrender not because the Anglo-American forces assailed it from France, as some bourgeois historians strive to prove today, but because its vaunted Wehrmacht was torn to ribbons on the Soviet-German front. Winston Churchill admitted it at the time. "The Red Army," he wrote, "celebrates its twenty-seventh anniversary amid triumphs which have won the unstinted applause of their Allies and have sealed the doom of German militarism. Future generations will acknowledge their debt to the Red Army as unreservedly as do we who have lived to witness these proud achievements."[*]

When the Soviet troops were preparing the offensive on Berlin from the Oder-Neisse line, a series of important questions clamoured for a solution. The most important of them was the matter of the surrender terms and Germany's post-war structure. So the heads of the Big Three Powers gathered in Yalta, in the Crimea, in the early half of February 1945 to hammer out a common line.

At the Yalta Conference the Allies worked out an agreed plan for the final defeat of Germany, outlined her future and passed a number of other important decisions. There were points of difference and acrimonious controversy, notably over the post-war arrangement in Germany. The U.S. and British delegations were

---

[*] *Correspondence Between the Chairman of the Council of Ministers of the U.S.S.R., and the President of the U.S.A. and the Prime Minister of Great Britain During the Great Patriotic War of 1941-45*, Vol. I, pp. 305-06.

all for partitioning Germany, but the Soviet Union won its point and it was decided to preserve a united Germany, disband the Nazi Party, the armed forces and the General Staff, and to promote Germany's development as a peace-abiding democratic state. The Report of the Yalta Conference pointed out on this score that "only when nazism and militarism have been extirpated, will there be hope for a decent life for Germans, and a place for them in the community of nations".*

The conference examined the matter of reparations, the question of the Soviet-Polish border and the restoration to Poland of her western territories.

It outlined the plan to establish the United Nations Organisation with the purpose of ensuring international peace and security. It also adopted a declaration on liberated Europe, which acknowledged the right of the peoples liberated from fascism to create democratic institutions of their own choice.

To reinforce the security of its Far Eastern borders and speed the end of the war, the Soviet Government undertook to enter the war against Japan two or three months after V-E Day. A special decision passed by the conference stipulated that after the surrender of Japan Southern Sakhalin and the Kuriles would be returned to the Soviet Union.

The Crimean Conference dealt a death blow to all the hopes the Hitlerites had nurtured of a separate peace and of a split in the anti-Hitler coalition, although behind-the-scenes diplomatic activities continued between nazi diplomats and reactionary groups in the United States and Britain. Defying jointly assumed commitments, Churchill, too, stuck to his perfidious policy in an effort to hold up the Red Army advance.

In the final stage of the war the Germans virtually ceased their resistance in the West, while fighting on ferociously for every inch of land on the Soviet-German front and prosecuting what were in effect scorched earth tactics.

In February and March the Red Army wiped out the enemy force in East Prussia (save a few seats of resistance), smashed the East Pomeranian enemy group, liberated the Silesian industrial area and all of Poland, and repulsed a German counter-offensive in Hungary. Hungary and the eastern section of Austria, including Vienna, were liberated in late March and early April.

In April 1945, the Red Army was poised to deliver nazi Germany and her armed forces the final and crushing blow.

To capture Berlin, the Soviet troops had to pierce a strong deeply fortified defensive zone along the Oder and Neisse and

---

* *Report of the Crimean Conference*, February 11, 1945, Miscellaneous, No. 5 (1945), London, 1945, p. 4.

pound the three annular lines of the Berlin fortified area, and the city itself, which had been prepared for a long and tenacious resistance. The German armies defending Berlin had nearly a million officers and men, 8,000 guns and mortars, over 1,200 tanks, siege guns and other armour, and 3,300 planes. Their backs to the wall, the Hitlerites fought with the desperation of the condemned.

The Soviet Command, for its part, massed for the final assault an incredible amount of heavy arms—40,000 guns and mortars, 6,300 tanks and self-propelled guns, 7,300 planes and many other weapons.

The battle for Berlin began on April 16 and lasted until May 2. Troops of the First Byelorussian Front under Marshal Georgi Zhukov, and of the First Ukrainian Front under Marshal Ivan Konev, later joined by the Second Byelorussian Front under Marshal Konstantin Rokossovsky, breached the enemy defences in a series of powerful thrusts, moved forward rapidly and completed the investment of the enemy force at Berlin on April 25. The nazis in the Berlin pocket numbered about 200,000 officers and men with 3,000 guns and mortars, and 250 tanks and siege guns. Rather than cease the futile bloodshed, the nazis drove their troops into action in the streets of the capital. On Hitler's orders bills were hung out on walls and fences saying that "anyone suggesting measures liable to impair resistance, or anyone who merely agrees to such measures, is a traitor and shall be shot or hanged on the spot".

Colonel-General Weidling, an artillery commander, was put in command of the Berlin garrison, but it was Hitler who, in effect, directed the action from his hide-out in the imperial chancellory bunker.

After the nazi Command turned down a surrender offer, the Soviet troops began the assault on Berlin.

Fierce fighting proceeded in the streets of the German capital for ten days and nights. The Soviet soldiers assailed block after block, street after street, district after district, converging from several sides on the Reichstag building, the heart of the city. At long last, Soviet soldiers hoisted the Victory Flag over the Reichstag on April 30. An hour later, Adolf Hitler committed suicide, and Goebbels killed his wife and children before taking his own life. The Berlin garrison surrendered on May 2, 1945.

The Anglo-American bomber force staged ferocious raids on cities in what had been designated beforehand as the Soviet occupation zone, all but razing to the ground the cities of Dresden, Halle and Dessau, and many other industrial centres. In the meantime, Anglo-American ground forces advanced unhindered to the Elbe, making contact on its bank with Soviet troops advancing from the east early in May.

On May 8, representatives of the German High Command signed the instrument of unconditional surrender in Karlshorst, a Berlin suburb. However, in Czechoslovakia a group of nazi formations under Fieldmarshal Schörner would not lay down its arms, and clung to Prague with the intention of destroying it. On May 9, a Soviet task force made a whirlwind thrust to the walls of the Czech capital, where the population had taken arms and was fighting the nazi occupation troops. The Soviet force helped the Czechs to clear Prague of invaders.

The nazi Reich collapsed under the powerful onslaught of the Red Army, which co-operated with the armed forces of France, Britain, the United States, Czechoslovakia, Poland, Yugoslavia, Albania, and Rumanian, Bulgarian and Hungarian units, which joined in the fighting later. The war in Europe was over.

On May 9, millions of Soviet men and women celebrated the long-awaited Victory Day.

After the war in Europe was over, the Soviet Government did its utmost to create conditions that would rule out a new war by the German militarists. An understanding was reached to convene a Three-power Conference in Berlin. But the U.S. Government procrastinated. It turned out later that President Harry Truman was waiting for the test of the first atomic bomb, which the Americans intended to explode on July 15 in Alamogordo, New Mexico, to strengthen his hand and intimidate his Allies at the negotiations. With the atomic bomb in its pocket and with an eye to Soviet war losses, the United States hoped to lay down the law in Berlin.

The Conference of the Heads of Government of the U.S.S.R., Great Britain and the U.S.A. opened on July 17, 1945, in Potsdam, and continued until August 7. Despite Truman's expectations, the propositions worked out in Yalta prevailed and were made more specific. Germany was to be disarmed, her war industry dismantled, and the Nazi Party disbanded in order to give the German people a chance of reorganising their country along democratic peaceful lines. A start was made in framing peace terms for Germany and her allies—Italy, Rumania, Bulgaria, Hungary and Finland. Agreement was reached, too, on German reparations and on changes of Germany's frontiers. The conference turned over part of East Prussia with the city of Königsberg (now Kaliningrad) to the Soviet Union, fixed Poland's western frontier along a line running from the Baltic Sea west of Swinoujscie (Swinemünde) along the rivers Oder and Western Neisse to the Czech frontier, and including the territory of Danzig (Gdansk) and part of East Prussia.

On the insistence of the Soviet delegation, the conference decided to speed the trial before an international tribunal of the chief nazi war criminals.

German prisoners of war in Moscow

Flag of Victory over the Reichstag

Veterans of the French Normandy-Niemen Regiment with Soviet
generals

The Potsdam Conference was a triumph for peace-abiding, progressive humanity. It laid what could have been a solid foundation for European peace, provided the agreements reached there have been fulfilled in good faith by all concerned.

Defeat of Imperialist Japan. World War Ends

In May 1945 the war in Europe was over. But it raged on in the Pacific Ocean, next door to the Far Eastern frontiers of the Soviet Union. When the three months after the surrender instrument was signed by nazi Germany had run out, the Soviet Union, always faithful to its commitments, came to the assistance of its Allies in the war against imperialist Japan.

Although Japan was not at war with the Soviet Union, it had at all times since the outbreak of the war been an ally of nazi Germany and kept her large Kwantung Army near the Soviet border, threatening to invade the Soviet Far East. The U.S.S.R. was compelled to concentrate a considerable force (as many as 40 divisions) in the area. Neither could the Soviet Government overlook the fact that before the war all of Japan's military preparations were aimed against the U.S.S.R. As pointed out by Oshima, former Japanese Ambassador to Germany, for 20 years all the plans of the Japanese General Staff were focussed on an assault on Russia. In 1938 the Japanese militarists attempted a large-scale provocation at Lake Hasan, and in 1939 they attacked the Mongolian People's Republic, a state friendly to the U.S.S.R., in the Khalkhin Gol area. During the war, the Japanese Navy interfered with Soviet commercial shipping and, in effect, blockaded the ports and maritime frontiers of the Soviet Far East.

The Japanese intelligence service supplied Germany with whatever information it obtained. According to Japanese ex-War Minister Hideki Tojo, Japan was to have attacked the Soviet Union after "the military power of the U.S.S.R. had been completely sapped by the German onslaught, thereby easing to the maximum the conquest by Japan of the Soviet Far East". That was how Japan intended to "adhere" to the neutrality pact which it had signed with the U.S.S.R. in April 1941. When its term ran out on April 5, 1945, the Soviet Government refused to prolong it and said that "in the circumstances, the neutrality pact between Japan and the U.S.S.R. is senseless, and its prolongation impossible".*

On August 8, 1945, the Soviet Government declared war on imperialist Japan. The purpose behind this move was to reinforce

---

* Vneshnaya politika Sovetskogo Soyuza v period Otechestvennoi Voiny (Soviet Foreign Policy During the Patriotic War), Vol. III, p. 166.

the security of the Soviet Union in the Far East, help the Chinese people in their struggle against the Japanese invaders, and bring closer the end of the Second World War. The Japanese Ambassador in Moscow was told that as of August 9 the Soviet Union would consider itself in a state of war with Japan.

Three fronts were engaged for the Japanese campaign—the Transbaikal Front which included troops of the Mongolian People's Revolutionary Army, the Second Far Eastern Front along the Amur, and the First Far Eastern Front in the Maritime Territory. The Pacific Fleet and the Amur flotilla were also engaged. The operations were put under the charge of the High Command of Soviet troops in the Far East, headed by Marshal of the Soviet Union Alexander Vasilevsky. Three operations were planned—one in Manchuria with the objective of smashing the Kwantung Army and liberating North-East China and North Korea, the other in Southern Sakhalin with the objective of driving out the Japanese from Southern Sakhalin, and the third was the Kurile Islands landing. The first of the operations was the decisive one, for it was to settle the issue with the Kwantung Army.

At the beginning of the Manchurian operation troops of the three Soviet fronts, investing the territory occupied by the Kwantung Army, were able to strike inwards in converging directions from a huge semicircular perimeter. The Soviet Command meant to pierce the enemy defences in the north-west by the Transbaikal Front and in the south-east by the First Far Eastern Front, to crush the enemy troops and cut off the main strength of the Kwantung Army from North China and Korea in converging attacks, to surround them in the Manchurian lowlands and annihilate them piecemeal.

The drive into Manchuria began early in the morning of August 9. Active operations were launched on August 10 by the 8th and 4th Chinese People's Liberation armies and partisan groups headed by Communists.

Making the most of the experience gained in the war against fascist Germany, the Soviet troops pulverised the fortified border areas and, crushing bitter enemy resistance, advanced rapidly into the heart of Manchuria. The offensive developed in very adverse weather. Downpours had begun on August 8, mountain streams had burst their banks and bad roads held up the advance. The retreating enemy troops blew up bridges and river crossings, gutted towns and villages, and fought back ferociously. But nothing could stop the Soviet soldiers. In a mere 10 days the bulk of the Kwantung Army was smashed, and had no choice but to surrender. In the latter half of August 1945, Soviet troops liberated Manchuria, the city of Dalny (Dairen), Port Arthur, and North Korea. They captured Southern Sakhalin and the Kurile Islands.

When the Soviet advance against the Kwantung Army became a reality, the U.S. air force staged all-out raids on some parts of Manchuria, where U.S. airmen had dropped no bombs throughout the war. The situation resembled that of what had been designated as the Soviet occupation zone in Germany, where cities were also indiscriminately bombed.

On August 6 for no good reason at all, at least in the military sense, the U.S. air force exploded an atomic bomb over the Japanese city of Hiroshima, which claimed the lives of at least 247,000 civilians, mostly children, women and old people. On August 9, when the Red Army mounted its offensive, an atomic bomb was dropped on Nagasaki. This time some 200,000 people were killed or wounded. Humanity will never pardon or forget this savage and disgraceful act.

The rout of her ground forces in Manchuria, defeats in China, naval losses and the utter futility of fighting on compelled Japan to lay down her arms. On September 2, 1945, Japanese representatives signed the instrument of unconditional surrender. The end of the Second World War had come.

* * *

Bourgeois war historians have written piles of books in an effort to explain the reasons for the disastrous defeat of nazi Germany and the amazing victory of the U.S.S.R. Western literature harps on the legend of Hitler's mistakes, brought forward by West German writers. These were blamed for Germany's military collapse. But that is a falsification, an attempt to whitewash the German generals, to belittle the Soviet people and their army, and to prove that a new war against the U.S.S.R. could be won if the mistakes Hitler made are avoided.

However, it is not a matter of mistakes made by the one or the other side, though such mistakes did take place and did affect the progress of the war. It was the unbending determination of the Soviet people to safeguard their freedom and independence that decided the issue. The nation was united by the common urge to protect the Soviet Union, the world's first socialist country. The mass heroism, self-sacrifice, and contempt of death in the name of freedom, shown in the war by the Soviet people are without precedent in history. Even when taken prisoner, when deported far from their homeland, when languishing in nazi camps, Soviet men and women continued the fight with all the means at their disposal. They organised uprisings, escaped from POW camps, and sabotaged measures taken by the nazi authorities.

In the Soviet rear, the people devoted all their energy to supplying the battle lines with arms, ammunition, food and all the means necessary to defeat the enemy and end the war.

In the Great Patriotic War the Soviet people fought to protect the great gains made by socialism and to safeguard their Soviet statehood and the socialist system.

When the nazi leaders prepared the war against the U.S.S.R. they fooled themselves into believing that the Soviet system was unstable. But the facts proved that the Soviet state, based on the alliance of the working class and the peasants, the alliance and friendship of all the peoples, was the strongest in the world. No other state could have converted the nation into a united military camp in so short a time and in adverse circumstances, reorganised its economy along wartime lines and marshalled all its forces against the enemy.

The high economic level of the Soviet Union was another source of the victory. The country's industrialisation, featured by the priority development of heavy industry, enabled the Soviet Union to produce superior weapons in desired quantities. The Soviet Army gained a military victory over the nazi troops. Likewise, people in the Soviet rear gained an economic victory in their combat against Hitler Germany and her allies. Production capacities kept growing throughout the war, especially in the country's eastern areas. In the last three years of the war the German aircraft industry produced 80,000 planes, while Soviet industry produced as many as 120,000. Similarly, many more tanks, guns, mortars, submachine guns and other war matériel were produced in the U.S.S.R. than in Germany.

Socialist agriculture, too, coped with the task of supplying food and raw materials.

Soviet warcraft was of a superior standard to that of the German Wehrmacht. A galaxy of brilliant Soviet generals developed during the war, winning fame with their prowess and valour. More than 7,000,000 officers and soldiers were decorated with Orders and medals in the course of the war, nearly 11,000 of them being conferred the title of Hero of the Soviet Union.

The Soviet war effort was led by the Communist Party. By word and deed, the Communists gave the Soviet people splendid leadership. The prestige of the Party rose from day to day, and its bonds with the people grew closer. As many as 5,319,000 candidate members and more than 3,615,000 members were admitted to the Party during the war.

Chapter Six

POST-WAR ECONOMIC REHABILITATION
AND DEVELOPMENT
(1945-53)

Internal Development

Rehabilitation of Liberated Areas

As the end of the war drew closer, peaceful rehabilitation began of the territories cleared of the enemy. The Soviet people applied their energies to restoring industrial plants, collective and state farms, machine-and-tractor stations, and dwellings. The general effort followed the principles laid down in the decision of the Council of People's Commissars of the U.S.S.R. and the Central Committee of the Communist Party, of August 21, 1943, "On Urgent Measures for the Rehabilitation of the Economy in Areas Liberated from German Occupation."

While the war was still on, the Soviet Government allotted considerable resources for economic rehabilitation, laying emphasis on the coal and steel industry of the Ukraine, the light and food industries, municipal and social services, cultural institutions, and housing. Engineers, technicians and skilled workers were recalled from the Red Army, and tens of thousands of collective farmers and workers were marshalled, too, from the eastern regions.

The devastation left behind by the fleeing nazis was cyclonic. Stalingrad lay in ruins. Nearly all the housing was destroyed in Voronezh. In Poltava, Kharkov, Kremenchug, Zaporozhye and Ternopol the nazis had gutted or blown up some eighty per cent of all the dwellings and public buildings. In Kiev, the capital of the Ukraine, they had demolished 940 government and other public buildings, more than 6,000 dwellings and over 800 factories. Kreshchatik, the main thoroughfare and Kiev's pride, had been almost entirely demolished.

The devastation in the towns and villages of Byelorussia was almost as complete. Nearly all the factories, all the machine tools and all the plant at power stations had been destroyed. Minsk,

Gomel, Vitebsk, Polotsk, Orsha and most of the other towns had suffered incredible damage. More than 400,000 farmers' cottages, thousands of the collective-farm buildings and all the machine-and-tractor stations lay in ashes.

Leningrad had lived through 900 days and nights of a savage enemy siege. Brutal artillery bombardments and countless air raids had caused terrible damage in the city and its environs, the suburbs of Petrodvorets, Pushkin, Pavlovsk and Kolpino. Yet all this was only a fraction of the wanton damage the German invaders had inflicted on the Soviet people.

The rehabilitation of the liberated areas required immense effort and sacrifice.

More than 620,000,000 cubic metres of water had to be pumped out of the coal mines in the Donets Basin, an amount six times greater than the French coal industry had to cope with after the First World War. Equipment and all other mining facilities, and the supply of power, had to be almost wholly rebuilt, and manpower had to be brought in to do the job.

Reconstruction began in 1944. The whole country chipped in to help revive the nation's oldest coal basin.

The miners laboured with the utmost devotion. Taking their lives into their hands, men descended into the perilous mines and worked under water to extract dozens of tons of scrap iron cluttering up the passages and tracks. In two years they put 129 big mines and 889 medium and small ones back into operation.

The steelworkers of the South restored 77 blast- and open-hearth furnaces, three Bessemer converters and nine electric furnaces in 1944 and 1945. Power stations totalling 2,300,000 kw were restarted after restoration work, including the Novomoskovsk, Volkhov, Shterovka and Zuyevka developments. Work also proceeded to restart the big Dnieper Hydropower Station.

Stupendous work was done to restore the country's transport, electrical industry, agricultural machine-building, the municipal services, and the housing in town and countryside.

The women of Stalingrad started the patriotic movement of rendering volunteer help to the builders. It was initiated by A. Cherkasova, the wife of a front-line soldier. The first volunteer women's team helped builders restore the famous Pavlov House. It published an appeal for volunteers to the women of the city in the local newspaper, and before long had evoked a nation-wide response.

Volunteers contributed more than 2,000,000 man-hours in the Donets Basin, helping build dwellings and public buildings.

It was a matter of honour for every citizen of Kiev to assist in the reconstruction of his city. In 1944 alone, the people of the Ukrainian capital put in some 230,000 unpaid man-hours in rebuilding the Kreshchatik.

In 1944, after the blockade was lifted, Leningraders did volunteer work totalling 25,000,000 man-days to restore their city.

The collective farmers and the workers and employees of the state farms and machine-and-tractor stations laboured selflessly to bring the farms back to normal.

The eastern republics and regions of the U.S.S.R. came to their aid. Seed, tractors, implements, draught animals and other livestock were shipped to the Ukraine, Byelorussia, Moldavia and Karelia. The people of the Gorky and Ivanovo regions and of the Khakass Autonomous Region helped the farmers of Kalinin Region, and the latter, too, shared their seed supplies with the collective farms of Kursk and Smolensk regions, giving them 4,800 tons of grain.

The difficulties which the Soviet people had to cope with in the first few years of rehabilitation were incredible. Towns and villages lay in ruins. There was an acute shortage of machines and manpower, food and clothing. But the people did not lose heart. The advantages of the socialist system and the nation's determination to erase the scars of war won through.

Focus on Peacetime Development

On May 9, 1945, the Soviet people joyously celebrated the victory over German nazism, the deadly enemy of humanity, Peace was restored to the U.S.S.R.

On June 22, 1945, the Twelfth Session of the Supreme Soviet examined the question of demobilising soldiers of the higher age groups from the regular army. A special law was passed to that effect. And two days later, on June 24, a Victory Parade was held in Red Square. Units of the three services, generals covered with glory, and Heroes of the Soviet Union filed past the stands in an impressive demonstration of the strength and valour of the Soviet Armed Forces. The battle standards of the defeated nazi regiments and divisions were cast down before the Lenin Mausoleum.

The consequences of this, the bloodiest of all the wars in history, were ghastly. The Soviet nation had lost more than 20,000,000 men and women. Scarcely a family in the land had been spared the grief of bereavement. The loss of property was staggering. The direct recorded material damage alone caused by the nazis to the Soviet state amounted to the colossal sum of 679,000 million pre-war rubles. The losses from the stoppage of factories, offices, and farms amounted to 2,569,000 million rubles in pre-war prices. Hundreds of towns and tens of thousands of villages had been demolished, two-thirds of the coal mines in the enemy-occupied areas had been put out of action, and some of the country's biggest power stations and iron-and-steel works lay in ruins. Agriculture had suffered heavily. The nazis had destroyed 98,000 collective farms, 1,876 state farms and 2,890 machine-and-tractor stations, and had shipped out or slaughtered 7,000,000 horses and 17,000,000 head of cattle.

By the end of 1945 the country produced 90 per cent of the pre-war output of coal, 62 per cent of oil, 59 per cent of pig iron, 67 per cent of steel and 41 per cent of textiles. The crop acreage had shrunk from 150,400,000 hectares in 1940 to 113,600,000 hectares, and the cattle herd diminished from 54,500,000 to 47,400,000 head. The aggregate farming output was 60 per cent of pre-war.

The governing groups in the West hoped the Soviet Union would not cope with economic rehabilitation on its own, and that they would get in on the ground floor and make the U.S.S.R. economically dependent on the capitalist countries. But their expectations were dashed. The Soviet people eliminated the grim consequences of the war without outside assistance.

The culmination of the war against imperialist Japan gave added impetus to the general rehabilitation effort. On August 19, 1945, the *Pravda* announced that the Central Committee of the Communist Party and the Council of People's Commissars of the U.S.S.R. had authorised the State Planning Commission to draw up a Five-Year Plan of Economic Rehabilitation and Development for 1946-50, providing for "the full restoration of the economy in areas that had suffered German occupation, a post-war reorganisation of the national economy and the further development of all regions of the U.S.S.R. with the object of considerably surpassing the pre-war economic level of the U.S.S.R." This was the only directive issued in relation to the Fourth Five-Year Plan. The projected targets and questions of post-war conversion were not discussed at any Party congresses or conferences, or at any plenary meetings of the Central Committee. The initiative of Party, government and economic bodies was considerably hemmed in. This was why grave errors of judgement were made in the plan.

The plan was not properly balanced as regards all the basic elements. Some elements were overlooked in the distribution of available resources. Economic development did not fully exploit co-operation between the various economic areas. Resources were dispersed, specialists were slow to return to their industries, and there were delays in restarting the rehabilitated enterprises. These deficiences and difficulties were combated by the people and the Party. The Soviet Union resumed its advance to communism, interrupted by the war.

The Fourth Five-Year Plan (1946-50)

The Fourth Five-Year Plan was passed at the First Session of the Supreme Soviet of the U.S.S.R. in March 1946. Its chief objective was "to restore the country's war-ravaged areas, to regain the pre-war level in industry and agriculture, and then to surpass this level by significant amounts".

The pre-war industrial output was to be surpassed by 48 per cent. It was planned to increase the force of factory and office workers from 27,300,000 in 1945 to 33,500,000, to boost labour productivity by 36 per cent over the pre-war figure and to reduce costs of production 17 per cent as compared with 1945.

The plan laid considerable emphasis on the country's continued electrification. Major hydropower stations were projected, including the Kuibyshev, Volgograd and Gorky stations, in addition to a number of thermal powerhouses.

The plan gave prominence to the rehabilitation of the war-ravaged areas, for which it set aside 40 per cent of the projected capital investments. Furthermore, it envisaged sweeping economic development for the new Soviet republics of Lithuania, Latvia and Estonia, and for parts of Siberia and the Far East.

A seven per cent rise over the pre-war grain yield and a 25 per cent rise in the production of industrial crops was envisaged, the livestock was to be increased considerably, and the farms were to get more tractors, farming machinery and mineral fertilisers.

The return to normal economic life and the fresh upsurge of all branches of the economy paved the way for a considerable improvement of the living and cultural standard. The five-year plan provided for a 30 per cent increase of the national income and a 28 per cent growth of the commodity turnover over pre-war. Housebuilding was to proceed on a grand scale. It was planned to build 72,400,000 sq m of housing in five years, which amounted to something like half of all the housing available in the country in 1913.

The First Session of the Supreme Soviet of the U.S.S.R. passed a law converting the Council of People's Commissars into the Council of Ministers, for the new name was more consistent with the generally accepted governmental designations.

New Upsurge of Industry

In the Fourth Five-Year Plan period industry had to cope with three major tasks: post-war reconversion, rehabilitation of demolished enterprises in the war-ravaged areas and the large construction programme.

The peacetime reconversion of industry involved a number of formidable problems. Wherever new items were to be manufactured, entirely new equipment, raw materials, new techniques, and contacts between related or ancillary plants were called for. Yet there were sad disproportions in the development of the various branches of industry, and resultant shortages of fuel, electric power and metal. Stoppages caused by power shortages harassed the Petrovsky Steel Mill in Dnepropetrovsk, the steel mill in Makeyevka and the Ilyich Works in Zhdanov, all of them factories of major importance. Even in some parts of the Urals and Siberia factories putting out key materials were supplied no more than 40 to 50 per cent of their electricity needs.

The reconversion to peacetime production called for a reorganisation of management. The People's Commissariats of the tank, mortar and ammunition industries were closed down in 1946 and 1947, and replaced by People's Commissariats (later ministries) of agricultural and transport engineering, and of machine and instrument building. The reorganisation took time and inevitably caused drops in output. The cumulative effect was that the aggregate 1946 industrial output was 17 per cent lower than that of the year before and amounted to just 77 per cent of pre-war. Output of peacetime goods increased 20 per cent over that of 1945.

But despite all these difficulties, the post-war reconversion of industry was in the main completed in 1946. The 1947 plan set its sights on eliminating the disproportions and envisaged a more intensive development of the fuel, steel, electric power and consumer industries than provided for in the five-year plan. In 1947, industry fulfilled the annual plan. In the last three months of the year output reached the pre-war level, and the lag with respect to the five-year plan targets was eliminated. The following year the pre-war level was surpassed.

Pride of place in the rehabilitation effort went to the reconstruction of power stations, the coal industry and the steelmaking works in the country's south. The Dnieper Hydropower Station was the most important and the biggest rehabilitation project. Its machine room, and most of its spillway piers and sluices, had been blown up. The nazis had put 360 tons of explosive into the body of the dam. The amount of work involved in putting the station back into operation was titanic. Thousands of workers, technicians and engineers laboured on restoring this first big industrial project built under socialism in the thirties. F. Loginov, a prominent industrial organiser, headed the reconstruction of the Dnieper Hydropower Station, which was restarted in record time. Its first section began operating in March 1947, and the last in June 1950. After its reconstruction the station produced more power than all the power stations of pre-revolutionary Russia combined. Also restored were the Zuyevka and Kurakhovka stations in the Donets Basin, the Niva Hydropower Station in Murmansk Region, and the power stations in Tiraspol, Kharkov and Krivoi Rog. All the power stations in the Donets Basin, the Dnieper area, and in Kiev, Kharkov, Krasnodar, Voronezh, Bryansk and other cities which suffered from German occupation were back in operation by the end of the five-year plan period.

The rehabilitation effort launched in the Donbas in 1944 and 1945 proceeded on a grand scale in the subsequent five years. The whole country backed the miners. New machines were sent there, such as hammer drills, coal planes and coal combines. In 1949, the basin's coal output was back at the pre-war level.

The speedy rehabilitation of the Donets and Moscow coal basins, increased mechanisation, new mines in the Donbas, in the Urals, the Kuzbas and Karaganda, coupled with the hard work and enthusiasm of the miners, helped the coal industry back on its feet. It overfulfilled its five-year plan target, and extracted 57 per cent more coal in 1950 than in 1940 and 75 per cent more than in 1945.

Blast- and open-hearth furnaces were brought back into action in the iron and steel industry, the iron and manganese ore mines were rehabilitated in Krivoi Rog and Nikopol, respectively, and the big steel mills in the south of the country were put back into operation. The eyes of the country were on Zaporozhstal, the giant iron and steel works in the south of the country, whose wartime stoppage had affected many industries. More than 10,000 young men and women came from Moscow, the Urals and other industrial areas to help in the reconstruction of this mammoth plant.

The plant's thermal powerhouse, its open-hearth furnaces, slab mill, cold-rolling mill, sheet rolling mill and other shops were restored in short order. The speedy reconstruction of the Ukrainian iron and steel industry helped step up pig iron, steel and rolled stock production 100 to 150 per cent.

Industrial rehabilitation proceeded apace in Kiev, Kharkov, Minsk, Stalingrad, Leningrad and the other war-ravaged cities.

At the close of 1945, the government passed a special decision to stimulate the restoration of fifteen war-damaged ancient Russian towns. The Y.C.L. volunteered to assist in the nation-wide effort. Tens of thousands of youths and young women worked on the rehabilitation of Stalingrad, Leningrad, Minsk, Kiev, Voronezh and many other cities. More than half a million young men and women helped rehabilitate the Donets mines, the steel mills in the Ukraine, the Dnieper Power Station, and the factories in the liberated areas.

Just as before the war, the Soviet Union was comparable to a giant building site. Power stations went up on the Syr Darya River in Uzbekistan, on the Irtysh in Kazakhstan, at Khrami and Sukhumi in Georgia, at Krasnaya Polyana in Krasnodar Territory, at Lake Sevan in Armenia, at Mingechaur in Azerbaijan, Rybinsk near Moscow, at Tsimlyanskaya, etc. The Y.C.L. gave great help in all these power projects. In 1947, the Ust-Kamenogorsk Hydropower Development, for example, was proclaimed a Y.C.L. project. More than 4,000 Y.C.L. members, or 80 per cent of the labour force, worked on the project in 1950. The Y.C.L. of Azerbaijan made a great contribution to the building of the Mingechaur Hydropower Project, and the same was true in every republic and region where construction proceeded under the five-year plan. In the latter half of 1950, the Soviet Government announced the decision to build a Volga-Don Canal, two hydropower stations on the Volga and one at Kakhovka on the Dnieper. Young people from all over the country took part in the building. Some enlisted at the building sites, others helped produce the equipment for them. It was the heroic labour effort of the Y.C.L. youth, and the nation's youth in general, that gave the main impetus to the fulfilment of the Fourth Five-Year Plan ahead of schedule.

Considerable oil development was under way between the Volga and the Urals. At the close of the five-year plan period new towns, such as Oktyabrsky and Ishimbai, appeared on the map, and such old towns as Syzran, Bugulma and Buguruslan, too, grew into prominent oil centres. The gas pipelines laid from Saratov to Moscow (843 km) and from Dashava to Kiev (500 km) improved the country's fuel supply.

The post-war building gradually changed the face of the country and its industrial geography. An iron and steel works was built in the town of Rustavi in Transcaucasia, and another in Begovat, Uzbekistan. Pipe-rolling works were started up at Sumgait in Azerbaijan and in Nikopol in the Ukraine.

The Leningrad industries changed from top to bottom. When the five-year plan got under way, Leningrad's industries were producing no more than 32 per cent of what they had produced in 1940. Under the five-year plan the pre-war level was to be reached and then considerably surpassed.

Leningrad's factories had to be brought up to date technically. Pride of place went to the shipyards and the specialised engineering plants.

In the past, Leningrad's industries were hamstrung by the lack of local raw materials and the absence of large power-generating plants. Shipping metals from the Urals and coal from the Donbas involved additional costs, and the power supplied by the peat-burning powerhouses and local hydropower stations fell woefully short of the demand. This situation was remedied in the Fourth Five-Year Plan period by boosting coal output for Leningrad in the Pechora Coal Basin, expanding production and the manufacture of peat bricks, and increasing the extraction of shale and shale gas in Estonia and Leningrad Region. A gas pipeline was built from Kokhtla-Järve to Leningrad.

Lignite production leaped after new mines were sunk at the Borovichi, Nelidovo, Selizharovo and other coalfields adjoining Leningrad Region. Coal, too, was used more extensively to produce electric power. Preparations were under way in 1948 to build the Cherepovets Iron and Steel Works.

Through the selfless efforts of the Leningrad workers and the vast organising work of the city's Party organisation, Leningrad's industries reached their pre-war level in 1948, and considerably surpassed it in 1950.

Leningrad's output of equipment for the metallurgical, oil and coal industries, and of powerful turbines for the country's hydropower projects increased steadily. The city became the nation's centre of specialised engineering and instrument-making. The disproportion that had prevailed between the manufacturing industry and the fuel and metal supply was eliminated.

New lines of production were initiated at many of the country's older factories. The Azov Steel Works installed a blooming mill and a rail-structural mill. A big bloomery was also started up at the Novo-Tagilsky Works. New aluminium plants went up at Bogoslovsk in the Urals and Kananer in Armenia, and a lead and zinc plant was built at Ust-Kamenogorsk in Kazakhstan. A tractor and automobile works was built in Minsk, the capital of Byelorussia, a motor works in Kutaisi, a tractor works in Lipetsk and an agricultural machinery works at Rubtsovsk in the Altai Territory. In the five years the nation's basic productive assets increased at least 50 per cent over 1940.

The rapid industrial upsurge of the war-ravaged areas was greatly facilitated by the industrial potential of the country's eastern areas, which had been built up before the war and greatly expanded in wartime.

At one time it had been the central republics that helped the people of the Soviet East to develop industrially and culturally. After the war, as in 1944 and 1945, it was the turn of the Eastern regions, particularly the Central Asian republics, to help the war-ravaged areas of the Russian Federation and the other republics. This fraternal assistance and friendship of the peoples helped surmount the grave difficulties of the post-war five-year period.

The working class grew numerically at a rapid rate. Servicemen demobilised from the Army and Navy, totalling more than 9,000,000, swelled its ranks, together with school-leavers and young people from the vocational and factory schools. In the first four years of the five-year plan period as many as 11,600,000 people joined the country's labour force, chiefly in industry and building. In 1950, the Soviet economy had 38,895,000 factory and office workers.

But due to the difficulties of rehabilitation and irregularities in the system of emoluments there was fluidity of labour. The Soviet Government stepped in with measures to combat labour fluidity and eliminate the reasons for it. People employed in industry, building and mining were offered social insurance advantages and supplementary emoluments. While state-financed housebuilding proceeded, long-term credits were furnished to people wishing to build their own homes. Mechanisation of arduous jobs considerably improved working conditions, and facilities for occupational training were extended.

A far-flung movement arose among the people for the promotion of new labour methods, which was evidence of a rise in their political consciousness and proficiency. Go-ahead workers of the Fourth Five-Year Plan period set their sights on improving techniques, raising labour productivity and the quality of production, and securing profitable operation. V. Seminsky, a turner at the Krasny Ekskavator Plant in Kiev, fulfilled 20 times as much in the five-year plan period as he was to have done in a year and introduced 47 innovations. These yielded an economy of 300,000 rubles. Many Ukrainian engineering workers followed his example. Grigory Nezhevenko, an Odessa lathe operator, fulfilled 23 annual assignments in the same time, and Konstantin Kislyakov, a Kharkov turner, operated simultaneously several machine tools and exceeded his assignments three or four times over.

Nikolai Rossiysky, foreman of Moscow's Kalibr Works, developed a conveyor technique which boosted output 750 per cent. He taught his method to all the workers in his shop, with a resultant threefold rise in its labour efficiency and a reduction of production cost by one-half.

The textile and steel workers, miners and builders and men of other trades initiated numerous good trends in the socialist emulation movement. There are countless examples to illustrate the wholesale heroism, initiative and inventiveness shown by the workers, engineers and office employees in the nation-wide rehabilitation effort. Here is one. At the Azovstal Iron and Steel Works the nazis had demolished the biggest blast furnace. It had shifted 1.3 metres, had sunk more than 3.5 metres and listed at an angle of 20 degrees. Inspection committees thought it would be easier to tear it down and build a new furnace in its place. But the engineers suggested an audacious experiment. They planned to lift the furnace with hydraulic hoists, straighten it out and move it to its former place. Their project was accepted and carried through. The furnace, weighing 1,300 tons, was hoisted and moved in 18 working shifts. This was an unprecedented accomplishment, for it would have taken at least 6 months to restore it in the conventional manner. On September 10, 1946, it yielded its first smelt of iron.

The socialist emulation movement of the Fourth Five-Year Plan period was marked by a variety of forms, an intensive creative search for new production techniques and a growth of the innovation movement. By the end of that period as many as 90 per cent of the workers had joined in it heart and soul.

Fulfilment of the Fourth Five-Year Plan industrial targets was spotlighted by a widespread introduction of new machinery. Labour-consuming jobs were mechanised in the iron and steel industry. Coal extraction was mechanised too. New machinery was developed for oil drilling, and is still renowned as the world's best. Industry made wider and wider use of electric power, and electronic engineering made its first appearance.

New mass-production and automatic techniques appeared in the engineering industry. A fully automated factory was built to manufacture pistons for automobile engines. Soviet engineers and technicians developed more than a thousand different highly efficient machine tools, automats and other machinery. Leningrad workers initiated a movement for closer co-operation between science and production. Thousands of scientists, researchers, engineers and innovators blazed new trails in science and technology, putting their accomplishments to good use in industry. A striking example of this is the development of a new method of automatic electric welding by the associates of the Institute of Electric Welding of the Academy of Sciences of the Ukraine. The new method was rapidly put to use in Soviet industry.

In collaboration with engineers and workers, Soviet scientists discovered methods of producing atomic energy and of using it for peaceful purposes. The building of the world's first industrial atomic power station of 5,000 kw was begun in the Fourth Five-Year Plan period in the Soviet Union. The station was put into operation on June 27, 1954. The use of atomic energy in industry ushered in a deep-going technical revolution.

The industrial targets of the Fourth Five-Year Plan were fulfilled well ahead of schedule in a matter of 4 years and 3 months thanks to the vast effort put in by Party and public organisations in promoting new technology, training personnel, and encouraging the socialist emulation and innovation movements. As many as 6,200 rehabilitated or newly built industrial enterprises were put into operation. Aggregate industrial output climbed 73 per cent over the pre-war level, against the 48 per cent originally planned. Heavy industry made particularly good headway. The 1950 output of iron was 19 million tons, steel more than 27 million tons, coal more than 261 million tons, oil about 38 million tons, and electric power more than 91,000 million kwh. This surpassed the production figures of pre-war 1940. The accomplishments of industry reinforced the material and technical basis of socialist society.

The industrial output in all the Union republics exceeded the pre-war level—by 15 per cent in the Ukraine and Byelorussia, 91 per cent in Lithuania and 100 per cent in Moldavia. Big steel and rolling mills were built in Kazakhstan, Uzbekistan, Georgia and Latvia. Labour productivity in industry climbed 37 per cent.

The new industrial advance was spurred by the labour enthusiasm of the working class and the advantages of the planned system of socialist production.

It should be noted, however, that some of the key industries did not fulfil the five-year plan targets. This was due to mistakes in gauging the country's actual possibilities when framing the post-war plan in the personality cult environment.

The Fourth Five-Year Plan and Agriculture

The collective farmers faced tasks of immense proportions in the first post-war five-year period. On top of the war's aftermaths came a terrible drought in 1946, embracing the south-west and north of the Ukraine, the central chernozem area, the lower reaches of the Volga and a few other regions. The Ukraine, for example, had a worse harvest that year than in 1921. This was due, besides the drought, to the ravages of the nazi occupation. In addition harmful violations occurred of the collective-farm statutes. The democratic principle of farm management was scorned, work-day emoluments were incorrectly distributed, public land and collective-farm property were squandered and misappropriated. On many collective farms the principle of incentives was neglected.

In September 1946, the Council of Ministers and the Party Central Committee issued a decision "On Measures Eliminating Violations of the Rules of the Agricultural Artel". It was designed to rectify the deviations from Party policy concerning the management of collective farms.

In February 1947, a Plenary Meeting of the Communist Party adopted a set of measures to strengthen agriculture in the post-war period. In the main, the measures concerned the development of farming as envisaged in the Fourth Five-Year Plan, and provided for greater assistance to collective and state farms in the way of material and machinery, personnel and Party guidance at village level.

But the decision of the C.C. Plenary Meeting also contained wrong notions typical of the Stalin cult period, some of which were put down on his personal insistence.

For example, the decision described the practice of calculating procurement quotas proportionately to the area of arable as conflicting with "the interests of agricultural development". Procurement quotas for the collective farms, the decision said, should be proportionate to land development, meaning that collective farms developing land and disposing of a sufficient labour force should

Rehabilitated Kiev

Housing development for the Donbas miners built in place of
those destroyed by the nazis, 1955

Fallen Heroes Square, Stalingrad (now Volgograd)

Palace Square in Leningrad with its war wounds healed

turn in more grain to the state procurement agencies, while those that did not should turn in less grain.

In practice, this meant that the procurement plans were met at the expense of the more prosperous collective farms. This virtually removed the incentive for improving land cultivation and increasing grain production.

The advice to sow summer wheat not only in Siberia, the Urals and the north-eastern regions of Kazakhstan, where it yielded good harvests, but also in the Ukraine, had a similar effect.

All the same, Soviet agriculture managed to put the difficulties of the post-war period out of the way and, in the main, had reached its pre-war level. All the collective and state farms, and all the machine-and-tractor stations were rehabilitated, and some new ones were founded. By the end of the five-year plan period all peasant farms in the western parts of the Ukraine, Byelorussia and Moldavia, and those of Lithuania, Latvia and Estonia had gone over to collective farming.

On vacant land the Soviet Government organised 827 new state farms and 1,345 machine-and-tractor stations, raising the number of state farms to 4,988 in 1950. The government assisted farming considerably with supplies and technical resources. In five years, the factories delivered 308,000 tractors to the countryside, bringing their number up to 595,500 in 1950 as against 531,800 in 1940. There were also more harvester-combines and other farming machinery than in 1940.

Amalgamation of smaller collective farms into bigger ones was a milestone in the history of Soviet collective farming. This was a highly effective measure, because the smaller collective farms, some of them consisting of as few as 20 to 30 households (the national average being 80 households) could not use the available up-to-date farming machinery to the best advantage. Besides, the cost of maintaining an office staff was too heavy a burden for them. Their amalgamation into bigger units, started in 1950, reduced the number of collective farms.

The crop area increased 20 per cent during the Fourth Five-Year Plan period, but was still short of the pre-war figure. The aggregate grain yield amounted to 78,400,000 tons, or to 32,000,000 tons more than in 1945. State grain procurements totalled 32,000,000 tons a year. The aggregate production and the procurements were not large enough to meet the nation's food requirements. The cities were short of potatoes, vegetables and fruit as well. The procurements of animal products were two or three times greater than in 1945, but also fell short of the rising demand.

The fact that agriculture fell down on some of the Fourth Five-Year Plan targets was due not only to the ravages of war, but also to the many serious errors and deficiencies of management typical of the Stalin cult period.

The Living Standard Rises

Industrial growth and the recovery of farming in the Fourth Five-Year Plan period, coupled with reduced military expenditures, gave the Soviet Government a chance to improve the condition of the working people in town and countryside, and concentrate on raising the cultural standard. The planned development of the Soviet economy enabled the country to avoid the crises and unemployment that harassed the capitalist West in the post-war period. On the contrary, the number of gainfully employed rose steeply, surpassing the 1940 figure by 7,700,000. This alone is a striking indication of the rise in the living standard.

The towns and villages ravaged by the fascists were restored in a very short time. New towns appeared on the map, such as Sumgait, Krasnouralsk, Novaya Kakhovka, etc. In 1951, the U.S.S.R. had 1,451 large towns and 2,320 small ones, which considerably exceeded their number in 1941.

The urban population swelled, its growth being stimulated by the rehabilitation of old and the appearance of new towns, by industrial growth and new industrial developments. In 1941, the urban population was 60,600,000. By 1951, it increased to 71,400,000. In the five-year plan period houses aggregating 102,800,000 sq m of floor space were built in towns and cities, overshooting the five-year plan target by 21 per cent. In addition, more than 2,700,000 cottages were built in the countryside. People were better off than before the war, but the rapid growth of the urban population precipitated an acute housing shortage. The death rate dropped to half of what it was in 1940, and to one-third of 1913. The birth rate climbed. The natural growth of the population increased. The Soviet Union ranked first in the world for the average number of marriages.

In December 1947, the Soviet Union abolished rationing of food and other consumer goods, and carried through a money reform. During the war, the government had issued a large amount of paper money, whose purchasing value decreased due to the shortage of consumer goods. Besides, a vast sum of counterfeit money had been put into circulation by the nazis. The money reform reinforced Soviet finances, raised the purchasing capacity of the Soviet ruble, facilitated the abolition of rationing and paved the way for unrestricted retail trade at considerably reduced prices. Three successive price reductions in the Fourth Five-Year Plan period impelled a considerable rise in the real incomes of factory and office workers, and of the collective farmers.

The rise in the living standard is illustrated, too, by the growth of the national income, which in 1950 surpassed that of 1940 by 64 per cent.

The government allocated vast sums each year to social and cultural development. The hospitals, sanatoria and holiday homes destroyed during the war were restored. New ones were built. The number of doctors in 1950 was 265,000, against 155,000 in 1940.

The post-war five-year plan fortified the country appreciably, paving the way for the completion of the building of socialist society. *wasn't this completed in 1936*

Socio-Political Developments in 1946-53

After the war, the socio-political trend in the country changed. During the war all mass organisations concentrated on rallying the nation for the war effort. In the post-war period, it was economic, cultural and educational matters that came to the fore. The Communist Party directed the nation's resources on reaching the targets of the post-war five-year plan and on completing the building of socialism. It sought to stimulate the work of the Soviets, the trade unions, the Young Communist League and the other mass organisations. But this was impeded by the fact that some Party organisations were inclined to handle many of the economic problems on their own, and ignored the Soviets, trade unions and the Y.C.L. *explain*

The Central Committee intervened, ordering the local Party organisations to mend their ways. Party conferences were held at district, city, region and territory levels. The Communist Parties of the Union republics held congresses. This helped speed the reconversion of the Party organisations to peacetime methods and to improve Party work in the newly arisen situation.

The Party lifted the wartime restrictions on inner-Party democracy, but the Stalin cult retarded democratic development. *how*

Ideological work advanced to the forefront in Communist Party activities. Victory in the war demonstrated the superiority of Soviet ideology. During the war and after it, Soviet people displayed a deep sense of purpose in their labour, a sense of duty, and a fervent love of country.

But survivals of bourgeois mores and morals, the profit-craving psychology of the private proprietor, were still evident among some sections of the population. Elements of nationalism still existed, and some people showed a reluctance to work for the common weal. This called for special efforts in the ideological field.

In 1946, the Party had a membership of 6,000,000, more than half of whom had joined the Party during the war. The newly admitted members were in need of political education.

The Communist Party took the matter up in all earnest. From 1946 to 1952, a large section of Party and government functionaries passed orientation courses. A far-flung network of Party political education schools and courses was developed.

In 1946-48, the Central Committee adopted decisions "On the Journals *Zvezda* and *Leningrad*", "On the Repertoire of Drama Theatres and Measures for Improving It", "On the Motion Picture *Big Life*" and "On the Opera *Great Friendship*". They condemned the apolitical mood, lack of ideological orientation, sordid flavour and other failings evident in some of the works of art and literature, and formulated measures to improve the nation's ideological development, particularly that of the youth. The principle of Party allegiance in art and literature was underscored with fresh emphasis. The social responsibilities of art and literature were stressed, too, and a call was sounded for close and viable bonds with the life of the nation.

The steps taken by the Party to carry through these decisions did a lot to raise the ideological level of Soviet culture. People's interest in questions of art, literature and science increased considerably.

The cult of the Stalin personality took deep root after the war. It tainted all aspects of Party work, and the work of its central bodies. The Leninist principles of collective leadership went by the board. Only one plenary meeting of the Central Committee was held in the post-war years, and no Party congress was convened, although none had been held for fourteen years. In the circumstances, many fundamental questions of Party policy were not given deep enough study, and the solutions took no account of what the Party membership thought. Mostly, decisions were taken by Stalin on his own.

In the ideological field, the Stalin cult created a rift between theory and practice. The collective thought of the Party was ignored. Stalin thought no one but he was qualified to deal with matters of theory. The works of Marx, Engels and Lenin were, in effect, relegated to relative obscurity. No written works of any worth appeared in the fields of political economy, philosophy and history.

The Young Communist League played a prominent part in the country's socio-political affairs. When the war ended, the fields in which Soviet youth could apply their enthusiasm and ability were truly boundless. Y.C.L. members came out with many valuable initiatives designed to speed industrial development, the restoration of towns and villages and agricultural production.

In appreciation of the Young Communist League's services to the country, the Presidium of the Supreme Soviet decorated it with the Order of Lenin on October 29, 1948. This was the fourth Order and the second Order of Lenin awarded to the youth organisation.

The Eleventh Y.C.L. Congress took place in March-April 1949.

It was convened 13 years after the previous congress, held in 1936. In the interim, the Y.C.L. membership had climbed from 3,981,780 to 9,283,289. In addition, some 13,000,000 children were members of the Young Pioneer organisation. The Rules of the Y.C.L. and the decisions on Y.C.L. work in schools, passed by the Congress, defined the tasks of the Y.C.L. in the fields of education and production.

But alongside the telling Y.C.L. successes, there were woeful shortcomings. As later noted in the decisions of the Twentieth Congress of the C.P.S.U., a noisome beating of drums and blaring of bugles was the catchword in all matters, interfering with vital day-to-day work.

All the same, even during the period of the Stalin cult, the Y.C.L. lived up to its tradition of active assistance to the Party in all Party undertakings.

The trade unions, the most massive of the people's organisations, had to cope with many difficult post-war tasks. They had to deal with economic matters, educational work among the masses, and improvement of the living conditions of their members. During the war the drop in the number of factory and office workers also reduced the trade union membership. But the rapid rehabilitation and a certain improvement of trade union organisation had the effect of boosting the membership. In 1948 it totalled 28,500,000. The post-war tasks of the trade unions were defined in the decisions of the Fourteenth (December 1945) and Fifteenth (April 1946) plenary meetings of the U.S.S.R. Central Council of Trade Unions. The Council focussed all efforts on the socialist emulation movement, which would draw the many millions of factory and office workers into the fulfilment of the 1946-50 Economic Development Plan. The trade unions were also called upon to work for the improvement of living conditions and of the cultural level of their membership.

The trade unions worked very hard to organise the socialist emulation movement, to develop a movement of innovators and inventors, to build collaboration between science and production and to better the working and living conditions of factory and office workers. In 1945, the trade unions set up commissions to control workers' proposals for the improvement of production and expedite their implementation. On the suggestion of the Party Central Committee the practice of collective agreements, which existed from 1917 to 1933, was revived in 1947. The Sixteenth Plenary Meeting of the Central Council of Trade Unions, held in April 1947, ruled that collective agreements should govern all trade union work. Much was done in the field of culture and education. The trade unions restored the war-damaged clubs and libraries. Propaganda of advanced production methods and courses for the improvement of skills were organised on a large scale.

The Tenth Trade Union Congress convened in Moscow in April 1949. It reviewed the work done by the trade unions over the preceding 17 years. The vast trade union membership had helped build socialism in the U.S.S.R., and then assisted in driving the enemy out of the country during the war. After the war it had worked might and main to mend the damage.

But trade union work fell short of the mark in many respects. There were elements of formalism in the socialist emulation movement. Innovators' ideas were too often neglected. Too few workers participated in the production conferences, and the cultural endeavours of the trade unions lagged behind the growing requirements. The Tenth Congress endorsed a new set of trade union rules and defined the place of trade unions in socialist society.

After the Tenth Congress, the trade unions improved their guidance of the socialist emulation movement, the innovators' movement, and cultural work. These issues were also dealt with at plenary meetings of the Central Trade Union Council. In 1945 there were as many as 139 trade unions in the country, many of which then amalgamated, bringing the total down to 66 by 1949. But due to the occupational principle in their structure, the factory and office workers of, say, the iron and steel and engineering industries had as many as 12 different trade unions, while the employees of the country's primary and secondary schools had 11 trade unions and government employees and shop's attendants had seven.

The trade unions coped poorly with their function of protecting the labour rights of their members, and were not active enough in the field of production and labour organisation. But due to the Stalin cult little was done to remedy the situation.

The war victory offered splendid opportunities for the development of Soviet democracy and the lifting of wartime restrictions. The day after the victory over imperialist Japan, the Presidium of the Supreme Soviet of the U.S.S.R. passed a decree terminating the nation-wide state of emergency and dissolving the State Defence Committee. The latter's affairs were turned over to the Council of People's Commissars.

In February 1946, elections were held to the Supreme Soviet of the U.S.S.R., and a year later to the Supreme Soviets of Union and Autonomous republics, and at the close of 1947 and in early 1948, to the local Soviets. Subsequently, elections to the Soviets were held as stipulated in the Constitution. They renewed the composition of the Soviets and drew fresh millions of Soviet citizens into active political life. Suffice it to say that 38,446 electoral commissions were set up during the 1947 campaign for election to the Supreme Soviets of Union and Autonomous republics. Some 10,000,000 citizens took part in the election campaign.

The elections touched off a wave of political and labour enthusiasm. Election meetings were held everywhere, outgoing deputies reported on their work, and electors briefed their nominees. The political awareness of Soviet citizens is illustrated by the following figures. In 1946, as many as 99.85 per cent of the electorate cast their votes in the elections to the Supreme Soviet of the U.S.S.R. and as many as 99.96 per cent in 1950. In 1946, 97.67 per cent of the votes were cast for the bloc of Communists and non-Party people, and 99.72 per cent in 1950.

The same was true of the elections to other Soviets. The finest sons and daughters of the nation were elected to them. In 1946, the 1,339 deputies elected to the Supreme Soviet of the U.S.S.R. comprised 511 workers (38.05 per cent), 349 peasants (26 per cent), and 479 intellectuals, office and other employees (35.95 per cent). The high percentage of intellectuals and employees evidenced a rise in the nation's cultural level.

After the war, the Soviets handled a multiplicity of matters related to the rehabilitation and building of industry, the municipal services, the work of machine-and-tractor stations, the state and collective farms, and the living standard.

But there were many deficiencies in their work due to the Stalin personality cult. The college of opinion was scorned and the Supreme Soviets did no more than perfunctorily discuss and approve budgets and endorse decrees passed by their Presidiums. The role of the Soviets was minimised and the rights of republican, regional and other local Soviets were curtailed. Many local matters were settled in the centre. Often, Stalin took decisions on key issues of domestic and foreign policy completely on his own.

The machinery of state cultivated red tape and a bureaucratic style of work. Staffs were inflated. Frequently, the bodies of state did not provide competent and timely leadership to economic development.

In the years after the war Stalin grossly violated socialist legal procedure and abused his power. This was starkly illustrated by the so-called Leningrad case, fabricated by the adventurists Beria, Bagirov and others who had wormed themselves into positions of power. Many guiltless men and women were framed, including prominent Party functionaries, such as Nikolai Voznesensky, member of the Political Bureau of the C.C. and Chairman of the State Planning Commission of the U.S.S.R., Alexei Kuznetsov, Secretary of the Central Committee of the Party, and M. I. Rodionov, Chairman of the Council of Ministers of the R.S.F.S.R.

The Nineteenth Party Congress and the Fifth Five-Year Plan

The Nineteenth Party Congress convened in October 1952, nearly 14 years after the previous congress. Major events had occurred in the intervening years. There was the Great Patriotic War and the successful post-war rehabilitation, which demonstrated the strength of the Soviet system and the correctness of Communist Party leadership. The close bonds between the Party and people, which did not weaken even in the grimmest days of the war, were underscored by the growing Party membership. At the time of the Eighteenth Party Congress the membership totalled 2,477,666. This figure had nearly trebled, climbing to 6,882,145 by the day the Nineteenth Congress opened.

The membership of the Young Communist League, too, had grown from 8 million in 1939 to 16 million in 1952. In the interim, more than 4,000,000 Y.C.L. members had joined the Party.

The Central Committee report to the Congress summed up the results of post-war economic development and pointed out the close ties established with the Soviet Union by all the forces of peace and democracy. The economic successes of the U.S.S.R. were too obvious to be denied. But industrial management was not coping with its job, and the report pointed to the shortcomings. Some factories did not fulfil their plans. Output was irregular. Equipment and plant were not used to their full capacity, and mechanisation of production, as well as labour productivity, increased too slowly, etc. But the cardinal failings born of the Stalin cult, such as red tape, inflated staffs, excessive centralisation, etc., were not mentioned. The situation in some branches of the economy was obviously window-dressed. The woeful miscalculations made in planning and in capital construction were not mentioned either.

The situation in agriculture was dressed up beyond all reason. Georgi Malenkov told the Congress that in 1952 the aggregate grain crop totalled 128,000,000 tons and that the "grain problem has been solved once and for all". He based his exaggerated claim on estimates of the unharvested crop, while the actual harvest had been much smaller. According to the more authentic figures obtained from state and collective farms, the 1952 grain crop amounted to some 89,600,000 tons.

Malenkov also quoted exaggerated figures for the increase of the cattle herd from 1945 to 1952, and made no mention of the dismal failure of the three-year livestock development plan (1949-51) passed by the Council of Ministers and the Party Central Committee. In the meantime the Leninist principle of material incentives had been grossly violated, and the prices of farm products were much lower than was economically justified. These and many other grave errors had an adverse effect on agriculture.

Malenkov made no mention whatsoever in his report of the way in which Stalin and his associates had violated the constitutional rights of many thousands of Soviet citizens, and even entire peoples of the Union. Neither did he say anything about the so-called Leningrad case, a frame-up which he had helped to engineer.

The Central Committee report to the Nineteenth Congress and most of the speeches eulogised Stalin beyond all proportion.

The Congress passed directives for the Fifth Five-Year Plan for 1951-55. This plan was focussed on a new advance in all branches of the economy. Aggregate industrial output was to be increased 70 per cent, the output of heavy industry 80 per cent, and the output of consumer goods 65 per cent. Capital investments were to be about double those made under the Fourth Five-Year Plan. Large hydropower developments, including the Kuibyshev, Kama, Gorky and Ust-Kamenogorsk stations, were to be put into operation.

In agriculture, the yields were to be raised still more, and the aggregate output of grain was to be increased 40-50 per cent. It was planned to increase the cattle herd and their productivity, and to complete the mechanisation of the main jobs on the farms.

The productivity of labour was to be increased 50 to 55 per cent and the national income 60 per cent. Plans were also made to improve the living and cultural standard.

The Nineteenth Party Congress decided to rename the Party the Communist Party of the Soviet Union or, in abbreviated form, the C.P.S.U. It discussed the question of amending the Party Rules. The new Rules defined the main tasks of the Party in the period of the completion of socialist construction and the transition to communism. They stressed the leading role of Communists in Soviet society. The Congress modified the structure of the central Party bodies, creating a Presidium of the Central Committee in place of the Political Bureau and a Secretariat in place of the Organisation Bureau. To enhance Party control over violations of Party and government discipline by Communists, the Commission of Party Control was reorganised into the Party Control Committee.

In 1951 and 1952, the Soviet people put their shoulder to the wheel to fulfil the Fifth Five-Year Plan. The 101-kilometre Volga-Don Canal was put into operation in 1952, and the construction of hydropower stations proceeded apace. The people showed considerable initiative in resolving the difficult task of socialist construction.

Soon after the Congress, on March 5, 1953, Stalin died. Certain Western groups hoped that after Stalin's death there would be confusion and vacillation among the Party and government leadership. They hoped the Soviet Government would completely alter its domestic and foreign policies.

But these expectations did not materialise.

Men came to the helm of the country who were quite capable of combating the negative consequences of the Stalin cult and leading Soviet society along the Leninist path to communism.

Foreign Policy of the Soviet Union

New Situation in the World

The gallant four-year war fought by the Soviet state against nazism enhanced the international prestige of the Soviet Union and its role in world affairs. The Soviet Union had delivered mankind from fascist slavery at the price of great sacrifices. Millions of people in all countries had their eyes opened to the realities in the socialist state and shook off their groundless prejudices.

The defeat of Hitler Germany and fascist Italy, the mainstays of reaction in Europe, induced a new upsurge of the revolutionary movement. While the fascists were still in control of most European countries, a resistance movement emerged there, touching off an armed struggle against the occupation forces. The liberation of the Central and South-East European countries by the Soviet Army was marked by a further development of the national liberation struggle against foreign invaders and local traitors and reactionaries. In Poland, Czechoslovakia, Bulgaria, Rumania, Hungary, Yugoslavia and Albania the people took power.

Thanks to its strength and international influence, the Soviet Union safeguarded the People's Democracies from a foreign reactionary intervention. But it was domestic causes that lay at the bottom of the revolutionary changes in the East European countries. The working people of Poland, Bulgaria and some other East European countries were the poorest and most oppressed on the continent. The war had added to their hardships. In the meantime, the ruling classes in those countries had discredited themselves by their undisguised collaboration with the fascist occupation forces.

The common struggle against foreign invaders brought together the workers, peasants, progressive intellectuals and large sections of the petty bourgeoisie in a united front of struggle against fascism. The masses were not content any longer to just drive out the occupation troops. They were eager to obtain deepgoing socio-economic and political changes. Communists everywhere acted as the boldest and most dedicated fighters for the general national interests. They won the confidence of the people, assumed leadership and led their nations to victory.

The People's Democracies carried through important democratic changes, agrarian reforms, the nationalisation of big industry and of the banks, and embarked on socialist development. The emergence of the People's Democracies meant that socialism was gradually growing into a world system. The countries that were once cast as links in the sanitary cordon along the Soviet frontiers, became loyal friends of the U.S.S.R.

Socialism won important victories in Asia too. The people of Vietnam triumphed over the colonialists in August 1945 and put a People's Government headed by Communists into power. Important democratic changes occurred in North Korea, and the Communists of China were in control of areas with a population of 100 million on the day the Second World War ended.

Two camps appeared on the world scene. One was the socialist democratic camp, and the other was imperialist and anti-democratic. The new breaches in the capitalist front showed that the shrinking of spheres for capitalist exploitation proceeded at an increasing rate and ushered in a second stage in the general crisis of capitalism.

The crisis of the colonial system deepened as a result of the Second World War. More than half the world population became involved in the struggle for the independence of their respective countries. In some countries, such as Indonesia and Malaya, full-scale wars were fought between the colonialists and the people's armies. The struggle of the Indian people was crowned with success in 1947, when India became an independent country. Burma and Ceylon won their independence in 1948. Vast colonial empires, the pillars of British, French and Dutch wealth, were falling apart.

The war changed the balance of power among the chief imperialist countries. Germany and Japan no longer belonged among the Great Powers, at least for a time. Of the three major imperialist states involved in the war against the fascist bloc, Britain and France emerged from the war weaker than they were before it. Only the United States of America had gained considerable military and economic strength. U.S. war losses were relatively small. U.S. territory had not been bombed at all. U.S. industry had steeply increased its output. The U.S. monopolies had added vastly to their capital. The financial dependence of Britain and France on U.S. imperialism increased during the war and after it. In the latter half of the 1940s the United States reigned supreme in the capitalist world. The Second World War, triggered by the uneven development of the capitalist countries, added to this unevenness.

Within each capitalist country contradictions between the working class and the bourgeoisie grew more acute. After war's end the masses gravitated leftward. In France and Italy large sections of the population gave their votes to the nominees of the Communist and Socialist parties. Communists were put into offices of responsibility in their governments. The Labour Party, which promised to carry through many important social and economic reforms, came to power in Britain, where the workers defeated the Conservative Party.

All in all, the balance of world strength tilted strongly in favour of democracy and socialism as a result of the Second World War.

The Soviet Union at the Paris Peace Conference

Unlike 1919, when the Big Three tried to settle all international problems at Versailles with utter disregard of the socialist state, no major issue of international politics after the Second World War could be resolved without the Soviet Union participating.

The victor states had to draw up peace treaties with Germany's former allies, Italy, Hungary, Rumania, Bulgaria and Finland. The drafting of treaties was undertaken by the Council of Foreign Ministers. Grave differences arose at sessions of the council between the Western powers and the Soviet Union. The spokesmen of the capitalist countries flung overboard the inspiring formulas of the Atlantic Charter and the decisions of the Yalta and Potsdam conferences. The selfish interests of U.S. and British Big Business assumed paramount importance in their designs. The British spokesmen suggested that all Italian colonies be put under British control.

The U.S. and British delegates insisted on peace terms that would give them an enduring hold on the economies of the defeated states. They spoke at the Foreign Ministers conferences and at the Paris Peace Conference, which opened on July 29, 1946, about "equal opportunities", "economic freedom", etc. The purport of their proposals was to deprive the war-ravaged economies of the defeated countries of all safeguards against the economic incursions of the American and British monopolies.

Everything the American and British delegates did indicated their wish to exert pressure on Rumania, Hungary and Bulgaria. Threatening notes were sent by London and Washington to the governments of these East European countries concerning their domestic policies. But they flirted with Italy and Finland, and wanted the peace terms for those two countries to be made "milder". All Western proposals concerning Rumania, Hungary and Bulgaria were so designed as to inflict the greatest possible damage to their economy and sovereignty.

Britain made no bones about supporting Greece's claims to a large slice of Bulgarian territory. Moreover, behind the scenes, the Western delegates suggested dividing Albania among the neighbouring countries.

But all these expansionist designs fell through. The Soviet Government did not want the new system of treaties to duplicate the injustices and humiliations of Versailles. Its main purpose was to eradicate the survivals of fascism in all the countries that had fought on Germany's side in the war.

All Western attempts to bend the Soviet Union to the will of the big Western powers were repelled. The Soviet delegation championed the cause of Bulgaria and Albania against Greek claims, and squashed all Western attempts to formalise their "right" to interfere in the economic affairs of the five former German allies. Reparations, as suggested by the U.S.S.R., were governed by the principle of partial compensation for war losses.

The Paris Conference did not settle all the controversial issues, and a new Foreign Ministers' Conference had to be called (New York, November-December 1946) to complete the drafting of the peace treaties. In February 1947, the peace treaties were finally signed. They were democratic in tenor and secured the free and independent development of the countries concerned. This was a major accomplishment of Soviet foreign policy.

The West Starts the Cold War

The peace negotiations revealed the two basic trends in international politics.

Soviet foreign policy, like the foreign policy of any other country, was tied up with the country's internal development. The Communist Party set the country's sights on post-war rehabilitation and further economic development. Peace was an essential condition for the fulfilment of the Soviet economic plans.

The Soviet Union took an active part in the establishment of the United Nations Organisation, the international body designed to maintain world peace, and stated time and again that it wanted friendly relations with the United States and Great Britain. This was, in effect, an invitation to the peaceful coexistence of the two systems.

The United States and the other imperialist powers, however, followed an entirely different course.

During the joint war against the powerful bloc of fascist countries, the members of the anti-Hitler coalition succeeded, as a rule, in reaching agreement on the key issues of foreign policy. But after the war was over, the groups that were unwilling to cooperate with the Soviet Union took the upper hand in the bourgeois countries.

A few weeks after V-E Day, on May 22, 1945, Sumner Welles, U.S. Under-Secretary of State, said in a radio speech: "In five short weeks since the death of President Roosevelt the policy which he had so painstakingly carried on has been changed."

It is absolutely clear today that the inhuman atomic bombing of Hiroshima and Nagasaki was one of the initial acts of the cold war against the Soviet Union. It had not been a military necessity. President Harry Truman, who was then at Potsdam, waited impatiently for the explosion of the first atom bomb over Japan. He told the other U.S. delegates: "If it explodes, as I think it will ... I'll certainly have a hammer on those boys."* The "boys" he meant were the Soviet delegates. Soon after war's end U.S. newspaper writers and officials voiced the claim of U.S. imperialism to "world leadership". They were backed by the U.S. captains of heavy industry, the manufacturers of atomic bombs and heavy bombers, who had made fabulous profits during the war. In 1946 and 1947, while the matter of peacetime economic reconversion was still being discussed, the industrialists of the United States, Britain and France were, as the bourgeois press described it, "gripped by a genuine dread of peace".

On March 5, 1946, speaking in Fulton, Winston Churchill was the first openly to fling down the gauntlet at his wartime ally. His appeal to oppose the Russians with "a show of force" and unite the English-speaking world against "Eastern communism" won the ready support of the U.S. President.

A year later, in his so-called Truman Doctrine, President Truman declared the U.S. "right" to interfere in the domestic affairs of other countries. The Truman Doctrine was exploited for the first time in Greece, where home-grown fascists and monarchists received generous U.S. aid. The next to fall within the operational field of the Truman doctrine was Turkey, a neighbour of the Soviet Union. In April 1947, Walter Lippmann pointed out that the United States had picked Turkey and Greece not because they were sparkling models of democracy, but because they formed the strategic gate to the Black Sea and the heart of the Soviet Union.

In the summer of 1947 U.S. State Secretary Henry Marshall announced a plan of economic assistance to the European countries. The main purpose of this plan was to reinforce the war-ravaged capitalist system and to put it under United States leadership for a struggle against the Soviet Union. In 1947 and early 1948 the Marshall Plan was exploited in an attempt to split the East European People's Democracies. It was hoped that the grave post-war economic difficulties would drive some of them (such as Czechoslovakia) into the orbit of the U.S. plan.

Under the Marshall Plan, U.S. aid would be attended by U.S. control over the foreign trade and, partly, over the industry and finance of the recipient countries, with restrictions on trade with the Soviet Union and other socialist states. The administration established to supervise the Marshall Plan was bent on reviving the economic potential of Western Germany, which was quickly moulded into the kernel of all anti-Soviet alignments and alliances in Europe, rather than assisting the countries ravaged by the Hitler aggression. Initially, a Western bloc was formed of Britain, France,

---

* William Appleman Williams, *The Tragedy of American Diplomacy*, N.Y., 1959, p. 169.

Belgium, Holland and Luxembourg (March 1948), and a year later, early in April 1949, the United States, Canada, the countries of the Western bloc, Italy, Norway, Denmark, Iceland and Portugal, concluded the North Atlantic Alliance Treaty.

The architects of this aggressive bloc made no secret of their intention to deal with the Soviet Union from positions of strength and, above all, atomic strength. President Truman went so far as to express the hope that the United States would for all time preserve the secret of nuclear arms manufacture. The Hiroshima explosion ushered in a period of "atomic diplomacy" that lasted several years. The substance of this "diplomacy" was to exert continuous pressure on the Soviet Union and the People's Democracies.

At that time, the Soviet Union had no atomic bomb. But the Soviet Government did not give way to Western threats and intimidation, and worked tirelessly against the architects of a new war. It rallied all the peace-loving forces of the world to the fight against aggression. In so doing, Soviet diplomacy made good use of bilateral and multilateral negotiations, and of the rostrum of the United Nations.

Soviet Foreign Policy in 1946-49

The Soviet delegation to the United Nations raised many important questions related to the maintenance of peace. To each session of the U.N. General Assembly the Soviet Government submitted proposals for the banning of nuclear weapons and reducing conventional armaments. In four years, the Soviet delegates made five well-reasoned proposals for the banning of the manufacture and stockpiling of atomic weapons. Ever since 1947, the Soviet Union has been suggesting an international control body with extensive powers. But the advocates of "atomic diplomacy" responded with what they knew to be unacceptable proposals for the "registration of national armaments", and the establishment of an international or supranational authority with almost unlimited rights to interfere in the economic affairs of all countries (the so-called Baruch Plan). They invented the formula, "first confidence, then disarmament". The Soviet Union, on the other hand, believed, and rightly so, that the arms drive was instrumental more than anything else in undermining international confidence.

The state of affairs in the U.N. Atomic Energy Commission set up by the General Assembly on January 24, 1946, may be illustrated by the following episode. In the summer of 1947, the British delegation declared in the Working Committee of that Commission that it agreed to the proposition that "all atomic weapons should be destroyed and their nuclear fuel used for peaceful purposes". This attitude coincided with that of the Soviet Union. Australia and Canada, too, backed this point of view. The only

271

delegation to refuse to subscribe to the idea of banning nuclear weapons was that of the United States. But this was enough to make the delegates of Britain and the other bourgeois countries beat a retreat, withdraw their proposals, and follow the U.S. lead in this crucially important matter for the future of the world.

At the close of 1947, after a long diplomatic battle, the General Assembly accepted the Soviet proposal for the prohibition of war propaganda. Soviet diplomats in the United Nations and elsewhere actively championed the interests of the small countries. They called for an end to the intervention in Greece and Indonesia, and gave moral support to the Arab countries fighting for their independence.

The Soviet policy of peace, proletarian internationalism and defence of the independence and sovereignty of big and small nations was embodied in the relations which emerged between the Soviet Union and the People's Democracies.

In 1945-48 the Soviet Union concluded friendship and mutual assistance treaties with Poland, Rumania, Hungary, Bulgaria and Yugoslavia along the lines of a similar instrument signed with Czechoslovakia in 1943. These accords stipulated immediate mutual military and other assistance in case of involvement in a war with Germany or any other state allied with that country. The terms also envisaged consultations on all important international issues of mutual interest, and called for expanding cultural and economic relations.

The development of the relations between the Soviet Union and the People's Democracies was spotlighted in early 1949 by the establishment of the Council for Mutual Economic Aid. It is the purpose of the Council to organise economic co-operation among its member-countries, to promote exchanges of economic experience and technical assistance, and to aid each other with raw materials, food, machinery, equipment, etc.

Soviet policy towards the Federative People's Republic of Yugoslavia took an unfortunate course. During the war against the common enemy and in the first few years after the war Soviet-Yugoslav relations were of the friendliest. In 1948, however, the C.P.S.U. and a few other Communist and Workers' Parties levelled strong criticism at the Yugoslav Communists. This criticism soon lost its friendly tenor. In effect, an attempt was made to oppose the Yugoslav people to their leaders. The bad blood between the Communist Parties of the Soviet Union and Yugoslavia also affected relations between the two governments. This conflict, one of the upshots of the Stalin cult and of Stalin's subjective views, lasted several years. It was not until 1953-55, that is, after Stalin's death, that the relations between the U.S.S.R. and Yugoslavia returned gradually to normal.

Kuibyshev Hydropower Development Project, 1955

Mining ore at the Kursk Magnetic Anomaly, 1960

Virgin land development in Kazakhstan, 1955

Harvesting wheat in Stavropol Territory

The German problem held a prominent place in Soviet policy throughout the period from 1945 to 1949. The Soviet approach to German affairs was based on the Yalta and Potsdam decisions. In Eastern Germany, the zone of Soviet occupation, all democratic parties and organisations were given an opportunity to function normally, and this soon produced unity within the working class. A united Marxist party, the Socialist Unity Party of Germany emerged.

The Soviet Military Administration worked hand in hand with the working class and other progressive forces in Eastern Germany to root out the survivals of the Hitler regime. All cartels, trusts and syndicates were dissolved, and the property of all war criminals was confiscated and turned over into the possession of the people. By spring 1948, German governing bodies had nationalised almost all the mining industry, more than 60 per cent of the power stations, half the engineering works, etc. Monopoly capital, one of the pillars of German militarism, was thus extirpated in the eastern part of Germany.

The Soviet Military Administration disbanded all fascist organisations. More than half a million active nazis were removed from office.

The land reform in Eastern Germany was a progressive act that put an end to the large landed estates and delivered a strong blow to the other pillar of German militarism, the Junker system.

The educational reform did a lot to root out nazi influences on the minds of the younger generation. All nazi teachers were dismissed and textbooks and readers of the Hitler period were withdrawn.

All these measures smoothed the way for the further development of the eastern part of Germany along the lines of peace and progress.

The Soviet Government worked assiduously on the international scene for a fair peace treaty with Germany and for a united, peace-abiding democratic German state.

But the Western powers threw their weight on the other side of the scales. No agrarian reform was carried out in Western Germany. The monopolies were allowed to carry on, and former nazis were left unmolested in their offices. Washington, London and Paris followed a deliberate policy designed to split the country.

In 1946 and 1947, the British and American occupation zones were merged, and a little later the French zone, too, was merged with them. This set the scene for a far-reaching involvement of Western Germany in anti-Soviet military blocs.

Spokesmen of the United States, Britain and France declared in so many words at the Moscow session of the Council of Foreign

Ministers in March-April 1947, that they would not abide by earlier decisions pertaining to Germany. The U.S. delegation turned down Soviet proposals concerning Germany's demilitarisation and democratisation, her economic and political unification and undelayed drafting of a German peace treaty. In 1948, the quadrilateral control of Germany established under the Potsdam terms, died a natural death due to Western attitudes and actions, which soon brought about a dangerous "Berlin crisis".

The "Berlin crisis" was provoked by the Western occupation authorities, who carried through a separate money reform in June 1948. The Western powers were fully aware of the grave implications of their unilateral measure. They disregarded the fact that an all-German monetary reform was then being discussed and prepared by the four occupation authorities, the U.S.S.R. included.

Here is how the events developed. On June 20, 1948, a secretly prepared separate money reform was suddenly announced in the three Western zones. The devaluated old German marks instantly flooded Eastern Germany, creating a danger to its economy.

The Soviet occupation authorities were compelled to take urgent measures. To block off currency profiteers all vehicles and passengers arriving from Western Germany were thoroughly checked. At the same time, the Soviet Military Administration offered to supply food to West Berlin and thus prevent added hardships to the population. But the Western occupation authorities rejected the offer.

The United States organised an "air bridge" to supply West Berlin by planes. This undertaking had far-reaching propaganda aims and was meant to intensify the cold war.

It was the restraint and skill of the Soviet diplomats that averted a breach of peace in those alarming months. On May 12, 1949, the Soviet Government lifted the restrictions on entry into West Berlin. This move was taken to facilitate mutual understanding with the United States, Britain and France. But the Western powers were completing preparations for the establishment of a separate West German state, and in September 1949, inaugurated the Federal Republic of Germany.

This was what the policy "from positions of strength", on which the U.S. Government was pinning its fondest hopes looked like in practice.

Yet world history was developing rapidly in the post-war years. Every year brought new failures to the policy "from strength" and new successes to the socialist cause.

In China decades of unrelenting struggle against foreign oppression and the domestic reactionaries culminated in a complete victory of the people, and the proclamation on October 1, 1949, of the People's Republic of China. The remnants of the Kuomintang troops, the big compradores and the top Kuomintang officeholders fled to Taiwan to escape the wrath of the people.

Towards the close of 1949, socialism turned into a world system with a population of over 800,000,000, that is, over one-third of the world population, and a territory comprising about 27 per cent of the earth's land surface.

A new peace-loving state also arose in the heart of Europe that year. As a counter-measure to the establishment by the Western powers of a revenge-seeking West German state, the People's Council of Germany, elected by the population of East Germany, proclaimed the founding on October 7, 1949, of the German Democratic Republic. For the first time in history, a peace-loving state, a bulwark of struggle for Germany's democratic and peaceful development and a strong barrier to revanchism and aggression, appeared on German soil.

The world-wide Peace Movement came into being in 1949 and soon won the allegiance of hundreds of millions of people in all countries. In its vanguard stood such well-known public leaders and scientists as Frédéric Joliot-Curie, Yves Farge, Pablo Picasso, John Bernal and William Du Bois. This gave the movement an immense power of attraction and prestige. It rapidly became a mighty politico-moral force.

Last but not least, 1949 was marked by yet another historical development—the end of the U.S. nuclear arms monopoly. The U.S.S.R., too, came into possession of nuclear weapons, and much sooner than Western politicians had expected.

This was striking evidence of Soviet scientific progress. It added to Soviet prestige and altered the balance of strength in the world. The day the first Soviet atomic bomb was tested was, in effect, the last day the U.S. policy "from strength" had any foundation. After that, it became absolutely meaningless.

Soviet Union Works for an International Detente

The development of nuclear arms by the U.S.S.R. was a forced measure aimed at safeguarding the nation's security. The U.S. ruling circles had ringed the Soviet Union with military bases and were rattling their sabre, leaving the Soviet Government no other choice but to strengthen its defences. However, after having developed its own atomic weapons, the U.S.S.R. declared time and again that it was ready to destroy all its weapons of mass annihilation, provided the Western Powers did the same. Between 1950 and 1953, as before, the Soviet Government worked perseveringly for an atomic weapons ban. But its peaceful proposals, aimed at relieving international tensions and settling all controversial issues by peaceful means, were turned down out of hand by the bourgeois rulers. Dreading the rapid growth of the world socialist system, the latter stepped up their efforts to do what they described as "rolling back communism". The U.S. monopolists were also disgruntled by the grave recession in 1949 of U.S. industry. They demanded that the U.S. Government increase its war orders and organised a far-flung press campaign to persuade the American people that nothing but war, or large-scale war preparations, could avert an economic crisis.

The U.S. Government did the bidding of the monopolies and in 1950 increased war allocations several dozen times in excess of the pre-war level. They amounted to $300 per head of population against $79 in the 1947/48 fiscal year and $12 in 1938/39. The Truman administration spent more money on arms in its first six years in office (1945-50) than all the preceding U.S. governments combined in the 150 years before the Second World War. U.S. ruling circles continued to build military bases in different parts of the world and began arming them with nuclear weapons. In September 1949, the U.S. Government officially admitted that the Soviet Union had the atomic bomb, but did not draw the logical conclusions and refused to reassess its policy. On the contrary, the Joint Congressional Committee on Atomic Energy declared in December 1949 that the U.S.A. must from now on produce more bombs, more powerful bombs and more quickly.

This ushered in the atomic arms race. War hysteria gripped the United States. People were told that a Soviet attack on Western Europe and the United States would occur within weeks.

At the same time the U.S. reactionaries launched a massive campaign against all progressively minded Americans. The witch-hunt ruined very many people. They lost their jobs, some of them lost their freedom, and some even their lives. The frantic anti-communist campaign created a favourable climate for repressions and acts of terrorism not only in the United States, but also in other countries. A number of foul crimes were committed in 1949-51 against prominent working-class leaders. Terrorists gravely wounded Palmiro Togliatti, the Italian Communist leader, assassinated Jorge Calvo, secretary of the communist organisation of Buenos Aires, and Julien Lahaut, the chairman of the Belgian Communist Party.

In 1951, U.S. Congress baldly proclaimed that subversion in the socialist countries was part of U.S. official policy. It allotted $100 million to finance reactionary émigré groups, anti-government propaganda and sabotage and subversion in the socialist countries.

That, in the main, was how the "free world" comported itself in the world arena.

But the U.S. intervention in the civil war in Korea (June 1950) was the biggest threat yet to world peace. Organised under the U.N. flag, with the participation of a few other imperialist powers, it created a direct menace to the People's Republic of China. At the end of 1950, when the invading troops approached the Chinese border, Chinese volunteers came to the assistance of the friendly Korean nation and soon helped it to drive back the enemy to his initial positions along the 38th parallel. But the war continued. It escalated into an acute international conflict. The United States used the Korean war as a pretext for establishing undisguised control over the Chinese island of Taiwan occupied by the Kuomintang clique. Thus, a new seat of tension appeared. The bloody war against the Democratic Republic of Vietnam, started in 1947 by the French bourgeoisie, continued too. In 1951, the Western Powers, without the Soviet Union, concluded a peace treaty with Japan. A Japanese-American treaty on mutual security, under which U.S. troops stayed in Japan, was also signed at that time.

In Europe, the plan for bringing West Germany into the military bloc was pressed ahead. General Dwight Eisenhower (then already a presidential nominee), declared on September 4, 1952, that it was in the interest of the U.S.A. to provide the German army with the opportunity of attacking in any direction Americans may consider necessary.*

The North Atlantic Pact admitted Turkey and Greece, two countries located close to the Soviet frontier and far away from the Atlantic. Furthermore, the U.S. intensified its commercial blockade of the socialist camp countries. In September 1951, it annulled its trade agreement with the Soviet Union, which had been in force since 1937.

In these circumstances, which were fraught with serious military dangers, the Soviet Government worked vigorously against the intrigues of the enemies of peace, and advocated accommodation of all controversial issues by negotiation.

Conclusion of an alliance with the People's Republic of China was one of the most important acts of Soviet foreign policy in that period. In February 1950, in Moscow, the two countries signed a treaty of friendship, alliance and mutual assistance. Under an agreement signed in 1953, the Soviet Union undertook to help China build or reconstruct 141 large industrial plants. The Soviet Union gave China credits on easy terms and instituted regular exchanges of scientific and technical information. Specialists were trained in the U.S.S.R. for China's national economy.

Friendly relations between the Soviet Union and the other socialist countries continued to expand.

The U.S.S.R. gave up all its assets in the People's Democracies, reduced to a minimum reparations due to it from Rumania and

---

* See *Frantsiya i "yevropeiskaya armiya" (France and the European Army)*, collection, translated from the French, Moscow, 1954, p. 96.

Hungary, and turned over to the socialist countries a vast quantity of scientific and technical papers. The Soviet universities and institutes trained thousands of their students. By 1952, Soviet exports of machinery and equipment to the socialist countries had increased tenfold since 1946. Purposeful co-ordination of the economic plans of the socialist countries and other forms of economic and cultural co-operation were an important and progressive factor. The Soviet Union acted as a powerful pillar for all the socialist countries, both in their economic and cultural development, and in protecting their rights and interests from the incursions of the imperialist powers.

The Korean conflict was the most acute international problem of the early fifties. The U.S. aggression against the people of Korea created a most precarious situation. From the first, the Soviet Union did its utmost to localise the conflict, to prevent it from spreading, and to achieve a cease-fire. On July 4, 1950, the Soviet Government published a detailed statement on the Korean events. It gave an account of how the U.S. intervention was prepared, and demonstrated that the U.N. Security Council resolution on the Korean question was illegal. The Soviet Union urged a stop to the military intervention of foreign powers and the withdrawal of their troops from Korea.

Later, too, the Soviet Union issued insistent calls for a peaceful settlement of the Korean question.

It was on the basis of Soviet proposals, that armistice negotiations were launched between the belligerents on July 10, 1951. The negotiations continued for two years and broke down several times due to the resistance of the U.S. Command. In the meantime, the interventionist troops tried to achieve their objectives in the battlefield. They attempted to breach the front at different points, attacked soldiers of the Korean People's Army and the Chinese volunteers, and bombed North Korean cities. At the time of the armistice negotiations the Soviet delegation to the 6th and 7th U.N. General Assemblies in 1951-52 and 1952-53 again submitted proposals for the final and complete discontinuance of military operations. The persevering diplomatic effort of the Soviet, Polish and a few other delegations, pressing for a peaceful solution of the Korean problem, was crowned with success. In April 1953, the 7th U.N. General Assembly passed a resolution on whose basis an armistice was concluded on July 27 of the same year. This was a new setback for the aggressive policy of the United States and a victory for the forces of peace and democracy.

The Soviet Union worked just as perseveringly for a fair solution of all other international problems. Time and again the Soviet Government demanded that representatives of the Kuomintang be removed from the United Nations and that the legitimate rights of the People's Republic of China in that organisation be restored. It backed the Chinese demand on the withdrawal of U.S. Armed

Forces from the Chinese island of Taiwan. Acting on the principle of the freedom and independence of all peoples, Soviet delegates to the United Nations supported Iran in its struggle against the foreign oil monopolies and backed the Arab countries which protested against colonial repressions in Northern Africa. The U.S.S.R. also backed the Burma Government, which demanded that Kuomintang troops ensconced in Burma territory cease their aggressive acts.

The Soviet Government persevered in its efforts to achieve a solution of the German problem, the chief problem of the post-war world. A series of measures was carried out to consolidate the German Democratic Republic. In May 1950, the Soviet Government announced a reduction of the remainder of the reparations due to it by 50 per cent, that is, by more than $3,000 million, and in August 1953 absolved the G.D.R. of further reparations. Dozens of Soviet-owned enterprises in G.D.R. territory were turned over to the German Democratic Republic and credits were granted to that country on easy terms. At the same time, the Soviet Union sought to speed the drafting of a just and democratic peace treaty with Germany and thus facilitate the country's reunification.

In October 1950, a conference of the Foreign Ministers of the eight European socialist countries was held in Prague on the initiative of the Soviet Government. A joint statement issued by the conference pointed out that the decisions to remilitarise West Germany, passed at a New York conference by the United States, Britain and France in September 1950, conflicted with the Potsdam Agreement.

The Prague Conference advanced a number of proposals designed to mitigate the German problem. It called on the powers occupying Germany to issue a joint statement that they would not allow the country's remilitarisation and would adhere to the Potsdam Agreement. The Prague Conference also suggested lifting all restrictions relating to the development of a peaceful German economy, restoration of German unity, and conclusion of a German peace treaty drafted with the help of the German people itself. But the Western powers scorned all these proposals. They also turned down the Soviet suggestion, made in November 1950, of convening the Council of Foreign Ministers to examine the implementation of the Potsdam Agreement.

In the years to follow, the Soviet Government made other important public statements concerning the German problem. In March 1952, it published a draft of the basic principles governing the German peace treaty. This draft envisaged Germany's reunification, withdrawal of occupation forces not later than a year after the treaty enters into force, lifting of all restrictions on the development of the country's peaceful economy, and establishment of national armed forces essential for Germany's defence. Germany, for her part, was to pledge that she would not enter into any military alliances against any of the countries of the wartime anti-Hitler coalition. Special articles provided safeguards for the democratic rights of the German people, and envisaged the banning of all organisations hostile to democracy and peace. The draft pointed out that after Germany's reunification the Allied Powers would render their good services for her admission to the United Nations.

The United States, Britain and France did not make any direct reply to the Soviet proposal, and continued to prepare the Paris and Bonn treaties, which envisaged the inclusion of West Germany in the European Defence Community, a military alliance of the West European countries.

Chapter Seven

FINAL ESTABLISHMENT OF SOCIALISM.
THE FULL-SCALE BUILDING
OF COMMUNISM BEGINS IN THE U.S.S.R.

Restoration of Leninist Standards and Principles of Leadership

The successful completion of the Fourth and Fifth Five-Year Plans brought within view the completion of the Soviet socialist construction programme and paved the way for a gradual transition to communism.

The Soviet Union had made distinct progress in developing the material and technical basis for socialism, particularly as regards industry. In 1953, it produced 27,400,000 tons of pig iron, 38,100,000 tons of steel, 320,400,000 tons of coal and 134,400 million kwh of electric power. Soviet industry employed more than 17,000,000 workers, technicians, engineers and other employees. The nation kept increasing the rate of industrial development and continued to catch up with the foremost Western capitalist countries, the U.S.A. included, in industrial production per head of population.

The production of farm products, however, did not yet meet the needs of the population, although in 1953 the aggregate grain harvest amounted to 80,000,000 tons, and the output of meat (dressed weight) was 5,800,000 tons, the output of milk 36,500,000 tons, and of butter 497,000 tons.

A fresh economic advance and considerable improvement in the living and cultural standards was essential to complete the building of socialism and begin the full-scale building of communism.

The times dictated a radical reorganisation of Party, government and public work along Leninist lines, and removal of the deeply ingrained deficiencies in the country's political and economic leadership bred by the personality cult. After Stalin's death on March 5, 1953, the Communist Party laid bare what hindered the nation's advance to communism and revived the Leninist principles of leadership, making them conform to the new situation. It organised the masses to combat shortcomings in industrial, scientific and educational development.

The revival of Leninist standards and of the principles of collective leadership in Party and government work did not occur overnight. It took some time to examine and appraise the state of affairs in Soviet society, to probe the harm done by the Stalin cult and to remove the errors and deficiencies that sprang from it.

The exposure of the criminal activities of Beria, the political adventurer who had won control over the country's security service, was a crucial factor in the battle against the consequences of the Stalin cult, for the enemies of socialism pinned their hopes on Beria in their efforts to weaken the Soviet state.

Beria, who had wormed himself into a position of authority in the Party and Government with Stalin's backing, had inflicted untold damage on the Communist Party and the Soviet people. After Stalin died, Beria concentrated on disrupting the alliance of the working class and the peasants, undermining the collective-farm system and impairing the friendship of the peoples of the U.S.S.R. He attempted to place the security service above the Party and Government, to use it against the Party leadership, and continued to fabricate "cases" against honest citizens and officials in gross disregard of the standards of socialist legality. But the criminal activities of Beria and his accomplices were exposed. The offenders were brought to trial and punished. The Party's collective leadership triumphed. The C.C. C.P.S.U. Plenary Meeting of July 1953 approved the firm action taken by members of the C.C. Presidium against the Beria group and passed a set of measures to fortify Party guidance of the machinery of state at all levels.

Acting on the decisions of that Plenary Meeting, the Central Committee set its course firmly on restoring and developing the Leninist standards and principles of Party life. The work of the central Party bodies was reorganised. The principle of collective leadership was revived. Plenary meetings of the Central Committee were called regularly, and the Central Committee itself became a standing body expressing the will of the Party as a whole.

The structure of the governing bodies of the Central Committee was altered. One body, the Presidium of the C.C. C.P.S.U., replaced the previous two—the Presidium and Bureau of the Presidium.

The Central Committee established the office of First Secretary of the C.C. C.P.S.U.* Nikita Khrushchov was elected to this office in September 1953. The Central Committee took measures to considerably extend inner-Party democracy. The method of running the country by decree was eliminated in Party work, Party

---

* The 19th Congress of the C.P.S.U. (1952) had abolished the office of First (or General) Secretary of the C.C. C.P.S.U.—*Ed.*

282

activists multiplied in number, and rank-and-file Communist Party members were called upon more extensively to help frame the major Party decisions. The Party worked assiduously to enhance the role of the mass organisations in the country's political affairs.

All the doubtful criminal cases fabricated during the Stalin cult period against Communist Party members and other citizens were re-examined by a decision of the Central Committee, and all persons found guiltless were released and reinstated. The so-called Leningrad case, too, was reviewed.

The Central Committee of the Party devoted itself to improving the work of the state and Party machinery, and came out strongly against red tape and excessive bureaucracy. The rights of government ministers and administration chiefs were extended, the structure of ministries and government departments was altered, and the administrative personnel was considerably reduced. The work of drawing up technical and financial plans for individual enterprises was repatterned and improved.

These measures added to the responsibility of managers for the fulfilment of production plans and promoted greater creative initiative by eliminating excess centralisation.

The distortions in the nationalities policy, witnessed during the war years with regard to some of the Soviet peoples, were denounced by the Party, and the national autonomy of the Balkars, Kalmyks, Chechens, Ingushes and Karachayevs was restored.

The rights of the Union republics in planning and in financial and economic matters were considerably expanded. Violations of Soviet legality were rectified and strong measures were taken to ensure rigorous observance of legal procedure.

The struggle against the consequences of the personality cult in public, government and Party life fortified Soviet society and enhanced the role of the Party in the country's development.

In 1953, the Soviet people celebrated the fiftieth anniversary of the Second Congress of the Russian Social-Democratic Labour Party, which gave birth to the Bolshevik Party.

In March 1954, elections were held to the Supreme Soviet of the U.S.S.R. More than 120,000,000 people came to the ballot boxes, with 99.8 per cent voting for the nominees of the bloc of Communists and non-Party people. The nation once more demonstrated its allegiance to the Party and the Soviet system.

The celebrations marking the 300th anniversary of the reunification of the Ukraine and Russia were nation-wide. They demonstrated the undying friendship of two brother nations. Orders of Lenin were conferred upon the R.S.F.S.R. and the Ukrainian Soviet Socialist Republic for outstanding accomplishments in political, economic and cultural development.

On February 19, 1954, the Supreme Soviet of the U.S.S.R. endorsed bills submitted by the Supreme Soviets of the R.S.F.S.R.

and the Ukrainian S.S.R. concerning the transfer of the Crimean Region from the R.S.F.S.R. to the Ukraine for geographic, economic and cultural reasons. This was yet another token of the unbreakable bonds between the Russian and Ukrainian peoples.

Soviet People Work for Further Socialist Economic Development

The further development of socialist economy held pride of place in the work of the Party and the Soviet people. This applied first and foremost to agriculture. There were many deficiencies in post-war farming. Its growth rate was much slower than that of industry, and this threatened to become a grave impediment to the country's economic progress and the improvement of the living standard.

The Communist Party did not hesitate to reveal all the failings that obtained in agriculture. It probed the causes for these failings, and examined why the level of farming failed to meet the country's needs.

To begin with, there was a number of objective causes. When industrialising the country, the Soviet state was not yet able to put big enough resources into farming. Before the war, part of the metal intended for the manufacture of farming machinery had to be redirected to the defence industries. Besides, the nazi invaders had inflicted immense damage on Soviet agriculture.

The country's population had increased. In 1956, the population of the U.S.S.R. was 200,200,000 (against 159,200,000 in 1913). Life expectancy in the Soviet Union had risen too (from 32 in pre-revolutionary Russia to 69 years). The population structure had changed. In 1913, 82.4 per cent of the population lived in the countryside, while in 1956 only 56.6 per cent of the population was rural and the remaining 43.4 per cent lived in the towns. Between 1950 and 1954 the urban population increased by 17,000,000, of which 9,000,000 came from rural areas.

The nation had made spectacular strides since the Revolution in farming mechanisation. It was nothing short of a technical revolution in the countryside. But the level of mechanisation attained still fell short of the mark. The Soviet Union was far behind the United States in the number of tractors in use. The United States had 1,500,000 of them in 1940, while the U.S.S.R. had 531,000, and in 1953 the figures were 4,100,000 and 744,000, respectively. The United States thus had one tractor per 88 hectares of land in 1940, while the U.S.S.R. had one tractor per 283 hectares. True, tractors were used more effectively in the U.S.S.R., but mechanisation of crop farming was still incomplete. In 1953, combines harvested no more than 78 per cent of the grain crop, with almost all the post-harvest jobs being done manually. Animal husbandry, too, was not mechanised.

But until the end of 1953, there were also subjective causes obstructing the growth of agricultural production. Among these were the big errors in agricultural management born of the Stalin cult. Stalin did not really know how people lived in the collective-farm villages, and the men he assigned to supervise agriculture, one of whom was Malenkov, concealed the real state of affairs from him.

The prevailing system of government procurements did anything but stimulate greater farm output. The procurement quotas pegged to the number of hectares, established before the war, existed no more than nominally. In fact, the procurement agencies took as much grain from the collective farms as they could get. As a result, too little grain was left for distribution among the collective farmers, for cattle fodder, and for sale at the market. This state of affairs discouraged the collective farmers and dampened their interest in production.

Faulty planning of grain procurement was another brake on collective-farm production. The farms were compelled to pay much more in cash and kind for the services of the machine-and-tractor stations than provided for in the state plans, and more than any of them could afford. This created backlogs in grain deliveries to the state.

The low prices set on grain, vegetables, fruit and animal produce were another factor that retarded agricultural production. They did not cover the outlay in labour and material, and as a result the work-day unit (the standard measure of payment) at the collective farms amounted to very little in both cash and kind. The collective farmers did not get the rewards they expected for their work on the collective farm and laboured reluctantly. Another damper on the initiative of the collective farmers was the practice of centralised planning, which did not take account of local conditions.

Lenin's ideas about the electrification of the countryside were also neglected in large measure, and the rate of electrification was much too low. Until August 1953, the state-operated power supply agencies did not service any of the collective farms and machine-and-tractor stations.

The labour force, too, was not of a very high standard. Machinery was entrusted to seasonal workers appointed by the collective farms for the field jobs. As a result, there was a very high rate of labour turnover, maintenance of machinery was poor, and productivity was low. Specialists with secondary and higher training were not used to best advantage. Most of them were concentrated at upper levels, and only 68,500 of the 350,000 specialists were employed directly on the collective farms and at the machine-and-tractor stations.

The Ministry of Agriculture and the central Party and government offices were poorly informed of the state of affairs in the countryside. Often, they took decisions that did not reckon with the opinion of the Party membership and the governments of the Union republics.

Cumulatively, these factors created a big gap between what the farms produced and the country's needs. They also unbalanced the rates of development in industry and farming.

At its Plenary Meeting in September 1953, the Central Committee of the C.P.S.U. discussed the state of farming and revealed the deep-going faults in its development. A comprehensive programme was worked out to promote a rise of crop farming and animal husbandry.

Most important was grain. But to raise the grain harvest it was not enough to raise the yields on cultivated land. New land had to be brought under the plough, because the situation demanded a swift and substantial increase in the grain output. The Communist Party therefore decided to develop virgin and waste land in Kazakhstan, Siberia, the Urals, the Volga area and the North Caucasus. This did not call for large investment and promised a considerable grain harvest in the minimum of time. The C.C. C.P.S.U. Plenary Meeting in February-March 1954 ruled that at least 13,000,000 hectares of virgin and waste land should be developed in 1954 and 1955. This plan met with the enthusiastic support of the population.

Members of the Young Communist League and young people of the city of Moscow and Moscow Region were the first to respond to the appeal of the Party. Thousands of young Muscovites pocketed their Y.C.L. assignments and set out for the virgin land developments. The example of the Moscow youth was quickly followed by that of other cities and regions. When the Twelfth Congress of the Y.C.L. opened in March 1954, sixty thousand Y.C.L. members had already departed for the land development areas, while more than 500,000 youths applied for similar assignments. Veteran mechanics, collective farmers and state-farm workers, too, went there in large numbers, and by the summer of 1954 more than 350,000 people set to work there.

The virgin land development scheme became a national cause. All the brother republics helped Kazakhstan develop its virgin land. In the two years of 1954 and 1955, as many as 452 large new state farms were organised, each with 20 to 30 thousand hectares of arable. More than 200,000 tractors were supplied to them, and 18,000 harvester-combines and other machinery. By the end of 1955, more than 33,000,000 hectares of new land had been put under the plough, yielding an annual average of some 32,000,000 tons of grain.

The virgin land development was a big victory for the Party and the Soviet people.

The Soviet Government also carried through other measures to develop Soviet farming. Investments in agriculture were increased, and the material and technical equipment of the farms was augmented.

Many first-class organisers, workers and specialists were sent from the towns to the countryside—over 120,000 agronomists and cattle-breeders, 23,000 engineers and technicians, and among them more than 30,000 Communists. Seasonal workers employed by the machine-and-tractor stations were replaced by the end of 1955 by some 2,000,000 permanent employees.

The material incentives factor is always important in any programme of boosting farm production. So the approach to it was changed. The government raised the procurement prices more than 450 per cent for cattle and poultry, 100 per cent for milk and butter, 150 per cent for potatoes and an average of 25 to 40 per cent for vegetables. In 1953 already the incomes of collective farmers had gone up by 13,000 million rubles, by 50,000 million rubles in 1954 and by 75,000 million in 1955.

The state of animal farming was particularly deplorable. A new effort was required to bring it out of its protracted slump.

In January 1955, a Plenary Meeting of the C.C. C.P.S.U. specially discussed ways and means of increasing the output of animal products, and set the sights primarily on raising the output of cattle fodder. Net output (of meat, milk and eggs) per 100 hectares of farmland was made the basic criterion in the planning of animal husbandry.

The entire approach to planning was altered. Plans were based on the amount of marketable produce collective and state farms could sell to the state, and were to be drawn up at local level. It was pointed out that government guidance and co-ordination should leave room for, and encourage, local initiative.

Early successes on the farms served to increase cash payments for work-day units earned by the collective farmers, but the earlier method of distributing collective-farm incomes among members only after the end of the production year did little or nothing to encourage the farmers in their work. So the C.C. C.P.S.U. and the Soviet Government passed a decision to pay collective farmers monthly advances and additional emoluments amounting to 25 or 30 per cent of the cash income of the collective farm. This made the agricultural workers much keener. A socialist emulation movement sprang up for higher yields and quicker sowing and harvesting. Machine operators learned additional trades. They became proficient at operating tractors, combines and other machinery, and strove to make more efficient use of them. Besides, they learned how to repair and overhaul them.

Many of them won nation-wide renown for their accomplishments, notably Mark Ozyorny and Yevgenia Dolinyuk in the Ukraine, M. Yefremova in the Altai, etc.

In the Fifth Five-Year Plan period the crop areas were increased by nearly 40,000,000 hectares, with 23,600,000 hectares being allotted for grain. A large number of new machines, tractors, lorries and grain harvester-combines were supplied to the countryside. Electrification made some progress. Power consumption by the farms increased more than 50 per cent, with 25 per cent of the collective farms, 98 per cent of the machine-and-tractor stations and 90 per cent of the state farms being supplied with electricity.

Many of the collective and state farms soon began to pay their way and show a profit. There were also some advances in animal husbandry. Milk, meat and wool procurements in 1955 exceeded those of previous years.

On August 1, 1954, an All-Union Agricultural Exhibition, in effect a university of advanced farming techniques, opened in Moscow.

The tide began to turn in Soviet agriculture. But the gap between actual output and the targets had not yet been closed by the end of the five-year plan period.

The early successes in the agricultural effort had a political, and not only economic, impact. They solidified the alliance between the working class and the peasants. The countryside was helped enormously by the cities in terms of machines and specialists. The collective farmers saw their living standard rise. Greater trade strengthened the economic bonds between town and country.

As before, heavy industry was the leading sector of Soviet economy. For this reason, the Party and the Soviet people saw to it that its priority growth continued.

The country's industrial potential expanded all the time. Soviet engineering made excellent progress. Each year, between 600 and 700 new types of machinery and machine tools were developed, enabling the country to mechanise all labour-consuming processes. However, the extent of mechanisation and automation was still insufficient. New production techniques were being introduced too slowly, and so were the accomplishments of Soviet and foreign science and technology. The cause for this lay in faulty guidance by ministries and departments. Some of the factory managers and department chiefs underrated the scientific and technological achievements made in the capitalist countries.

The C.C. C.P.S.U. Plenary Meeting held in July 1955 discussed the ways of advancing Soviet industry, promoting technical progress and improving the organisation of production. Foremost workers, scientists and technologists were invited to take part.

Flocks graze in a highland pasture, Kazakhstan

Picking tea-leaves in Georgia

The Ferghana Canal waters desert land

Bringing in cotton grown in Tashkent Region

Sverdlov Silk Mills,
Moscow

Khojent Carpet Mill,
Tajikistan

These large diamonds come from Yakutia

Timber is the wealth of the North of the U.S.S.R.

The Central Committee pointed out that many factories, whole industries even, did not cope with the state plan targets. The extent of co-operation between industrial plants, too, was unsatisfactory. Engineers and technicians were not always employed to the best advantage. Too many of them were concentrated in the managerial apparatus, rather than in production. The managerial machinery was too ramified and over-centralised. Some of the research institutes neglected the basic problems, the solution of which would have yielded great economic and technical benefits.

The C.C. C.P.S.U. Plenary Meeting called on all concerned to intensify research and designing in all branches of industry, to replace and modernise outdated equipment and to mechanise and automate production. The Central Committee asked all relevant departments and ministries, as well as the Academy of Sciences of the U.S.S.R., to organise scientific and technical information services and to extend their contacts with research institutions abroad. The Communist Party defined as the main trend in industrial development the course for better technology and continuous technical progress. A decision was passed to organise a permanent exhibition of scientific accomplishments and advanced techniques. The purpose of the exhibition was to demonstrate and disseminate achievements registered in Soviet industry, agriculture and building. The exhibition, known as the Exhibition of Soviet Economic Achievement, was soon opened.

The C.C. C.P.S.U. Plenary Meeting devoted itself to improving industrial management, eliminating superfluous organisational links, bringing the managerial superstructure closer to production, and extending political and organisational Party work in industry.

The decisions of the Plenary Meeting gave impetus to a new upsurge in all branches of the economy and speeded the building of communist society.

The Historic Impact of the Twentieth Party Congress

The Twentieth Congress of the C.P.S.U., which opened in Moscow on February 14, 1956, and closed on February 25, holds a special place in the history of the Soviet people and that of the world communist movement. It was attended by 1,436 delegates representing more than 7,200,000 members and candidate members, and guests from fifty-five foreign Communist and Workers' Parties.

The Congress heard the C.C. C.P.S.U. report, which contained an exhaustive analysis of the internal and external situation of the U.S.S.R. and outlined the prospects of communist construction.

The Congress stressed that the main feature of the contemporary epoch was that socialism had transcended the framework of one country and become a world system. The balance of strength had changed in favour of the Soviet Union and the rest of the socialist camp. The socialist countries had left the capitalist countries far behind in rates of industrial development, and their industrial basis had grown.

The capitalist economy was described in the report as unstable. The contradictions within it, it was shown, had grown more acute and the pillars of world capitalism had weakened considerably.

The Twentieth Congress summed up the new elements in the life of contemporary society and brought forward many new propositions on the basic questions of international development. It elaborated on Lenin's thesis on the peaceful coexistence of countries with different social systems.

The peaceful coexistence of countries with different social systems implies economic competition between them, and competition in the field of science and culture. There is only one field, the field of ideology, in which peaceful coexistence is impossible. Competition between the two systems does not signify that the class struggle in the world is abandoned or mitigated, and inasmuch as the class struggle continues, the struggle between the socialist and bourgeois ideologies is inevitable. But it is a struggle with peaceful means. Ideological and political controversies between countries should not be settled by war. Marxists believe that socialism wins as a result of the internal development of contradictions and of the class struggle in each capitalist country. Export of revolution goes against the spirit of Marxism-Leninism.

The Congress drew the important conclusion that in modern times war may be averted. Although the danger of aggressive wars persists due to the continued existence of imperialism, war is no longer fatally inevitable and the peace-loving forces all over the world, leaning on the powerful socialist camp, have a realistic opportunity of preventing a new world war.

The Congress developed and extended Lenin's proposition that the forms of transition to socialism can vary from country to country and pointed out that socialist revolution is possible by peaceful means.

The basic propositions worked out by the Congress concerning the key problems of contemporary international development were of great practical and theoretical impact. They gave the working class and all progressives fresh prospects in their efforts to maintain and strengthen peace and in their struggle for the revolutionary reorganisation of capitalism into socialism, for the independence of the peoples, for democracy, against imperialist oppression.

The Congress examined the results of the Fifth Five-Year Plan, which was fulfilled ahead of schedule, in four years and four months. Industrial output had increased 85 per cent over the 1950 level. The Fifth Five-Year Plan targets were considerably surpassed for the output of steel, rolled stock, electricity, coal, oil, etc. Housebuilding was in progress all over the country on a grand scale. As many as 150 million sq m, or 5,000,000 flats, had been built in 5 years.

The Congress issued a directive to proceed with the cardinal economic task of the U.S.S.R., that of catching up and surpassing the most developed capitalist countries in a short space of time in output per head of population. The Congress decisions outlined the specific ways of fulfilling this task.

The Congress examined the question of the Stalin cult and its consequences. The Central Committee report contained an exposure of the errors born of the Stalin cult.

The cult of an individual is foreign to the spirit of Marxism-Leninism. It is the people who are the true makers of history. "The intelligence of tens of millions of creators," wrote Lenin, "creates something immeasurably higher than the greatest and most brilliant foresight."[*]

Marxism-Leninism does not deny the important role played by the leaders of the working class, but condemns any magnification of personalities, because such magnification inevitably relegates the people and the Party to the background and belittles their role in history.

Acting on these Marxist-Leninist propositions and guided by the Leninist principle of candid criticism and rectification of errors, the Party firmly denounced the Stalin cult and set about eliminating its consequences.

The Central Committee exposed the gross violations of socialist legality and abuses of power that occurred in Stalin's time, and decided to tell the Party and the people about them from the rostrum of the Twentieth Congress. It knew that this might create bitterness, even some discontent, among a certain section of people. It knew too that its candid criticism of errors may be used by enemies for anti-Soviet ends. But it had no choice, because it had to eliminate the conditions in which violations of democracy and of the principles of collective leadership, the abuses of power and other acts alien to Soviet society had been possible. Valid guarantees had to be created that such things would never recur within the Party and the country.

While criticising the errors and distortions made by Stalin, the Party gave him due credit for his previous services to the country and the international working-class movement. The Twentieth Congress produced a model of Party criticism, whose ultimate

---

* Lenin, *Collected Works*, Vol. 26, p. 474.

goal it was to strengthen socialism and encourage the creative initiative of the masses in communist construction.

The Twentieth Congress signified its approval of what the Central Committee had done to restore Leninist principles and standards in Party and government life and to remove the consequences of the Stalin cult. It instructed the Central Committee to implant the standards initiated by Lenin in all fields of Party, government and ideological work.

In order to promote the initiative of the masses, the Congress called for an expansion of Soviet democracy, improvement of the work of central and local Soviet government bodies and a strengthening of their bonds with the masses.

The Congress approved the actions taken by the Central Committee in extending the rights of the Union republics in economic management and recommended additional measures in that direction. It passed decisions about improving the communist education of the working people and Party ideological work generally.

The Twentieth Congress was thus a historic event, a turning point in the life of the Party, the Soviet state, and the world communist and working-class movement. It embarked boldly upon the Leninist course in international politics and in the building of communism in the U.S.S.R.

New Forms of Economic Management

Changes occurred in the Soviet Union from 1956 to 1958 in pursuance of the historic decisions of the Twentieth Congress.

A law passed by the Seventh Session of the Supreme Soviet in May 1957 modified the pattern of management of industry and building.

Industrial management was reshaped to follow the territorial principle. Economic administration areas were established, each of which was run by an economic council. This reform was carried through by the Union republics.

The central planning agencies were also reorganised.

The trade union bodies at the factories and offices, too, had to cope with new tasks. The Plenary Meeting of the C.C. C.P.S.U. in December 1957 discussed the work of the trade unions and their role in production management and communist construction. An important role was assigned to standing production conferences at factories, building projects and offices. It was their purpose to spur the fulfilment of plans, to marshal all available resources and to create the right conditions for higher labour productivity.

The measures taken between 1953 and 1958 did a lot to strengthen the collective-farm system.

This called for changes in the technical servicing of the farms. The C.C. C.P.S.U. Plenary Meeting held in February 1958, which dealt with the further development of the collective-farm system, recommended a reorganisation of machine-and-tractor stations. The meeting noted the big part played by machine-and-tractor stations in strengthening the collective-farm system, but arrived at the conclusion that in the new conditions machine-and-tractor stations no longer helped farm production expand and that, on the contrary, they tended to slow it down. The fact that there were two masters to the same land—the machine-and-tractor station and the collective farm—impaired proper organisation of labour and proper use of machinery, and, in addition, involved the unnecessary expense of maintaining parallel administrations. The Plenary Meeting decided to reorganise the machine-and-tractor stations into repair and maintenance stations, and sell their machinery directly to the collective farms. However, it was decided that the new ruling would not apply for the time being to the weaker and poorer collective farms, which would be serviced by machine-and-tractor stations as before.

The decision of the Plenary Meeting was discussed throughout the country and wholeheartedly endorsed. So in March 1958, the Supreme Soviet of the U.S.S.R. passed a law reorganising the machine-and-tractor stations in the way described above.

The session appointed N. S. Khrushchov, who also remained First Secretary of the Central Committee, to the post of Chairman of the Council of Ministers of the U.S.S.R.

The reorganisation of machine-and-tractor stations required the system of farm procurements to be changed as well. The principle of procurements per hectare had been perfectly viable before, but the procedures it involved were complicated and different prices existed for the same products. It was therefore decided to introduce a new system of state procurements at single economically justified prices.

The Plenary Meeting of the C.C. C.P.S.U. held in May 1958 passed important measures for the development of the chemical industry in the U.S.S.R. It noted that the latest scientific discoveries made it possible to use national resources more fully in producing synthetic materials for shoes, clothes and household goods. The chemical industry, therefore, would play a very big part in the building of the material and technical basis of communism. The Plenary Meeting called on the U.S.S.R. Government and the governments of the Union republics to provide in the 1959-65 economic development plan for appropriate investments and high rates of development in the chemical industry with the object of increasing the output of key chemicals by 100-200 per cent and the output of artificial and synthetic fibre and plastics by 350 to 700 per cent.

The economic advances made it possible to carry out measures for the improvement of the living standard of the people. The Soviet Government set itself the task of providing the population with consumer goods in ample quantities within 5 to 6 years, and ending the housing shortage within 10 to 12 years.

After the Twentieth Congress important changes took place in the structure of the state. The powers of the Union republics were considerably extended. In May 1956, more than 3,500 enterprises were turned over by all-Union agencies to the respective Union republics, and these were given sole powers as regards their economic management and planning.

Supervision of enterprises became the job of the economic areas administrations and the Union republics. This was a big step forward in the development of socialist democracy. In February 1957, the Council of Nationalities of the Supreme Soviet of the U.S.S.R. formed an Economic Commission on which all the Union republics were represented to carry out a closer study of what the republics needed and to co-ordinate their economies more effectively.

The Communist Party took measures to improve the work of the Soviets of Working People's Deputies, which are the pillar of the machinery of state. Local Soviets were given greater powers in economic planning, production, distribution of the production of local and co-operative industries, supervision of housebuilding and the building of cultural and service premises and roads, and in financial matters. The Soviets became more active also in marshalling the efforts of the masses for communist construction.

Many of the functions earlier vested in the state were transferred to the mass organisations. Management of health resorts, cultural institutions and sports, for example, was gradually turned over to the trade unions and other mass organisations. Important measures were taken to improve the work of the state machinery and the economic administrations, to enhance the role of trade unions, of the Young Communist League, the co-operatives and the various cultural societies. That is the general trend in the development of the Soviet state. Government by the state combines more and more in the U.S.S.R. with public self-administration. The Communist Party has always pursued the goal of making every Soviet citizen an active participant in the administration of society.

These modifications tended to improve forms and methods in the work of the Soviet state and furthered the development of socialist democracy. They were designed to remove the harmful consequences of the Stalin cult and align the methods of economic and political leadership with the level attained in social development.

The Leninist policy set out in the decisions of the Twentieth

Congress of the C.P.S.U. was opposed by Vyacheslav Molotov, Lazar Kaganovich, Georgi Malenkov and other factionalists. The Party condemned the anti-Party conduct of the group.

The Party closed its ranks, fortified its bonds with the masses, and marshalled all forces for the full-scale building of communism.

Final Victory of Socialism.
Celebrations of the 40th Anniversary of the Revolution

The twentieth century will go down in history as the socialist century. In the 1930s socialism won in the Soviet Union. In the forties it transcended the bounds of one country and materialised into a powerful system of socialist countries embracing more than one-third of mankind. The late fifties were marked by the complete and final victory of socialism in the Soviet Union. The U.S.S.R. entered the period of full-scale communist construction.

The victory of socialism in the U.S.S.R. in the thirties was not yet final, because it was the only socialist country in the world and was surrounded by hostile capitalist countries. A continuous threat of armed intervention by the imperialist countries hung over it, with the consequent forcible restoration of capitalism by international reaction. The capitalist countries that surrounded the Soviet Union surpassed it economically and militarily.

But after the Second World War, when the world socialist system appeared, the balance of strength in the world changed radically. No longer is the Soviet Union surrounded by capitalist countries. The capitalist world is relatively weaker than it was before the Second World War. Today, too, the U.S.S.R. is not guaranteed against an armed attack by the capitalist countries, but the relation of forces has changed and the Soviet land is strong enough to repulse the attack of any enemy.

In November 1957, the peoples of the U.S.S.R. and working people all over the world celebrated the 40th anniversary of the October Revolution. The Soviet people marked this glorious occasion with fresh accomplishments. New factories were put into operation and the socialist emulation movement for the fulfilment of the 1957 plan ahead of schedule yielded excellent results. Party and government delegations of all the socialist countries came to the celebrations in Moscow, and so did representatives of fraternal Communist and Workers' Parties of 64 countries. Representatives of various other parties, mass organisations, and prominent personalities from many countries of the world, also attended. An endless stream of messages and congratulations arrived from foreign friends of the Soviet state.

The anniversary session of the Supreme Soviet of the U.S.S.R. opened in Moscow on November 6, 1957, and adopted an appeal to the peoples of the Soviet Union and an appeal to all working people, to political and social leaders, to men of science and culture, and to the parliaments and governments of the world.

The building of socialism in the U.S.S.R. was a feat of truly historic significance. For the first time in history socialism had become a reality, a mode of life. The complete and final victory of socialism was won by the Soviet people under the leadership of the Communist Party. This victory was the main result of the work done by the Party and the people in the years of Soviet power.

The radical changes that had been rung in in the social and economic life of society served as a basis for the rapid elimination of the country's age-long backwardness. In a mere 22 years (for 18 of the 40 years the Soviet land was preoccupied with wars and post-war economic rehabilitation), the Soviet Union had developed economically to an extent that would have taken a capitalist country at least a hundred years. Aggregate industrial output had risen 33-fold over 1913, and production of means of production increased 74 times over. This meant that the Soviet Union had won its initial victory in the peaceful economic competition with the capitalist countries. With this victory to back it, the Soviet Union was now able to tackle a new task—to catch up and surpass the most developed capitalist countries in production per head of population in a matter of 15 to 20 years.

As a result of the final victory of socialism in the U.S.S.R., a new historical communion has emerged, uniting people of different nations, best described as the Soviet people, with common features as regards economy, class structure, ideology, spiritual mould and psychology. The living conditions of the Soviet people have changed beyond recognition. Poverty, unemployment and the slums in which the workers had lived, and the ruinous state of the peasants from land hunger and an excessive tax burden have become a thing of the past. The real wages of the workers have increased 480 per cent, while the incomes of peasants have increased 500 per cent. Electricity, gas, radio, television, books and newspapers are part of the working people's way of life. Taxes are being gradually abolished, and the housing problem is being swiftly resolved. The Soviet Union has the lowest house rents in the world. The average life expectancy has risen steeply.

Its economic and socio-political successes have enabled the Soviet Union to enter a new period of development, the period of full-scale communist construction. Socialist relations have begun to develop into communist social relations.

This has brought about far-reaching changes in the substance of the Soviet state. From a dictatorship of the proletariat it has grown into a state of the whole people. The state of the whole people is based on all the classes and sections of society, with the

Saami, indigenous dwellers of the North, inhabit the village of
Tuloma, which is situated within the Arctic Circle

Segezha Pulp and Paper Mill, Karelia

Twenty-Second Congress of the C.P.S.U. in session, Moscow, October 1961

Dam of the Twenty-Second C.P.S.U. Congress Hydropower
Station on the Volga, 1964

Power station machine room

working class playing the guiding role, and successfully represents the common interests of all working people against the capitalist world, performing its internationalist tasks in relation to the socialist and other friendly countries.

Ever since its inception, the dictatorship of the proletariat contained features of universal socialist democracy. It was the first democracy for the working people, the vast majority of society. As socialism advanced, these features came out in bolder relief, and when its victory was complete and final they became determinative.

Soviet successes in the building of communism had an immense impact on the world. A Conference of the Communist and Workers' Parties of the socialist countries was held in Moscow in 1957, followed closely by a Meeting of the Communist and Workers' Parties of 64 countries. Important documents were adopted —a Declaration of the Communist and Workers' Parties of the Socialist Countries, and a Peace Manifesto of the Communist and Workers' Parties.

The Declaration reaffirmed the conclusions of the Twentieth Congress of the C.P.S.U. concerning the international situation and summed up the experience of the masses in the struggle for socialism and peace. It was also a token of the identity of opinion prevailing among the Communist and Workers' Parties. The Declaration defined the main objective laws governing the struggle for socialism: the leading role of the working class and its vanguard, the Marxist-Leninist party; socialist revolution and establishment of the dictatorship of the proletariat; the alliance of the working class and the peasants; abolition of capitalist property and establishment of socialist ownership of the basic means of production. These are features common to the development of all the countries that have embarked on socialism, but they are applied in each country to fit its specific historical conditions and national characteristics.

The Declaration struck a painful blow at opportunists and focussed attention on the struggle against revisionism and dogmatism in the Communist and Workers' Parties. It pointed out that the main danger came from revisionism, a manifestation of bourgeois ideology in the working-class movement, and also dogmatism and sectarianism, which weaken the ranks of the working class and undermine the revolutionary movement. The Peace Manifesto called on the peoples of the world to step up the struggle for world peace.

These two documents demonstrated the unity of all the fraternal parties on the rock-like foundation of Marxist-Leninist ideology and showed the strength of proletarian internationalism. Both had the support and approval of the overwhelming majority of Communist and Workers' Parties of the world.

The period since the adoption of these documents has been marked by new successes in the socialist countries and by a growth of the world communist movement. This again confirmed the principles set out in the Declaration and the Manifesto.

The National Effort to Fulfil the Seven-Year Plan

In the autumn of 1958 targets were being set for a Seven-Year Economic Development Plan for 1959-65.* The central bodies of the Party and the Government, and local Party, government, trade-union and Y.C.L. organisations took part in this work. In November 1958 a Plenary Meeting of the C.C. C.P.S.U. examined the theses of the projected Seven-Year Plan, and approved them.

They were published in the Soviet press, and more than 70,000,000 people took part in the ensuing public discussion of them. The publication of the Seven-Year Plan draft targets stimulated the nation-wide socialist emulation movement for the fulfilment of plan assignments ahead of schedule.

The Extraordinary Twenty-First Congress took place in Moscow from January 27 to February 5, 1959. The Congress heard and discussed the Central Committee report on the control figures of the projected Seven-Year Economic Development Plan, and endorsed them.

It was pointed out at the Congress that the main purpose of the Seven-Year Plan was to secure a further powerful advance in all branches of the economy on the basis of a priority growth of heavy industry, to increase the country's economic potential, and achieve a considerable improvement of the living standard.

By 1965, the aggregate industrial output was to increase 80 per cent over 1958, with the average annual rate of growth being 8.6 per cent. Such an increase in production was to be achieved by improving plant, modernising existing factories and building new ones. Investments in new construction and modernisation were set at a sum approximately equal to the total investments made in all the preceding Soviet years.

The plan envisaged accelerated rates of development for the iron and steel and non-ferrous metals industry, for engineering, instrument-building and the radio-electronics industry. An accent was laid on the development of the chemical industry, and in particular on the production of polymer materials. The Soviet economy was to be almost completely electrified. With this purpose in

---

* The replacement of the directives for the Sixth Five-Year Plan, adopted by the Twentieth Congress, with a Seven-Year Plan was due to the discovery of new mineral resources, whose development had not been provided for in the Sixth Five-Year Plan. When drawing up the Sixth Five-Year Plan, the State Planning Commission had made serious mistakes. Its targets were excessive.—Ed.

view, output of electric power was to be raised 110-120 per cent and integrated grids were to be set up to cover the more important areas of the country. Industrial use of atomic energy and the consequent building of atomic power stations was provided for. Engineering was to be developed in order to improve production techniques, to complete the mechanisation of labour-consuming jobs and to automate production.

The Seven-Year Plan set big tasks for agriculture, whose output was to increase 70 per cent.

Provisions were made to boost the output of the consumer industries by 50 to 70 per cent. Public consumption funds were to increase 60 to 63 per cent and the incomes of factory and office workers and collective farmers 40 per cent. Taxes paid by the population were to be gradually lifted, the minimum pensions were to be raised and community services were to be improved. In the seven-year period 15 million flats were to be built in the cities and towns and 7,000,000 houses in the countryside.

The Seven-Year Plan envisaged an advance in public education, science and culture.

The Seven-Year Plan ushered in a new stage in the economic competition with capitalism. It was the basic target of the plan to make the greatest possible gain in time in the peaceful economic competition between socialism and capitalism.

By passing the Seven-Year Plan, the Twenty-First Congress equipped the nation with a programme of communist construction.

Friends of the Soviet Union hailed the plan as an instrument for the further consolidation of the socialist camp and a reliable guarantee of world peace.

The Seven-Year Plan was recognised all over the world. Many Western bourgeois leaders and economists and the Western press admitted that the plan was realistic and that the Soviet Union had immense potentialities in its peaceful competition with the capitalist countries.

In assessing the international impact of the Seven-Year Plan, the Twenty-First Congress of the C.P.S.U. pointed out that it underscored the peaceful trend of Soviet policy and that its fulfilment would tilt the scales in the international arena in favour of peace and socialism.

The Seven-Year Plan inspired Soviet people to perform new feats on the labour front.

The movement of communist work teams and shock workers grew in scale. Not only individual workers, teams and sections joined the movement, but also shops and factories. The first to win the distinction of being named a shop of communist work was the repair shop of the Moscow Marshalling Yard, which had initiated the movement. The workers of the shop had decided to make the most of advanced techniques and the latest technology in securing good production, continuously to improve their cultural and technical level, and to be models at work and at home.

By the summer of 1960, when an all-Union conference of communist work teams and shock workers was held in Moscow, more than 5 million factory and office workers and collective farmers had joined the movement under the slogan, "Learn, Work and Live the Communist Way".

Who were these members of the communist work movement, and what were they determined to achieve? Take Hero of Socialist Labour, Nikolai Mamai, a Donets coal miner. His team pledged to extract 2.5 tons of coal per team member in excess of the monthly plan in the first year of the Seven-Year Plan period, and to lower the cost per ton of coal by 1.50 rubles. His team lived up to their pledge honourably, and the following year undertook to use a coal-mining combine instead of perforation hammers and to completely mechanise coal extraction. They kept their word.

The initiative of the workers and engineers of the Novo-Kramatorsk Works is another good example. They decided to draw up technical projects and manufacture more than 3,000 tons of equipment in excess of the plan for the modernisation of existing rolling mills. The initiative of the Novo-Kramatorsk Works was picked up by workers in Leningrad, Baku, Moscow, Gorky and other cities.

The ranks of innovators and inventors swelled. They were intent on improving the organisation of labour and advancing technology. They did so not for the sake of personal gain, but because of their devotion to the communist system. The splendid initiative of Valentina Gaganova, a worker of the Vyshny Volochok Cotton Mill, proves this point conclusively. In October 1958, she asked to be transferred from an advanced work team with high wages to a backward team, and by April 1959 had turned it into an advanced team. This modest initiative, extremely important in all respects, was highly commended by the Soviet Government, and Valentina Gaganova was conferred the title of Hero of Socialist Labour. Gaganova has many followers. At her own mill, 80 of the foremost workers volunteered to join the backward teams and teach them to work better. Following Gaganova's example, the Donets miners Nikolai Mamai and and A. Kolchik transferred to backward teams.

Gaganova's initiative met with response also among other professions. A group of doctors in Rostov-on-Don—P. Kovalenko, P. Nikolsky, V. Davydov and F. Skvortsov—decided to receive patients after office hours at the city polyclinic without additions to their salaries. Doctors and professors in many Soviet cities are following their example today, and receive patients without additional payment. This new movement is typical of the Soviet man, who strives to work the communist way, for the common weal, in the name of the future.

The most notable result of the socialist emulation movement, which embraces some 85 per cent of the nation's factory and office workers, is the fact that the annual targets of the Seven-Year Plan have been fulfilled.

Rapid economic development released additional resources for consumer goods production, development of the consumer industries and improvement of the living standard.

Visible progress was made in the countryside. The effort to increase agricultural production was stimulated by the country's general economic upsurge. The Soviet Government rendered the farmers every possible assistance and allocated considerable funds for this purpose.

The collective farmers initiated an emulation movement for the fulfilment of the Seven-Year Plan targets ahead of schedule. Many new names appeared in the list of Heroes of Labour. The Party and the Government called on the people to match the accomplishments of the foremost workers in socialist farming.

Increasing farm yields became a national cause.

The working class began a movement to produce in excess of the plan to meet the needs of agriculture.

The material and technical basis of Soviet farming is expanding from year to year. In 1960, for example, the collective and state farms received more than a quarter million tractors, 66,000 lorries, 55,000 self-propelled harvester-combines and many other farm machines. The farmers strove to make the best possible use of their machinery. A movement got under way among innovators and inventors to mechanise all farming jobs. The example of Hero of Socialist Labour Nikolai Manukovsky, a tractor operator, was followed all over the country, with the result that thousands of tractor teams mechanised all their field work.

The Soviet Government set fair prices on farm products, giving added stimulus to the growth of farm production. The prices of farm machines and implements, spare parts and fuel, on the other hand, were considerably reduced, and this, too, worked to the advantage of the collective farms.

The newly developed virgin and waste land areas took a prominent place in the country's agriculture. From 1954 to 1962 the government had invested 6,700 million rubles in developing them, and the profit on this investment over the same period amounted to something like 10,000 million rubles, the newly developed areas supplying the country with an additional 131,200,000 tons of grain. To improve the administration of the newly developed farm areas of Kazakhstan, the C.C. C.P.S.U. and the Council of Ministers of the U.S.S.R. formed the Tselinny Territory in the north of Kazakhstan at the close of 1960.

Farming made good progress in the first two years of the Seven-Year Plan period. However, it still lagged behind the growing

Soviet industries and the mounting demand, and was still a branch of production that claimed the attention of the Party, Government and people.

Congress of the Builders of Communism

In January 1961, the Central Committee decided to convene the Twenty-Second Congress of the Communist Party in the coming October.

Word of the forthcoming congress was received with joy all over the country. It had become a tradition in the Soviet Union to mark scheduled Party congresses by special work and the fulfilment of production assignments ahead of schedule. The Twenty-Second Congress was no exception.

The workers and collective farmers were joined by professional people and intellectuals in the preparations for the Twenty-Second Congress of the C.P.S.U.

"Let us honour the Twenty-Second Congress in the Communist way!" was the motto of all people in town and country.

The socialist emulation movement grew to unprecedented dimensions. Millions upon millions of working people and thousands of teams, sections, shops, factories, Economic Councils, towns, regions, territories and republics joined in the effort to fulfil individual and collective pledges in celebration of the Twenty-Second Congress.

By decision of the Central Committee of the C.P.S.U., the drafts of the new Party Programme and of the Rules of the Communist Party of the Soviet Union were published in the Soviet press on July 30, 1961, for public discussion. The draft of the new Programme contained a concrete plan for the building of communist society in the U.S.S.R.

The draft Programme created an immense and lively interest among working people in the Soviet Union and abroad. The progressive press abroad described it as a "document of optimism and hope". Ill-wishers were unable to belittle its impact, however hard they tried.

Soviet people welcomed the project of a new Programme. About 73 million people attended the more than 500,000 meetings held at factories, collective farms, offices and army units to discuss the drafts of the new Party Programme and the new Party Rules. They voted for the new Programme not only by word, but above all by their deeds, their successes in production.

As the date of the Twenty-Second Congress drew nearer, the working people of the U.S.S.R. showed their determination to fulfil the Party Programme for the building of a better future.

The Twenty-Second Congress of the Communist Party, held in Moscow from October 17 to October 31, 1961, summed up the past successes of the Soviet Union, adopted the new Programme of the C.P.S.U., the new Party Rules, and elected the higher bodies of the Party.

It was the most representative congress in the history of the C.P.S.U. Nearly 5,000 delegates, representing the 10 million Soviet Communists, attended it. Also present were numerous guests from the fraternal Communist and Workers' Parties.

The Congress heard the report of the Central Committee. The report noted that the time between the Twentieth and Twenty-Second congresses was marked by a further consolidation of the might of the U.S.S.R. The international prestige of the Soviet Union as the standard-bearer of peace and of the friendship and happiness of the peoples had grown immensely.

Soviet industrial production had risen by nearly 80 per cent. As before, the Soviet Union was far ahead of the United States in rates of industrial growth and had begun to surpass it, too, in the physical growth of production in many important fields. In the six years from 1956 to 1961, the average annual rates of industrial growth were 10.2 per cent in the Soviet Union and only 2.3 per cent in the United States. In the same period steel output in the Soviet Union increased by 26 million tons while that of the United States decreased by 15 million tons, and Soviet oil output increased by 95 million tons while that of the United States increased by about 20 million tons. By the end of 1961 Soviet industrial output amounted to more than 60 per cent of that of the United States, while a mere ten or eleven years before the Soviet Union produced less than 30 per cent of what the U.S. produced. At the time of the Twenty-Second Congress, the Soviet Union accounted for almost one-fifth of the total world industrial output, and for more than Britain, France, Italy, Canada, Japan, Belgium and Holland combined.

Agriculture had made satisfactory progress. Output of grain, meat, milk and other farm produce had increased considerably. This had also contributed to a steady improvement of the living standard of the collective farmers.

The Central Committee report to the Twenty-Second Congress quoted facts and figures to illustrate the general rise in the living standard and the progress of science, education, art and literature.

The Soviet national income per head of population had grown much more rapidly than in the developed Western countries. The real incomes of Soviet factory and office workers had increased since 1956 by 27 per cent and those of the collective farmers by 33 per cent. In their efforts to improve the life of the people, the Communist Party and the Soviet Government had revised the wage scale, put all factory and office workers on a 7- and 6-hour working day, improved the pension scheme, etc.

Housebuilding proceeded on an unheard-of scale. Twice as many flats were built in the Soviet Union per 1,000 population as in the

United States and France, and more than twice as many as in Britain and Italy.

The schooling and labour training of the younger generation had improved considerably after the reorganisation of public education and the extension of bonds between the school and real life.

The Congress summed up the results of the first years of the Seven-Year Plan period. The average annual increase of industrial output in the first three years had exceeded the target. Industrial output in excess of the plan for 1959-61 was worth about 19,000 million rubles.

The historic importance of the Twenty-Second Congress of the C.P.S.U. lies in the fact that it adopted a concrete, deeply and scientifically reasoned programme for the building of communism in the U.S.S.R.

The new Party Programme is indeed the Communist Manifesto of modern times. It sums up the experience gained in the building of a new society in the countries of the socialist system, the experience of the world communist movement, and of the liberation movement as a whole. Like all the other documents of the Twenty-Second Congress, it epitomises the creative development of Marxism-Leninism in our time.

The Programme analyses the objective laws governing the transition of mankind from capitalism to communism. Having breached the imperialist front, the Great October Socialist Revolution ushered in a new epoch in the history of mankind—the epoch of the collapse of capitalism and the victory of socialism.

In its second Programme, adopted in 1919, the Communist Party had set itself the task of building socialist society. The complete and final victory of socialism in the U.S.S.R. marked the fulfilment of this second Programme. Dealing with the development of all mankind, the new Programme pointed out that the victory of socialism in the U.S.S.R. has equipped mankind with a science, tested by experience on the making and development of socialism. It is now easier for other peoples to advance to socialism.

The chief feature of world development is that the forces of socialism, all the forces of world progress, are growing, and the peoples are breaking away from imperialism more and more resolutely.

The Programme of the C.P.S.U. outlined the tasks of the Communist Party in the building of communism and defined the main laws governing communist construction.

It gave priority to electrification. By 1980, the Soviet Union is to produce 50 per cent more electric power than all the other countries of the world produced in 1961. Power consumption per worker will by then increase 8- to 9-fold, with the effect of considerably improving technology and organisation of social production

Sumgait Petro-Chemical Plant under construction, 1964

Oilfield in Azerbaijan

Artificial fibre plant at Kirovokan, Armenia

Turbines for the giant Krasnoyarsk Hydropower Station made at the Leningrad Metal Plant, 1964

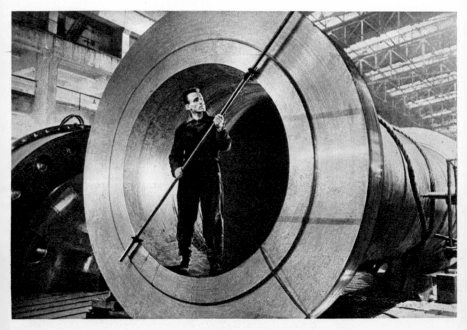

in industry and agriculture. This will give substance to Lenin's formula: "Communism is Soviet power plus the eletrification of the whole country."

Other factors that play a big role in the building of the material and technical basis of communism include higher labour productivity, comprehensive mechanisation and automation of production, extensive use of chemicals, greater production of all fuels, of steel, and the proper distribution and rational use of the country's productive forces. The organic fusion of science and production and the continuous improvement of the cultural and technical level of the workers will secure rapid rates of scientific and technical progress and will enable the country to attain a high productivity of labour.

The Programme deals at length with the development of heavy industry. At the same time, it envisages that the light and food industry will considerably increase output of consumer goods on the basis of the growth of heavy industry.

Agriculture is a part of the country's economy. In the period of socialist construction, the Soviet Union had built up a developed system of collective and state farms. The next task was to attain an abundance of high-quality products for the nation and of raw materials for industry.

State and collective farms would continue to exist and develop in the Soviet Union throughout the period of communist construction. The Programme stressed that it was essential to exploit the advantages inherent in the collective-farm system. The collective farms are a school of communism for the peasants. Economic prosperity of the collective-farm system paves the way for a gradual coming together, and ultimately a fusion, of collective-farm property and property of the whole people into a single system of communist property.

The development of state farms is also important. They are the leading socialist enterprises in the countryside and should be models of advanced farming techniques.

The farm labourer's work has become a variety of industrial labour.

The essential differences between physical and mental labour will be eradicated. Scientific and technical progress will create new conditions for communist work. Hard, unskilled physical labour will disappear. The worker's duties will be confined to controlling complicated machinery. By virtue of higher labour productivity, the working day will be considerably reduced. This will create conditions for the cultural and technical development of people employed in industry and farming. Labour will be creative and will become an inner urge for all sound men and women.

The purpose of the new Programme of the C.P.S.U. is to create the best possible living conditions for all people. Everything in the name of man, everything for the benefit of man—that is the supreme expression of communist humanity.

The Programme of the C.P.S.U. sets its sights on securing the highest living standard in the world for Soviet people. All Soviet working people will enjoy prosperity, want will be wiped out completely for the first time in history, and low-paid employment brackets will disappear totally. The Soviet Union will have the world's shortest working day, and the country's housing problem will be completely resolved. Every family in the land will be provided comfortable modern housing with the basic amenities and community services free of charge.

Throughout the period of communist construction payment for work done will remain the main tool in satisfying the material and cultural needs of the people. At the same time, social consumption funds, from which all members of society are entitled to benefit, will be extended. Children and all incapacitated persons will be maintained at the expense of society. Free education and medical treatment will be supplemented by free use of sanatoria by the sick, and free dispensation of medicines. Public transport facilities, too, will be free.

The Programme of the C.P.S.U. sets specific tasks in industry, transport and agriculture. It traces the path to a higher living standard. Then it goes on to show the future development of social relations, of the Soviet state, of the relations between the nationalities of the Soviet Union, and of science and culture. Among other things, it indicates the ways of moulding the new man of communist society.

Communism is a classless society with one form of public ownership of the means of production and full social equality of all members of society, put into effect through the formula, "From each according to his ability, to each according to his needs". It calls for a high level of economic development to carry this formula into practice. It also calls for the moulding of the new man, living and working in the communist way. He will develop and live in accordance with the moral code of the builders of communism set out in the Programme. This code lays down the moral and ethical standards of communist society, based on collectivism and humanism, as expressed in the following mottos: "One for all, and all for one", and "Man is to man a friend, comrade and brother".

The moral code of the builders of communism also encompasses such important principles as devotion to the communist cause, love of their socialist motherland and of the other socialist countries, and conscientious labour for the good of society. The code also contains the principles that should govern relations between the peoples—friendship and brotherhood of all the peoples of the U.S.S.R., intolerance of racial and national prejudice, fraternal solidarity with the working people of all countries, and with all peoples, and an uncompromising attitude to the enemies of communism and as regards peace and the freedom of nations.

The Programme of the C.P.S.U. is the basis not only for all Party work, but also for everything the Soviet people will do. Having made a realistic survey of the possibilities of the Soviet people and of the advantages of the Soviet system, the Communist Party solemnly proclaimed that the present generation of Soviet people would live to see communism.

The Twenty-Second Congress also endorsed new Rules of the Party, which had become a Party of the whole people as a result of the victory of socialism in the U.S.S.R. and the grown unity of Soviet society. The Rules adjust the Party's organisational principles to fit the tasks of the period of full-scale communist construction. It is stressed in the Rules that the C.P.S.U. adheres in its work to the Leninist standards of Party life: the principle of collective leadership, all-round development of inner-Party democracy, activity and initiative of Communists, criticism and self-criticism. The organisational principles defined in the Rules will facilitate the fulfilment of the Programme and further the unity and cohesion of the Party as the militant vanguard of the Soviet people, the builders of communism.

The Twenty-Second Congress gave much of its attention to the consequences of the Stalin cult. When the Twentieth Congress condemned the Stalin cult, it had authorised the Central Committee to remove the consequences of the cult in all spheres of Party, government and ideological work and to revive the Leninist standards in Party and government affairs. The Central Committee of the Party did a considerable amount of work in this direction and reported to the Twenty-Second Congress on what it had done.

At the time of the Congress a monument was festively unveiled in Moscow to Karl Marx, the brilliant thinker and founder of scientific communism.

Representatives of 80 Communist and Workers' Parties, who were present as guests at the Congress and expressed their solidarity with the C.P.S.U., commended its good work as the vanguard of the world communist movement. The C.P.S.U. constantly promotes friendship and co-operation between all the fraternal Communist and Workers' Parties upon the foundation of Marxism-Leninism.

The Twenty-Second Congress dealt at length with questions of foreign policy. The Congress reasserted the Twentieth Party Congress decisions on theoretical questions related to Soviet foreign policy and international relations. The central tasks of Soviet foreign policy were defined as strengthening of the community of socialist states and all-round support of the national liberation movement. The Congress pointed out that the Soviet Union followed firmly the Leninist policy of peaceful coexistence.

The Communist Party of the Soviet Union, the Congress resolutions said, would continue to do everything in its power to preserve and strengthen peace and friendship among the peoples, so that the lofty ideals of social progress and the happiness of the peoples might triumph.

The conclusions of the Twentieth and Twenty-Second congresses concerning basic questions of international relations and the international working-class movement were acclaimed by Communists all over the world. They were also reflected in the decisions of the high-level Moscow conferences of Communist and Workers' Parties in 1957 and 1960.

The Focus on Progress

Labour Enthusiasm of the Masses

After the Twenty-Second Congress closed the Soviet people set about with a will to translate its historic decisions into reality.

The efforts of the nation were concentrated, first and foremost, on the building of the material and technical basis of communism. The working class occupied itself with redoubled vigour fulfilling the industrial targets of the Seven-Year Plan.

It was of crucial importance to develop progressive labour techniques, raise efficiency and promote technical progress. The movement for communist work stimulated this effort. By the close of 1963 it had been joined by 26 million factory and office workers. More than 2,600 factories, 50,000 workshops, departments and farms, and 400,000 teams had won the proud title of communist work collectives. In addition, more than 6 million factory and office workers had gained the title of communist work shock-workers.

In 1960 members of the communist work movement were the trail-blazers, but by the end of 1963 they comprised an army of many millions of builders of communism.

Numerous feats of labour were performed in industry and building. The Zaporozhstal Steel Works, whose personnel was contesting the title of a communist work collective, produced as much steel in 1962 as it was targeted to produce at the end of the Seven-Year Plan period.

The powerful Kremenchug Hydropower Station, an important link in the Dnieper hydropower chain, was started up long ahead of schedule in July 1962. The builders of the Krasnoyarsk Hydropower Project in Siberia, the first of a chain of powerful stations projected on the Yenisei, dammed the river on March 25, 1963, and directed it along a new bed.

The fifth and sixth years of the Seven-Year Plan period went down in history as years of vast construction. In each of these two years more than 600 major industrial projects were completed.

The government allocated some 35,000 million rubles annually for capital construction, which exceeded the aggregate investments made in the three pre-war five-year plan periods.

The Seven-Year Plan effort produced new forms of popular activity.

A nation-wide movement for the pre-schedule starting of new plant in the chemical industry was launched by the personnel of the Lugansk Khimstroi in 1963.

The movement for higher labour productivity expanded. The blast-furnace operators of the Magnitogorsk Works achieved the world's highest labour productivity in the fourth year of the Seven-Year Plan period.

We could list numerous other examples of the dedicated work done by Soviet workers. The experience of innovators and the foremost work groups reveal the immense possibilities of the socialist economy.

Volunteer unpaid organisations at factories, set up to resolve problems of production and management, attracted a large membership and operated in a variety of fields. Their role in the economy is growing continuously. By the end of 1962, there were 118,000 standing production conferences with a membership of 5,000,000. Each year they submitted some 2,000,000 recommendations and suggestions.

In 1963 more than 16,000 after-work design and technological groups, 14,000 economic analysis bureaus, 8,000 technical information bureaus and thousands of innovation councils were active at research institutes and laboratories on an unpaid, volunteer basis, consisting of more than a million engineers, researchers and advanced workers. The communist work movement played a decisive part in the successful fulfilment of the annual plans in the concluding years of the Seven-Year Plan period.

The effort to advance agriculture was no less intensive.

After the Twenty-Second Congress, conferences of farm workers and leading Party and government functionaries were held in all the important farming zones of the country. They examined the possibilities of increasing output of farm products in every republic, territory and region.

Rank-and-file workers showed a lively concern for the efforts to rally the nation's moral forces for the fulfilment of the great national programme. This was, indeed, a distinctive feature of the new stage of communist construction in the U.S.S.R., which began after the Twenty-Second Party Congress. In August 1962 Nadezhda Zaglada, a 69-year-old collective farmer and Hero of Socialist Labour, who was a team leader at the May Day Collective Farm of Zhitomir Region, appealed to all crop farmers through the press to live and work honourably and conscientiously.

The Soviet youth showed models of dedicated labour. After the

Fourteenth Congress of the Young Communist League held in April 1962, 150 of the country's biggest building projects were declared all-Union shock objectives. More than 3,000,000 young men and women were employed at the numerous building sites. In 1962 alone, some 150,000 young people responded to the Y.C.L. appeals and left their homes to work on the shock projects. That same year, 150 industrial projects were completed with Y.C.L. help and put into operation.

On the farms Y.C.L. members worked assiduously to produce high yields and to mechanise animal husbandry. In June 1962 the Y.C.L. members in the industrial centres supervised and assisted in the building of new shops and the modernisation of operating factories of the engineering and tractor industries in order to supply agriculture with efficient machinery.

Young people were still hard at work, too, developing the wealth of the newly settled farming areas. In 1962, more than 70,000 Y.C.L. members harvested the virgin land development areas, working hand in hand with the older generation to create the material and technical basis of communism.

The uplift of the Soviet economy stimulated a rapid development of the more progressive branches of industry.

The latest scientific and technological achievements, coupled with the industrial practice of the last few years, are an indication of the big part the chemical industry plays today in economic development. Accelerated development of the chemical industry and extensive use of the chemical products in the economy make it possible to refashion the key branches of industry, to increase the output of consumer goods, improve their quality and reduce production costs.

The December 1963 Plenary Meeting of the C.C. C.P.S.U. charted the modernisation of more than 500 operating plants, with a resultant rise in the output of the chemical industry by 200 to 300 per cent in seven years. A particularly important place was assigned to the chemical industry in boosting agricultural production.

The Party programme for the accelerated development of the chemical industry and the chemicalisation of the economy is making good progress. In 1964 more than 200,000,000 rubles' worth of chemical products were manufactured in excess of the plan.

Alongside industry, the Soviet Union devoted a great deal of attention to the development of agriculture.

In particular, the Plenary Meeting of the C.C. C.P.S.U. in February 1964 examined questions related to the further intensification of farming.

Until then farming developed largely by increasing the crop areas, because this was the quickest way of increasing the harvest, particularly of grain. Greater production of mineral fertilisers, extensive irrigation, mechanisation of all farm jobs and the raising of the machinery-to-worker ratio now enables the country to boost agricultural output through a better use of the land and through higher per acre yields. The Plenary Meeting stressed in its decisions that "a further uplift of agriculture is of cardinal importance for the fulfilment of the tasks of communist construction and the improvement of the people's standard of living".

Moulding the New Man

In the course of socialist construction the Marxist-Leninist doctrine took firm root in the Soviet land and became the ideology of the whole Soviet people. The bourgeois world outlook, a leftover from the old society, was completely eradicated, and survived only in the consciousness of a negligible section of people. Marxist-Leninist ideology has stood the test of time. It is the basis of the spiritual life of the Soviet people, their weapon in the struggle for a new world. A new man has developed in Soviet society, moved by the noble ideals and lofty moral principles embodied in the moral code of the builder of communism.

The Party attaches great importance to ideological work. It believes that the higher the political awareness of the members of socialist society, the greater will be their creative activity in building the material and technical basis of communist society, that the higher is the level of the people's consciousness, the higher the rate of the development of society.

Questions of communist education were in the spotlight at the June 1963 Plenary Meeting of the C.C. C.P.S.U. The Plenary Meeting passed a resolution entitled "The Current Tasks of Ideological Party Work", stressing that the moulding of the new man who harmoniously combines spiritual wealth, moral purity and physical perfection, was the most important aspect of ideological and cultural development in the period of full-scale communist construction. Moulding the new man, the citizen of communist society, is bound up closely with the struggle against survivals of the old code of morals, against old habits and the left-overs of nationalism and Great-Power chauvinism, against the attempts of reactionary imperialist ideology to influence the minds of Soviet people.

The Communist Party adheres consistently to the principles of proletarian internationalism and devotes itself untiringly to instilling in Soviet people a spirit of friendship and revolutionary solidarity with the peoples of other countries.

Splendid revolutionary and labour traditions have sprung from the struggle of the Soviet people for the new society, and it is part of the ideological work to bring up the working people, particularly the youth, on these traditions.

Communism and labour are indivisible. The path to communism

implies continuously rising labour productivity and participation in labour of all able-bodied citizens. Instilling in every Soviet citizen affection and respect for socially useful labour, breeding in him a sense of responsibility for public property, constitutes the core of the ideological work done by the Party, the trade unions, the Soviets and the Young Communist League.

The Plenary Meeting defined the tasks of the press, radio, television and cinema in ideological work, and raised high the banner of allegiance to Party and people, to the principles of socialist realism in Soviet art.

Changes in the Management of the Economy

The building of communism in the U.S.S.R. in pursuance of the general line of the Party set out in its Programme, calls for effective organisational forms and methods of Party guidance in all sectors of communist construction.

The general aim in the further improvement of the organisational side of the economy is defined in the Party Programme, which says:

"The Party will continuously improve the forms and methods of its work, so that its leadership of the masses, of the building of the material and technical basis of communism, of the development of society's spiritual life will keep pace with the growing requirements of the epoch of communist construction."*

Yet this can only be achieved if the task is tackled scientifically, if the objective laws governing social development are taken properly into account and if the Leninist standards and principles of Party and government life, democratic centralism, all-round development of inner-Party and Soviet democracy, collective leadership and consideration for the opinion of the Party membership and the general public, are strictly observed.

Changes were carried through in the sphere of economic management in 1962. In March, new organs were set up to administer farming, known as collective- and state-farm production boards. In November, by decision of a Plenary Meeting, the previously constituted Economic Councils were reconstituted into larger units.

By the same decision Party organisations were structurally reconstituted along the so-called production principle, which replaced the territorial-production principle inscribed in the Party Rules.

Also in November 1962, the Party Central Committee restored the Leninist structure of the bodies of control by creating a united Party and government control machinery—the Committee of Party and Government Control of the C.C. C.P.S.U. and the Council of Ministers of the U.S.S.R., and its corresponding local bodies.

---

* The Road to Communism, p. 584.

The Growing Role of the Communist Party

After the Twenty-Second Congress, the Communist Party membership increased. The finest and most politically conscious section of the citizens of the U.S.S.R. joined the Party.

In 1965 the C.P.S.U. had twelve million members and candidate-members. The Party works for still stronger bonds with the people. The Communists strive to live up to Lenin's precept: live in the *thick* of the masses, know their *mood*, know *everything*, understand the masses, know how to approach them, win their *absolute* trust.* Success in communist construction depends on the work of the Party; its role and significance as the leading and motive force of Soviet society is growing year after year.

The C.P.S.U. has achieved considerable successes in all fields of communist construction, and in strengthening the international position of the Soviet Union. After removing the consequences of the Stalin cult, the Party has worked hard to restore the Leninist principles and standards of Party leadership.

The decisions of the Twentieth and Twenty-Second Party congresses have done much to reinstate Leninist standards in Party affairs and to develop inner-Party democracy, and have promoted greater creative activity among Communists. The Party returned to normal in its life and work.

But the faults born of the preceding period were not removed overnight. Some of the leaders were still apt to overrate successes, to push through subjective ideas, and to overlook the boons offered by science and practical experience.

The C.C. C.P.S.U. Plenary Meeting of October 1964 censured these deficiencies. It cleared the path for the enforcement of the decisions of the Twentieth and Twenty-Second Party congresses and the Party Programme, producing yet another model of fidelity to principle and intolerance of shortcomings. It put into effect additional guarantees against excessive concentration of power in the hands of individuals and against subjectivism in the treatment of important issues of state.

The Plenary Meeting relieved Nikita Khrushchov of the offices of First Secretary of the C.C. C.P.S.U. and Chairman of the Council of Ministers of the U.S.S.R. Leonid Brezhnev was elected First Secretary, and Alexei Kosygin was recommended for the post of Chairman of the Council of Ministers.

Undeviating and consistent implementation of the Leninist general line is the cornerstone of Party success in the guidance of communist construction. The decisions of the Plenary Meeting of the C.C. C.P.S.U. in October 1964 speak of the solid unity of the Communist Party.

* See *Lenin*, "On the Role and Tasks of Trade Unions in Relation to the New Economic Policy", *Collected Works,* Vol. 44, p. 497.

The next Plenary Meeting, held in November 1964, made a thorough study of the two years' experience of Party, government, trade union and Y.C.L. organisations divided under the so-called production principle. The Plenary Meeting came to the conclusion that the reorganisation carried through in 1962 had been ill considered and hasty. Two years of work showed that it had created certain difficulties, complications and deficiencies. It impaired co-ordination between Party and government bodies and prevented them from concerting their actions in economic and political matters. Locally, the bodies supervising retail trade, public education, health and the cultural services were, in effect, deprived of due Party guidance. A confusion of functions, terms of reference and responsibilities arose between Party, government and economic bodies.

Due to the reorganisation, the machinery of the regional and territory bodies became unwieldy. So did the structure of Party and government bodies in the towns and rural areas. The most efficient personnel were concentrated in the regional and territory bodies, while the district level was weakened. The artificial division of Party organisations into industrial and rural created difficulties in staffing rural Party organisations with personnel of a working-class background.

Furthermore, the reorganisation impaired the work of the Soviets, curtailed their role in economic development and was not conducive to strengthening co-operation between the working class and the peasants.

The November 1964 Plenary Meeting of the C.C. C.P.S.U. issued a ruling to realign the structure of Party bodies with the provisions of the Rules of the C.P.S.U. and the realities of Soviet society. In December 1964 regional and territory Party bodies were reunified, and this was followed up by extensive work in reunifying and strengthening bodies at district level.

The same was done with regard to the Soviets of Working People's Deputies, the trade unions and the Y.C.L.

The committees of Party and government control of the industrial and rural regional and territory Party committees and regional and territory Soviets of Working People's Deputies were also reunified.

Seven-Year Plan Nears Completion

The labour effort of the Soviet people, their deep sense of patriotism, coupled with the extensive organisational and ideological work done by the Party, have been crowned with success. The industrial targets of the Seven-Year Plan are being duly reached. Aggregate industrial production will be 84 per cent higher than the plan's starting figure, instead of the originally planned 80 per cent. The average annual rate of industrial growth in the 1959-65 period has been 9.1 per cent. This contrasts favourably with the 3.9 per cent industrial growth rate of the United States in the past seven years (up to and including 1964). Soviet production capacity has expanded appreciably as old enterprises were modernised and new ones were built. The Soviet Union has built and started up more than 5,500 large industrial enterprises in the seven years of the plan. The fixed assets of the state have nearly doubled. Considerable production increases were attained in power, steel, oil and gas, engineering, metal working and the chemical industry.

New industrial areas, particularly in the East of the Soviet Union, are being developed.

The accelerated technical progress achieved under Party leadership, has had a strong bearing on economic development. Manufacture of up-to-date equipment has enabled the country to re-equip the leading branches of the economy.

The structure of industry has improved. Big advances were registered in the gas industry, electronics, and the production of plastics, chemical fibres and artificial diamonds. The country's fuel balance has changed, with oil and gas gaining appreciably in the aggregate production of the key fuels.

Soviet science and technology, which hold vanguard positions in many important fields, have made impressive headway. The imposing successes of Soviet space exploration are well known.

But for all the indubitable successes, serious deficiencies came to light in the development of Soviet industry during the Seven-Year Plan period. Oversights in the projecting and planning of capital construction created delays and added to the cost of building. The lag of agriculture tended to slow up the industrial development rates, particularly in industries producing consumer goods. A slight drop was also registered in the growth of labour productivity.

A number of far-reaching measures was taken in carrying out the Seven-Year Plan to raise the standard of living.

The working day has been reduced, the average wage has grown, the tax on factory and office workers' incomes has been either lifted or drastically cut for some brackets, and pensioning has been introduced for collective farmers.

The Fourth Session of the Supreme Soviet of the U.S.S.R., convened in July 1964, passed a law increasing salaries to teachers, physicians and other people employed in services catering directly to the population. Before the end of the year, the wages and salaries of more than 9 million employees had been increased 23 to 25 per cent. Approximately the same number of employees had their wages and salaries raised in the beginning of 1965, some six months earlier than planned. Today, about 6,800,000 collective farmers are receiving old-age pensions.

Housebuilding and the building of cultural facilities and community services proceeded on a large scale. In the first six years of the Seven-Year Plan period about one-third of the country's population improved their housing conditions.

The Fifth Session of the Supreme Soviet of the U.S.S.R. met in December 9-11, 1964, and passed the economic plan for 1965, the last year of the Seven-Year Plan period.

On the recommendation of the C.C. C.P.S.U., the Supreme Soviet appointed Alexei Kosygin to the office of Chairman of the Council of Ministers of the U.S.S.R.

Considerable attention was devoted to agriculture in the Seven-Year Plan period. The crop area was considerably expanded through the development of virgin and waste land, the yields increased in some zones, and, coupled with government help to the collective and state farms in the way of machinery, this boosted grain production and state grain procurements. This applies mainly to the first five years after the September 1953 Plenary Meeting of the C.C. C.P.S.U. Due to a drought in some of the country's leading grain zones in 1963 the harvest was low and the government stocked less grain than the year before.

The good harvest in 1964 enabled the farmers to fulfil the state purchasing plan. But all in all, the growth rate in agriculture has dropped considerably in the past five years.

Livestock breeding is still the most backward branch of farming. In the last five years the rate of growth of the cattle herd has decreased by half as compared with the previous five years. The number of pigs, sheep and poultry has decreased, too, and the production of milk on the collective and state farms has dropped.

In substance, the uplift witnessed in agriculture before 1959 has ceased.

The March 1965 Plenary Meeting of the C.C. C.P.S.U. laid bare the main reasons for the lag in farming seen in the last few years. It demonstrated that the objective economic laws governing the development of socialist economy had not been observed and pointed out violations of the principles of the proper combination of public and personal interests, and of the principle of material incentives, which make the worker interested in the results of production.

The tasks set for socialist farming were not always backed by economic measures. The prices for agricultural produce were unjustifiably low. On many collective and state farms crop rotation was neglected and even elementary farming practices were often scorned. Frequent reorganisations of bodies that administer farming, the weakening of Party guidance and insufficient use of scientific practices and of the knowledge of specialists acted cumulatively as a brake on agricultural production.

Having bared these grave causes for the lag in farming, the Plenary Meeting worked out a set of urgent economic and political measures to remedy the situation.

The procedure of state grain purchases has been altered. There will now be a fixed target operative for a number of years ahead. Besides, the basic state purchasing prices have been considerably increased. Marketable surplus food crops in excess of the plan will be purchased by the state at substantially higher prices. This economic stimulation of the production of some of the food crops will yield added profits to the collective and state farms.

Considerable additional funds are being put into animal husbandry through increases of purchasing and procurement prices of animal products.

As much as 71,000 million rubles is to be put into farming to expand its material and technical foundation. This is a very big sum, equalling the aggregate investment in farming in the first 19 post-war years.

Mechanisation and chemicalisation are a key to higher labour productivity and the efficiency of farming. Within the next five years, therefore, the production of tractors will be doubled over that of 1965, while the output of grain combines, lorries, machines and equipment for animal farms, and other farm machinery will be considerably increased.

The Plenary Meeting outlined a series of measures designed to strengthen the collective and state farms organisationally, to better the use of scientific practices in farming and to elevate the standard of Party and government work in rural areas.

All this will enable the country to achieve high productivity in farming.

The agricultural programme drawn up at the Plenary Meeting of the C.C. C.P.S.U. in March 1965 is making headway.

Its sights set on the building of communism in the U.S.S.R., the Communist Party is determined to make the most of the economic laws and vast possibilities of the Soviet system in the interests of the people. The decisions of the C.C. C.P.S.U. Plenary Meeting in September 1965 were fresh evidence of this.

Impressive facts and figures were quoted at the Plenary Meeting to illustrate the growth of Soviet industry.

But the Communist Party and the Soviet people cannot rest on their oars. Neither can they afford to suffer the serious deficiencies still harrassing economic development. Fuller use of all the potentialities of industry is called for to continue raising the level and rate of industrial development, accelerating technical progress and improving the people's standard of living.

The foremost task facing Soviet industry is to raise the efficiency of production, increase returns on capital investments and fixed assets, improve the quality of products, and eliminate wasteful and unproductive expenses.

Steadily rising labour productivity is of crucial importance for economic, particularly industrial, development. Yet insufficiently vigorous introduction of scientific and technical achievements and deficiencies in organisation act as a brake on labour productivity.

The decisions of the Plenary Meeting are centred on these cardinal tasks. They provide for measures to improve planning and management, enhance the economic incentives of factories and broaden their powers and initiative.

In planning, a special accent is laid on strict adherence to the economic laws of socialism, ensuring proportionality in the development of the economy and obtaining the maximum of output at the minimum of outlay.

Administration of industry on the territorial principle has been replaced with administration by branches of industry, for which purpose Union-Republican and all-Union Ministries have been established for the various branches of industry.

The territorial principle of management, through regional economic councils, was introduced in 1957. This structure had positive sides, but has not justified itself on the whole. It extended the possibilities of inter-industry specialisation and co-operation to a slight extent within the economic areas, but acted as a brake on branch specialisation between factories located in different economic areas. Also, it created a barrier between science and production and produced too many administrative levels.

A steady rise in the technical level of industry and rapid introduction of the foremost achievements of science and technology in production calls for competent management of the various branches, securing a single technical policy for every branch.

It should be noted that this is not a mechanical return to the old system which obtained before the economic councils were set up. It is a new system of branch management based on new principles of planning and the enhancement of economic levers through a sensible combination of centralised management with extended functional and economic independence of the factories.

Until now the method of directives held precedence in industrial management to the detriment of economic methods. Now, a system of economic stimuli (genuine profitability and financial self-sufficiency, material encouragement of factories and of every employee for higher production results) will pave the way for a higher productivity of labour, better quality of production, and greater efficacy of operation.

Excess limits to the independent activity of enterprises are being put out of the way, and the number of plan indices set by central bodies to factories is being reduced. From now on enterprises will be set only the key targets: the amount of production they have to sell, the main items they have to produce, the wage fund, the size of centralised investments, and a few others. The enterprises will work out their own plans as regards such indices as size of personnel, labour productivity, cost of production, etc.

This will enable enterprises to take a fuller account of their potential reserves for greater production and to make a better use of such crucial economic levers as profit, price, bonus and credit.

While enhancing the role of economic stimuli in economic development, the Plenary Meeting stressed, the Communist Party will continue to work for greater communist consciousness among the people and to promote a communist attitude to labour.

The Plenary Meeting decisions, which follow the Leninist approach to the root problems of Soviet economy, were received with approval by the Soviet people. The Sixth Session of the Supreme Soviet of the U.S.S.R. in October 1965 unanimously passed a law on the reorganisation of organs of industrial management and some other organs of the state. The Plenary Meeting decisions will secure a new powerful upswing of the country's productive forces and will strengthen the international position of the Soviet Union, of the socialist community as a whole, to a still greater extent.

Foreign Policy of the U.S.S.R.

Initial Soviet Successes in Combating the Cold War

The measures taken to restore Leninist standards in government and Party life also enlivened the foreign policy of the Soviet Union. To begin with, the Soviet Government took steps to improve relations with the neighbouring countries. In May 1953, it informed the Turkish Government that it was abandoning all the territorial claims made on Turkey after the war, and suggested concerted measures to establish good neighbour relations between the two countries. A proposal to improve relations was also made to Iran. An agreement was concluded with Afghanistan early in 1954 granting credits and assistance to that country in building a number of industrial projects. The first long-term trade agreement with India was signed at the close of 1953. These moves had the effect of improving the international climate.

With active Soviet support, the Korean People's Democratic Republic and the People's Republic of China succeeded in concluding an armistice in Korea in July 1953. But as long as the war in Indochina continued, world peace was still in jeopardy.

On the initiative of the Soviet Government a Conference of Foreign Ministers of the U.S.S.R., U.S.A., Britain and France was held in Berlin in January-February 1954 after a very long interval.

Urging an end to the wars in Korea and Indochina, the Soviet delegation suggested a special Five-Power Foreign Ministers' Conference with the People's Republic of China participating. The French setbacks in Indochina and domestic political motives induced Britain and France to accept the Soviet proposal. The objections of the United States were outvoted and it ultimately joined the majority.

At the Berlin Conference, the Soviet Union came forward with the idea of an all-European collective security treaty, and soon after the conference. it suggested that the United States join the treaty as well.

The Soviet Union proposed that a Provisional All-German Government be set up, consisting of representatives from the parliaments of the German Democratic Republic and the Federal Republic of Germany. This all-German body, the Soviet proposal said, could prepare the ground for, and carry through free elections and act as Germany's spokesman during the framing of the peace treaty, whose principles were suggested at the conference by the Soviet delegation. Reunified Germany, it was stipulated, should not be a party to any military alliances.

The Western powers, in the meantime, insisted on a plan which provided for Germany's participation in the U.S.-sponsored military alignments set up in Europe. No agreement was possible on these terms.

In relation to the Austrian problem, the Soviet delegation in Berlin proposed that Austria undertake to stay out of military alignments and not make its territory available for foreign military bases. This Soviet proposal was well received by all concerned and quickly won the support of the majority of the Austrian people. But like the plan for Germany, the Western powers turned it down.

The Foreign Ministers of the five Great Powers gathered in Geneva on April 26, 1954, to examine the Korean and Indochina problems. Representatives of the other countries concerned were invited to attend.

The Soviet Union, the Korean People's Democratic Republic and the People's Republic of China advocated the establishment of a unified Korean state, and suggested elections to the National Assembly of Korea. However, the objections of John Foster Dulles, the U.S. representative, dashed all hope of a solution for the Korean problem in Geneva. After the U.S. State Secretary's attempts to prevent a discussion of the Indochina problem fell through, he walked out of the conference.

The Soviet Government did everything in its power to clear the path for a cease-fire in Indochina. Under pressure of public opinion at home and due to the painful defeat of French arms at Dien Bien Phu on May 7, 1954, the French Parliament dismissed the government that was stalling the negotiations and demanded

Sixty-five-ton auto-train made at the Byelorussian Auto
Works

Lenin Nevsky Engineering Works. It produces huge installations for the
metallurgical and chemical industries

At Popov Radio Plant, R█

an immediate end to the dirty war by a majority vote. The armistice in Indochina was concluded on July 20, and the following day all the delegates to the Geneva Conference, save those of the United States, signed a Closing Declaration, which envisaged free elections in Vietnam, Laos and Cambodia.*

The German problem was still a sore point in Europe.

The policy of the United States and the other Western powers in respect of the Federal Republic of Germany gravitated, in substance, towards a revival of German militarism.

True, the French National Assembly on August 30, 1954, turned down the Paris Treaty, which was designed to pave the way for a rapid renascence of a rearmed West Germany in the capitalist part of Europe. But the architects of West German remilitarisation set to work again the day after their debacle in the French Parliament. Their "new" military scheme also included Britain.

On October 23, 1954, new Paris agreements were concluded, inaugurating a West European alliance of France, Britain, the F.R.G., Italy, Belgium, Holland and Luxembourg.

In early 1955, the F.R.G. Government began to build up an army, the Bundeswehr. More than a hundred former Hitler generals were invited to top posts in the new West German military establishment. Revenge-seeking propaganda was launched on a lavish scale.

The German monopolies that had brought Hitler to power in the 1930s set about with United States, British and French assistance to rebuild a strong war machine, creating a grave peril to the neighbouring countries and the rest of the world.

Between November 1954 and January 1955 the Soviet Government issued three successive notes to the Western powers, in which it gave its view of the Paris agreements. The Soviet Government warned, among other things, that if these agreements were ratified, Germany's reunification through free all-German elections would become impossible. The Soviet Government pointed out that if the Paris agreements were not ratified and both parts of Germany not entangled in any military alignments, the Soviet Union would agree to hold free elections in Germany under international supervision. The Soviet Government noted that the Paris agreements were incompatible with the treaties of alliance concluded during the war by Britain and France with the U.S.S.R. The Soviet Union repeated its proposal of a European collective security treaty and suggested an international conference to discuss it.

The Western governments rejected the idea of such a conference.

---

* A temporary demarcation line was drawn across Vietnam south of the 17th Parallel. Due to the resistance of the U.S.A. and its reactionary puppets in South Vietnam, the reunification of the country is still hanging fire.—*Ed.*

Alarmed by the mounting war threat in Europe, the European socialist countries held a conference in Moscow from November 29 to December 2, 1954. The conference declared that if the Paris agreements were ratified, the conferring countries would take measures to ensure their security, not short of concluding a multilateral treaty and setting up a joint military command. In defiance of all these actions by the international peace-abiding forces, and of the widespread opposition of the working class, peasants and intellectuals in the capitalist countries party to the Paris agreements, the latter were ratified.

In view of this development, the Soviet Government on May 7, 1955, annulled the Soviet-British Treaty of Alliance concluded in 1942 and the Soviet-French Treaty of Alliance and Mutual Assistance concluded in 1944. On May 14, in Warsaw, eight European countries—the U.S.S.R., Bulgaria, Hungary, the German Democratic Republic, Poland, Rumania, Czechoslovakia and Albania—concluded a Treaty of Friendship, Co-operation and Mutual Assistance for a term of 20 years. They established a Political Consultative Committee and a Joint Command for the armed forces assigned to it.

The peace-abiding character of the Treaty was underscored in a number of articles, one of which provides that it is open "to the accession of other states, irrespective of their social and political systems". The signatories agreed that if a system of collective security should be established in Europe and a General European Treaty to that effect should be concluded, the Warsaw Treaty would automatically cease to be operative. Furthermore, the Government of the German Democratic Republic declared that if Germany is reunified, G.D.R. commitments under the Warsaw Treaty would become null and void. The establishment of the multilateral alliance strengthened the forces of peace and enabled them to combat the war threat more effectively.

At about the same time, the Soviet Government acted as the initiator of a State Treaty with Austria. In April 1955, when Austria's top political leaders visited Moscow, the Soviet Government reaffirmed its readiness to end the occupation of Austria and fully restore Austrian sovereignty, provided the Austrian Government declared her neutrality. This meant abandoning important strategic positions in Central Europe, which was yet another token of faith in the possibility of preventing a war and settling all controversial problems by negotiation. After a provisional agreement was reached in Moscow, matters advanced speedily. On May 15, 1955, representatives of the Soviet Union, the United States, Britain and France gathered in Vienna to sign with the Government of Austria a State Treaty terminating Austria's occupation and restoring her sovereignty. Shortly after the treaty was concluded, Austria proclaimed her neutrality. This was an important development, and it markedly improved the international climate.

But no real relaxation of tension had yet been achieved. The cold war continued. The United States Government had not abandoned its designs despite its diplomatic defeat at the 1954 Geneva Conference. In September, a military bloc was established, composed of the United States, Britain, France, Australia, New Zealand, Pakistan, Thailand and the Philippines, known as SEATO. Early in 1955, Britain, Turkey, Iraq, Iran and Pakistan concluded the Baghdad Pact. Formally, the United States was not a member of this military alliance, but in fact came to play a leading part in it soon after it was set up. At the close of 1954 and early in 1955 the situation in the region of the Chinese island of Taiwan and the off-shore islands near the Chinese mainland held by Chiang Kai-shek, grew very tense. The situation in Europe, too, looked alarming, for in May 1955 West Germany officially joined the North Atlantic bloc.

Fresh actions were needed to improve the atmosphere and compel the bourgeois politicians to abandon the notions and customs of international intercourse that had emerged in the ten years of the cold war. The Soviet Government ranged itself on the side of world public opinion, which clamoured for a renewal of the contacts which the heads of the Allied governments had abandoned after the war. The Western powers were unable to resist the combined pressure of the advocates of a conference and of the dynamic Soviet diplomacy.

On July 18, 1955, the Heads of Government of the U.S.S.R., the U.S.A., Britain and France met in the Palace of Nations in Geneva to examine the German problem, the problem of European security, disarmament and the question of great contacts between the two world systems. The Soviet Government again came forward with the proposal of concluding a general European collective security treaty with, at first, the two German states and, later, reunified Germany as co-signatories.

The Soviet Government suggested that the member-states of the North Atlantic Pact and the West European Alliance, on the one hand, and the Warsaw Treaty countries, on the other, should conclude a treaty that would formalise their common undertaking not to employ armed force against each other. At the same conference, the Soviet delegation proposed that the armed forces of the United States, the Soviet Union and the People's Republic of China should be reduced to 1-1.5 million men, and those of Britain and France to 650,000 men, while the armed forces of all other countries should not exceed 150-200 thousand men each. After the armed forces and conventional armaments would have been considerably reduced (some 75 per cent of the agreed reduction), the Soviet proposal said, atomic and hydrogen weapons should be totally banned and withdrawn in due course from the armouries of states, and destroyed.

The U.S. delegation came forward with a plan for unrestricted air inspections of Soviet territory ("open skies" plan). In the opinion of the Soviet Government this plan, far from securing disarmament, had the underlying motive of facilitating espionage and reconnaissance.

The Heads of Government produced agreed texts of directives to their Foreign Ministers, who were to continue the discussion of the issues raised at the conference. Subsequently, the Western powers refused to adhere to the agreed directives, but, all the same, the Geneva summit conference did go a long way in improving the international situation.

The Soviet Government came out with the initiative of expanding personal contacts between statesmen, public leaders, scientists and stage performers of different countries. After 1955 Soviet leaders paid visits to India, Burma, Indonesia, Afghanistan, Poland, the German Democratic Republic, Czechoslovakia, Hungary, Bulgaria, Rumania, the People's Republic of China, Finland, Britain, France, the United States, the United Arab Republic and other countries. Leaders of dozens of countries came to the Soviet Union to hold negotiations.

At the close of 1959 an agreement was reached to convene in May 1960 a conference of the Heads of Government of the Soviet Union, the United States, Britain and France.

In preparing for the projected summit conference, the Soviet Government strove to ensure its success. One of the Soviet measures to that effect was a unilateral reduction of the Soviet Armed Forces by one-third. But influential U.S. groups, who dreaded a detente, laid covert plans to torpedo the summit conference. On the eve of the new year (1960) President Eisenhower refused to prolong the moratorium on nuclear weapons tests, which expired on December 31, 1959, and on May 7, 1960, a few days before the summit conference opened, announced that the U.S. Government had decided to resume underground nuclear tests. To top this, a Japanese-American military treaty was concluded in Washington in January 1960.

Vice-President Nixon, State Secretary Herter and Under-Secretary of State Dillon made bellicose speeches on the eve of the conference, and urged that the conception of peaceful coexistence be "flung overboard", while President Eisenhower, for his part, said these speeches set out the foreign policy of the United States.

On April 9, 1960, the U.S. authorities dispatched a reconnaissance plane into Soviet air space, followed on May 1 by another. The latter was shot down near Sverdlovsk by Soviet rocket units, and the spy-pilot, Garry Powers, who had bailed out, was arrested by the Soviet authorities. The U.S. Government announced that flights of a similar nature had taken place before, and would be continued. The Soviet Union demanded that President Eisenhower reprove the aggressive U.S. action against the Soviet Union, punish the offenders, and guarantee that such actions would not recur. However, the U.S. President turned down this legitimate demand, and thereby scuttled the summit conference.

The Soviet Government was not discouraged and continued to expand contacts with Western statesmen.

The Soviet Union and the German Problem

The Government of the Soviet Union, whose people had suffered heavy losses from the German-fascist invasion, gave pride of place in its foreign policy to the German problem, the questions of a final peace settlement in Europe.

As we have seen, the Soviet Government worked very hard after the war to pave the way for a united peaceful Germany.

But in 1948-49 the Western powers engineered a split of that country into two economically and politically separate parts, each of which developed along different lines. The bourgeois order, dominance of monopoly capital and large Junker landholdings were the basic features in the west of Germany, while workers' and peasants' power and socialist construction were the basic features in the east. After the Federal Republic of Germany joined the West European alliance and NATO, the road to reunification became more thorny still. It became impossible to achieve a mechanical integration of the two parts of Germany.

The Soviet Government believed that it was impossible to unify Germany through the efforts of the Great Powers and that it was the Germans themselves who could make the greatest contribution to their own unity. The U.S.S.R. gave strong support to everything the German Democratic Republic did in its striving for a rapprochement with West Germany, in particular the proposal of a confederation of the two German states. However, all the G.D.R. proposals were rejected out of hand, or left unanswered. At the Geneva Foreign Ministers' Conference attended by representatives of the U.S.S.R., U.S.A. Great Britain, France, the German Democratic Republic and the Federal Republic of Germany (May-August 1959), the Soviet Union came forward with the proposal of creating an All-German Committee with representatives from the G.D.R. and F.R.G. Such a committee could apply its efforts to promoting contacts between the two states and preparing a German peace treaty. But the Western powers turned these proposals down.

The question of the German peace treaty became one of the pivotal problems in international affairs, and understandably so.

Embers left over from the Second World War were left smouldering in the heart of Europe. Supported by the other socialist countries, the Soviet Government worked perseveringly for a peace treaty with Germany. A Soviet project for such a treaty was submitted to the Western powers on January 10, 1959.

This draft consisted of 48 articles. It envisaged that the G.D.R. and the F.R.G. should not enter into any military alliances of which the U.S.S.R., the U.S.A., Britain and France were not members jointly. Both parts of the country were to withdraw from NATO and the Warsaw Treaty respectively, and recognise the existing frontiers as final.

Specific articles were designed to make secure for all citizens the basic freedoms and rights of man and ban fascist and revenge-seeking organisations. The draft imposed certain military restrictions upon Germany and, among other things, prohibited that country to produce or acquire weapons of mass annihilation. According to the draft, the occupation of the country was to be ended and all foreign bases on German soil were to be closed down. Last but not least, the draft provided for a solution of the West Berlin problem and for that city's conversion into a demilitarised free city.

The Soviet Government pointed out that it wished the peace treaty to be signed by all members of the anti-Hitler coalition.

Why did the Soviet Union insist so strongly on the conclusion of a peace treaty? What did the peace-loving forces expect from it?

The signing of the peace treaty would make the political climate in Europe milder and more stable. It was the purpose of the peace treaty to give legal power to the frontiers, which would to some extent bridle the revenge-seekers of West Germany.

The peace treaty would also settle the question of West Berlin. Due to the unadjusted general situation, acute, tense and dangerous tensions arose in West Berlin time and again after the war. It became a nest of spies and the seat of subversive activities against the German Democratic Republic. The Soviet Government believed that the best solution was to turn West Berlin into a free city with no occupation troops and economically associated with both East and West. This solution, which should be set down in the peace treaty and thus have the authority of all the parties concerned behind it, would remove a seat of tension in the centre of Europe.

The peace treaty would also actuate a system of guarantees against the revival of German aggression and help to resolve many other problems.

It was the best way of consolidating peace in Europe, and all procrastination created the danger of a serious deterioration of the international situation.

If the Western powers were not prepared to sign a peace treaty with the two German states, an accommodation could be reached on the basis of two treaties. These did not necessarily have to coincide textually, but should contain the same stipulations on the key issues of the peace settlement.

The Soviet Union went to the length of suggesting that troops of neutral countries, or a U.N. force, could be temporarily stationed in West Berlin to replace the troops of the NATO powers.

The Western response to all these Soviet proposals was negative. The U.S., British, French and West German intelligence services reacted by intensifying their subversive activities against the German Democratic Republic, making the most of the almost uncontrolled access to the German Democratic Republic through Berlin's surface and underground transport services.

On August 13, 1961, the Government of the German Democratic Republic took steps to fortify its frontier with West Berlin. A wall was erected along the border that divides the city into two parts. An insuperable barrier was put up to keep out spies, saboteurs and profiteers from the West. The Western powers responded to this measure with war hysteria and demonstrations of strength. In the circumstances, the Soviet Union was compelled to increase its defence potential. This brought the Western militarist groups to their senses, and ended a dangerous crisis. In 1962, the governments of the U.S.S.R. and U.S.A. began negotiations on the German problem.

The developments of the last few years and, in particular, the international crisis of August-September 1961 over the Berlin issue, is strong evidence of the dangers nourished by the absence of a peace settlement with Germany.

A peace treaty would conform equally to the interests of the peoples of the socialist and capitalist countries.

After the "change of guards" in Bonn when Adenauer's place was taken over by Erhard, the foreign press predicted that F.R.G. policy would grow more pliant and realistic. But time went by and no change was forthcoming. At the same time, official and semi-official statements by West German politicians revealed that the "pliant" conception of the new Chancellor and his Foreign Minister, H. Schroeder, rested on the hope of isolating the G.D.R. from her allies and on a scheme of transacting a deal with the other socialist countries at the expense of the German Democratic Republic. In the meantime, the extreme reactionary politicians with neo-fascist inclinations continued to bank on an "X-day", which would give them an opportunity of absorbing the G.D.R.

On June 12, 1964, all these plans were knocked into a cocked hat. That day in Moscow the Soviet Union and the G.D.R. concluded a Treaty of Friendship, Mutual Assistance and Co-operation. This treaty states solemnly that the immunity of G.D.R. frontiers is one of the main factors of European security.

If either of the signatories, the treaty says, is made the object of an armed attack in Europe by any country or group of countries, the other signatory shall render it instant assistance in accordance with the provisions of the Warsaw Treaty.

The two signatories took guidance from the incontestable fact that two German states and an independent political entity, West Berlin, existed on German soil. They declared (Article 2 of the treaty) that they would work on perseveringly for the removal of the survivals of the Second World War, for a German peace treaty, and for the normalisation on this basis of the situation in West Berlin.

New Type of International Relations

After the emergence of the socialist camp, a new type of international relations, heretofore unknown, arose between the socialist countries.

Soviet policy in relation to the other socialist countries is based on the principles of equal rights, respect for political independence and sovereignty, and non-interference in domestic affairs. It is imbued with the spirit of international friendship, socialist internationalism, and concern for world peace.

Acting on its internationalist duty, the Soviet Union helped the Hungarian Revolutionary Workers' and Peasants' Government headed by János Kadar to suppress the counter-revolutionary uprising in the autumn of 1956, and to restore order in that country.

Soviet policy toward the fraternal socialist countries is set out and formalised in documents issued by the Soviet Government and the Communist Party, and notably in the decision of the Plenary Meeting of the C.C. C.P.S.U. in the summer of 1955.

"In our relations with the People's Democracies," this decision says, "our government and Party bodies, and all our officials abroad must adhere rigorously to the Leninist principles of socialist internationalism, complete equality, respect for national sovereignty and regard for the national distinctions of the countries concerned."

This was reaffirmed in the resolution of the Twentieth Party Congress and the Soviet Government Declaration concerning the foundations of friendship and co-operation between the Soviet Union and the other socialist countries issued on October 30, 1956.

In the last few years, the economic bonds of the Soviet Union with the other socialist countries have grown stronger still. The socialist countries co-ordinate their economic plans and carry through an international division of labour within the socialist camp according to plan. The development of the socialist countries proceeds at a higher rate than that of the capitalist coun-

Construction in Moscow

The Rossia Hotel, Moscow, under construction

Nuclear power icebreaker *Lenin*

tries. Their industrial output is increasing by about 15 per cent annually, while that of the capitalist countries is increasing by 3.5 per cent. It will not be long before the socialist system produces more than half of the world's industrial output. This rapid development of countries most of which had only recently been economically backward has been facilitated by fraternal mutual assistance.

The economic and trading relations between the Soviet Union and the other socialist countries have little or no resemblance to conventional commercial transactions. They are based on the principle of fraternal mutual assistance and are impelled by a desire to assist the economic development of the partner. Yet under agreements with other socialist countries, the Soviet Union is supplying complete equipment for several hundred new industrial undertakings. The steel mills built in the socialist countries with Soviet help produce about 15 million tons of steel a year, whereas before the war the countries concerned aggregated some 6 million tons. The Soviet Government gives the socialist countries either interest-free credits or credits on highly advantageous terms for 2 per cent annual interest, no interest being paid in the first few years of the credit period. By 1962, the total of credits and loans granted by the Soviet Union to the socialist countries exceeded 7,800 million rubles.

The U.S.S.R. and the other socialist countries have a standing arrangement for the exchange of scientific and technological information. Besides, the socialist countries account for about 80 per cent of Soviet foreign trade.

The conferences of the Council for Mutual Economic Aid member-countries in June 1962 and July 1963 have gone a long way in extending the economic co-operation of the socialist countries. They passed decisions on collective co-ordination of national economic plans and on the establishment of an International Economic Co-operation Bank for multilateral trade settlements between the member-countries of the Council for Mutual Economic Aid.

The Soviet Union has rendered the people of China extensive economic and technical assistance. More than 200 large industrial enterprises, shops and other projects equipped with the latest machinery have been built in China with Soviet co-operation. New branches of industry have been developed, such as the aviation, automobile and tractor industries, power generation, heavy and precision engineering, instrument-building, radio engineering, and various branches of the chemical industry. The Soviet Union helped China by supplying her with a large number of specialists for terms of various lengths and thousands of Chinese engineers, technicians and workers were trained in the Soviet Union.

The world socialist system is the principal product of the international working class and, at once, its main support and hope.

Unity of the chief revolutionary forces of our time—the world socialist system, the international working class and the national liberation movement—is a basis and guarantee of success in the peoples' struggle for peace and for social and national emancipation.

The Soviet Union and the National Liberation Movement

The Soviet Union renders moral and material support to the peoples fighting for their liberation. This international policy accords completely with Soviet internal policy, the emancipation of scores of nationalities of old-time tsarist Russia. The previously backward peoples in the non-Russian areas have in a short period of history received extensive help and support from the Russian and other Soviet peoples, and have become economically prosperous industrial areas. This excellent practice—assistance to the backward—is also applied by the Soviet Union and the other socialist countries on the international scene.

The help of the socialist countries, including supplies of arms, has facilitated the victory of the peoples of Algeria, the Yemen and a few other countries. The existence of the world socialist system gives the peoples of the newly free countries a prospect of national revival, of the elimination of age-long backwardness and achievement of economic independence.

For years, Soviet spokesmen at the United Nations have championed the cause of the young Indonesian Republic, which was attacked by the Netherlands. Vigorous Soviet moves in the Security Council helped to end the foreign occupation of Arab countries and expedited restoration of sovereignty in two Arab states, Syria and the Lebanon. The Soviet Union backed Egypt in 1956 during the Anglo-Franco-Israelian aggression, and has come to the aid of Middle East countries whenever their independence was imperilled by Western "gun-boat policy".

The Indonesian Republic had the sympathy and understanding of the Soviet Government and the peoples of the Soviet Union in its efforts to liberate Western Irian, a part of its territory, which culminated in a complete triumph in 1962. And the people of the young Congo Republic, too, had Soviet support in their struggle against the colonialists.

In 1960, on the initiative of the Soviet Government, the 15th U.N. General Assembly adopted a Declaration on the Granting of Independence to the Colonial Countries and Peoples. The 16th General Assembly discussed how this Declaration was being implemented.

The peoples of the Asian, African and Latin American countries rightly consider the Soviet Union as their true and well-meaning friend.

The United States and other imperialist powers conduct an entirely different policy. Even U.S. State Department officials, those at least who compiled the brochure, *Foreign Aid. Facts and Fallacies*, admit the self-seeking and purely military complexion of U.S. aid to the developing countries. They write that a decision on foreign aid depends on whether the aid contributes to U.S. security, for example, by giving the United States the right to use an important military base or military installation on the territory of the country in question.

Many politicians and publicists in the United States and other Western countries regard the small countries (particularly the developing countries) as a convenient site for cold war battles against the socialist camp. "The United States," writes John Spanier, a U.S. professor, "must take the lead, as before, in formulating policies which will create situations of strength among the underdeveloped countries of Asia, the Middle East, and Africa."*

It is not too long since the publication of the U.S. Alliance for Progress programme, purporting to assist the Latin American countries, yet it is now quite obvious to all concerned, as pointed out by Leonel Brizola, a progressive Brazilian leader, that it is a neo-colonialist programme and a cold war instrument or, more precisely, a method of organising political coercion against Latin America. The American Peace Corps scheme has evoked similar comment in the developing countries. The publicity given to this ostensibly altruistic body helped to unlock the doors of some Asian and African countries for the U.S. Peace Corps "volunteers". In December 1961, its first 26 "members" landed in India. In describing how this new breed of U.S. missionaries comported themselves in the Punjab, the weekly *Hindi Times* wrote: "The activities of these 'volunteers' may be qualified as the worst kind of propaganda and as an ideological offensive on the Punjab peasants to instil the American cold war spirit."

The highly advertised assistance rendered by the imperialist powers to the economically undeveloped countries is really very small. The sum allocated by the United States to finance the "aid" programmes of the 1961-62 fiscal year was described by the authors of the above-mentioned State Department brochure as a mere "two-thirds of what Americans annually spend on tobacco and about half of what Americans spend on liquor".

The lessons of independence have not been lost on the peoples of the new countries. They have realised that in the present circumstances, too, the imperialist countries have not changed their spots. Like Goethe's Mephistopheles they set a very high price

---

* J. W. Spanier, *American Foreign Policy Since World War II*, New York, 1960, p. 178.

on their often purely illusory assistance and strive to control the very "soul", the internal development and foreign policy, of the newly independent countries.

The socialist countries, on the other hand, do not attach any political or military strings to whatever assistance they give to the young countries. Their aid is invariably friendly, selfless and advantageous.

The United States, Britain, France, West Germany and other bourgeois countries grant credits at 4 to 7 per cent interest, while the usual interest charge on Soviet credits is 2.5 per cent. Since 1954, the Soviet Union has granted large credits to India, the United Arab Republic, Algeria, Indonesia, Iraq, Cuba, Ghana, Guinea, Mali, etc. Soviet credits to Afghanistan account for 70 per cent of that country's external revenue. Soviet credits to the U.A.R. have enabled that country to tackle the Aswan High Dam Project, the first section of which has already been completed, and the construction, among others, of five steel works and six engineering enterprises. Ceylon used the finance afforded by the U.S.S.R. to build a steel works and a tyre factory, Indonesia used it to build two steel mills, and India to build several large heavy industry enterprises and power plants.

The Soviet Union is rendering economic and technical assistance to 23 former colonial and dependent countries in Asia, Africa and Latin America. It is helping these countries to build about 500 different projects, of which one-fifth are already in operation. The Soviet credits, extended on easy terms, exceed a total of 3,000 million rubles. Soviet assistance is expediting the development of an independent economy in India, the United Arab Republic, Indonesia, Iraq, Afghanistan, Mali, Guinea, Ghana, Somalia and many other countries. In just the African countries, Soviet aid will go into more than 60 enterprises of heavy industry, 20 power stations and 37 educational establishments. This brief list shows that the Soviet Union is helping the developing countries build up the basic and decisive branches of economy, on which their economic independence will hinge.

Besides credits, the Soviet Union renders direct technical help to the young Asian, African and Latin American countries. The Bhilai Steel Mill in India, which produces one million tons of steel a year, is an example of such co-operation. Early in 1962 a contract was concluded in Delhi under which the Soviet Union will supply the Bhilai Mill with equipment and material to boost its output to 2.5 million tons a year. By 1965, when the Indian state-owned refineries will be processing 4,750,000 tons of oil, all of 4 million will come from refineries built with Soviet assistance. Soviet excavators, vehicles, earth-diggers, bulldozers, technical documentation and, last but not least, Soviet specialists, are employed on the Aswan Dam Project. Soviet engineers and skilled workers are both helping to build installations and train local workers, technicians and engineers in many countries.

Thousands of students from the developing countries are being trained at institutes in Moscow, Leningrad, Kiev and other cities, and notably at the Lumumba Friendship University in Moscow.

Furthermore, trade between the Soviet Union and the newly independent countries has been expanding rapidly in the last few years.

Growing economic ties with the U.S.S.R. and assistance from the socialist camp are enabling the young Asian and African countries to carry through an independent foreign policy, and to defy the threats and intimidation of the imperialist powers.

The national liberation movement and the neutralist policy of most of the young countries are a powerful factor in the struggle for peace and the prevention of a new world war.

The success of the national liberation movement has been promoted in our time by the emergence and consolidation of the world socialist system and the defeat in the Second World War of imperialism's strike force—Hitler Germany, fascist Italy and militarist Japan. The liberation revolution of the peoples in the colonial and dependent countries has the continuously mounting support of the working class and all working people in the metropolitan countries.

Experience has taught the peoples of the newly free countries, and those of the colonial countries as well, to seek the friendship of the world socialist system and the Soviet Union.

Alliance with the peoples that have thrown off the colonial yoke is one of the basic principles of Soviet foreign policy.

The solidarity of the socialist countries and the nations fighting for national liberation has been illustrated by the developments in Indochina. For ten years the U.S. Government has been supporting extreme reactionaries in the countries of that peninsula: Bao Dai and Ngo Dinh Diem in South Vietnam, Phoumi Nasavan in Laos, and the pro-American elements in Cambodia. It sent arms and military instructors to South Vietnam, where the vast majority of the people opposed the reactionary regime, plied its puppets there with money and, in effect, assumed guidance of the puppets' war against the people.

However, this could not sustain the cankered Saigon regime. Political coups followed in quick succession, and outside the capital large territories came under the control of National Liberation Front detachments. At the close of 1964 developments entered a new phase. The administration of U.S. President Lyndon Johnson sent tens of thousands of troops to take direct part in the fighting. U.S. warplanes began bombing towns and roads in the Democratic Republic of Vietnam in gross violation of international law. The U.S. campaign was outright international piracy. The U.S.

Government gave to understand that it interpreted the policy of peaceful coexistence to mean peace between just the two strongest states of the two camps—the U.S.S.R. and U.S.A.

As far as the other countries were concerned, the U.S. Government arrogated the right to interfere in their affairs, send its navy and marines to their shores, and shuffle their governments as and when it saw fit. A U.S. intervention in the Dominican Republic coincided in time with the attack on Vietnam.

The Soviet Union condemned the U.S. aggressions in Indochina and Latin America. It gave much more than just moral and political support to the people of Vietnam, carrying through a series of measures to buttress the defence potential of that fraternal country. Furthermore, it announced that if the U.S. aggression would not cease, it would allow Soviet volunteers wishing to assist in the struggle against the American militarists to go to the Democratic Republic of Vietnam.

This decision was one of many tokens of the fraternal solidarity and internationalism that pervade Soviet foreign policy.

The Soviet Union and Disarmament

So long as the armaments race continues, people cannot have peace of mind. In this age of nuclear arms with its vast stockpiles of monstrously destructive weapons, the danger of a war breaking out by evil intent or accident is unusually great. Besides, if the arms race is not checked, the number of countries possessing nuclear weapons will proliferate and these dangerous weapons will fall into the hands of generals and politicians in dozens of lands. In that case, the threat of war will become greater still.

The Soviet Government considers disarmament to be the "question of questions" in international relations. At the close of the forties and in the early fifties the Soviet Government made repeated proposals to reduce the armaments and armed forces of the five Great Powers by one-third and to ban nuclear weapons. The Western powers rejected these proposals on the pretext that the Soviet Union would then allegedly gain a military advantage. They drew up their own plan for reducing conventional armed forces to a certain level (1-1.5 million men for the U.S.S.R., U.S.A. and China and 700-800 thousand men for Britain and France). They suggested that atomic weapons should not be banned at the time of the reduction of conventional armaments, but at some later stage.

The Soviet Government consented to these proposals in principle. In a statement on May 10, 1955, the Soviet Union announced that it would accept the Western strength levels for the armed forces with a slight amendment as regards Britain and France. The Soviet draft named precise dates limiting each stage of disarmament. Posts were suggested at ports, railway junctions, motor roads and airfields to control disarmament. The same proposals were also submitted by the Soviet side to the summit conference at Geneva in July 1955.

The projects of the two sides had come so close together that a realistic possibility appeared of an agreement. But the purely propaganda nature of the widely advertised Western proposals was soon revealed. As soon as the Western powers realised that agreement was imminent, their spokesmen went back on their own projects and demanded as a precondition the consent of the Soviet Union to aerial photography throughout its territory. Thereby, the Western powers deliberately disrupted the looming agreement, and have kept to these tactics ever since.

In 1958, the United States, Britain and France suggested raising the level of the armed forces for the U.S.S.R., U.S.A. and China from 1.5 to 2.5 million men. Eager to start an arms reduction, the Soviet Government consented, although it realised the limitations of this proposal. The sponsors of the Western project reacted by declaring that disarmament should not begin at all as long as unsolved political problems, particularly the German problem, continued to exist.

In response to the Western suggestions of "partial measures", the Soviet Government submitted a series of concrete proposals to discontinue nuclear weapons tests, publicly reject the use of atomic and hydrogen weapons, reduce the strength of foreign troops on German territory, cut down the troop strength of NATO and Warsaw Treaty armed forces, etc. Lastly, the Soviet Government agreed to aerial inspections over a wide stretch of Soviet territory in Europe and Asia.

The Soviet Government started in on a series of bold unilateral disarmament measures. From 1955 to 1958 it announced three reductions of its armed forces, the three totalling 2,140,000 men. It wound up its military bases in other countries, withdrew all its troops from Rumania, and reduced the armed forces stationed in the German Democratic Republic and Hungary. In January 1960 the Supreme Soviet of the U.S.S.R. announced a new reduction of the Soviet Army by 1,200,000 men, bringing the armed forces down to 2,423,000. Military expenditure comprised less than 13 per cent of the Soviet 1960 Budget, whereas in 1955 it amounted to 19.9 per cent. This came on the heels of a decision in 1958 to discontinue nuclear weapons tests, which the U.S.S.R. urged the other powers to imitate.

Despite all these peace-loving steps of the Soviet Union, the Western powers continued to sabotage disarmament. Whenever Soviet disarmament drafts accentuated the banning of nuclear weapons, the bourgeois politicians and the monopoly press urged the retention of "deterrent weapons" or weapons of "massive retaliation". And whenever the Soviet Union, eager to reach an agreement, suggested a reduction of conventional armed forces for a start, the propagandists and politicians of the Western powers declared that at the present time conventional armed forces had altogether lost their importance.

The bourgeois press wrote prolifically about the alleged traps set in the Soviet project and said that by advancing its disarmament plans the Soviet Union hoped to weaken other countries and gain military advantages. The Soviet Government responded by bringing forward entirely new proposals, designed to end all these apprehensions.

On September 18, 1959, the Soviet Government submitted to the 14th U.N. General Assembly a plan for general and complete disarmament. The Soviet Union suggested carrying through the complete disarmament of all countries in three stages over four years: to disband the armies, destroy all types of weapons, wind up war production, ban weapons of mass annihilation and the means of delivering them to targets once and for all, and to wind up military bases in foreign territories. The reduction and ultimate dissolution of conventional armed forces and military bases abroad was to be carried out in the first two stages, while the destruction of nuclear and rocket weapons, and of the air forces, would take place in the third stage.

This proposal seemed certain to eliminate many of the obstacles to an agreement. General and complete disarmament would yield no advantages to any country over another. The danger of sudden attack would disappear. Control and inspection would no longer contain any element of military intelligence, and the broadest of all-embracing international control could then be established.

The U.N. General Assembly voiced its approval of the ideas brought forward by the Soviet Government, and unanimously passed a resolution on general and complete disarmament. The U.S. delegates, too, voted for it.

The governments and peoples of the socialist countries declared their support of the Soviet Government proposals. In the capitalist countries they were received approvingly by the workers and peasants, and also by many bourgeois leaders and the press.

To meet the wishes of the French and a few other governments, the Soviet Union made some amendments to its project. The somewhat altered Soviet proposals of June 2, 1960, envisaged that disarmament should begin with the banning and destruction of all means of delivering nuclear weapons to targets. In them, too, the Soviet Government consented to the establishment of an international police force under the U.N. Security Council. Lastly, it submitted detailed plans for international control.

Soviet artificial earth satellite, 1957

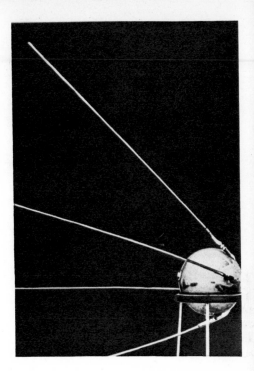

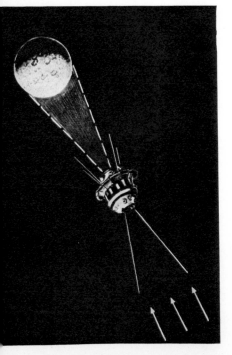

Position of an automatic interplanetary
station in space when it photographed
the far side of the moon, 1959

Team of Soviet spacemen. *Left to right*: Vladimir Komarov, Konstantin Feoktistov, Yuri Gagarin, Alexei Leonov, Herman Titov, Valery Bykovsky, Valentina Tereshkova-Nikolayeva, Pavel Popovich, Pavel Belayev, Boris Yegorov and Andrian Nikolayev

Models of Soviet artificial earth satellites on display at the Exhibition of Economic Achievement of the U.S.S.R., Moscow

But for all this the Disarmament Committee of ten countries set up by the United Nations in 1959 made no progress towards an agreement. The Western delegations suggested, in effect, that the nations should confine themselves to control over armaments, that is to a system of legal espionage.

In the circumstances, the fruitless debates in the Ten-Nation Committee were tantamount to deception, to misleading the peoples. So at the close of June 1960 the Soviet Union and the other socialist countries withdrew from it. The U.S.S.R. suggested discussing disarmament at the U.N. General Assembly and called on the Heads of Government to come to New York and participate in its work. Heads of states and governments, and the leaders of scores of countries, took part in the 15th U.N. General Assembly which opened in September 1960.

The draft of a General and Complete Disarmament Treaty brought forward by the Soviet Union at the General Assembly, like the Soviet proposals of June 2, 1960, envisaged the complete termination of the manufacture and the destruction of all means of delivering nuclear weapons to targets in the first stage, and also the removal of all foreign military bases from foreign territories. The project envisaged the reduction of the armed forces of the United States and the Soviet Union to 1,700,000 men. In the second stage, the signatories would completely prohibit nuclear and other weapons of mass annihilation, stop manufacturing them and destroy their existing stockpiles, reduce conventional weapons and armed forces and, finally, in the third stage, complete the disbandment of the armed forces of all countries, shut down all military establishments, and end military budgets. The Soviet Union suggested an effective system of international control, but announced that if a general and complete disarmament agreement were reached, the Soviet Government would consent to any type of control. The Soviet position was confirmed in Vienna in July 1961 when Khrushchov met Kennedy. This statement should have satisfied all those who claimed that control was the focal issue of the projected agreement. But nothing of the sort happened. The 18-Nation Disarmament Committee set up by a U.N. decision, held dozens of sittings in Geneva from March 1962 onward, but made no progress whatsoever.

The 1962 Crisis in the Caribbean

In the spring of 1962 provocative actions by the U.S. militarists created a perilous situation in the Caribbean area. The attempts made by the United States since 1959 to strangle revolutionary Cuba by economic means ended in failure, because the Soviet Union and the other socialist countries rendered the young republic prompt assitance. Unrefined sugar, Cuba's main item of export, which the United States refused to buy, was purchased by the Soviet Union, Czechoslovakia and the German Democratic Republic. After the United States ceased delivering oil to Cuba, dozens of Soviet tankers lifted anchor for that far-away revolutionary island. An attempt to crush the Cuban revolution with a landing force of counter-revolutionary mercenaries trained and armed in the United States, fell through as well. Units of the People's Army led by Fidel Castro, Cuba's national hero, routed the interventionists in a matter of three days.

In the autumn of 1962. the U.S. Government decided to send large U.S. armed forces against Cuba. It exploited the question of the Soviet medium-range rockets delivered to Cuba as a pretext for an intervention. In October 1962 the U.S. Command announced a naval blockade of the island, expecting to cut it off from all sources of economic and military assistance, then to bombard it, and to begin an invasion. The Soviet Government acted swiftly to squash this "export of counter-revolution". It publicly pledged to help Cuba in the event of an intervention.

This created the most acute crisis since the war, generated by the aggressive action of the U.S. governing group in the Caribbean. The situation grew tenser by the hour. At this point, the Soviet Government again demonstrated its love of peace and desire for greater international security.

On its initiative an understanding was reached to terminate the blockade of Cuba and thus substantially relieve the situation. The Soviet Government agreed to ship all rocket weapons out of Cuba, though these were delivered to the island for defence purposes. For his part, President Kennedy promised that the armed forces of the U.S.A. and those of its allies would not undertake any invasion of Cuba. This was a beneficial solution for the people of Cuba, and for the rest of the world. It was a sensible compromise in international relations, and, at the same time, demonstrated the far-reaching changes that had occurred in the world since the war ended. "Gunboat diplomacy", of which the bourgeois governments were so fond in the centuries of their rule, had suffered defeat. The existence of the powerful socialist system offered new opportunities of national and social liberation to the small or militarily weak peoples.

The Moscow Treaty of August 5, 1963

The Caribbean crisis revealed to the world the immense dangers implicit in the cold war and the arms race. Many Western political leaders realised that it was necessary to abandon the policy of "rolling back", "containment" and other formulas framed at the time when the U.S. had a monopoly on atomic weapons, which had become obsolete by the 1960s.

Soviet space successes and the development of modern weapons betokened the vast scientific and technological progress made by the Soviet Union, and the immense growth of the Soviet defence potential.

The late U.S. President Kennedy admitted the radical changes in the balance of world forces in a speech at American University in June 1963. "We must deal with the world," he said, "as it is and not as it might have been had the history of the last eighteen years been different."

This was a level-headed and realistic statement.

The Soviet Government took advantage of the modifications in U.S. policy to reach agreements in the interests of peace.

No progress had been made in the matter of a nuclear test ban for a number of years. By 1962 techniques for detecting nuclear explosions had been perfected. Highly sensitive instruments could detect explosions at immense distances. To all intents and purposes, every government could have a national system of control located in its own territory. In addition, the Soviet Government announced its consent to the installation of automatic seismological stations in Soviet territory. However, the spokesmen of the United States, Britain and other Western countries insisted on the right to send groups of inspectors to the Soviet Union in order to control the observance of the nuclear test ban treaty. Such inspections were, in effect, no longer needed, but, eager to reach an agreement, the Soviet Government announced at the end of 1962 that it was prepared to allow two or three inspections a year on its territory. This conformed closely to the number of inspections (3 or 4) suggested by the Western powers during the negotiations. However, as soon as the Soviet proposal was made public, the U.S. Government declared that it considered 7-8 inspections a year necessary. This gave reason to believe that what the Western powers wanted was an opportunity to make reconnaissance flights over Soviet territory, rather than conclude an equitable agreement.

There was considerable controversy over a ban on underground testing. The Western powers erected new barriers to the discontinuance of all nuclear tests on the pretext that underground tests were not easily detectable.

The Soviet Government wanted to make a beginning in the matter, and undertook a new important step. On July 2, 1963, it announced its willingness to conclude an agreement on the banning of nuclear tests in the atmosphere, in outer space and under water.

This impelled new developments and by the end of July the text of a Treaty banning tests of nuclear weapons in the atmosphere, in outer space and under water was agreed by representatives of the U.S.S.R., U.S.A. and Britain. On August 5, 1963, the Treaty was signed in Moscow by the Soviet Foreign Minister Andrei Gromyko, the British Foreign Minister Lord Home and U.S. Secretary of State Dean Rusk. The Treaty was left open for all other countries to accede to, and by February 1, 1964, representatives of 105 countries had affixed their signatures to it. Only two of the big countries—France and the People's Republic of China—refused to sign the treaty. The French Government had begun frantically to develop its own nuclear weapon and continued testing in defiance of protests in France and all over the world. President de Gaulle sought to justify his stand by his professed wish of "ending the nuclear monopoly" of the U.S.A., the U.S.S.R. and Britain. However, French policy in this matter may set off a "chain reaction" and induce a further proliferation of nuclear weapons, creating an added threat of nuclear war.

Conclusion of the Moscow Treaty was a big success for the forces of peace and a defeat for the forces of war. It put a stop to the contamination of the air and water with radioactive substances harmful to health. Besides, it erected an obstacle to the further proliferation of nuclear weapons, whose development calls for repeated test explosions. All in all, it may impel new important agreements designed to strengthen peace.

As soon as the Treaty was signed, the Soviet Government came forward with a series of fresh proposals. It suggested a non-aggression pact between the NATO countries and the member-countries of the Warsaw Treaty. It proposed a number of measures to prevent sudden attack and, among others, the establishment on a reciprocal basis of control posts at airfields, railway junctions, motor roads and big ports.

In the 1964 fiscal year Soviet military expenditures were reduced by 600 million rubles, and preparations were announced for a further reduction of the armed forces.

The beginning of 1964 was marked by a new Soviet peace initiative. The Soviet Union proposed that an international treaty be signed rejecting the use of force in settling territorial and border disputes. This proposal was received with approval by the general public and by the governments of dozens of countries. U.S. President Lyndon Johnson, who had succeeded the late John Kennedy, assassinated in November 1963, welcomed this proposal.

Important new steps to reach an understanding on disarmament were taken by the Soviet delegation at the 18th U.N. General Assembly. Before the Assembly opened the Western powers had expressed "apprehensions" that in the process of complete disarmament some country may be tempted to use concealed stockpiles of nuclear weapons and missiles. Other opponents of disarmament demanded that the "equilibrium of strength" be preserved as a basic condition for disarmament. To allay these "apprehensions", the Soviet spokesman at the General Assembly made a new proposal: until the end of the disarmament process the U.S.S.R. and the U.S.A. should retain a limited number of intercontinental, anti-missile and ground-to-air rockets, a project described in the press as a "rocket umbrella".

In 1963 and 1964 certain steps were taken to ease international tension, such as the U.N.- approved Soviet-American understanding not to fire into orbit missiles or satellites carrying nuclear war-heads and the Soviet, American and British undertaking to reduce the manufacture of fissionable materials for military purposes.

At the 19th U.N. General Assembly the Soviet Government sub-mitted a memorandum concerning measures for a further easing of international tension and limiting of the arms drive. It envisaged a reduction of the military budgets of a number of countries by 10 to 15 per cent, the withdrawal or reduction of foreign troops in territories abroad, the winding up of foreign military bases, prevention of any further proliferation of nuclear weapons and a ban on their use, creation of nuclear-free zones, conclusion of a non-aggression pact by member-countries of NATO and the signatories of the Warsaw Treaty, and the like.

Successes of the policy of peace and peaceful coexistence encounter furious resistance on the part of the bellicose groups in the capitalist countries. The latter bring forward various provo-cative plans aimed at foiling the improvement that began in inter-national relations. The Washington plan for a multilateral nuclear force is one of them. It envisages that long-range Polaris rockets would be installed on surface ships camouflaged as merchant ves-sels and manned by officers and men of the American, British, West German and other NATO navies. This would mean that the revenge-seeking groups of the Federal Republic of Germany gain access to nuclear weapons, and thereby vastly increase the danger of a world nuclear war.

To meet this situation, the member-countries of the Warsaw Treaty convened a conference of their Political Consultative Committee in Warsaw in January 1965.

The conference warned the architects of the multilateral nuclear force plan that if they proceeded with it, the Warsaw Treaty coun-tries would be compelled to take appropriate measures to ensure their security. The conference warned that any attempt to carry through the West German revenge-seeking plans would inevitably escalate into a nuclear war, and added that the Warsaw Treaty countries would continue "to promote in every way a relaxation of tension, disarmament, peaceful coexistence and a peaceful future for all nations".

The latest steps of the Soviet Government are consistent with the aims proclaimed by the Warsaw Treaty countries. Late in March 1965 the U.S.S.R. proposed that the U.N. Disarmament Commit-tee be reconvened. It is up to this Committee, on which all the

U. N. member-countries are represented, to outline a path towards progress in the disarmament negotiations.

The Treaty of Alliance and Mutual Assistance concluded by the Soviet Union and the Polish People's Republic in March 1965 also serves the purposes of peace in Europe. The treaty formalises the immunity of Poland's frontier along the Oder and Neisse and delivers a fresh blow at the designs of the Bonn revenge-seekers.

The jubilee 20th Session of the U.N. General Assembly, held in autumn 1965, opened in a tense atmosphere created by the U.S. aggression against the people of Vietnam and the armed conflict between India and Pakistan. In Europe, too, apprehensions increased over various plans to put the Federal Republic of Germany into possession of nuclear weapons.

The Soviet Government used the U.N. rostrum to campaign for peace. It demanded that the United States cease its intervention in Vietnam and suggested that the Assembly adopt a special declaration on the impermissibility of interference in the internal affairs of states and on protection of their independence and sovereignty. The Soviet Union offered its good services in settling the India-Pakistan conflict and suggested that the leaders of the two countries meet each other on Soviet territory. The Soviet Government devoted special attention to the peril of the further proliferation of nuclear weapons. In an effort to block all channels for such proliferation, the Soviet delegation to the 20th General Assembly submitted the draft of a treaty on the non-dissemination of nuclear weapons.

* * *

The Soviet Government has on many occasions shown the world that the policy of peaceful coexistence proclaimed by Lenin, the great founder of the socialist state, is feasible and realistic. The main result of the intensive and single-minded foreign policy pursued by the Soviet Government and Communist Party is that peace has prevailed on earth and that conditions have been created for its further consolidation.

Chapter Eight

THE CULTURAL REVOLUTION IN THE U.S.S.R.

The cultural revolution was a part of Lenin's plan for the socialist construction of the U.S.S.R.

What the cultural revolution stands for is a thorough change in the spiritual life of society. In substance, it represents rapid elevation of the educational and cultural standards in the country, and the moulding of active and conscious builders of the new way of life. It created a socialist culture and will in due course create a communist culture—the highest level of mankind's cultural development. Born of the new social system, this new culture helps to consolidate it and to secure its final victory.

The development of Soviet culture proceeded in close interaction with the radical socio-economic changes. The years of socialist construction were also the determinative period of the cultural revolution.

The workers and peasants, under the guidance of the Communist Party, took a direct part in the cultural revolution in the U.S.S.R.

Radical Changes in the Spiritual Make-Up of the Working People

The First Steps of the Cultural Revolution

The cultural revolution in the U.S.S.R. began on the day of the Great October Revolution. Its main purpose was to educate and mould the new man and to create a new and truly popular culture.

The establishment of the Soviet system in Russia was in itself a most important cultural factor and a dynamic medium for the political education of the masses. Millions of people of all the nationalities inhabiting Russia, freed from oppression, surged forward to a new life. In a matter of years, just a few decades, the Soviet system, as Lenin put it, had to "pay the cultural debt of many centuries".*

To perform its cultural tasks, the Soviet Republic had to

---

* Clara Zetkin, *O Lenine* (*About Lenin*), Moscow, 1933, p. 25.

extirpate the survivals of feudalism and national oppression, emancipate the women, eradicate mass illiteracy among the adult population, establish a secondary and higher school consistent with the socialist system and elevate the educational standard of the masses, train a people's intelligentsia, and secure a rapid development of science, art and literature, putting them into the service of socialism. It was essential to bridge the abyss that had gaped in the past between the millions of workers and peasants and the gains of culture, to place the artistic wealth and the achievements of science into the total possession of the working people, and to provide opportunities and scope for the development of popular talent.

Lenin, the leader of the October Revolution, proclaimed to the whole world at the Third All-Russia Congress of Soviets:

"In the old days, human genius, the brain of man, created only to give some the benefits of technology and culture, and to deprive others of the bare necessities, education and development. From now on all the marvels of science and the gains of culture belong to the nation as a whole, and never again will man's brain and human genius be used for oppression and exploitation."*

After the October Revolution, the "prophecies" of the opportunist leaders of the Second International and the Russian Mensheviks exploded in their faces, for they had insisted that the proletariat would not be able to carry out a political and social revolution, let alone build a new society, before it achieved a "definite cultural level". Before the Revolution they wasted reams of paper in trying to prove that the working people were incapable of cultural endeavour and of governing the country "due to a lack of culture".

Then the Revolution came about.

The undisguised enemies of the Soviet system predicted the "collapse of civilisation" and "the destruction of culture" in Russia. They flung mud at the new system and described the Bolsheviks as barbarians who would destroy and plunder, sell the artistic treasures of the land, and squander its cultural wealth.

This was a malicious slander. Nothing was more foreign to the October Revolution than vandalism.

It was the former landowners, industrialists, merchants and bureaucrats, thrown out by the Revolution, who were responsible for the loss and ruin of many of the country's cultural treasures. As a rule, they bent every effort to prevent the cultural treasures that had once been their sole property, from falling into the people's hands. This is why they often wrecked and destroyed what they had not managed to conceal or sell abroad.

Time showed that throughout its long history, Russia has never

---

* Lenin, *Collected Works*, Vol. 26, pp. 481-82.

Vladimir Rogozhnikov (U.S.S.R.) and N. Rataya (India) work side by side
at the Bhilai Iron and Steel Works

Bhilai Iron and Steel Works, built with Soviet assistance

Opening of the World Peace and Disarmament Congress,
Moscow, 1962

Housebuilding plant, built
in Kabul, Afghanistan,
with Soviet assistance

Huge Soviet tip-up lorries
damming the Nile at
Aswan on May 13, 1964

had so devoted and considerate a caretaker of its cultural wealth as the revolutionary masses headed by the Communist Party, who were the new master of the country.

Valuable monuments of Russian culture, the theatres and museums, the old manors and castles, the palaces and parks, the art galleries and ancient manuscripts, libraries and academies, collections of historical objects and laboratories, etc., were placed under the protection of the state.* Shipment of cultural treasures out of the country was prohibited by a decree of the Council of People's Commissars. Considerable funds were allotted by the government for cultural needs. In December 1917, 15,000 rubles were earmarked for the protection of the treasures of the Winter Palace. The Military Revolutionary Committees and the Soviets treated all objects of historical value with utmost care. At the proposal of the peasants of Yasnaya Polyana, the Council of People's Commissars passed a decision putting Leo Tolstoi's estate there under government protection, and turning it over for life-long use to his wife.

The Bolshevik Party applied considerable efforts to put the riches of science and culture within reach of all working people. The doors were flung wide open for the workers and poor peasants at schools and libraries, museums, theatres, institutes, laboratories, art galleries and clubs. School tuition was abolished at once. Students of technical schools and university-level establishments were given monthly grants. Measures were taken to educate the previously oppressed peoples, who were granted the right to learn in school in their native language.

As the Revolution developed, the reactionary press was shut down and a popular press appeared. Cultural and educational work proceeded among the population on a large scale—at clubs, reading rooms, libraries, and people's houses. Newspapers and magazines, books and political pamphlets were circulated in the thousands (usually free), presenting to the people the truth about the policy and goals of Soviet power.

The young proletarian state did its utmost to improve the housing and living conditions of the people. Workers' families were removed from damp cellars to the comfortable villas and residences that had formerly belonged to factory owners, landowners, merchants and priests. Lenin initiated a number of important government acts to combat child destitution.

The government introduced social insurance, labour protection,

---

* The Commission for Museums and the Protection of Monuments of Art and of the Past, set up by the Soviet Government, had the explicit function of protecting the cultural wealth of the country. The Tretyakov Art Gallery, the Hermitage, the Shchukin art collection, the Museum of the Academy of Art, the Palace of Count Sheremetyev (Ostankino Museum) and the Moscow and Petrograd conservatoires, etc., were declared national possessions.—*Ed.*

and free medical treatment. The workers' and peasants' state repealed all laws prejudicial to women's equality and granted women free access to education and science for the first time in history. The Declaration of the Rights of the Peoples of Russia, adopted by the Council of People's Commissars on November 2, 1917, proclaimed the equality and sovereignty of the peoples and lifted all national restrictions and privileges. On November 12, 1917, the government issued a decree abolishing the social estates and civil ranks.

The decree separating the church from the state and schools from the church (passed on January 20, 1918, by the Council of People's Commissars) had an immense revolutionising effect on the socio-political and cultural life of the country, and the way of life and consciousness of the nation.

Those were the first steps of the cultural revolution.

The culture of the new society did not arise on empty ground. It sprang from all the progressive elements of the Russian and world culture, which it critically digested. The Party censured the followers of the so-called Proletkult,* who denied the progressive classical culture of the past and clamoured for a "purely proletarian culture". Condemning nihilistic treatment of the nation's cultural heritage, Lenin wrote:

"Proletarian culture must be the result of the natural development of the stores of knowledge which mankind has accumulated under the yoke of capitalist society, landowner society, bureaucratic society."**

Lenin urged the broad enlistment of the services of bourgeois specialists. They were employed in the economy and conducted cultural and educational work, and many of the old military experts served in the Red Army.

The tasks of cultural construction could not be carried through overnight. It was not easy to begin building a new culture on the vast territory of the former tsarist empire, inhabited by numerous, generally backward peoples. The armed intervention against Soviet Russia, which began soon after the October Revolution, multiplied the difficulties and also affected cultural development. To begin with, the Soviet Republic was short of material resources, of economic and industrial experts, scientists and teachers. The schools and universities lacked adequate premises, fuel and teaching aids. Furthermore, the class enemies went out of their way to obstruct mass education.

---

* Proletkult (proletarian culture)—a cultural and educational organisation founded in September 1917. The theorists of the Proletkult (Alexander Bogdanov, V. Pletnyov, etc.) denied the principle of succession in cultural development and discoursed fatuously about the creation of a new proletarian culture free from all elements of the old culture.

** Lenin, *Selected Works*, Vol. 3, p. 506.

But all these obstacles were surmounted because millions of workers and peasants joined in the march for culture. In that early period their efforts were focussed chiefly on eradicating the most hateful and disgraceful legacy of the past—the mass illiteracy of the adult population.

"Down with Illiteracy!"

The mass illiteracy inherited from the old world was truly a national calamity. Pre-revolutionary Russia was in that sense one of the most backward countries in Europe. The all-Russia census of 1897 showed that only some 20 per cent of the adult population could read and write. The state of affairs among the non-Russian nationalities was particularly dreadful. As many as 99.5 per cent of the Tajiks were illiterate, 99.4 per cent of the Kirghizes, 99.3 per cent of the Yakuts, 99.3 per cent of the Turkmens and 98.4 per cent of the Uzbeks. The journal *Vestnik vospitaniya* estimated in 1906 that at the then prevailing rate it would take Russia 180 years to achieve total literacy of the male population and 280 years for the female population. The tsarist government allocated ridiculously meagre funds to education. Just before the Revolution, much less money was spent on building educational establishments than on building and repairing prisons.

The October Revolution put an end to the spiritual oppression of the people. The campaign against illiteracy was declared a national cause. Lenin, the head of the Soviet Government, called on all citizens to join the campaign against illiteracy.

The nation-wide educational offensive opened within the first few months after the establishment of Soviet power. The People's Commissariat for Education headed by Anatoly Lunacharsky, a prominent Party leader, statesman and a man of varied knowledge, an excellent speaker and publicist, literary critic and dramatist, theorist in education and aesthetics, and a distinguished art connoisseur, worked with dogged pertinacy to organise the mass campaign for universal literacy.

On December 26, 1919, the Council of People's Commissars issued a decree signed by Lenin on the elimination of illiteracy among the population of the R.S.F.S.R. "In order to afford the entire population of the republic an opportunity to participate consciously in the country's political life," the decree said, "the Council of People's Commissars has decided that all citizens of the republic between 8 and 50 years of age who do not know how to read and write, shall be obliged to learn reading and writing either in their native language or, if they so choose, in Russian."

Amidst the hardships of the Civil War and the economic dislocation, the Soviet administration built up a far-flung network of educational institutions—reading-and-writing schools, reading rooms and various other types of literacy circles. Illiterates were taught at the cost of the state and on study days were let off work two hours earlier without prejudice to their earnings.

Professional teachers and thousands of volunteers from among students, factory and office employees, peasants, researchers, scientists and senior schoolchildren joined the crusade against illiteracy in response to the Bolshevik Party appeal.

In the first 12 months after Lenin's decree was issued, nearly 3 million people were taught to read, write and count.

The battle against illiteracy proceeded most intensively in the Red Army.

The finest of the Russian intellectuals gave much of their strength and energy in those years to combat illiteracy, such as the writers Maxim Gorky, Alexander Serafimovich and Alexander Neverov, the poets Demyan Bedny, Vladimir Mayakovsky and Valery Bryusov, the prominent psychiatrist Academician Vladimir Bekhterev, etc.

In July 1920, the government established the All-Russia Extraordinary Commission for Combating Illiteracy under the R.S.F.S.R. People's Commissariat for Education, and in the autumn of 1923 a mass society, Down with Illiteracy, was founded, under Mikhail Kalinin, Chairman of the Central Executive Committee of the U.S.S.R. Lenin, too, joined the society. Active in its work were such prominent Bolshevik Party leaders as Nadezhda Krupskaya, Anatoly Lunacharsky, Andrei Bubnov and Nikolai Podvoisky. By 1925 the Down with Illiteracy Society had a membership of 1,600,000 (and of over 5,000,000 in 1932).

In the first ten years of Soviet power some 8,000,000 adults were taught to read and write, but the Soviet Union still ranked 19th in Europe for literacy.

The years of the First Five-Year Plan were a decisive period in the fight against this grim legacy, for a vigorous campaign was mounted throughout the country for total literacy. The Young Communist League set out on a cultural crusade under the motto, "Each literate teach an illiterate!" The Soviet public responded enthusiastically. Volunteer teachers taught more than 34,000,000 people to read and write from 1928 to 1932. There was scarcely any place in the country where illiterates did not learn their ABC. In the mountain auls of the Caucasus and the kishlaks of Tajikistan, the nomad yurtas of Kazakhstan and the Kalmyk steppes, the huts of the Ukraine and the chooms of Chukotka people of different nationalities learned reading and writing. So did nationalities that had had no written language of their own before the Revolution. In the Second and Third Five-Year Plan periods illiteracy was practically wiped out among the adult population of the Soviet Union. All in all, some 50 million men and women were taught to read and write in the twenty years from 1920 to 1940.

Universal literacy was thus achieved in the U.S.S.R. in an unheard-of short time.

As they gained knowledge, millions of Soviet men and women became active builders of the new life. Khamra Tahirova, a common Tajik woman, once an illiterate, became Minister of Urban and Rural Construction of the Tajik S.S.R. M. Yegorov, a Yakut, was illiterate when the October Revolution broke out. Today, he is a prominent scientist-farmer and a winner of the State Prize. A blacksmith at the Gorky Auto Works, Alexander Busygin, who was one of the initiators of the Stakhanov movement, surpassed existing standards in the manufacture of crankshafts in the mid-thirties. "Crankshaft wizard" was what the foreign press called him, and it is hard to believe, though true, that this adept in automobile making was still barely literate at the time. Speaking at the First All-Union Conference of Stakhanovites in the Kremlin in November 1935, Busygin said: "There is nothing I want more than learning. I am very eager to get ahead. I want to be more than a blacksmith. I want to know how a steamhammer is made, and to learn making steamhammers." The worker saw his dream realised. He learned to read, write and count with astounding tenacity, and finally became a qualified engineer. His is the story of many thousands of factory workers, and many thousands of farmers too, in the Soviet land.

The General Census of 1959 confirmed once more that the Soviet Union is now a country with total literacy.

Development of the New School

Elimination of illiteracy among the adult population was only a start in cultural development. A new school for the rising generation had to be built up. The Soviet power could not rest content with the system of education that prevailed in the old school, which was divorced from the realities of life and was based on the class principle, inequality of the sexes and national oppression.* Yet the Bolshevik Party was intent on turning to advantage all the valuable elements accumulated by the pre-revolutionary school.

From the first, the people's power set its sights on reforming the system of education. All cultural activities and school education were administered by the People's Commissariat for Education.

In 1918, the Constitution of the R.S.F.S.R. introduced legislation guaranteeing the workers and peasants the right of "full, comprehensive and free education". The former division of schools was abolished by a government decision inaugurating one type of

---

* According to 1913 figures, four-fifths of the workers' children of school age did not go to school.—*Ed.*

school. The school was flung open to all the peoples of the republic. Its proclaimed purpose was to train the rising generation for productive labour and educate young men and women to be conscious builders of the new society.

At the outset there were many difficulties, notably a shortage of trained teachers. Development of the new school in the outlying regions was strongly hampered by the general economic and cultural backwardness of the local population, absence of a written language in the case of many of the peoples, and active resistance by the priesthood and the bourgeois nationalists.

But nothing could dampen the craving for knowledge that fired the people.

In the first three years after the Revolution 13,000 new schools, and a vast number of children's homes where thousands of homeless children found shelter, were set up in the country. The number of pupils increased many times over, particularly in the national minority areas. In Kirghizia alone, the number of pupils among the native population increased eight times over. Twenty-three primers were compiled in different languages and published in large editions for children of the national minorities. Teachers' courses were founded in many gubernias and 55 teachers' colleges were restored or newly established. The number of teachers in 1920 already considerably surpassed the pre-revolutionary figure (400,000 against 73,000 in 1911).

The Political Education Board, headed by Nadezhda Krupskaya,* was established in November 1920 by decision of the Council of People's Commissars under the People's Commissariat for Education to promote and control mass cultural, educational and political work. By the end of 1920 the country had nearly 34,000 rural reading rooms, a large number of public libraries, People's Universities and culture clubs.

In the twenties the schools were being reorganised. The school provided not only an education, but was also a seat of communist training for the rising generation.

Vocational and professional schools to train specialists and skilled workers grew rapidly in number at that time. Schools for peasant youth, which provided general knowledge and specialised training in agronomy and livestock-breeding, were opened in the countryside.

Enemies of the Soviet system did their utmost to obstruct the development of the new school. They stopped at nothing, not even at terrorist acts against teachers. The Soviet authorities and the

---

* Nadezhda Konstantinovna Krupskaya (1869-1939), a prominent leader of the Communist Party, Marxist theorist in pedagogics, organiser of public education in the U.S.S.R. The wife of V. I. Lenin. From 1929 she was Deputy People's Commissar for Education of the R.S.F.S.R. Author of books on teaching.—*Ed.*

working people took strong action against these reactionary outbursts.

Each year the government increased its allocations for education. In many districts, the population initiated self-taxation, working people voluntarily contributing a certain portion of their income for public education. In addition, at public meetings people volunteered to repair and equip school premises, provide schools with fuel, and the like. Factories undertook to help educational establishments with school equipment and with winter fuel for schools and teaching staffs, etc. By the end of the rehabilitation period (1925-26) the aggregate school enrolment climbed to 9,000,000. The nation-wide problem of homeless children created by the Civil War was eliminated by that time. The people's power picked its young citizens, who had lost their parents in the years of hunger and hardship, off the streets, provided them with an education and brought them up as upright citizens. Many former delinquents, raised in children's homes, became prominent scientists, cultural workers, factory managers, and generals. The famous historian Academician Boris Rybakov, the distinguished conductor People's Artiste of the U.S.S.R. Konstantin Ivanov, General A. Lobachov, Corresponding Member of the Academy of Sciences Nikolai Dubinin, poet Pavel Zheleznov and many others had been street urchins.

When the country embarked on industrialisation, public education was faced with new and more formidable tasks. The rapidly growing industry required numerous competent personnel. Vocational and professional training, therefore, was intensively developed in the First Five-Year Plan period, and the training of teachers, too, grew in scale. Expenditure on education in 1929-30 was ten times that of 1925-26, and the building of schools proceeded in high gear.

Industrial and agricultural development was instrumental in reducing the term fixed earlier for the introduction of obligatory universal primary education. By a directive issued by the Sixteenth Party Congress (1930), universal four-year education was introduced in the U.S.S.R. as from the 1930-31 school year. This was a milestone in the cultural revolution.

At about the same time, obligatory seven-year education was instituted in the cities and towns for all children with four years of schooling. This required many new school buildings. More than 20,000 new schools, almost as many as tsarist Russia had built in 200 years, were opened in the U.S.S.R. between 1933 and 1937, inclusive.

Striking changes occurred in the non-Russian republics and regions of the U.S.S.R. In the first 15 to 20 years of Soviet rule more than 40 nationalities in just the Russian Federation developed their own written languages. In Turkmenia, the school enrolment increased 15 times over the pre-revolutionary mark, 39 times in Tajikistan, and 40 times in Uzbekistan.

The Soviet authorities laid an accent on strengthening the bonds between the school and production. In the thirties public education concentrated on improving educational work among pupils and introducing the rudiments of polytechnics in the school curriculum.

The decisions of the Central Committee of the Party issued in the early thirties "On the Primary and Secondary School", "On Curricula and Regulations in Primary and Secondary Schools", "On the Work of the Young Pioneer Organisation", etc., played an important part in improving instructions. The Central Committee ruled that school curricula were to be revised in order to secure lasting and systematic knowledge of the rudiments of science and to bring education closer to practice. Lessons in class became the chief form of the educational process.

In combating erroneous trends prevailing here and there, Soviet pedagogics developed and improved. Soviet teaching made the most of the progressive elements in home and foreign pedagogics, and applied itself to developing the educational theory of socialist society. Nadezhda Krupskaya, Anatoly Lunacharsky, Mikhail Kalinin and Andrei Bubnov* contributed greatly to the development of pedagogics. The writings of Nadezhda Krupskaya, who had devoted all her strength and knowledge to the development of Soviet culture after the Revolution, were particularly popular among educationalists.

Considerable credit for improving the educational system is due to the gifted educationalist and innovator Anton Makarenko,** and to Stanislav Shatsky, Pavel Blonsky and many other educationalists who were at once skilled teachers and gifted theorists.

The strengthening by the Party of the theoretical foundations of the Soviet school improved the level of instruction by the teachers, helped by the school Y.C.L. and Young Pioneers.

Universal seven-year education in the countryside was enforced in the years of the Second and Third Five-Year Plans (1933-41), while ten-year secondary education expanded considerably in town and country. Government allocations for the further development of public education were continuously increased. Shortly before the war a start was made in enforcing universal obligatory secondary (10-year) education in the cities, while the introduction of seven-year schooling in the countryside was successfully completed. In the late thirties school enrolment totalled 35 million. There

---

* Andrei Bubnov (1883-1940), prominent Communist Party leader. People's Commissar for Education of the R.S.F.S.R. from 1929 to 1937.—*Ed.*
** Anton Makarenko (1888-1940), distinguished Soviet pedagogue and writer. As head of children's colonies (Gorky Colony and Dzerzhinsky Commune) he developed a scientific system of youth education through labour, in the collective and in the family.—*Ed.*

Young workers apply for enrolment at institutions of higher
learning, 1928

Vocational training at the Krasny Bogatyr Works, 1925

Nadezhda Krupskaya among women delegates at a Congress of
non-Russian republics, 1922

Collective farmers at a school for the abolition of illiteracy,
Turkmenia, 1931

were more than 1,230,000 teachers, an imposing total when compared with the barely 80,000 teachers in the country before the Revolution. In 1939-40 the Soviet Union had 3,733 technical schools with more than 1,000,000 pupils. By then there were in the Soviet Union more than 13,000,000 people with a secondary education, of whom half were women.

The system of pre-school education had also expanded considerably, comprising infant nurseries, kindergartens, children's playgrounds, etc. Young Pioneer palaces and clubs, Young Technicians' and Young Naturalists' clubs, Young Pioneer summer camps, children's sports schools and the like, established under Soviet power, were highly effective in building the health of children and in the educational field.

The rate of development in Soviet public education was unprecedented.

The Soviet general school paved the way for a rapid growth of university-level education and accelerated training of personnel vitally needed in the different fields of the rapidly growing national economy.

The Rise of a Socialist Intelligentsia

The rise of a Soviet intelligentsia was a major accomplishment of the cultural revolution. The proletariat of pre-revolutionary Russia had neither the facilities nor the opportunities to develop its own intelligentsia.

After winning political power, the working class set its mind on enlisting the services of the old specialists to work in the machinery of state and the national economy. At that time Lenin stressed over and over again that it was in the interest of the workers' and peasants' state to learn patiently from the bourgeois specialists and to make the most of their experience. But this was not easy.

The old intelligentsia had mixed feelings about the Revolution. The top stratum was distinctly hostile and fought the new system tooth and nail. A large section of this anti-Soviet intelligentsia emigrated abroad.

Among the émigrés were some honest people who loved their country but were unable at the time to grasp the purport of the Revolution; including such distinguished men of Russian culture as the singer and actor Fyodor Chaliapin, composer Sergei Rakhmaninov, artist Ilya Repin, chess master Alexander Alyokhin, writer Ivan Bunin, chemist Vladimir Ipatyev, and others. Some of them suffered mental anguish over their mistake.

Many émigré intellectuals returned to the Soviet Union. Among these were the famous writer and former count Alexei Tolstoi, the gifted composer, pianist and conductor Sergei Prokofiev, and the renowned film director Yakov Protazanov. In their old age, well-known writers like Alexander Kuprin and Stepan Skitalets, and the former War Minister of the Provisional Government, General A. Verkhovsky,* returned to the Soviet Union as well. So did the distinguished sculptor Sergei Konenkov, in his creative prime at the time, soon earning the title of People's Artist of the U.S.S.R. and Hero of Socialist Labour, and winning the Lenin Prize in 1957.

Many teachers, doctors and office employees looked askance at the Soviet power after the October Revolution. They were not able at once to grasp the substance of the proletarian revolution and the goals of the workers' and peasants' government.

But there were also among the old intelligentsia many progressive people, who welcomed the Revolution. World-renowned scientists Kliment Timiryazev, Ivan Pavlov, Nikolai Zhukovsky, Alexei Bakh, and Vladimir Bekhterev, distinguished Russian men of letters Alexander Blok, Valery Bryusov, Vikenty Veresayev, Konstantin Trenyov, the artists Isaak Brodsky, Igor Grabar, the actors Prov Sadovsky, Leonid Sobinov, and Maria Yermolova, the architects Alexei Shchusev, Ivan Zholtovsky, and many others, joined the nation's creative effort from the first days of Soviet power and devoted all their experience, knowledge and talent to the people. Their example influenced the mood of the intelligentsia as a whole, and brought it closer to the triumphant masses. The role played by Alexei Maximovich Gorky in enlisting the old intelligentsia, above all the men of letters, for the building of a new life, was inestimable.

The Bolshevik Party followed a policy of persuasion towards the still vacillating intellectuals, striving to dispel their doubts and to win them over to the Revolution. This policy and the cultural crusade led by the Bolshevik Party gradually convinced the progressive section of the old intelligentsia that it was their duty to serve the Soviet people.

Naturally, the problem of training personnel for the new society could not be resolved merely by attracting and re-educating the old specialists. What the Soviet land needed was personnel for the economy and for cultural work with a working-class or peasant background. The Soviet state tackled this difficult problem from the very beginning. It was the chief means of creating a new intelligentsia.

The Soviet power boldly promoted the best workers and peasants to offices of responsibility. Many of them were employed in the first years of the Revolution in government institutions, mass organisations and responsible posts in the Red Army. The steadily increasing need for organisers prompted the setting up of new

---

* On returning from his self-imposed exile, Verkhovsky took an appointment as professor of the Red Army Military Academy. The last War Minister of the tsarist government, General D. Shuvayev, also aligned himself with the Soviet power and became an instructor at the Red Army Infantry School.—*Ed.*

types of educational establishments, such as Soviet and Party schools and Communist Universities, which provided trained Party and government personnel.

The Soviet higher school and the specialised secondary school were veritably factories for the production of the new intelligentsia. A decree of the Council of People's Commissars signed by Lenin and issued on August 2, 1918, abolished the rules of admission to higher educational establishments previously in force and lifted all the restrictions that had existed in pre-revolutionary Russia for the enrolment of workers and peasants to university-level schools. Tuition was free and students were provided a monthly living allowance.

Workers' faculties (rabfaks), a special type of secondary school, were set up at the university-level establishments on the initiative of the working people to prepare young men and women for entrance to the higher schools. Not only young men and women, but also adults with years of service in industry and agriculture, joined the rabfaks. In a matter of three or four years they passed the curriculum of a secondary school. In 1920, the country had 32 rabfaks with a total enrolment of 17,000 students.

The rabfaks breathed new life into the higher school. In the time that they existed they prepared 2,327,000 people for admission to the higher schools.*

The higher school reform prompted a mass influx of women to the university-level educational establishments. Already in 1919 female students in Moscow University made up one-third of the total. A start was made in specialised secondary and in higher education in the remote non-Russian areas. In the twenties and thirties secondary professional and higher educational establishments were founded in Byelorussia, Armenia, Azerbaijan, Kazakhstan, the Central Asian republics and the capitals of the autonomous republics and regions. More than 100 institutes and universities were established by the Soviet authorities in the ten Soviet republics that had had none before the Revolution. The Institute of the Peoples of the North was founded at the same time.

Before the October Revolution there was not a single technical school in the territory of what are now Turkmenia, Tajikistan and Kirghizia. The same applied to Kazakhstan and Uzbekistan. Yet by the end of the thirties these five republics of the U.S.S.R. had 325 specialised secondary educational establishments with an enrolment of 66,400. They graduated many thousands of local specialists.

The socialist reconstruction period was marked by many major

---

* Corresponding Members of the Academy of Sciences Vasily Yemelyanov and Maxim Kim, the writer Alexander Fadeyev, People's Commissar of Shipbuilding and then of Metallurgy Ivan Tevosyan and many other prominent Soviet intellectuals and leaders had begun their education at rabfaks.—Ed.

accomplishments in the training of competent specialists. In the 1933-34 school year the Soviet Union had more than 700 higher educational establishments, or nearly seven times as many as tsarist Russia had on the eve of the Revolution: In 1939, the enrolment in the specialised secondary schools of Moscow alone amounted to 37,900, which surpassed the total pre-revolutionary enrolment in the whole country.

The rate at which Soviet higher education developed was much more rapid than that of the developed capitalist countries. There were more students in the Soviet Union before the last war broke out than in 22 European countries combined, including Britain, France, Germany and Italy. In 1940-41, Soviet university-level establishments had an enrolment of 812,000 students, with women comprising more than 50 per cent of them, whereas in the 22 countries of Europe they then comprised as little as 19.8 per cent.

In the pre-war years the institutes trained some 2,000,000 specialists. When the Great Patriotic War broke out the Soviet intelligentsia totalled 14,000,000, with all nations and nationalities of the Soviet Union represented.

Science Serves the Socialist Cause

Science held an important place in the building of socialist culture in the U.S.S.R. The Soviet power did its utmost to promote scientific development and put science within the reach of the millions of working people.

The situation in the scientific world in the first months of the young Soviet Republic was also very complicated. Many scientists viewed the October Revolution with misgivings and did not at first wish to co-operate with the new authorities. But the work of the Communist Party, the heroic history of the reconstruction of Russia, showed them how wrong they were and induced most of them to join in the building of the new life.

The measures of the Soviet Government indicated from the first that science, no longer a privilege of the nobility and bourgeoisie, had a strong and faithful champion. The Academy of Sciences suggested enlisting scientists for the investigation of the country's natural wealth, and in April 1918 Lenin prepared an "Outline Plan of Scientific and Technical Work", which defined the main goals of the young Soviet science, linked closely with the country's production needs. A month later the government allocated a considerable sum of money for the needs of the Academy of Sciences.

Acting on Lenin's plan, the Soviet authorities gave pride of place to the investigation of the country's natural wealth. Oil prospecting began in the large area between the Volga and the Urals. A comprehensive survey was made of the Kursk Magnetic

Anomaly under Academicians Pyotr Lazarev and Ivan Gubkin. Geological research headed by Alexander Fersman was undertaken in the Urals, the Soviet Far East and the Kola Peninsula. In an environment of appalling ruin, the Civil War raging all round, the workers' state established a number of new research institutes, such as the Central Aerohydrodynamic Institute, the Physico-Technical Institute, the Institute of Roentgenology and Radiology, the Optical Institute, the Silicates Institute, and the Institute of Fertilisers. It also established scientific centres in the non-Russian areas. In 1919, an Academy of Sciences, whose first President was Academician Vladimir Vernadsky, a distinguished mineralogist and geochemist, was instituted in the Ukraine, and institutes of physiotherapy and bacteriology were founded in Tashkent. All in all, 117 new science institutions were founded in the first two years of Soviet power.

Measures were taken to advance the social sciences. On May 25, 1918, a decision was passed to organise the Socialist Academy, and in February 1921 the Institute of Red Professorship was founded to train instructors in the humanities. In 1924, the V. I. Lenin Institute was established to collect, keep and publish the literary heritage of Vladimir Lenin and works of scientific communism. In its campaign for scientific progress the Bolshevik Party depended on a group of distinguished scientists who, as we have already noted, had aligned themselves with the victorious people.

Soon after the Revolution, Kliment Timiryazev, an outstanding follower of Charles Darwin, published a book, *Science and Democracy*, in which he ranged himself firmly with the new system. He gave frequent public lectures, and in 1920 Moscow's working people elected him Deputy to the Moscow Soviet of Working People's Deputies. Dmitry Chernov, a world-known scientist and founder of metallography, was another distinguished scientist faithful to his people. Undaunted by the hardships of life in the war-ringed Soviet Republic, he turned down the lucrative offers of foreign industrialists. He refused to board the destroyer sent specially for him by the British to Yalta, where the scientist was receiving medical treatment. The well-known veteran lawyer, Academician Anatoly Koni, a friend of Turgenev's, Goncharov's, Nekrasov's and Dostoyevsky's, also welcomed the October Revolution. In spite of his age and state of health (he moved about on crutches), Koni spoke with enthusiasm at public lectures to workers, Red Army men and seamen.

Many gifted engineers of old Russia joined in the reconstruction of the young republic. A big part was played in the development of socialist science by such prominent Bolsheviks as the art critic and publicist Anatoly Lunacharsky, power engineer Gleb Krzhizhanovsky, literary critic Vaclav Vorovsky, historian Mikhail

Pokrovsky, pedagogue Nadezhda Krupskaya, astronomer Pavel Sternberg, economist and historian Ivan Skvortsov-Stepanov, physician Nikolai Semashko, literary critic Mikhail Olminsky, historian and publicist Yemelyan Yaroslavsky, engineer Leonid Krasin, lawyer Dmitry Kursky, economist and agricultural expert Alexander Shlikhter and geographer Otto Schmidt.

Despite the immense difficulties facing the country, the government and Lenin did their utmost to afford normal working and living conditions to the scientists. A commission for the improvement of scientists' living conditions, in which Maxim Gorky worked actively, was instituted in December 1919. In a hunger-stricken, ruined country, scientists were supplied food rations equal to those of the Red Army men in the battle lines.

In January 1921, the Council of People's Commissars passed a special decision "On Providing Conditions for the Scientific Work of Academician Ivan Pavlov and His Associates" and on the publication of his works. On January 27, 1921, Lenin received a delegation of scientists (which included Maxim Gorky) and consulted them on how to improve conditions for scientific research in the country.

Tangible successes were achieved in the scientific field already in the first years of Soviet power. The republic learned to produce its own aluminium and at the Optical Institute Professor Dmitry Rozhdestvensky and Abram Joffe experimentally split an atom of lithium. In shipbuilding Academician Alexei Krylov made good progress, while Nikolai Zhukovsky and Sergei Chaplygin obtained good results in aerodynamics, and Mikhail Bonch-Bruyevich conducted research in radio engineering, etc.

The Central Labour Institute, headed by scientist and poet Alexei Gastev, worked on problems of labour organisation.

The All-Union Association of Research and Technical Workers for the Promotion of the Socialist Construction of the U.S.S.R., founded on the initiative of Academician Alexei Bakh in 1927, was prominent in drawing the bulk of scientists into Soviet economic development. By 1932 it had a membership of 11,000. The Soviet Government awarded scientists with Lenin Prizes and the title of Labour Hero for distinguished work. It showed a paternal interest in the training of young, highly-qualified researchers and scientists and the development of scientists with a working-class or peasant background. Botanist Vasily Kuprevich, a very prominent scientist, had previously been a seaman. At the time of the armed uprising in October 1917 in Petrograd he fought tenaciously for the establishment of a Soviet state. Today, Kuprevich is President of the Academy of Sciences of the Byelorussian Soviet Socialist Republic.

The system of post-graduate study has developed many prominent scientists, such as Academicians Mstislav Keldysh (now

President of the Academy of Sciences of the U.S.S.R.), Alexander Nesmeyanov, Ivan Petrovsky (now Rector of Moscow University), Yevgeny Zhukov, and many others. Between 1925 and 1934 some 7,000 people passed through post-graduate courses. Wholesale training of specialists proceeded on a large scale in the non-Russian republics of the Soviet Union before the war. This produced such prominent scientists as technician Boris Paton (Ukraine), mathematician Nikolai Muskhelishvili (Georgia), geologist Kanish Satpayev (Kazakhstan), astrophysicist Victor Ambartsumyan (Armenia), chemist Sabir Yunusov (Uzbekistan), etc. The Byelorussian Academy of Sciences and branches of the Academy of Sciences of the U.S.S.R. in Azerbaijan, Kazakhstan and Tajikistan, were founded in the beginning of the First Five-Year Plan period. The number of women scientists and researchers in the republics of the Soviet Union kept growing steadily and reached 10,000 by 1937.

The range of research widened continuously in all scientific fields.

The distinguished scientist Konstantin Tsiolkovsky, who made brilliant discoveries in aerodynamics and rocketry, worked fruitfully at this time, and was the first to prove that space navigation was possible. In the thirties, the earth's atmosphere was essayed by the first Soviet experimental rockets.

Physics was advanced before the war by such Soviet scientists as Sergei Vavilov, Abram Joffe, Leonid Mandelstam, Dmitry Skobeltsyn, Pyotr Kapitsa, and Lev Mysovsky. Intensive research proceeded on the atomic nucleus.

The research done by the prominent chemists Nikolai Zelinsky, Nikolai Kurnakov, Alexei Favorsky, Alexei Bakh, Sergei Lebedev and others was of vast importance. Industrial methods of manufacturing synthetic rubber were developed in the country, and considerable progress was made in developing mass production of artificial fibre, plastics, organic products, etc.

The new advances made by the Soviet physiological school headed by Ivan Pavlov, who worked out a definitive teaching on the higher nervous activity, won world acclaim. A wonderful chapter in biology was inscribed by Ivan Michurin, the audacious naturalist whose works enabled people to shift many southern plants far north. He cultivated more than 300 new varieties of fruit.

Outstanding advances in biology were made before the war by Academician Nikolai Vavilov, who headed the Institute of Plant Research. Some 350 varieties of grain, industrial, fodder, vegetable and fruit crops were developed under his guidance. Considerable accomplishments also fell to the credit of the biologists Dmitry Pryanishnikov, Nikolai Tsitsin, Vasily Williams and Nikolai Tulaikov.

The Marxist historian Mikhail Pokrovsky played a leading part in the development of Soviet historiography. He wrote *A Very Brief Outline of Russian History* and a number of other valuable investigations. Studies of the history of the Bolshevik Party were made by Alexander Bubnov, Yemelyan Yaroslavky, Vladimir Adoratsky, and Mikhail Lyadov. Vyacheslav Volgin, Nikolai Lukin, Boris Grekov, Vasily Struve, Yevgeny Tarle, Yevgeny Kosminsky, Anna Pankratova, and others, worked on the history of the U.S.S.R. and other countries. Institutes of History and Philosophy were founded by the Academy of Sciences of the U.S.S.R. in 1936, and in 1937, it founded the Institute of Ethnography. The Soviet historians portrayed the masses as the prime movers of progress.

Mass training of engineers was highly important in the conquest of technical independence. The scientists and researchers of the Academy of Sciences of the U.S.S.R. contributed greatly to the construction of new giant factories and the development of new types of machinery.

The work of the Soviet polar explorers in the thirties was acclaimed all over the world. Reports about the Arctic expeditions of the Soviet ships *Chelyuskin* (under Academician Otto Schmidt) and *Georgi Sedov* were followed all over the world, and so were reports about the research done by four daring explorers under Ivan Papanin (1937) on a drifting ice-floe in the proximity of the North Pole.

The rapid scientific and technical progress in the U.S.S.R. before the war is strikingly illustrated by the first section of the Moscow Metro (subway), put into operation in 1935, and the non-stop flights of Soviet airmen, above all those by Valery Chkalov, Mikhail Gromov, Valentina Grizodubova, and others. Soviet warcraft was particularly important in the continuously deteriorating international situation (works by Mikhail Tukhachevsky, Boris Shaposhnikov, Vasily Blücher, Iona Yakir, Ivan Isakov, etc.).

In the early 1940, the U.S.S.R. had more than 1,800 research institutions. Many gifted men and women left industry and agriculture to join the army of scientists. Scientific and technical achievements added to the strength and power of the Soviet Union.

Soviet science developed in the course of socialist construction and won cardinal importance in the economic and cultural life of the world's first workers' and peasants' state.

Art and Literature Belong to the People

The socialist content of Soviet culture is mirrored in art and literature.

The victory of the October Revolution in Russia created vast opportunities for the writers, artists, composers and actors who wished to serve the cause of freedom and progress. The Soviet

Konstantin Tsiolkovsky

Ivan Pavlov

Kliment Timiryazev

Letter from Lenin to Timiryazev

Ivan Michurin

Alexander Popov

Ilya Mechnikov

Dmitry Pryanishnikov

Sergei Vavilov

Igor Kurchatov

power condemned the harmful theory of "pure art", "art for art's sake" and various formalistic and anarcho-nihilistic attitudes towards classical art. Lenin proclaimed, "art belongs to the people". The rich artistic legacy of the past was put by the Revolution into the possession of the people. The new burgeoning socialist art developed with the active participation of the workers and peasants.

The Bolshevik Party laid stress on the development of a new literature. By the end of 1917, no more than a few months after the Revolution, mass editions of classical Russian and world prose and poetry had been published in the Soviet Republic. The Communist Party appealed to the writers time and again to write books that would appeal to all people and be understandable by all.

Maxim Gorky was the founder of Soviet literature. He joined at once in building the new life and helped the workers' and peasants' state devotedly in carrying out revolutionary changes. The great writer persuaded many pre-revolutionary men of letters and artists to take the side of the Revolution. He urged "all the living forces of the land to respond to the rallying call for difficult but magnificent labour". Lenin highly commended the creative and organisational work done by Gorky.

The young Soviet literature, whose nucleus consisted of Maxim Gorky, Demyan Bedny, Alexander Serafimovich and Vladimir Mayakovsky, was soon joined by Valery Bryusov, Konstantin Trenyov, Alexander Blok, Sergei Yesenin, Alexander Neverov, Vikenty Veresayev, and many others. On the other hand, writers far removed from the people, men who peddled decadence and mysticism, such as Mikhail Artsybashev, Zinaida Gippius and Dmitry Merezhkovsky, stayed on the other side of the barricades.

The reactionary men of letters mounted a fierce attack on the writers who co-operated with the Soviet power. Bryusov and Serafimovich were ostracised, and the assault on Maxim Gorky was vociferous and vehement. But the frantic efforts of the hostile forces to obstruct the development of a new literature, devoted heart and soul to the people, were in vain, because the new literature had the wholehearted support of the people. An All-Russia Union of Proletarian Writers was founded in August 1918. The literature of the Soviet Republic took strength from its close bonds with the Russian writers and the democratic writers of the other peoples in the country.

Forceful works breathing faith in socialism, soon appeared. Poetry, highly varied in form and content, developed. The gift of the proletarian poet, Demyan Bedny, flowered. His verse inspired the masses in their revolutionary effort. His poetry and satire became an effective weapon against enemies. He was the first of the revolutionary poets to be awarded the military Order of the Red Banner.

The development of the young Soviet literature was influenced considerably by *The Left March, Order of the Day to the Art Army, 150,000,000,* and other verses and poems by Vladimir Mayakovsky, who hailed the revolutionary reconstruction of the old world and affirmed the invincibility of the workers' and peasants' system. Alexander Blok's *The Twelve,* Eduard Bagritsky's *Reflections on Opanas,* Valery Bryusov's poem, *Such Days as These,* and some of the verse written by proletarian poets, are among the finest specimens of early revolutionary poetry.

In the 1920s, when peaceful reconstruction was in full swing, the new literature developed in a mass environment of political and cultural enthusiasm. Many writers and poets devoted themselves to the heroic topics of the October Revolution and the Civil War. The working man became the chief hero in fiction. Alexander Serafimovich's *The Iron Flood,* Alexander Fadeyev's *The Rout,* Dmitry Furmanov's *The Mutiny* and *Chapayev,* Vsevolod Ivanov's *Partisan Tales,* Mikhail Sholokhov's *Don Stories, And Quiet Flows the Don,* Alexei Tolstoi's *1918* and other works of fiction gave an exposition of the finer qualities of the Soviet people.

At the time of the country's economic rehabilitation, fiction demonstrated the uplift of free labour and the creative work of the people (*Blast Furnace* by Nikolai Lyashko, *Cement* by Fyodor Gladkov, *The Week* by Yuri Lebedinsky, etc.). Gladkov's novel, *Cement,* portrayed the working class as the master of the new life. Many books told how age-old habits and traditions were being rooted out in the villages, and how a new psychology was emerging among the working peasants. Poet Sergei Yesenin, the wonderful bard of Russian nature, reached his apogee in the twenties. Also in the twenties, the writers Leonid Leonov, Konstantin Fedin, and Lydia Seifullina, and the poets Nikolai Aseyev, Nikolai Tikhonov, Alexander Bezymensky and Mikhail Isakovsky published their first big books.

Vladimir Mayakovsky was at the peak of his poetic powers. His poems *Vladimir Ilyich Lenin, Good* and *A Verse About the Soviet Passport* were among the best of his writings. Mayakovsky had a keen sense of the new and articulately opposed all that obstructed progress. He extolled the labour of the nation of builders.

The writings of Maxim Gorky, who was receiving treatment in Italy after 1921 on Lenin's insistence, left a strong imprint on the Soviet literature of that period. It was in Italy that he completed his autobiographical trilogy, which he had begun before the Revolution, and wrote his essay, "V. I. Lenin", his novel *The Artamonovs* and began working on the epic *Life of Klim Samgin.* Though far away from his land, the writer considered himself a participant in the grand reconstruction of Russia.

The thirties, the time of the early five-year plans, saw Soviet literature on the upgrade.

In the early thirties, Nikolai Ostrovsky, a seriously ill, bed-ridden Civil War veteran who had lost his eyesight, wrote an unforgettable book, *How the Steel Was Tempered*, about the heroic life and struggle of the youth for the victory of Soviet power and the socialist cause.*

The progress made in the construction of the world's first socialist land, the new human relations that sprang up in it, its collectivism and the labour feats of its people opened broad horizons for the writer. Many men of letters went to the forward zone of the fight for the new life—the building sites of the first industrial giants, the newly organised collective farms and the new towns. Creative collective labour was extolled in Marietta Shaginyan's novel *Hydrocentral*, Leonid Leonov's *The Bog*, Valentin Katayev's *Time Go Forward!*, etc. Teacher and writer Anton Makarenko described labour and the collective as the educational medium of the new man in his books, *Road to Life* and *Learning to Live*.

A realistic picture of the new collective-farm life was painted by Mikhail Sholokhov in the first part of *Virgin Soil Upturned*, Fyodor Panfyorov in his novel, *Bruski*, and the poet Alexander Tvardovsky in his poem, *Muravia*. The socialist transformation of the countryside was described in books that appeared in Armenia (Nairi Zaryan's *Atsavan*), Georgia (Leo Kiacheli's *Gvadi Bigva*), Kirghizia (T. Sadykbekov's *Kensu*), Byelorussia (Yakub Kolas's *Drygva*), and other republics of the Soviet Union.

Many of the writers turned to the topics of the Revolution, the defence of the young republic, and the country's historic past. Some time before the Second World War, Mikhail Sholokhov completed his epic *And Quiet Flows the Don*. Alexei Tolstoi completed his trilogy, *The Ordeal*, Alexander Fadeyev a novel, *The Last of the Udegehs*, Sergei Sergeyev-Tsensky *The Siege of Sevastopol*, M. Javakhishvili *Arsen from Marabda* and S. Aini *The Slaves*.

Poetry developed broadly at that time. The verse of Vasily Lebedev-Kumach, Mikhail Isakovsky, Lydia Seifullina, Jambul Jabayev, Samed Vurgun, and others was very popular. Satirical literature, too, made a considerable impact (Ilya Ilf and Yevgeny Petrov, Mikhail Koltsov, etc.), and good books appeared for children and the youth (Arkady Gaidar, Kornei Chukovsky, Samuel Marshak, etc.).

Gorky, who had returned to the U.S.S.R. in 1931, wrote

---

* In 1935 the Soviet Government decorated Ostrovsky with the Order of Lenin. In 1936, a few days before his death, he completed the first book of a new novel, *Born of the Storm.—Ed.*

prolifically.* His articles and speeches rallied progressives all over the world against the threat of fascism, the offensive of reaction and the war danger. His appeal to the intellectuals of the world, "Who Are You with, Masters of Culture?", was a highlight of his campaign.

The victory of socialism saw the method of socialist realism** take root once and for all in the Soviet multinational literature. The First Congress of Soviet Writers (1934) did much to consolidate the country's literary forces. The congress created the Union of Soviet Writers, and Maxim Gorky was elected its first president.

The rapid spread of literacy in the country raised the demand for books. In 1937 the total printing amounted to 677,800,000 copies. By the end of the second decade of Soviet power, books had been published in the 110 languages of the peoples of the U.S.S.R.

Public libraries grew in number. In the late thirties they totalled more than 70,000. Books became an indispensable part of life, an unfailing companion of the Soviet man.

The new Soviet multinational literature, which played a prominent part in the spiritual life of many millions of people, was one of the biggest gains of the cultural revolution.

The theatre, too, was an important sector in the fight for popular art. By a decree of the Council of People's Commissars, of August 26, 1919, the country's theatres were proclaimed a national possession. It became their cultural purpose to further the education and enlightenment of the masses.

The finest artistes served the people with joy. The new audience that thirsted for art—the workers, peasants and soldiers—were a fact of immense importance. Classical plays and political skits evoked a lively response among the working people who had replaced the satiated and bored audiences of the well-to-do.

To bring the stage closer to the masses many theatre companies went directly to their spectators. During the Civil War progressive actors from the Bolshoi, Maly, Art, Petrograd and Kiev theatres went to the front and performed for the soldiers in the battlelines. Famous performers, such as Fyodor Chaliapin, Leonid Sobinov, Antonina Nezhdanova, Yekaterina Geltser, Vasily Kachalov, Konstantin Marjanishvili, and others, held recitals in workers' quarters and Red Army barrack-rooms.

The development of the Soviet theatre proceeded in bitter conflict with the formalistic trend and the trend of spurious

---

* Maxim Gorky died on June 28, 1936, in the village of Gorki near Moscow, from a malady that had affected him for many years (tuberculosis of the lungs).—Ed.

** Socialist realism is a method of truthful and specifically historical portrayal of reality in its revolutionary development.—Ed.

innovation. The topic of the new life gradually won, forcing out decadent, listless plays from the boards.

Plays on timely political subjects were prominent in the early years of Soviet power, but classical plays, too, were popular (including those of Maxim Gorky). Some of the early plays about the Revolution may have been naïve in content, but the main thing was that their heroes were workingmen and champions of the people's freedom.

In the rehabilitation period, Soviet playwrights wrote a number of enduring contemporary plays, such as Vladimir Bill-Belotser-kovsky's *Storm* (1925), Konstantin Trenyov's *Lybov Yarovaya* (1926), Vsevolod Ivanov's *Armoured Train 14-69* (1927), Boris Lavrenyov's *The Break-Up*, Jafar Jabarly's *Seville* (1928) and Vladimir Mayakovsky's *Bed-Bug* and *Bath-House* (1928-29).

The artistic system of Konstantin Stanislavsky, the great stage-man, had a most beneficial influence on the development of realistic principles in the Soviet theatre. In concert with Vladimir Nemirovich-Danchenko, Stanislavsky defined the lofty mission of the new citizen-actor. A fighter for a genuinely popular theatre and an opponent of sterile professionalism and stereotype, Stanislavsky considered art a public service.

The period of full-scale socialist construction in the U.S.S.R. witnessed an uplift in stage art. The number of theatres and actors' studios in the centre and the non-Russian regions, increased considerably. The abyss that had once lain between the big city theatres and the provincial companies, began to close. The topics and images of Soviet playwriting grew more varied. Besides plays by foreign and home classics, the theatres produced new plays devoted to revolutionary topics and to the life and work of the Soviet man (Vsevolod Vishnevsky's *Optimistic Tragedy*, Alexander Korneichuk's *Platon Krechet*, Kondrat Krapiva's *He Who Laughs Last*, Vargash Vagarshchyan's *Encircled*, Vladimir Kirshon's *Bread*, etc.). Nikolai Pogodin's play, *The Man with the Rifle*, was acclaimed by all who saw it. It centred on the image of Lenin.

The accomplishments of Soviet stagecraft before the Second World War were closely associated with stage directors Vsevolod Meyerhold, Alexei Popov, Mikhail Kedrov and Yuri Zavadsky and the older generation of actors, such as Ivan Moskvin, Alexander Ostuzhev, Olga Knipper-Chekhova, Yekaterina Korchagina-Alexandrovskaya, Mikhail Tarkhanov, Alexandra Yablochkina, and the younger actors, Nikolai Mordvinov, Alla Tarasova, Akaky Khorava, Nikolai Khmelyov and Boris Shchukin.

By the beginning of 1941, the Soviet Union had 926 professional theatres (Russia had 153 in 1914). They performed in 50 languages of the peoples of the U.S.S.R. Ten-day festivals in Moscow by performers of the various Soviet republics were held to demonstrate and promote the progress of theatrical culture in the formerly backward non-Russian areas.

The Soviet system inscribed a new chapter in the history of the cinema, which was still in its infancy in pre-revolutionary Russia.

"The most important of all the arts" was how Lenin described the cinema in a conversation with Anatoly Lunacharsky. A government decree issued on August 28, 1919, gave a start to Soviet cinematography. An All-Russia Photo and Cinema Department was formed under the People's Commissariat for Education. The new department carried through the nationalisation of the film industry. A similar All-Ukraine Cinema Committee was established in 1919, and a Cinema Department of the People's Commissariat for Education of Georgia in 1921.

Cameramen travelled the length and breadth of the country with workers' teams, propaganda trains and Red Army units, filming the events of the Revolution and Civil War for posterity. In 1920, film director Dziga Vertov compiled a documentary film of 13 reels about the peoples' struggle for Soviet power.

In that difficult time the young Soviet cinema was still unable to create lasting productions. It was not until the rehabilitation period that these began to appear. Experienced film people who had taken the side of the Revolution were joined by young gifted directors and actors such as Sergei Eisenstein, Vsevolod Pudovkin, Nikolai Shengelaya, Alexander Dovzhenko, Amo Bek-Nazarov, and others. The foundations of a film industry were laid in Azerbaijan, Armenia, Byelorussia and Uzbekistan in 1923-25. Some of the Soviet films that appeared in that time won world fame, such as Pudovkin's *Mother* and Eisenstein's *The Strike*, and, particularly, *Battleship Potemkin*. In 1925, the International Exhibition of Applied Art in Paris conferred its highest awards on Eisenstein, Vertov, Protazanov and other prominent Soviet film people. The American Motion Picture Academy voted *Battleship Potemkin* the best film of 1926, and the Paris Art Exhibition awarded it a gold medal.*

Sound films, the first of which were *The Road to Life* (director Nikolai Ekk),** *Ivan* (Alexander Dovzhenko) and *Counter-plan* (Sergei Yutkevich), appeared in the early thirties, some of them in the non-Russian republics.

The thirties may be safely described as a time of great creative uplift in the history of Soviet cinematography. The possibilities of the film industry had grown considerably. The number of

---

* At the World Fair in Brussels in 1958 *Battleship Potemkin* was listed among the finest films of all times.—*Ed.*

** In 1932 *The Road to Life* won a prize at the First International Film Festival in Venice.—*Ed.*

cinemas in the country multiplied. *Chapayev,* a film that soon became a classic, directed by Georgi and Sergei Vasilyev, appeared in 1934 and is still a screen monument to the legendary Civil War era and a masterpiece of the world cinema.

The patriotic motif dominated in such highly artistic historical films as *Peter the First* (in two parts), *Alexander Nevsky, Suvorov, Minin and Pozharsky, Arsen, Bogdan Khmelnitsky* and *Stepan Razin.*

But the spotlight was focussed on the image of the free man born in the flames of the Revolution and building a new world. This was the pivot in such fine pre-war Soviet films as *Deputy from the Baltic, We Are from Kronstadt, Lenin in October, Lenin in 1918,* the Maxim trilogy, *Shchors, Member of the Government* and *The Great Citizen.* Many pre-war Soviet films were shown in Europe and America with considerable success.

A number of gifted film actors appeared in the country, notably Nikolai Cherkasov, Igor Ilyinsky, Nikolai Simonov, Boris Babochkin, Lyubov Orlova, Boris Chirkov, Mikhail Zharov and Grachia Nersesyan.

The Soviet cinema developed into a true champion of the finest human ideals.

In the early period after the Revolution popular revolutionary music developed in close association with the art of singing. Proletarian songs resounded throughout the country, augmented by new songs mirroring the heroic events of the time. Prominent composers and performers of old Russia stood at the source of Soviet music. They included such men as Reingold Gliyer, Alexander Glazunov, Konstantin Igumnov, Mikhail Ippolitov-Ivanov, Alexander Goldenveiser and Alexander Kastalsky.

The first symphonies and operas appeared at the time of the rehabilitation. The revolutionary theme was prominent in composer Nikolai Myaskovsky's Sixth Symphony (1923). Folklore motifs breathed new life into the opera and ballet. Gliyer produced the opera *Shah-Senem,* Zakhary Paliashvili wrote *Abesalom and Etery* and some of the other popular works were Alexander Spendiarov's opera *Almast,* and the very contemporary ballet by Gliyer, *The Red Flower.*

As the other arts, music, too, developed in the 1920s and 1930s in sharp conflict with the formalistic trend and all sorts of "novel" deviations alien to the people and ideologically contrary to the demands of the masses.

The Union of Soviet Composers, which championed socialist realism in music, was founded in 1932. The number of opera houses, philharmonic societies and conservatoires increased throughout the country. The uplift of musical culture in the pre-war period may be illustrated by the appearance of the opera *And Quiet Flows the Don* by Ivan Derzhinsky, the ballets *Flames of*

Paris and *The Fountain of Bakhchisarai* by Boris Asafyev, Marian Koval's musical epic *Yemelyan Pugachov*, Sergei Prokofiev's ballet *Romeo and Juliet* and cantata *Alexander Nevsky*, Yuri Shaporin's symphonic cantata *The Battle of Kulikovo*, Dmitry Shostakovich's Fifth Symphony, Uzeir Gajibekov's opera *Ker-Ogly*, etc.

The operas and ballets produced in Byelorussia, the Union republics of Central Asia and in some of the autonomous republics of the R.S.F.S.R. were a big gain for Soviet music. Russian composers rendered considerable help to musicians of the non-Russian republics.

Popular songs entered the people's lives. Songs of the Revolution and the Civil War were replaced by new songs extolling socialist construction. The songs and operettas of Isaak Dunayevsky became popular throughout the U.S.S.R. His song, "So Large Is My Country", is known all over the world.

The triumphs scored in 1927-38 by Soviet performers at international contests in Warsaw, Vienna, and Brussels testified to the creative progress made by the Soviet school of music.

New talent kept appearing from the thick of the people, reaching the summits of musical art. By 1940, the U.S.S.R. had 110 big amateur musical groups that bordered on the craftsmanship of professional musicians.

The Soviet fine arts, too, developed in a struggle for the truth of life.

Soviet posters propagating Party slogans, Lenin's ideas calling on the people to fight the counter-revolution, the economic ruin and the illiteracy of the people, played an immense political role at the time of the Revolution and during the war against the intervention and the whiteguards. Window displays of political drawings and cartoons issued by the Russian Telegraph Agency (later TASS) were popular throughout the country. They featured drawings by Victor Deni, Dmitry Moor, Mikhail Cheremnykh, and the poets Vladimir Mayakovsky, Demyan Bedny, etc. Propaganda through monuments, started on Lenin's initiative, had a great educational impact. The bulky monuments to tsars and old-time generals were replaced by monuments to revolutionaries and educationalists.

The young Soviet arts grew in the struggle against schools deeply alien to the people, such as cubism, futurism, etc.

"Beauty ought to be preserved," Lenin said in a conversation with Clara Zetkin. "It ought to be taken as a model, and it ought to guide, even though it may be old.... I just cannot consider the products of futurism, cubism and the various other 'isms' as works of artistic genius. I do not understand them. They give me no joy."

In 1922, the leading artists of the country organised the Association of Artists of Revolutionary Russia. Most of them took

Anatoly Lunacharsky

Maxim Gorky with workers,
1928

Vladimir Mayakovsky at a literary evening for Red Army men,
1929

Mikhail Sholokhov at the Krasny Bogatyr Works club, 1929

part in the propaganda through monuments advocated by Lenin (Leonid Sherwood, Sergei Konenkov, Vera Mukhina, Sergei Merkulov, etc.).

Drawing on the finest models of classical realism, the foremost Soviet artists and sculptors created works of a new art, closely related and comprehensible to the masses, though some were still somewhat naïvely allegorical. The foundations of socialist realism were laid in the 1920s by Isaak Brodsky (his works dedicated to Lenin, the painting *Execution of the 26 Baku Commissars*), painter of battle-scenes Mitrofan Grekov (*Machine-Gunner, Joining Budyonny*), sculptor Nikolai Andreyev (monument to Leo Tolstoi and the playwright Ostrovsky, a large series of portraits of Lenin, drawings and monuments), sculptor Ivan Shadr ("Cobblestone—the Proletarians' Weapon", "The Worker", "The Peasant"), painter Boris Yakovlev (*Transport Is Improving*), and other gifted artists. Many well-known sculptors and painters of the older generation, too, worked fruitfully at the time. It was in the 1930s that the first canvases and sculptures set in the Soviet times were produced by artists of the country's non-Russian regions (Yakov Nikoladze and Mose Toidze of Georgia, Stepan Agajanyan and Martiros Saryan of Armenia, Alexei Shovkunenko and Karp Trokhimenko of the Ukraine, Valentin Volkov and Zair Azgur of Byelorussia, Semen Chuikov of Kirghizia, Pavel Benkov of Uzbekistan, Azim Azim-zade of Azerbaijan, etc.).

Soviet reality offered ample scope for artists and sculptors to portray the new man, the people of labour. At the close of the 1930s, sculptress Vera Mukhina created a striking monument, "Worker and Collective Farmer", for the Soviet pavilion at the World Fair in Paris (1937). It was an anthem to free labour, symbolising the unbreakable alliance of the working class and working peasants.

Exhibitions of young artists and craftsmen helped to reveal new talent. The First All-Union Exhibition of Amateur Art was held in 1937.

All these successes of the Soviet people, made in the period of socialist construction, were undeniable proof that the proletarian Revolution had won decisive victories in the U.S.S.R. Progress could have been still more significant if the rapid cultural advance had not been impeded by the Stalin cult, which arose in the 1930s. Unpardonable errors were made at that time, which had an ill effect on cultural life. The work of many prominent Party officials in science and culture was belittled, in order to magnify the stature of Stalin. Many men and women dedicated to the Soviet system were classed as "enemies of the people" and fell victim to repressions. Books mentioned disapprovingly by Stalin disappeared from the shelves of libraries, and the valuable works of some scientists were banned.

Although the Stalin cult did untold damage to the country's cultural development, it was not able to halt the rapid growth of Soviet science and culture, or to alter their popular, socialist content. Socialist culture never lost its bonds with life, with the people, which is amply demonstrated by the historical victories of the socialist revolution.

A new culture—national in form and socialist in content—took shape during the socialist construction period in the U.S.S.R. But peaceful cultural development was interrupted by the sudden attack upon the Soviet Union of Hitler Germany on June 22, 1941.

Science and Culture at the Time of the Great Patriotic War

The grim years of the Great Patriotic War upset the life of all sections of the population, including that of Soviet science and culture workers. Many of them abandoned their microscopes, drawing boards, pens and brushes and took up the rifle. More than 2,000 workers of the Academy of Sciences of the U.S.S.R. were on active service with the army or in partisan detachments. The patriotism of science and culture workers is illustrated by the conduct of Lt.-General Dmitry Karbyshev, Doctor of Military Science. Professor Karbyshev (1880-1945) was a prominent scientist. A Lt.-Colonel in the old army, he sided with the Revolution from the first. In the beginning of the Great Patriotic War he was shell-shocked and taken prisoner by the nazis. Neither tortures nor life in a concentration camp could shake his loyalty to his country. On February 28, 1945, he was done to death at the Mauthausen (Austria) death camp, by ice-cold water being poured over him in the execution square on a winter morning.

The Soviet scientists who stayed in the rear in laboratories and institutes, devoted themselves to the nation-wide slogan, "All for the Front! All for Victory!"

The work of the Academy of Sciences of the U.S.S.R., the research institutes and the higher educational establishments was reorganised to suit wartime needs. In September 1941, the scientists of the U.S.S.R. founded a commission to explore and put to use the potential resources of the Urals, Western Siberia, and Kazakhstan. It was headed by Academician Vladimir Komarov, President of the Academy of Sciences, and was joined by over 800 of the most prominent scientists and technicians from 60 research institutions. The core of Soviet science was moved to the far rear, across the Volga to the Urals and Siberia. New centres of science appeared in the eastern part of the country.

The army needed new weapons. Soviet scientists co-operated with industry to create improved types of guns, tanks, automatic firearms, armour-piercing shells, bombs, communication facilities, warships and aircraft. The Soviet heavy IS tank and the medium T-34 were generally recognised the best tanks to come out of the Second World War (designers Zh. Kotin, A. Morozov, N. Shamshurin, etc.). The devastating Soviet rocket artillery, known as "Katyusha", struck terror into the nazis.

The Institute of Electric Welding of the Academy of Sciences of the Ukraine, headed by Academician Yevgeny Paton, helped considerably in organising the mass production of tanks and artillery. The new aircraft, superior in quality and quantity (designers Alexander Mikulin, Alexander Yakovlev, Sergei Ilyushin, Andrei Tupolev, Vladimir Petlyakov, Semen Lavochkin, etc.), added greatly to the striking power of the Soviet Armed Forces. Discoveries in radio engineering, optics, chemistry, physics and geology, too, contributed greatly to the war effort.

In difficult conditions, lacking many necessary materials and appliances, Soviet scientists stood a most trying wartime test. The medical profession performed miracles. More than 70 per cent of the seriously wounded returned to the ranks after treatment. The death-rate at Soviet army hospitals was several times lower than that of the First World War. The Leningrad scientists showed rare courage and stamina. They continued their research, delivered lectures and worked at army hospitals in the beleaguered city, despite hunger, artillery bombardments and air raids.

Social scientists, too, did important work in the battle against fascism. Historians, philosophers and economists bolstered the nation's patriotism and faith in victory with their various works, and exposed the reactionary theories of the nazi obscurantists.

Despite the wartime privations, the Soviet Government established academies of medicine and pedagogics, academies of Uzbekistan, and Armenia, and a West Siberian branch of the Academy of Sciences of the U.S.S.R. in order to promote scientific work. For their war effort, many scientists were conferred the ttitle of Hero of Socialist Labour or awarded Orders of the Soviet Union.

The war did not interrupt the work of the Soviet school—the higher school, the specialised secondary school and the general school. Hundreds of university-level educational establishments and secondary schools were evacuated to the East. But schools and clubs continued to function in the enemy rear as well, in the free "partisan territories" of Byelorussia, the Ukraine and the western regions of the R.S.F.S.R., where newspapers and bulletins were also regularly issued. The government amplified the system of special seven-year and ten-year evening schools for the working youth. Vocational, factory and trade schools trained personnel for the national economy (the latter two trained more than 2,250,000 young workers from 1941-45). The higher schools and specialised secondary schools trained 842,000 young specialists. Schoolchildren and students did their bit in the war effort by helping out at hospitals, factories and collective farms.

Soviet writers worked hard for victory. Hundreds volunteered for the army when the war broke out. Many became war correspondents, soldiers, officers and political workers (Mikhail Sholokhov, Alexander Fadeyev, Konstantin Simonov, Nikolai Tikhonov, Alexander Tvardovsky, Alexei Surkov, Boris Polevoi, Vsevolod Vishnevsky, Vladimir Stavsky, Arkady Gaidar, Leonid Sobolev, Maxim Tank, Petrus Brovka, etc.). The 80-year-old veteran Soviet writer, Alexander Serafimovich, frequently visited the front lines.

Many penetrating and forceful books were written during the war. The writers and poets were the mates of the soldier. War articles did a lot to rally the nation (articles and essays by Alexei Tolstoi, Mikhail Sholokhov, Ilya Ehrenburg, Leonid Leonov, Boris Gorbatov, etc.).

Soviet men of letters infused into the people a deep faith in victory, taught them courage and tenacity, and exposed the beastly nature of fascism. At the height of the war Mikhail Sholokhov published his short story, "The Art of Hating", and began writing a novel, *They Fought for the Homeland*, in which he portrayed the courage of his people in the grim fight against Hitler's cutthroats. Konstantin Simonov devoted his novel, *The Days and Nights*, to the heroic men who fought the Stalingrad battle. In his *Indomitables*, writer Boris Gorbatov depicted the unbending spirit of the Donets Basin working class. The 95-year-old Kazakh poet, Jambul Jabayev, addressed a flaming poetic "Message" to the population of Leningrad. Tvardovsky's poem, *Vasily Terkin*, a true epic of the tenacious Soviet soldier, breathed optimism and faith in victory, and won immense popularity.

Two hundred and seventy-five writers and poets fell in battle for the freedom and independence of the socialist land. Among them were Arkady Gaidar,* P. Lidov, E. Zozulya, Yevgeny Petrov, Alexander Afinogenov, Yuri Krymov, Vladimir Stavsky and Iosif Utkin. The prominent Tatar poet, Mussah Jalil,** died a hero's death in a fascist prison.

---

* Arkady Gaidar (1904-1941)—an eminent writer of children's books, veteran of the Civil War, a regimental commander at seventeen. Author of many fine books for the young, such as *School, RMC, Timur and His Squad*, etc. In 1941, he volunteered for the front, and was machine-gunner in a partisan unit. Killed in battle on October 26, 1941.—*Ed.*

** Mussah Jalil (1906-1941)—well-known Soviet Tatar poet. Joined the army at the outbreak of the war. Taken prisoner by the nazis after being seriously wounded, he continued to fight nazism tooth and nail in the concentration camps. For his courage and bravery Jalil was posthumously conferred the title of Hero of the Soviet Union. For a cycle of verses, *The Moabit Notebook*, which he wrote in prison, he was posthumously awarded the Lenin Prize in 1957.—*Ed.*

Some 500 writers were awarded wartime Orders and medals of the U.S.S.R., and ten were conferred the title of Hero of the Soviet Union.

Soviets musicians, too, stood shoulder to shoulder with the defenders of their land. In beleaguered Leningrad composer Dmitry Shostakovich wrote his famous Seventh (Leningrad) Symphony, a moving musical vehicle of the war. Composer Sergei Prokofiev wrote the overture *1941* and Yuri Shaporin completed his patriotic oratorio, *Tale of the Battle for the Russian Land.* Composer Aram Khachaturyan wrote two forceful symphonies and a temperamental ballet, *Gayaneh*. Andrei Balanchivadze, the Georgian composer, completed his First Symphony, and the Ukrainian composer Andrei Shtogarenko wrote a cantata, *My Ukraine.*

Many excellent songs were written at the time of the Great Patriotic War, instilling courage in the people and helping them to withstand the wartime hardships ("The Sacred War", "An Evening at Anchor", "Song of the Dnieper", etc.).

The Soviet artists, too, devoted their talent and energy to the fight against the nazi invaders. Their posters and political cartoons were an effective weapon. Many artists contributed to the army newspapers (Boris Yefimov, the Kukrynikses trio, Victor Koretsky, etc.). Many new paintings and sculptures were created, such as Sergei Gerasimov's "Mother of a Partisan", "Tanya" by the Kukrynikses, Arkady Plastov's "The German Has Flown Over", Matvei Manizer's sculpture "Zoya Kosmodemyanskaya", etc.

New plays were produced during the war by the country's theatres. The public acclaimed Alexander Korneichuk's *Front*, Leonid Leonov's *Invasion*, Konstantin Simonov's *Russian People* and Boris Lavrenyov's *Song of the Black Sea Sailors*. Theatre companies abandoned the city stage and went to the front lines to perform for the soldiers. Some of the best companies went to the front. So did special concert groups, who performed in hospitals, on warships, at conscription centres and war factories. As many as 450,000 concerts, recitals and performances were given directly in the trenches from 1941 to 1945.

Soviet film-makers responded to the war, producing war documentaries and feature films. The front-line cameramen displayed model courage. More than 100 film groups went to the front lines when the war broke out. Firmness of spirit and faith in final victory were buttressed by such Soviet films as *District Party Secretary*, *The Rainbow*, *Zoya*, *Two Soldiers*, *Wait for Me*, *Leningrad Fights On*, *German Defeat at Moscow*, and others, which told of the indomitable courage shown by Soviet men and women.

At the time of the Great Patriotic War, Soviet culture proved that it was closely attached to the interests of the people and the Communist Party, and played an important role in the country's war effort.

Science and Culture After the War

The nazis inflicted indescribable damage to the cultural wealth of the U.S.S.R. Nazi vandals destroyed 84,000 schools, hundreds of universities, research institutes and laboratories, and ravaged some 430 museums, 44,000 palaces of culture, libraries and clubs and hundreds of depositories of historical treasures of the Russian, Ukrainian, Byelorussian, Lithuanian, Latvian, Estonian and other peoples of the Soviet Union. The Tolstoi Museum in Yasnaya Polyana was defiled and plundered, and so were the Pushkin Museum in Mikhailovskoye, the Tchaikovsky Museum in Klin, the Turgenev Museum in Spasskoye-Lutovinovo, the Shevchenko Museum in Kanev and the Chekhov Museum in Yalta. From one library alone (that of the Academy of Sciences of the Ukraine) the nazis shipped out 320,000 rare books and manuscripts. They burned 1,500,000 books of the Byelorussian Lenin Library, and turned the building into a heap of ruins. Rich cultural monuments and magnificent buildings of the country's ancient towns were laid waste.

The Soviet Government did its utmost to restore what the Hitler invasion had ruined. In the recaptured areas work was begun immediately on restoring and developing cultural and educational facilities. Schools, clubs, libraries, kindergartens, hospitals, theatres, universities and museums reopened their doors. The cultural work interrupted by the war was restarted on a grand scale in all parts of the country.

Strengthening Bonds Between School, Labour and Production

The Soviet Government showed special concern for the rehabilitation and further development of public education. To begin with, it was necessary to remedy the acute shortage of school premises and provide places in school for all children.

The continuously growing allocations for public education show that the people's government was deeply concerned about educational needs. By the end of the first post-war five-year period educational allocations had increased by over 150 per cent over pre-war 1940.*

Between 1946 and 1950, inclusive, the nation built 18,500 schools seating 2,500,000 pupils, including premises for 1,300,000 pupils partially or wholly built on money contributed by the collective farms. In the first ten years after the war the country built or restored more than 30,000 educational establishments, with accommodation for 5,000,000. Obligatory seven-year schooling was enforced throughout the country in 1949 and the stage was

---

* In 1940 they amounted to 22,489 million rubles.—*Ed.*

set for universal ten-year education in the capitals of Union republics and the big cities. In the early 1950s all children of school age regained the opportunity to go to school. By 1952 the Soviet Union had, in the main, enforced universal, free seven-year schooling.

Training the younger generation for active participation in social production has always been the most important function of the Soviet school. In accordance with the directives of the Twentieth Party Congress, which again stressed the duty of the Soviet school to raise knowledgeable and honest working people, new subjects were added to the curriculum, such as work, practical classes at workshops, and the like. Schoolchildren were afforded broader instruction in the key industries and farming.

In September 1956, the C.C. C.P.S.U. and the Council of Ministers of the U.S.S.R. passed a decision to set up special boarding schools. At these schools, children, admitted only at the express wish of their parents, are maintained by the state. They live, learn, work and rest there. Boarding schools afford a general education, instil love of labour, and prepare their pupils for independent adult life. The first 300 boarding schools were opened in the autumn of 1957.

Although the Soviet school achieved incontestable successes, it had its weak sides, too, not the least being the rift between education and practice. The school had to be further improved to conform to the latest needs. It was essential to bring the school closer to the tasks of communist construction.

In the last few years the government has acted to accentuate the polytechnical trend in the school curricula. Its measures were aimed at improving the education of the new man.

On the strength of the new law the existing seven-year schools were replaced by obligatory 8-year polytechnical schools. The young people now get their secondary education at a) evening schools, while working, b) secondary general schools with production training after eight years of schooling, and c) technical schools.

An All-Russia Teachers' Congress (similar congresses were held in the Union republics) was held in Moscow in 1960. It discussed ways of improving the education of the rising generation.

Various ways of sensibly combining education and production have been devised in the last few years. In the towns, schools are attached to factories where senior pupils have an opportunity to learn to work. Production teams of schoolchildren have been formed at factories (repairing machines, etc.) in some districts. In the countryside, teams of senior pupils are given plots of land, implements and machines, and perform various farming jobs.

In the 1962-63 school year the seventh forms were not graduated. The enforcement of universal 8-year education in the U.S.S.R.

is a big stride in public education and constitutes an important milestone along the road to universal obligatory secondary education.

School-leavers enter life better prepared for work on collective and state farms, and in factories and mines.

In 1964 general schools, including schools for young workers and farmers, had a total enrolment of some 45 million. All in all, more than 68 million people, or one-third of the country's population, are enrolled in some form of educational institution.

The outstanding achievements of the Soviet people in the field of education are recognised even by people who have not the least sympathy for the socialist system. For example, William Benton, U.S. ex-deputy Secretary of State, wrote in the *New York World Telegram and Sun* that the Russians had in a colossal way concentrated their efforts on developing education and are forging ahead in their competition with the United States. The most powerful weapon of the Soviet Union, he wrote, is most probably its most innocuous weapon, education. Professor George Counts (U.S.A.), reputedly a specialist in Soviet education, writes in *The Challenge of Soviet Education,* a book containing many slanders against the U.S.S.R., that the growth of Soviet power would have been inconceivable without the truly phenomenal development of the Soviet educational system.

Continuous improvement of the Soviet system of education has become established practice. In the coming 20 years, as the Programme of the C.P.S.U. envisages, all Soviet children of school age will receive a 10-year secondary education.

Mass Training of Qualified Personnel

Rehabilitation of the higher educational establishments was begun on a grand scale as soon as the war ended. The prospective students, who had gone through the grim school of war, assisted with great enthusiasm in building premises for university-level schools. New higher educational establishments were being opened throughout the country. Universities opened in Vladivostok, Irkutsk, Novosibirsk and other cities. Fifty new higher educational establishments were founded between 1950 and 1955. The number of students rose constantly. As many as 350,000 people were admitted as first-year students in 1951. This figure is three times higher than Britain's. In the 1945-46 academic year, 730,200 students attended higher schools and a mere ten years later the number passed the 2,000,000 mark. Nearly as many students as there were in the whole of tsarist Russia (under Nicholas II) graduated from Leningrad higher schools in the one year of 1957.

The building of new blocks for Moscow's Lomonosov University began in the late forties by decision of the Soviet Government.

Leonid Sobinov, Antonina Nezhdanova and Konstantin Stanislavsky

Sergei Eisenstein

Sergei Konenkov

"Worker and Woman Collective Farmer", sculptor Vera Mukhina

Monument to Karl Marx, sculptor Lev Kerbel

The new premises were opened on September 1, 1953. The main block is 32 storeys high, and the department blocks around it are 18-storey buildings. The University has model educational facilities. Its 13 departments have an enrolment of some 25,000 students, representing dozens of different nationalities of the Soviet Unon, the socialist camp countries and other foreign states.

By the end of the fifties there were as many as 766 university-level establishments in the U.S.S.R., against 105 in pre-revolutionary Russia, and 2,200,000 students against 127,000 before the Revolution.

The educational reform begun in August 1958 has, in the last few years, helped the Soviet higher and specialised secondary school to keep abreast of life. The Council of Ministers of the U.S.S.R. decided to place all university-level and specialised secondary educational establishments under the governments of the various Union republics, where previously they had been an all-Union responsibility. By the early sixties, half of the student body in the Soviet higher educational establishments was working and studying at the same time. The admission rules give priority to young men and women who have already had some experience in production. This has tended to alter the composition of the student body. More than 60 per cent of the present-day students have at least two years' practical work behind them. The reorganisation of the educational process in the country's higher schools has largely been promoted by the demands of the rapidly developing economy. As time passes, the higher school is extending and strengthening its ties with factories, building sites, collective and state farms. A large number of young men and women have been sent to the higher schools by factories and collective farms. They will go back when they have completed their education.

Training of qualified personnel is growing in scale in all fields, but special stress is being laid on the technical professions. The enrolment of the higher and specialised secondary establishments in the Soviet Union today totals 6,200,000, with 3,300,000 attending university-level schools. In 1964 the higher schools graduated 350,000 specialists, and technical and other specialised secondary schools nearly 550,000. In just one year nearly 900,000 specialists with a higher or specialised secondary education reinforced the country's labour force. The educational level of women is mounting at a truly staggering rate. Seventy-five per cent of the country's physicians are women. So are 63 per cent of the teachers and 36 per cent of the science and research workers. Some 5,550,000 women graduated at higher and secondary technical schools are gainfully employed in the Soviet economy.

Higher education has gained unprecedented scope in the non-Russian republics of the U.S.S.R., where many new university-level establishments were opened after the war. By the early sixties, Uzbekistan had 36 higher schools, Kazakhstan 25, Byelorussia 23, Georgia 19, Azerbaijan 14, Lithuania 12, Armenia 13, Latvia 9, Tajikistan 8, Moldavia 7, Estonia 7, and Turkmenia 6. The 134 higher schools of the Ukraine have more students than those of Britain, France, Spain, Sweden and Austria combined, and ten times as many as those of Canada. Uzbekistan, too, has surpassed the countries of Western Europe, let alone countries of the East, in the scale of higher education, although the literacy figure there among the stock population before the Revolution had been barely 2 per cent. Today, 81 per 10,000 population have a higher education. This is double the figure of France, more than double the figure of Italy and the Federal Republic of Germany, seven times as high as that of Turkey and 28 times as high as that of Iran.

The Soviet Union is rendering considerable help to the young Asian, African and Latin American countries in training highly qualified national specialists. To promote this undertaking the Lumumba Friendship University was founded in Moscow on November 17, 1960. The name of Patrice Lumumba was given to it soon after its founding to commemorate the national hero of the Congolese people.

The Soviet Union has considerably surpassed the capitalist countries in the rates and levels of higher and specialised secondary education. There are twice as many students in the Soviet Union as in 14 European countries combined.* The Soviet Union has more than 120 students per 10,000 population (15 times as many as in pre-revolutionary 1914), whereas the United States has 111, France 44, and Britain 29. In 1959, engineers' diplomas were conferred on 108,000 people in the Soviet Union, whereas only 38,000 engineers were graduated that year in the United States. More than 125,000 engineers were graduated in the Soviet Union in 1963. About one-third of all Soviet engineers are women. According to the latest figures, the number of mental workers in the country surpassed 22,000,000, or one-tenth of the country's population.

The rapid rise in the general educational, cultural and technical level of the working class and the collective farmers is the most striking feature of cultural development in the U.S.S.R. A large number of schools, technical schools and institutes have been established at the larger factories on the initiative of their workers.

At many of the factories people campaign for the entire staff— all workers and office employees—to complete their secondary

---

* The latter include Britain, France, the Federal Republic of Germany, Italy, Switzerland, Portugal, Austria, Spain, the Netherlands, Denmark, Belgium, Sweden, Finland and Norway.—Ed.

education. More than 70 per cent of the workers employed at Moscow's Likhachov Motor Works, for example, have finished secondary school. By the latest estimates, 50 per cent of the country's gainfully employed population have a higher or secondary education (44 per cent of the workers, 26 per cent of the collective farmers, and 92 per cent of the specialists and office employees).

A process leading to the gradual eradication of the essential differences between mental and physical labour is under way in the Soviet land.

The Soviet state is applying considerable efforts to make all working people of the future communist society highly educated and harmoniously developed.

The Achievements of Soviet Science

The range of research in the various fields of science expanded continuously after the war. Vast funds were allocated for this purpose by the government. But the Stalin cult had an adverse effect on the development of Soviet science. In many respects, it handcuffed the creative thought of the scientists, fostered dogmatism and divorced theory from practice.

It was not until after the Twentieth Party Congress that scientific research was put on the right lines, as scientists were charged with new important specific tasks.

The number of research institutes of the Academy of Sciences of the U.S.S.R. increased rapidly. By the end of 1956 the Academy had 120 institutes, large-scale laboratories and observatories, and twelve major local branches. Research centres were set up in Yakutia, Sakhalin, Eastern Siberia, Daghestan and the Crimea. A new research centre was organised at Novosibirsk, stimulating and extending the scientific exploration of the productive potential of Siberia and the Soviet Far East. Republican academies of sciences were established after the war in Kazakhstan, Estonia, Latvia, Tajikistan, Turkmenia, Kirghizia, Lithuania and Moldavia. The expanding creative post-war co-operation of Soviet with foreign scientists is illustrated by the election to the Academy of Sciences of the U.S.S.R. of more than 40 prominent scientists of America, Europe and Asia. At the same time, many Soviet academicians and professors were elected honorary members of foreign national academies, societies and universities.

After the war, Soviet scientists made major discoveries of inestimable value to the economy, at improving living conditions and stimulating the material and cultural standard of the nation, and at fortifying the peace camp and the strength of the Soviet Union.

The state lays an accent on the study of the nation's natural wealth. Some time ago new diamond deposits, rich deposits of coal, iron ore, molybdenum and titanium were discovered in the east.

Arctic exploration proceeded on a big scale. Soviet polar scientists set up research stations North Pole-2, North Pole-3, North Pole-4 (1954) and North Pole-5 (1955). Another seven research stations have been established within the Arctic Circle more recently. Polar researchers are conducting many valuable observations that augment knowledge about the climate and nature of the Arctic Ocean.

Research has been started on a large scale for the first time in Soviet history in the Antarctic, the land of eternal frost. By decision of the Soviet Government, several well-equipped comprehensive research expeditions have been sent to that continent, where a number of South Pole observatories and stations have been established. The Soviet geophysical investigations are being carried on in close contact with explorers of many other countries.

An immensely valuable contribution to the country's economic development is being made by scientists in automation and telemechanics (Academician Vadim Trapeznikov and others). Progress in these fields is aimed at easing and replacing man's labour in operating various mechanisms and devices.

Towards the end of the fifties the Soviet Union left all other countries behind in the science and technique of welding (Academicians Yevgeny and Boris Paton).

In the last few years considerable advances have been made in engineering. A new science, cybernetics, has gained prominence (Academician Aksel Berg). High-speed electronic machines (Academician Sergei Lebedev) and investigations in the field of semi-conductors (Academician Abram Joffe) have impelled technical progress in the U.S.S.R. Tangible advances have been made in the development of chemical methods of processing materials. Manufacture of new materials, which are ousting natural ones (the polymer industry), has begun on a big scale.

The development of supersonic airplanes has been a triumph for Soviet technology. Up-to-date passenger aircraft, TU-104, TU-114, IL-18 and AN-10, have made their debut on the country's domestic and international airlines. Soviet planes have broken many world records and other marks.

Soviet scientists are making good progress also in other fields. Important discoveries have been made after the war in astronomy. New audacious hypotheses have been advanced on the origin of the earth and various phenomena in the Universe. Medicine has made major advances. So has mathematics and chemistry.

By virtue of its great discoveries of the utmost importance to the future of mankind, Soviet physics has legitimately won a leading place in the world. Extensive scientific experimental work is being done by the country's physicists in the realm of the atom and the use of its energy for peaceful purposes.

On June 27, 1954, the Soviet Union put into operation the world's first industrial electric power station operating on atomic energy. The scientists of the socialist countries have jointly founded an International Nuclear Research Institute in the town of Dubna, near Moscow. It is a first-class science centre with a wealth of equipment, turned over for free use to the Institute by the Soviet Government. The world's most powerful (at the time) accelerator of atomic particles was started up at the Institute in April 1957. A year later, a 100,000-kw atomic power station began operating in the Soviet Union and the construction was begun of a number of new larger atomic power stations. Academician Igor Kurchatov (1903-1960), thrice Hero of Socialist Labour, one of the great scientists of our time whose life has been a model of dedication, played an outstanding part in furthering the progress of nuclear physics.

A splendid example of the peaceful use of atomic energy and a turning point in the history of world shipbuilding was the construction in the U.S.S.R. of the world's first atomic ice-breaker, the *Lenin*, built at the Admiralty Shipyards in Leningrad and launched on December 5, 1957. On September 15, 1959, the atom-powered *Lenin* put out from the Neva on its shakedown cruise.

Since the mid-fifties the social sciences have also been making good progress. Publication of the many volumes of a *World History* has been completed. Many revealing monographies have come off the presses. The Institute of Marxism-Leninism of the C.C. C.P.S.U. has published a one-volume *History of the C.P.S.U.*, a *Biography of V. I. Lenin*, a five-volume *History of the Civil War in the U.S.S.R.*, and is putting out a complete 55-volume works of V. I. Lenin (5th edition). The six volumes of a detailed *History of the Great Patriotic War of the Soviet Union (1941-45)* have come off the presses. The first of the six volumes of a *History of the C.P.S.U.* has appeared and the Institute of History, of the Academy of Sciences of the U.S.S.R., has begun work on a 12-volume *History of the U.S.S.R. from Ancient Times to Our Day*. Scientific works are being prepared for print to mark the 50th anniversary of the October Revolution and the approaching 100th anniversary of Lenin's birth.

The first artificial earth satellite, which marked the beginning of space exploration, the age-old ambition of mankind, was launched from Soviet soil on October 4, 1957.

After the end of the war many Western scientists and "experts" of different kinds spoke with contempt about the level of science in the U.S.S.R. and claimed that the Russians were incapable of major scientific discoveries. The launching of the Soviet sputnik cut the ground from under their speculation. A month later, in the early morning of November 3, signals were flashed from outer space by a second sputnik, with an animal, the dog Laika, on board. The third Soviet artificial satellite, which the world press likened in size to a sedan car, was fired into space in May 1958.

The Russian word "sputnik" instantly entered all the languages of the world. The sputniks opened the eyes of those who had had no reliable information and were enmeshed in a web of lies about the U.S.S.R. People realised at once that accomplishments of such magnitude could only be achieved in a country with a high scientific and technical standard. The facts showed that in spite of the Hitler invasion, the Soviet land born of the October Revolution was developing rapidly as a great power.

Scientific and technical progress enabled Soviet people to penetrate deeper and deeper into the secrets of nature. In just one year, 1959, three space rockets were launched in the U.S.S.R. The first of them became the tenth planet of the solar system. The second reached the surface of the moon, delivering to the region of the lunar seas of Serenity and Tranquillity a pennant bearing the coat-of-arms of the U.S.S.R. and inscribed "The Union of Soviet Socialist Republics. September 1959". The third rocket put an automatic interplanetary station in orbit round the moon, and it photographed the invisible side of the lunar surface. After an exhaustive study of the photographs, the Academy of Sciences of the U.S.S.R. published a detailed atlas of the far side of the moon in 1960. A new Russian word, "lunik", instantly spread the globe and became just as popular as the word "sputnik".

The launching of rockets and heavy sputniks, coupled with intensive study of the possibilities of interplanetary flight, enabled Soviet scientists, engineers and technicians to launch several experimental spaceships of superior weight into orbit in 1960 and 1961. After performing their assigned tasks, these were landed by remote control at predetermined spots on the earth's surface. Animals, earth plants and insects were sent into outer space, and returned. The information gleaned from these experiments supplied fresh data for the impending manned flight into space. The offensive on the Universe gave rise to a new branch of science, space physics.

On February 12, 1961, the world learned about the launching by the Soviet Union of an automatic interplanetary station in the direction of the planet Venus.

Two months after the interplanetary station was sent to the Venus, mankind witnessed an event that ushered in the space era. A man from the planet Earth was sent out into outer space.

In the morning of April 12, 1961, the world waited with bated breath as the radio broadcast: "This is Moscow. All radio stations of the Soviet Union are on the air. On April 12, 1961, the world's first spaceship, Vostok, with a man on board, has been launched into orbit round the earth in the Soviet Union. The pilot-cosmonaut of the Vostok spaceship is a citizen of the Union of Soviet Socialist Republics, Major Yuri Alexeyevich Gagarin."

No sooner than these history-making words resounded, festive meetings and demonstrations occurred spontaneously throughout the country. The world's newspapers and radio and television broadcasts were full of reports about the great event. The rejoicing in the Soviet Union was matched by that of all progressive mankind. At 10.35 hours Moscow time the Soviet spaceship with the pilot-cosmonaut made a safe landing in a predetermined spot inside the U.S.S.R.

The space flight round the world had lasted 108 minutes. The spaceship Vostok had ascended to an altitude of 327 kilometres and flew more than 40,000 kilometres. The weight of the craft and the pilot totalled 4,725 kg, excluding the final stage of the delivery rocket.

People had dreamed for centuries about flights in outer space. The feat of Communist Yuri Gagarin, justifiably described as "the 20th-century Columbus", turned this audacious dream into reality.

The Soviet people do not consider their triumphs in space exploration as their sole possessions. "We gladly place them at the service of all peoples, in the name of progress, happiness and the welfare of all men on earth," said the Appeal of the C.C. C.P.S.U. and the Soviet Government to the population of the world. "We put our achievements and discoveries not into the service of war, but into the service of peace and international security."

In the morning of April 14, 1961, jubilant Moscow gave the world's first cosmonaut a hero's welcome.

Red Square, the scene of many past celebrations, witnessed a popular holiday unrecorded in any calendar. People listened with bated breath to what the first space traveller told them. "We dedicated our first flight into space to the Twenty-Second Congress of the Communist Party of the Soviet Union," said Yuri Gagarin. People were deeply conscious of the fact that if there had been no 10 days that shook the world in October 1917, there would not have been these 108 minutes in outer space which amazed the world in April 1961.

Gagarin's space flight opened broad vistas for the further exploration of space by man.* On August 6, 1961, at 9.00 in the morning, a powerful Soviet rocket put into orbit round the earth a new spaceship, Vostok-2, piloted by Major Herman Titov. Cosmonaut Titov circled the earth 17 times. He spent more than 25 hours high above the earth's atmosphere, covering more than 700,000 kilometres, that is, a distance almost double that from the earth to the moon, in a state of complete weightlessness. Spaceship Vostok-2 landed safely in the territory of the Soviet Union.

People all over the world expected fresh space triumphs from

---

* By decision of the Soviet Government, April 12 is annually celebrated as Space Day.—Ed.

Soviet science, and their expectations were not disappointed. On March 16, 1962, the first of a series of space exploration sputniks (Cosmos-1), was fired into space. Many times over, reports spread throughout the globe about the launching into orbit of new Soviet space vehicles. The space flight of Major Andrian Nikolayev and Lt.-Col. Pavel Popovich was the big event of the summer of 1962. The "stellar brothers" ascended into space on August 11 and 12, respectively, in the Soviet spaceships Vostok-3 and Vostok-4, performing the world's first group space flight. Nikolayev orbited the earth 64 times and Popovich 48 times. All in all, they covered a distance of 4,500,000 kilometres, while maintaining direct radio communications with each other, and landed almost simultaneously in a preset region of the U.S.S.R. The world quickly learned the names of the two daring Soviet cosmonauts, Nikolayev, a Chuvash, and Popovich from the Ukraine.

Fresh successes in space exploration came in quick succession. On November 1, 1962, an automatic interplanetary station, Mars-1, was launched towards the distant planet Mars. On April 2, 1963, an automatic Soviet station, Luna-4, was fired to the moon. Shortly, the world witnessed yet another triumph when a fresh many-day group flight was performed by Lt.-Col. Valery Bykovsky in the spaceship Vostok-5 and the world's first woman cosmonaut, Valentina Tereshkova, in Vostok-6. Vostok-5 was put into orbit on June 14 and Vostok-6 on June 16, 1963. In 119 hours Bykovsky orbited the earth 81 times, covering more than 3,300,000 km. This was a new world record. In her 71 hours in space, Tereshkova made 48 orbits and covered nearly 2,000,000 km.

On October 12, 1964, a new powerful booster rocket put in orbit the world's first piloted spaceship, Voskhod, with accommodation for three travellers, manned by Colonel Vladimir Komarov, researcher Konstantin Feoktistov and physician Boris Yegorov. This was a new stage in space exploration. For the first time, a scientist and a doctor made observations directly in outer space. The cosmonauts made their flights without spacesuits and had no ejection system.

On March 18, 1965, another Soviet spaceship, Voskhod-2, was put into orbit, writing a new startling chapter into the history of space exploration. For the first time a man abandoned his spaceship and made a sortie into outer space. This difficult experiment, which called for extraordinary courage, was made by Cosmonaut Alexei Leonov with the help of the spaceship commander, Cosmonaut Pavel Belayev.

These flights in outer space extended the limits of knowledge about the Universe and again proved that the Soviet spaceships, created by the genius of Soviet scientists, designers, engineers, technicians and workers, were reliable and effective.

In 1962-63 Soviet scientists sent radio signals to the planets Venus,

Sergei Prokofiev

Dmitry Shostakovich

Many foreign students study at Friendship University, Moscow. They are helped by their Soviet classmates

Moscow State University, Palace
of Science

Lecture on zoology at Moscow
State University

Galina Ulanova and Mikhail Gabovich

the Moon and Mercury. On April 3, 1964, TASS reported the launching in the U.S.S.R. of a multistage booster-rocket with the automatic satellite ZOND-1, and then the launching of guided manoeuvring vehicles Polyot-1, Polyot-2, and others.

* * *

The achievements of Soviet science embody the labours of scientists from all the republics of the Union. Yet before the Revolution, Kirghizia, for example, had not had a single research worker. By the early sixties it had more than 15,000. The Academy of Sciences of Kazakhstan has more than 30 research institutions under its auspices, and 550 research institutes and laboratories operate in the Ukraine. In 1962 the country had more than 450,000 researchers, including more than 11,000 Doctors of Science and more than 100,000 Candidates of Science. Socialism flung open the doors to science for women. Some 150,000 women in the U.S.S.R. are engaged in research and nearly 800 of them have the titles of Academician, Corresponding Member of the Academy of Sciences and Professor.

The Soviet Union, where living standards keep rising, where all working people are afforded free medical treatment and where unemployment and exploitation have been wiped out once and for all, is paving the way for a solution of the problem of longevity. Some 300 institutes and laboratories, and 38,000 medical workers in the country are working on the question of prolonging man's life span. The average life expectancy in tsarist Russia was a mere 32 years, while that of the Soviet Union today is 70 years. An army of physicians, 408,000 strong, stands guard over the health of Soviet citizens. In 1961 alone, as many as 20,000 doctors were graduated in the U.S.S.R.* There are medical services in even the most remote points of the Soviet Union. Since 1913 the number of doctors per 10,000 population has increased 34 times over in Turkmenia, 42 times in Kazakhstan and Uzbekistan, 66 times in Kirghizia and 112 times in Tajikistan. Annually some 6 million people spend their vacations at holiday homes and sanatoria, and nearly 3,500,000 children spend their summer holidays in countryside Young Pioneer camps. Such dread diseases as the plague, cholera, typhus, small-pox, leprosy, malaria and scurvy have disappeared, and tuberculosis and poliomyelitis have essentially been conquered.

The number of research institutions in the country is increasing continuously. In mid-1963 the U.S.S.R. had 4,476 scientific research institutes and laboratories, which is 13 or 14 times as many as tsarist Russia had in 1914.

---

* In the early 1960s there were some 20 doctors per 10,000 population in the Soviet Union, 12 in the U.S.A., 10.7 in France, 10.5 in Britain, 1.3 in Iran, 0.7 in Pakistan.—Ed.

The efforts of Soviet scientists are concentrated on the important tasks formulated in the Programme of the C.P.S.U. Under the socialist economic system, in which science figures as a decisive factor impelling the powerful uplift of the productive forces of society, the Soviet scientists are intent on making the most effective use of the riches and forces of nature for the benefit of the people and in the interest of world peace.

Art and Literature Serve the People

Soviet art and literature are promoting the spiritual development of the working people and instilling in them the finest human qualities. The Communist Party calls upon the writers, artists, composers and actors to reflect more deeply in their art the great deeds performed by the people who are building in their country the most just and attractive society. It urges them to invade all spheres of life more boldly, to criticise faults and to demonstrate the life-giving force of the new, the triumph of the new over the old.

The theme of the heroic war effort of the Soviet people predominated in the works of art of the early post-war period. Writers wrote books tracing the events of the recent war. Boris Polevoi depicted the tenacity of the Soviet soldier in his *A Story About a Real Man*. The well-known Soviet writer Alexander Fadeyev described the daring feats of an underground Y.C.L. organisation that operated in the nazi rear in the Donets Basin (Ukraine) from 1942 to 1943 in his novel *The Young Guard*. A number of other forceful books were popular at the time, in which the authors showed the sources of strength and heroism that moved the Soviet people in defeating Hitlerism, such as Pyotr Vershigora's *People with a Clear Conscience*, Victor Azhayev's *Far from Moscow*, Oles Gonchar's *Standard Bearers*, Emmanuil Kazakevich's *Spring on the Oder*, and others.

The years went by. The work of rehabilitation grew in scale. The writers turned their attention more and more to the daily deeds of a nation tending its war-inflicted wounds.

The Twentieth Congress of the C.P.S.U. had an immense impact on the development of Soviet art and literature. Removal of the consequences of the Stalin cult improved the climate in the various artistic societies, put an end to directives and rectified the injustices done to many gifted writers, composers and artists. The names and works of upright and honest men of letters and other artists who had been undeservedly abandoned to oblivion and repressed in the thirties and forties, were returned to the people.

The Soviet literary world, like the rest of the Soviet people, welcomed the Party's criticism of the personality cult and tackled the new tasks and challenges with redoubled energy.

Eager to portray the surrounding reality truthfully and forcefully, writers and poets did not confine themselves to depicting socialist achievements, and spoke of the contradictions and of the acute, as yet unresolved, problems. To be sure, creative failures and mistakes were unavoidable. Here and there, ideologically and artistically inferior works appeared. Some authors painted a one-sided picture of life, magnifying some of the negative sides beyond proportion and thereby perverting reality.

The men of letters in the non-Russian republics are working with enthusiasm. The subject-matter they deal with is now deeper and more versatile.

The Kazakh writer Mukhtar Auezov wrote one of the outstanding books of the last 15-20 years, the historic novel *Abai*, about the poet and educator Abai Kunanbayev (1845-1904). It is a veritable epic of the people. The life of the Latvian people was portrayed in the novels by Vilis Lacis, *The Storm* and *To the New Shore*. The Turkmenian writer, Berdy Kerbabayev, devoted his novel, *Nebit-Dag*, to the labour of the oilmen of his republic. An epic trilogy, *Bread and Salt*, about the life and struggle of the Ukrainian peasants through nearly half a century, was published by writer Mikhail Stelmakh.

The Soviet writers and poets of the older generation produced new, purposeful and gifted works in this period. Towards the end of 1956 Mikhail Sholokhov wrote a short story, "The Fate of a Man", depicting the spiritual beauty and ardent love of life of an ordinary Soviet man, unbroken by trials and privations. Somewhat later, the writer completed his novel, *Virgin Soil Upturned*, he had begun before the war, about the arduous path of collectivisation among the Don Cossaks. Among the epic works portraying the lot of dozens of people, are Leonid Leonov's novel *The Russian Forest*, Fyodor Gladkov's biographic trilogy, Konstantin Fedin's novels *The Unusual Summer*, *The First Joys*, etc.

Writers and playwrights wrote more and more about the scope, scale and pathos of present-day construction. Their books portrayed the true heroes of our time, people with a lofty sense of duty and audacious thinking, fighters for the new and progressive against the old and moribund. This applies to such works as Alexander Tvardovsky's *Distance Beyond Distance*, Galina Nikolayeva's *Battle on the March*, Vsevolod Kochetov's *The Zhurbins* and *The Brothers Yershov*, Valentin Ovechkin's *District Days*, Anatoly Kuznetsov's *A Legend Continued*, Yuri Bondarev's *Silence*, Daniil Granin's *Into the Storm*, and others.

The Second and Third All-Union congresses of Soviet Writers (1954 and 1959 respectively) did much to further the ideological and artistic progress of Soviet literature. Speaking at the Second Congress of Soviet Writers, Mikhail Sholokhov expressed the opinion and sentiment of his colleagues on this score: "Every one of us writes at the call of his heart, and our hearts belong to the Party and to our people, whom we serve with our art."

Soviet readers harshly and rightly criticise the occasional formalistic indulgences of some writers, artists, poets, film-makers, and composers, who try to breed individualism and ideological sterility under the guise of "innovation". This does not mean that an effort is being made to restrict artistic freedom, as some ill-wishers of the Soviet system strive to show. What it means is that every writer and every artist is given to feel his responsibility to society and is prompted to perform his mission, the spiritual moulding of the new man, more purposefully.

The Plenary Meeting of the C.C. C.P.S.U. in June 1963 was an important event in the struggle for the ideological integrity of Soviet literature and culture. It charted measures designed to advance the ideological integrity of art and literature as an important instrument of communist education of the masses.

All impartial people who know the state of Soviet literature, will realise how inept is the talk about a "crisis" in socialist art, spread by the ideological adversaries of socialism. The literature of the U.S.S.R. has scaled high summits of artistic creation and has won world acclaim. The number of forceful literary works is growing year in and year out in all the Union republics. The bonds between literature and the life of the people building communism grew distinctly stronger after the historic decisions of the Twenty-Second Congress of the C.P.S.U.

Each year on the birthday of V. I. Lenin (April 22), Lenin Prizes are awarded in the Soviet Union for the most gifted works of art and literature. Among the bigger works of recent years is the deeply humane poem *Man* by the Lithuanian poet Eduardas Miezelaitis, the stories of contemporary life by the young Kirghiz writer Chinghiz Aitmatov, the poem *The Verdict of Memory* by Yevgeny Isayev, the book of verse *Tall Stars* by the Daghestan poet Rasul Gamzatov, the novels *Bonfire* by Konstantin Fedin, *The Quick and the Dead* and *Soldiers Are Not Born* by Konstantin Simonov, Galina Serebryakova's three-volume *Life of Karl Marx*, and others.

The revolutionary changes taking place in the U.S.S.R. and the life of the people are today the main theme of Soviet literature.

The developments of recent times show that the absolute majority of Soviet writers and poets have taken the right attitude and overcome ideological errors in their work.

The writers of the U.S.S.R. respond to the solicitude of the Soviet power with redoubled creative work and with a greater sense of responsibility for what they are doing. The truthful mirroring of life has always been, and still is, the cardinal purpose of Soviet literature. It is inseparable from its people, who are building communism. Tvardovsky's *Distance Beyond Distance*, a poem of immense ideological integrity and highly militant in spirit, contains lines that carry deep purpose and deep faith in the advent of the great future:

> Year beyond year
> Milestone beyond milestone,
> Period beyond period,
> An arduous road.
> But the wind of the times
> Blows into our sails.

* * *

Art has become truly a people's possession in the Soviet Union. Music and painting, the theatre and cinema, sculpture and amateur art are within reach of all. Millions of people come to exhibitions of prominent Soviet and foreign artists. There are today more than 120 major art museums and galleries in the U.S.S.R.* Artists, film-makers, composers and architects hold congresses from time to time to discuss problems of art and deal with major political and ideological issues. The Party measures aimed at eradicating the consequences of the Stalin cult, and the decisions of the Twentieth, Twenty-First and Twenty-Second Party congresses have had a most beneficial influence on the progress of the arts.

The fine arts have outstanding accomplishments to their credit in the post-war period.

The founding of the Academy of Art of the U.S.S.R. (1947) has promoted artistic endeavour in the country. The finest painters have a Union of Artists (founded in 1957), which provides association and organisation to the nation's artists. New gifted artists and sculptors appear in all the republics of the Union. Artists are trained at the Repin Institute of Painting, Sculpture and Architecture in Leningrad, the Surikov Art Institute in Moscow, the Art Academies in Tbilisi and in Latvia, the art institutes in Kiev and Lithuania, and at many other educational establishments. The membership of the Artists' Union is over 10,000. Forty-three Soviet art exhibitions have been held over the years in 29 countries.

Soviet people prize those works which use the medium of art to mirror life truthfully and deeply. Soviet artists have created many profound and gifted canvases and sculptures. Their subject matter is versatile. Many of the works concern the nation's historic past. Many are dedicated to the highlights of the industrialisation period, many to the grim events of the past war, etc. There

---

* Among them are the Hermitage and the Russian Museum in Leningrad, the Tretyakov Gallery, the ancient Armoury, the Pushkin Museum of Fine Arts and the Museum of Eastern Cultures in Moscow, and the museums in Kiev, Tbilisi and other cities.—Ed.

is Alexander Bubnov's *Morning on Kulikovo Battlefield,* Vladimir Serov's *The Winter Palace Has Been Taken,* Yuri Neprintsev's *Respite After Battle,* the Kukrynikses' *The End,* Alexander Laktionov's *Letter from the Front,* Yevgeny Vuchetich's monument to the Soviet soldier in Berlin, and others.

An uplift was witnessed in art in the latter half of the fifties. This was a time when most of the artists centred their attention on contemporary themes, striving to mirror the peaceful life of Soviet people and their constructive labour. Many of the paintings and monuments are devoted to the most vital problem of our time—the struggle for peace and international friendship. More than 5,000 Soviet artists and sculptors participated in the exhibition held on the 40th anniversary of Soviet power. Some 8,000 canvases, drawings and sculptures were displayed. At the time of the Twenty-Second Congress a monument to Karl Marx by sculptor Lev Kerbel was unveiled in Moscow. An imposing obelisk (by A. N. Kolchin, M. I. Barshch and sculptor F. E. Faidysh) was erected in 1964 in the capital in commemoration of the space explorers.

Alongside professional art, various forms of popular art have taken deep root in the nation. An All-Union Exhibition of Amateur Artists, preceded by almost 6,000 local exhibitions, took place in 1961.

The Second All-Union Congress of Soviet Artists convened in Moscow in the spring of 1963. It reviewed the development of the fine arts over the preceding years and ranged itself with the public opposition to the signs of abstract art and ideological sterility that had appeared in the country, and outlined the ways and means of strengthening the bonds between the arts and the life of the people.

Soviet musical culture is on the upgrade. The country has 32 opera and ballet theatres, 22 conservatoires, 108 major philharmonic societies, 24 musical comedy and operetta theatres, 2 institutes of music, 126 comprehensive music schools and 1,200 primary music schools.

Soviet music affirms the ideas of peace and progress. The battle of the Soviet people against the German fascist invaders inspired such operas as Dmitry Kabalevsky's *The Family of Taras,* Yuli Meitus's *The Young Guard,* Sergei Prokofiev's *A Story About a Real Man,* etc. History is another prominent theme in the opera and ballet.

Songs have always been a fond companion of Soviet people in battle and in labour. The struggle for peace is a prominent theme. Highly popular are such songs as Anatoly Novikov's "Anthem of the Democratic Youth", Sergei Tulikov's "We Are for Peace", Isaak Dunayevsky's "Fly, Doves of Peace", Vasily Solovyov-Sedoi's "If All the Chaps in the World", Eduard Kolmanovsky's "Do the Russians Want War?", Vano Muradeli's "The Buchenwald Tocsin", etc.

A continuous process of mutual enrichment is observed in the U.S.S.R. between the national cultures in general, and music, in particular. At regular intervals, actors and musicians of the various republics perform in the bigger cities of the country. National song and dance festivals have become a tradition. Performers of the Union republics meet from time to time, and national 10-day festivals of art and literature are held regularly in Moscow.

The Second (1957) and Third (1962) All-Union congresses of Soviet composers focussed their attention on improving musical art in the country. Musicians, these forums stressed, want the life of Soviet people of our time to take precedence in their work.

Soviet music and musical interpretation has long enjoyed world-wide acclaim. In the last few years foreign contacts have expanded. The world press referred enthusiastically to guest performances abroad by the violinists David Oistrakh and Leonid Kogan, the virtuoso pianists Emil Gilels and Svyatoslav Richter, the conductors Yevgeny Mravinsky and Konstantin Ivanov, and many others. The guest tours in Britain, the United States, Belgium, and the United Arab Republic by the Bolshoi Theatre Ballet, featuring the famous ballerinas Galina Ulanova and Maya Plisetskaya, were a big success. The world-famous Folk Dance Ensemble of the U.S.S.R. directed by Igor Moiseyev, the Georgian Folk Dance Ensemble and the Beryozka Dance Company were acclaimed by foreign audiences.

Big changes were rung in in the country's theatre. Two-thirds of the repertoire featured contemporary plays. The post-war theatre has made the most of a variety of styles, forms and methods to fortify its bonds with life. Lenin's character was presented forcefully in Nikolai Pogodin's plays *The Kremlin Chimes* and *The Third Pathetic*. Highly popular among the recent Soviet plays are Alexander Korneichuk's *Wings* and *Over the Dnieper*, Alexei Arbuzov's *The Irkutsk Story* and *The City at Dawn*, Afanasy Salynsky's *The Drummer-Girl*, Sergei Alyoshin's *Everything Goes to the People* and Chinghiz Aitmatov's *Mother's Field*, etc. Performances of classical plays and some of the plays by foreign authors also attract large audiences.

The leading Soviet theatres produce plays of the people and for the people. The Soviet Union's more than 520 theatres perform in 40 languages of the peoples of the country. Many companies perform for the prototypes of their plays directly at building projects, collective farms and the state farms of the virgin land development area.

Amateur dramatics are making good headway. People's theatres, one of the highest forms of amateur dramatics, are a major vehicle for the aesthetic education of the working people. Tens of millions of Soviet people participate in amateur dramatic groups.

Soviet theatre companies have toured many countries of the world, such as the United States, France, the Federal Republic of Germany, Britain, Japan, the United Arab Republic, Yugoslavia, etc.

The Soviet cinema has made good progress after the war, and particularly in the last ten years.

Film studios have been founded in all the national republics of the U.S.S.R. The range of subjects treated in Soviet films has expanded.

The Soviet film industry has produced a number of good films in recent years, shown and acclaimed at home and abroad, such as *And Quiet Flows the Don* (Director Sergei Gerasimov), *The Fate of a Man* (Director Sergei Bondarchuk), *The Cranes Are Flying* (Director Mikhail Kalatozov), *The Communist* (Director Yuli Raizman), the trilogy *The Ordeal* (Director Grigory Roshal), *The Forty First, Ballad of a Soldier* and *Clear Skies* (Director Grigory Chukhrai), and others. Nearly all these films won prizes at the International Film Festivals in Venice, Cannes, Moscow, Brussels, Karlovy Vary, Mexico City, etc. It may be safely said that today the Soviet cinema is on the upgrade. Some highly artistic films have appeared recently, such as *The Quick and the Dead* (Director A. Stolper), *Silence* (Director V. Basov), *Optimistic Tragedy* (Director Samson Samsonov), *Everything Goes to the People* (Director G. Natanson), *Blood of the Blood* (Director M. Yershov), *Hamlet* (Director Grigory Kozintsev), and others.

The fact that the country's film-makers are concentrating on present-day realities, on subjects of civic impact, and that they strive to reflect the thoughts and aspirations of the people, opens broad horizons for the cinema and makes it a forum of popular thought.

* * *

The flowering of culture is a distinctive feature of Soviet reality. The thirst for the printed word is particularly great in the Soviet Union. Books are read everywhere—at libraries, clubs, reading-rooms, rest-homes and even in the subway, the buses, trams and trolley-buses and trains. This is something that strikes the eye of all visitors to the Soviet Union.

Let us look at a few figures. Every day Soviet readers get 3,000,000 copies of books. The country has a highly ramified system of libraries, totalling more than 390,000 and containing something like 2,000 million books. Every second citizen of the U.S.S.R. subscribes to newspapers and magazines. The aggregate newspaper circulation is 78 million daily, amounting to nearly one-third of the daily newspaper circulation of the world. Radio and TV broadcasting is in more than 60 languages of the peoples of the Soviet Union and 40 foreign languages. There are in the country tens of millions of radio receivers and loudspeakers. Today, the country has 100 TV broadcasting studios, whereas in 1950 it had only two. The radio audience totals about 150,000,000. The Soviet Union ranks first in the world for the number of periodicals. Books and magazines are issued in 89 languages of the country and 47 foreign languages.

The fact that cultural life flourishes in even the remotest corners of the country no longer surprises anyone. Only recently Chukotka was described as a land of icy desolation. The Soviet system has transformed it into a land of developed culture. In the early sixties Chukotka had 67 public libraries with 250,000 books, more than 100 clubs, 90 cinemas, a large number of schools, hospitals and holiday homes. The national minorities could not have dreamt of this before the October Revolution.

People's Universities, which offer the masses a systematised knowledge of aesthetics, literature and art, have taken firm root in the life of the people. At these universities, leading scientists, men of letters and artists lecture to factory and office workers and collective farmers as a public service, giving them an insight into the arts.

Physical culture and sports are highly popular in the U.S.S.R. Pre-revolutionary Russia had a mere 800 sports clubs and 50,000 to 60,000 sportsmen. Today, the U.S.S.R. has some 200,000 sports clubs with a membership of more than 25,000,000. The high achievements of Soviet sports are known throughout the world.

Soviet cultural contacts with other nations are expanding continuously. Tourism is developing. To strengthen and develop cultural bonds between the U.S.S.R. and other countries, a mass organisation, the Union of Soviet Societies for Friendship and Cultural Relations with Foreign Countries was founded in 1958.

The cultural revolution in the U.S.S.R. has entered its final stage of development. "Communist culture," says the Programme of the C.P.S.U. adopted at the Twenty-Second Party Congress, "which will have absorbed, and will develop all the best that has been created by world culture, will be a new, higher stage in the cultural progress of mankind. It will embody the versatility and richness of the spiritual life of society, and the lofty ideals and humanism of the new world."

The experience of the Soviet Union has fully confirmed Lenin's ideas about the construction of a popular socialist culture. It has demonstrated that the socialist revolution that gives people a progressive socio-political system also gives them a progressive culture.

CHRONOLOGY

1917

April 3	—Lenin returns to Russia
April 4	—Lenin speaks on "The Tasks of the Proletariat in the Present Revolution" (*April Theses*)
April 20-21	—Workers and soldiers demonstrate in Petrograd, demanding that Milyukov resign
April 25-29	—Seventh (April) All-Russia Conference of the R.S.D.L.P.(B.)
May 5	—A coalition government is formed in Russia
June 3-24	—First All-Russia Congress of Soviets of Workers', Soldiers' and Peasants' Deputies
June 18	—Start of an offensive on the South-Western Front. Anti-war demonstrations in Petrograd and other cities
July 3-4	—Workers, soldiers and sailors demonstrate under the slogans of "All Power to the Soviets!" and "Down with the Capitalist Ministers!"
July 6	—Members of the C.C. R.S.D.L.P.(B.), with Lenin presiding, meet to discuss the events of July 3-4
July 24	—The second coalition government is set up
July 26-August 3	—Sixth Congress of the R.S.D.L.P.(B.)
August 12	—In Moscow the Provisional Government convenes the so-called State Conference of representatives of trade and industrial circles, land-owners, clericals, etc.
August 25	—A counter-revolutionary uprising, led by General Kornilov, breaks out

September 14-22	—The Democratic Conference holds its sessions. A Pre-Parliament (Provisional Council of the Republic) is formed
October 10	—Meeting of the C.C. R.S.D.L.P.(B.). Lenin's resolution on an armed uprising is endorsed
October 12	—The Military Revolutionary Committee is set up in Petrograd
October 16	—The C.C. R.S.D.L.P.(B.) holds an extended meeting, which examines questions connected directly with preparations for an armed uprising
October 24	—An armed uprising begins in Petrograd
October 25	—The Great October Socialist Revolution triumphs
October 25-27	—Second All-Russia Congress of Soviets of Workers', Soldiers' and Peasants' Deputies
October 25-November 2	—Soviet rule is established in Moscow
October 26	—The Second All-Russia Congress of Soviets passes the decrees on Peace and on Land and creates a Council of People's Commissars (Soviet Government) headed by Lenin
November 1	—Defeat of a counter-revolutionary uprising near Petrograd led by Kerensky and Krasnov
November 2	—The Council of People's Commissars adopts the Declaration of the Rights of the Peoples of Russia
November 7	—On behalf of the Council of People's Commissars Lenin instructs the Commander-in-Chief Dukhonin to propose an armistice to the belligerent countries
November 8	—In notes to the ambassadors of the Allied powers, the People's Commissariat for Foreign Affairs proposes an immediate armistice and the initiation of peace talks
November 11	—A.R.C.E.C. and the Council of People's Commissars pass a decree

	abolishing the system of social estates and civil titles
November 11-25	—The Extraordinary All-Russia Congress of Soviets of Peasants' Deputies sits in Petrograd
November 14	—A.R.C.E.C. promulgates the Rules of Workers' Control
November 20	—The appeal of the Soviet Government "To All Working Moslems of Russia and the East" is published
December 2	—The Council of People's Commissars passes a decree On the Establishment of the Supreme Economic Council
December 18	—The Council of People's Commissars decrees the recognition of Finland's state independence
1918	
January 5	—The Constituent Assembly opens
January 10-18	—Third All-Russia Congress of Soviets of Workers', Soldiers' and Peasants' Deputies. It adopts the Declaration of the Rights of the Working and Exploited People
January 15	—The Council of People's Commissars decrees the formation of the Workers' and Peasants' Red Army
January 20	—The Council of People's Commissars promulgates a decree On Separating the Church from the State and the School from the Church
March 3	—Soviet Russia signs a peace treaty with the German bloc powers at Brest-Litovsk
March 6-8	—Seventh Congress of the R.S.D.L.P.(B.)
March 11	—The Soviet Government moves to Moscow
March 14-16	—Fourth Extraordinary All-Russia Congress of Soviets. It ratifies the Brest Peace Treaty
March	—Anglo-French-U.S. armed intervention begins in the north of Russia
April 29	—Lenin reports "On the Immediate Tasks of the Soviet Government"

June 11	—A.R.C.E.C. decrees the setting up of village and volost Poor Peasants' Committees
June 28	—The Council of People's Commissars decrees the nationalisation of large-scale industries and the railways
July 4-10	—Fifth All-Russia Congress of Soviets. It adopts the first Soviet Constitution
July 6-7	—Left Socialist-Revolutionaries stage an uprising in Moscow. The uprising is crushed
August 2	—The Council of People's Commissars passes a decree giving the children of workers and the poorest section of the peasantry priority in enrolment to institutions of higher learning
August 30	—An attempt is made on Lenin's life
September 2	—A.R.C.E.C. institutes a regime of Red terror against the counter-revolution
September 20	—British interventionists execute 26 Baku commissars
October 29	—The Young Communist League of Russia is founded
November 6-9	—Sixth Extraordinary All-Russia Congress of Soviets
November 13	—A.R.C.E.C. annuls the Brest Peace Treaty
December 31	—A Provisional Workers' and Peasants' Government is set up in the Ukraine

1919

January 1	—Byelorussia is proclaimed a Soviet Socialist Republic
January 11	—The Council of People's Commissars passes a decree on the requisitioning of surplus food
March 2-6	—First Congress of the Communist International
March 18-23	—Eighth Congress of the R.C.P.(B.)
April 12	—*Pravda* publishes the "Theses of the C.C. R.C.P.(B.) in Connection with the Situation on the Eastern Front". The first communist subbotnik is

	organised at the Marshalling Yard of the Moscow-Kazan Railway
April 28	—The Red Army launches a counter-offensive against Kolchak
June	—Yudenich is defeated near Petrograd
July 9	—The C.C. R.C.P.(B.) appeals for an all-out national effort against Denikin
August 24	—Lenin writes his letter "To Workers and Peasants in Connection with the Victory over Kolchak"
October	—The Red Army develops its offensive on the Southern Front
December 5-9	—Seventh All-Russia Congress of Soviets
December 12	—The Red Army liberates Kharkov
December 16	—Kiev is liberated from Denikin
December 26	—The Council of People's Commissars passes its decree On the Abolition of Illiteracy Among the Population of the R.S.F.S.R.

1920

January	—The first revolutionary labour army is formed to help the workers of the Ukraine
January 21	—The State Commission for the Electrification of Russia (GOELRO) is set up
March 29-April 5	—Eleventh Congress of the R.C.P.(B.)
April 6	—The Far Eastern Republic is formed
April 25	—Poland attacks Soviet Russia
April 26	—Soviet rule is proclaimed in Khoresm
April 28	—Soviet rule is proclaimed in Azerbaijan
May 20	—The theses of the C.C. R.C.P.(B.) "The Polish Front and Our Tasks" are published
June 5	—The First Cavalry Army begins a counter-offensive on the Polish Front
July 19-August 7	—Second Congress of the Communist International
September 7	—The Turkestan State University is opened in Tashkent

September 14	—Soviet rule is proclaimed in Bukhara
October 2-10	—Third Congress of the Young Communist League of Russia. Lenin speaks "On the Tasks of Youth Leagues"
October 14	—Soviet Russia and Finland sign a peace treaty
November 29	—Soviet rule is proclaimed in Armenia
December 22-29	—Eighth All-Russia Congress of Soviets
1921	
February 25	—Soviet rule is established in Georgia
February 26	—The Soviet-Iranian Treaty on the Establishment of Friendly Relations is signed
February 28	—The Soviet-Afghan Treaty on the Establishment of Friendly Relations is signed
March 8-16	—Tenth Congress of the R.C.P.(B.)
March 16	—The Soviet-Turkish Treaty of Friendship and Fraternity is signed
March 21	—A.R.C.E.C. passes a decree On the Replacement of Surplus Food and Raw Materials Requisitioning System by a Tax in Kind
March	—Soviet Russia and Britain sign a trade agreement
May 6	—Soviet Russia and Germany sign a trade agreement
June 22-July 12	—Third Congress of the Communist International
November 5	—Mongolia and Soviet Russia sign a treaty establishing friendly relations
December 23-28	—Ninth All-Russia Congress of Soviets
1922	
January 7	—The Italian Government invites the Soviet Government to attend the Genoa Conference
March 27-April 2	—Eleventh Congress of the R.C.P.(B.)
April 10-May 19	—Genoa Conference
April 16	—The R.S.F.S.R. and Germany sign the Rapallo Treaty
June 15-July 20	—Hague Conference

October 6	—A Plenary Meeting of the C.C. R.C.P.(B.) adopts a decree on the forms of uniting the independent Soviet republics
October 25	—Japanese invaders driven out of Vladivostok
November 5- December 5	—Fourth Congress of the Communist International
November 14	—The Far Eastern Republic merges with the R.S.F.S.R.
December 13	—The Transcaucasian Socialist Federative Soviet Republic is formed
December 30	—First Congress of Soviets of the U.S.S.R. The Union of Soviet Socialist Republics is formed
1923	
April 17-25	—Twelfth Congress of the R.C.P.(B.)
July 6	—The Second Session of A.R.C.E.C. adopts the Constitution of the U.S.S.R.
1924	
January 21	—Lenin dies
January 26- February 2	—Second Congress of Soviets of the U.S.S.R.
February 2	—Diplomatic relations are established between the U.S.S.R. and Britain
May 23-31	—Thirteenth Congress of the R.C.P.(B.)
May 31	—Diplomatic relations are established between the U.S.S.R. and China
June 17-July 8	—Fifth Congress of the Communist International
October 12	—The Moldavian Autonomous Soviet Socialist Republic is formed
October 27	—The Turkmenian and Uzbek Soviet Socialist republics are formed
October 28	—Diplomatic relations are established between the U.S.S.R. and France
1925	
January 20	—Diplomatic relations are established between the U.S.S.R. and Japan
May 13-20	—Third Congress of Soviets of the U.S.S.R.

December 18-31	—Fourteenth Congress of the C.P.S.U.(B.)
1926	
April 6-9	—A Plenary Meeting of the C.C. C.P.S.U.(B.) discusses the economic situation and the economic policy
July 12	—Foundation stone is laid in Stalingrad for the first Soviet tractor works
December 19	—The Volkhov Hydropower Station becomes operational
1927	
April 18-26	—Fourth Congress of Soviets of the U.S.S.R.
May 27	—Britain abrogates the Anglo-Soviet Trade Agreement of 1921 and breaks off diplomatic relations with the U.S.S.R.
June 7	—Pyotr Voikov, Soviet Ambassador to Poland, is assassinated
November 10-12	—World Congress of Friends of the U.S.S.R. is held in Moscow
December 2-15	—Fifteenth Congress of the C.P.S.U.(B.)
1928	
July 17-September 1	—Sixth Congress of the Communist International
October	—The First Five-Year Plan is launched
November 4	—The Electrical Engineering Plant in Moscow is placed in operation
1929	
May 9	—The C.C. C.P.S.U.(B.) passes a resolution on the organisation of socialist emulation at factories and mills
May 20-28	—Fifth Congress of Soviets of the U.S.S.R.
May 27	—Bandits attack the Soviet Consulate at Harbin
July 10	—Chinese militarists attack the Chinese Eastern Railway
October 3	—Diplomatic relations between the U.S.S.R. and Britain are restored

| December 5 | —The Tajik Soviet Socialist Republic is formed |

1930

January 5	—The C.C. C.P.S.U.(B.) passes a decree On the Rates of Collectivisation and on State Assistance to the Collective Farms
February 20	—The C.C. C.P.S.U.(B.) passes a decree On Collectivisation in the Republics of Transcaucasia and Central Asia and in the Non-Russian Regions of the R.S.F.S.R.
March 14	—The C.C. C.P.S.U.(B.) passes a decree On the Struggle Against Distortions of the Party Line in the Collective-Farm Movement
June 17	—The Stalingrad Tractor Works is placed in operation
June 26-July 13	—Sixteenth Congress of the C.P.S.U.(B.)
July 17	—The C.C. C.P.S.U.(B.) passes a decree On Universal and Compulsory Elementary Education

1931

January 1	—The Farm Machines Plant in Rostov becomes operational
March 8-17	—Sixth Congress of Soviets of the U.S.S.R.
October 1	—The Moscow Motor Works is reconstructed
December 10	—The Magnitogorsk Iron and Steel Works becomes operational
December 31	—The Saratov Harvester-Combine Plant is commissioned

1932

January 1	—The Gorky Auto Works is placed in operation
March 20	—The First Ball-Bearing Plant in Moscow starts production
April	—The Kuznetsk Iron and Steel Works is completed
May 1	—The Dnieper Hydropower Station begins generating electricity

August 7	—A.R.C.E.C. and the Council of People's Commissars pass a decree On the Protection of Socialist Property
November 29	—The U.S.S.R. and France sign a non-aggression pact

1933

January 7-12	—A Plenary Meeting of the C.C. and the Central Control Commission discuss the results of the First Five-Year Plan and the tasks of the political departments at the machine-and-tractor stations
July 1	—The Chelyabinsk Tractor Works becomes operational
July 15	—The Urals Heavy Engineering Works starts production
November 16	—Diplomatic relations are established between the U.S.S.R. and the U.S.A.
1933	—The Second Five-Year Plan is started

1934

January 26-February 10	—Seventeenth Congress of the C.P.S.U.(B.)
August 17-September 1	—First All-Union Congress of Soviet Writers
September 18	—The U.S.S.R. joins the League of Nations
December 1	—Sergei Kirov is assassinated

1935

January 28-February 6	—Seventh Congress of Soviets of the U.S.S.R.
May 2	—The U.S.S.R. and France reach agreement on non-aggression
May 16	—The U.S.S.R. and Czechoslovakia reach agreement on non-aggression
July 25-August 25	—Seventh Congress of the Communist International
November 14-17	—First All-Union Conference of Stakhanovite Workers

1936

March 12	—The U.S.S.R. and Mongolia sign a treaty on mutual assistance

November 25- December 5	—Eighth Extraordinary Congress of Soviets. It adopts the new Constitution of the U.S.S.R.
1937 June 18-20	—Valery Chkalov, Georgi Baidukov and Alexander Belyakov accomplish a non-stop flight from Moscow to Portland, U.S.A.
August 21	—The U.S.S.R. and China sign a treaty of non-aggression
1937-38	—The first Soviet drifting station conducts scientific observations in the Arctic Ocean
1938 July 21- August 11	—The Red Army routs Japanese troops at Lake Hasan
1939 March 10-21	—Eighteenth Congress of the C.P.S.U.(B.). The Third Five-Year Plan is adopted
May 11- August 31	—The Red Army, co-operating with the Mongolian People's Army, defeats Japanese troops at Khalkhin Gol
August 23	—Germany and the U.S.S.R. sign a treaty of non-aggression
September 1	—Germany attacks Poland. The Second World War breaks out
September 1	—The Fourth Extraordinary Session of the Supreme Soviet passes the Law on Universal Military Conscription
September 17	—The Red Army begins its liberation of Western Ukraine and Western Byelorussia
November 29	—War breaks out between the U.S.S.R. and Finland
1940 March 12	—The U.S.S.R. and Finland sign a peace treaty
June 28	—Bessarabia and Northern Bukovina become part of the U.S.S.R.

July 21	—The Latvian, Lithuanian and Estonian Soviet Socialist republics are formed
August 2	—The Moldavian Soviet Socialist Republic is formed

1941
June 22	—Germany attacks the U.S.S.R. without declaring war. The Soviet Government appeals to the people. The Presidium of the Supreme Soviet of the U.S.S.R. decrees the mobilisation of all reservists born between 1905 and 1918
June 30	—A State Committee for Defence is formed
September 29-October 1	—Moscow Conference of representatives of the U.S.S.R., the U.S.A. and Britain
December 6	—Rout of nazi troops begins at Moscow

1942
May 30	—The headquarters of the partisan movement is set up at the Headquarters of the Supreme Commander-in-Chief
July 17, 1942-February 2, 1943	—Battle of Stalingrad

1943
February 2	—Germans defeated at Stalingrad
July 5	—The Battle of the Kursk Salient begins
August 5	—Soviet troops liberate Orel and Belgorod
August 21	—The Council of People's Commissars and the C.C. C.P.S.U.(B.) pass a decree on urgent measures to rehabilitate the economy in areas liberated from German occupation
August 23	—Soviet troops liberate Kharkov
September 19-30	—Moscow Conference of Foreign Ministers of the U.S.S.R., the U.S.A. and Britain
November 6	—Soviet troops liberate Kiev

| November 28-
December 1 | —Teheran Conference of Heads of Government of the U.S.S.R., the U.S.A. and Britain |
| December 12 | —The U.S.S.R. and Czechoslovakia sign a treaty of friendship and mutual assistance |

1944

January	—The enemy siege of Leningrad is broken
March 23	—The State Committee for Defence passes a decree on the restoration of industry and municipal economy in Leningrad
May 12	—Soviet troops clear the nazi invaders out of the Crimea
June 6	—British and U.S. troops land in Normandy. The second front in Europe is opened
June 23	—Soviet troops start an offensive in Byelorussia
July 3	—Minsk is liberated
July 13	—Vilnius is liberated
July 18	—The State Committee for Defence passes a decree on measures to be taken to rehabilitate the Donbas
August 20	—Soviet troops launch an offensive south-east of Kishinev
August 31	—Soviet troops liberate Bucharest
September 16	—Soviet troops enter Sofia
September 20	—Tallinn is liberated
October 13	—Riga is liberated
October 20	—Soviet troops and troops of the National Liberation Army of Yugoslavia enter Belgrade
October	—Soviet troops liberate Budapest

1945

| January 17 | —Soviet troops liberate Warsaw |
| February 4-12 | —Yalta Conference of Heads of Government of the U.S.S.R., the U.S.A. and Britain |

April 11	—The U.S.S.R. and Yugoslavia sign a treaty of friendship and mutual assistance
April 21	—The U.S.S.R. and Poland sign a treaty of friendship and mutual assistance
May 2	—Berlin garrison capitulates. Berlin is captured
May 8	—Germany signs an unconditional surrender
May 9	—Day of Victory over nazi Germany
May 9	—Soviet troops liberate Prague
June 22	—The Twelfth Session of the Supreme Soviet of the U.S.S.R. decrees the demobilisation of the senior age groups from the army
July 7- August 2	—Potsdam Conference of Heads of Government of the U.S.S.R., the U.S.A. and Britain
August 9	—The Soviet Union declares war on imperialist Japan
August 19	—The Council of People's Commissars instructs the State Planning Commission to draw up the Fourth Five-Year Plan of Economic Rehabilitation and Development for 1945-50
September 2	—Japan surrenders unconditionally. The Second World War ends
October 24	—The Charter of the United Nations Organisation comes into force
1946 March 15	—The Council of People's Commissars of the U.S.S.R. is renamed into the Council of Ministers of the U.S.S.R.
July 29- October 15	—Paris Peace Conference
1947 February	—A Plenary Meeting of the C.C. C.P.S.U.(B.) passes a decision on steps to stimulate farming in the post-war period
End of 1947	—The U.N. General Assembly accepts the Soviet proposals for banning war propaganda

November 4	—The first section of the Rostov Farm Machines Plant is restored
1948	
February 4	—The U.S.S.R. and Rumania sign a treaty of friendship and mutual assistance
February 18	—The U.S.S.R. and Hungary sign a treaty of friendship and mutual assistance
March 18	—The U.S.S.R. and Bulgaria sign a treaty of friendship and mutual assistance
August 29	—The Kharkov Tractor Plant resumes production
1949	
March 29-April 7	—Eleventh Congress of the Young Communist League
April	—Tenth Congress of the All-Union Central Council of Trade Unions
August 25-27	—First All-Union Peace Supporters Conference in Moscow
End of 1949	—The Minsk Tractor Plant resumes production
1950	
February 14	—The U.S.S.R. and the Chinese People's Republic sign a treaty of friendship and mutual assistance
May 30	—The C.C. C.P.S.U.(B.) passes a decision "On Amalgamating Small Collective Farms and on the Tasks of Party Organisations in This Work"
1951	
March 12	—The Supreme Soviet of the U.S.S.R. passes a Law Defending Peace
November 27-29	—The Third All-Union Peace Supporters Conference. The Fifth Five-Year Plan is started
1952	
October 5-14	—Nineteenth Congress of the C.P.S.U.(B.)

| December 2-4 | —Fourth All-Union Peace Supporters Conference |

1953

March 5	—J. V. Stalin dies
End of the year	—The U.S.S.R. and India sign a long-term trade agreement
End of the year	—The U.S.S.R. and Afghanistan sign an agreement

1954

January 25-February 18	—Berlin Conference of Foreign Ministers of the U.S.S.R., the U.S.A. and Britain
February 23-March 2	—A Plenary Meeting of the C.C. C.P.S.U. passes a resolution on measures to further increase the grain output and to develop virgin and disused land
March 19-27	—Twelfth Congress of the All-Union Young Communist League
June 27	—The world's first atomic power station becomes operational in the U.S.S.R.
November 29-December 2	—Moscow Conference of representatives of socialist countries

1955

January 25-31	—A Plenary Meeting of the C.C. C.P.S.U. passes a resolution on measures to increase the output of animal products
May 14	—Warsaw Treaty of Friendship, Co-operation and Mutual Assistance Among Countries of the Socialist Camp is signed
May 15	—The U.S.S.R., the U.S.A., Britain and France sign a treaty ending the occupation of Austria
July 18-23	—Geneva Conference of the Heads of Government of the U.S.S.R., the U.S.A., Britain and France on European security, disarmament and the promotion of contact between countries

December 29	—The Kuibyshev Hydropower Station becomes operational

1956

February 14-25	—Twentieth Congress of the C.P.S.U.
June 30	—The C.C. C.P.S.U. passes a decision "On Surmounting the Personality Cult and Its Consequences"
July 14	—The Supreme Soviet of the U.S.S.R. passes a State Pension Law
July 16	—The Supreme Soviet of the U.S.S.R. appeals to the parliaments of all countries to work for disarmament
September 8	—The Council of Ministers of the U.S.S.R., the Central Committee of the C.P.S.U. and the All-Union Central Council of Trade Unions pass a decision "On Raising the Wages of Lower-Paid Categories of Workers and Employees"

1957

July 31	—The Central Committee of the C.P.S.U. and the Council of Ministers of the U.S.S.R. pass a decision "On the Development of Housing Construction in the U.S.S.R."
September 26	—The Central Committee of the C.P.S.U. and the Council of Ministers of the U.S.S.R. pass a decision "On Drawing Up a Seven-Year Plan of Economic Development for 1959-65"
October 4	—The U.S.S.R. launches the world's first artificial satellite
November 16-19	—Moscow Meeting of Representatives of Communist and Workers' Parties

1958

February	—The C.C. C.P.S.U. passes a decision on the further development of the collective-farm system and on the reorganisation of the machine-and-tractor stations
April 15-18	—Thirteenth Congress of the All-Union Young Communist League

May 7	—A Plenary Meeting of the C.C. C.P.S.U. adopts a decision to speed up the development of the chemical industry
May 20-23	—Moscow Meeting of Representatives of Communist and Workers' Parties of member-countries of the Council for Mutual Economic Aid
December 24	—The C.C. C.P.S.U. passes a decision "On Strengthening the Link Between School and Life"

1959

January 2	—The first multistage space rocket is launched in the direction of the moon
January 27-February 5	—Extraordinary Twenty-First Congress of the C.P.S.U.
May 11-August 5	—Conference of representatives of the U.S.S.R., the U.S.A., Britain and France on the conclusion of a peace treaty with Germany, Geneva
May 18-23	—Third All-Union Congress of Soviet Writers

1960

February 4	—The Declaration of the Warsaw Treaty Countries is signed
May 7	—Law on the Annulment of Income Taxes from Industrial, Office and Other Workers is passed
May 27-30	—All-Union conference of foremost workers in the emulation movement for the title of Communist Work Team and Communist Shock Worker
November 17	—Friendship University opens in Moscow
November	—Moscow Meeting of Representatives of Communist and Workers' Parties
December 9	—The Twenty-Second Party Congress Hydropower Station on the Volga becomes operational

1961

April 12	—Vostok-1 piloted by Yuri Gagarin, the world's first spaceman, accomplishes a flight in space

July 30	—Publication of the draft Programme and Rules of the C.P.S.U.
August 6-7	—Herman Titov accomplishes a space flight in Vostok-2
October 17-31	—Twenty-Second Congress of the C.P.S.U. The new Programme and Rules of the C.P.S.U. are adopted
End of the year	—The Bratsk Hydropower Station is commissioned
1962	
April	—Fourteenth Congress of the All-Union Young Communist League
August 12	—Andrian Nikolayev and Pavel Popovich accomplish a group flight in space in the ships Vostok-3 and Vostok-4
November 9-23	—A Plenary Meeting of the C.C. C.P.S.U. passes a resolution on economic development in the U.S.S.R. and on Party leadership of national economy
1963	
June	—A Plenary Meeting of the C.C. C.P.S.U. passes a resolution on the immediate tasks of the Party's ideological work
June 14	—Valery Bykovsky takes off on a space flight in Vostok-5
June 16	—Valentina Tereshkova, the world's first spacewoman, takes off on a space flight in Vostok-6
August 5	—The Foreign Ministers of the U.S.S.R., the U.S.A. and Britain sign a Treaty on banning nuclear weapons tests in the atmosphere, in outer space and under water
December 9-13	—A Plenary Meeting of the C.C. C.P.S.U. passes a decision to accelerate the development of the chemical industry for increasing farm output
1964	
February 10-15	—A Plenary Meeting of the C.C. C.P.S.U. passes a decision "On the

Intensification of Agricultural Production Through the Wide Use of Fertiliser"

April — The Kurchatov Atomic Power Station at Beloyarsk is commissioned

June 12 — The U.S.S.R. and the German Democratic Republic sign a treaty of friendship and co-operation

July 13-15 — A law is passed on raising the salaries of workers in education, public health, housing and communal services, trade and public catering

October 12 — Voskhod-1 takes off on a space flight with a crew of three—Vladimir Komarov, Konstantin Feoktistov and Boris Yegorov

October 14 — Plenary Meeting of the C.C. C.P.S.U.

1965
January — Conference of the Political Consultative Council of the Warsaw Treaty countries

March 18 — Pavel Belayev and Alexei Leonov take off on a space flight in Voskhod-2. Leonov becomes the first man in the world to walk in space

April 21 — The U.S.S.R. and Poland sign a treaty of friendship and co-operation

REQUEST TO READERS

Progress Publishers would be glad to have your opinion of this book, its translation and design and any suggestions you may have for future publications.

Please send your comments to 21, Zubovsky Boulevard, Moscow, U.S.S.R.

Printed in the Union of Soviet Socialist Republics